Learning To Be Employable

Learning To Be Employable

New Agendas on Work, Responsibility and Learning in a Globalizing World

Edited by

Christina Garsten

and

Kerstin Jacobsson

First published 2004 by
PALGRAVE MACMILLAN
Houndmills, Basingstoke, Hampshire RG21 6XS and
175 Fifth Avenue, New York, N.Y. 10010
Companies and representatives throughout the world

PALGRAVE MACMILLAN is the global academic imprint of the Palgrave Macmillan division of St. Martin's Press, LLC and of Palgrave Macmillan Ltd. Macmillan® is a registered trademark in the United States, United Kingdom and other countries. Palgrave is a registered trademark in the European Union and other countries.

ISBN 1–4039–0105–8

This book is printed on paper suitable for recycling and made from fully managed and sustained forest sources.

A catalogue record for this book is available from the British Library.

Library of Congress Cataloging-in-Publication Data
Learning to be employable : new agendas on work, responsibility, and learning in a globalizing world / editors, Christina Garsten and Kerstin Jacobsson.
    p. cm.
Includes bibliographical references and index.
ISBN 1–4039–0105–8 (cloth)
1. Occupational training—European Union countries.   2. Occupational retraining—European Union countries.   3. Continuing education—European Union countries.   4. Work ethic—European Union countries.   5. Labor market—European Union countries.   6. Manpower policy—European Union countries.   7. Occupational training—Sweden.   8. Occupational retraining—Sweden.   9. Continuing education— Sweden.   10. Labor market—Sweden.   11. Manpower policy—Sweden.   12. Globalization.   I. Garsten, Christina.   II. Jacobsson, Kerstin.
HD5715.5.E85L43 2003
331.12′042′094—dc21   2003053274

10   9   8   7   6   5   4   3   2   1
13   12   11   10   09   08   07   06   05   04

Printed and bound in Great Britain by
Antony Rowe Ltd, Chippenham and Eastbourne

Contents

Notes on the Contributors   vii

Preface   xi

1 **Learning To Be Employable: An Introduction**   1
Christina Garsten and Kerstin Jacobsson

2 **The Individualization of Labour**   23
Michael Allvin

3 **A European Politics for Employability: The Political Discourse on Employability of the EU and the OECD**   42
Kerstin Jacobsson

4 **Competition versus Regulation: Swedish Articulations of the EU Labour Market Discourse**   63
Lotte Faurbæk

5 **Lifelong Learning: A Clash Between a Production and a Learning Logic**   83
Lennart Svensson

6 **Constructing the Competent Individual: Trade Union Roles, Responses and Rhetoric**   107
Tony Huzzard

7 **'Do it Yourself': Making Up the Self-Employed Individual in the Swedish Public Employment Service**   131
Renita Thedvall

8 **'Be a Gumby': The Political Technologies of Employability in the Temporary Staffing Business**   152
Christina Garsten

9 **Teamworking and Emotional Labour in Call Centres**   172
Antony Lindgren and Per Sederblad

10 **Work as an Arena for Disciplining Mind, Body and Emotions: The Volvo Bus Plant Case**   189
Margareta Oudhuis

11   **Time for Competence?: Competence Development
     Among Interactive Media Workers**   210
     Fredrik Augustsson and Åke Sandberg

12   **Expertise and Employability in Management Consulting**   231
     Staffan Furusten

13   **Competing for Employability: The Media Ranking of
     Graduate Business Education**   252
     Linda Wedlin

14   **Conclusion: Discursive Transformations and the
     Nature of Modern Power**   274
     Christina Garsten and Kerstin Jacobsson

Author Index   291

Subject Index   297

Notes on the Contributors

Michael Allvin holds a PhD in Psychology and is a senior researcher in Work and Organization Psychology. He is currently doing research at the National Institute for Working Life in Stockholm on the individualization and increased flexibility of working life. Publications include *Det individualiserade arbetet: om modernitetens skilda praktiker* (*Individualization of Work: The Divided Practices of Modernity*, Symposion, 1997), and 'Do new generations imply the end of solidarity? Swedish unionism in the era of individualization' (with Magnus Sverke, in *Economic and Industrial Democracy*, 2000).

Fredrik Augustsson is a doctoral student of Sociology at the National Institute for Working Life in Stockholm. He is currently writing his dissertation about the organization of production in the Swedish market for interactive media production. Related research interests include social theory, economic sociology, organization theory, and technical development and its social and economic impacts. He is the co-author of *Interactive Media in Sweden 2001* (with Åke Sandberg, National Institute for Working Life, 2002).

Lotte Faurbæk holds a PhD in Political Science. She is currently teaching at Roskilde University. Her research interest concerns the relations between EU policy-making and national policy-making, especially in the field of EU social and labour market policy. She is the author of *Europæisk social-og arbejdsmarkedspolitik: Nationale EU-beslutningsprocesser og politikudvikling i Danmark og Sverige* (European Social Policy: National EU Decision-Making Processes and Policy Development in Denmark and Sweden, Copenhagen Business School, 2001).

Staffan Furusten holds a PhD in Business Administration and is research fellow at Score (Stockholm Center for Organizational Research), at Stockholm School of Economics and Stockholm University. His research is focused on the production and diffusion of popular management knowledge and on the construction and purchase of management consulting services. Another research interest is the standardization of organizational forms and regulation and professionalization of new forms of expertise. Recent publications include *Popular Management*

Books: How They Are Made and What They Mean for Organizations (Routledge, 1999) and *Managementkonsultation: reglerad expertis eller improviserat artisteri* (Management Consultation: Regulated Expertise or Improvised Art?, Studentlitteratur, 2003).

Christina Garsten is associate professor and senior lecturer at the Department of Social Anthropology, Stockholm University and research director of Score (Stockholm Center for Organizational Research) at Stockholm University and Stockholm School of Economics. Her research interests are in the anthropology of organizations and markets, with special focus on the globalization and flexibilization of employment. Recent publications include 'Trust, control and post-bureaucracy' (with Chris Grey, *Organization Studies*, 2001); and *New Technologies at Work: People, Screens and Social Virtuality* (co-edited with Helena Wulff, Berg, 2003).

Tony Huzzard holds a PhD in Business Administration from Umeå University. His research interests are organizational learning and change as well as critical perspectives on management and organizing. He currently works as a research fellow at the National Institute for Working Life in Stockholm where his research activities include organizational development and the quality of working life in a regional health authority as well as studies of social partnership and European works councils. Recent publications include: *Labouring to Learn: Union Renewal in Swedish Manufacturing* (Boréa, 2000) as well as a number of journal articles on trade union organization and learning.

Kerstin Jacobsson is associate professor of Sociology. She is a research fellow at Score (Stockholm Center for Organizational Research), Stockholm University and Stockholm School of Economics, and a senior lecturer at Södertörn University College. Her research interest is political sociology, with special focus on European integration. She is the co-author of *Mot en europeisk välfärdspolitik? Ny politik och nya samarbetsformer i EU* (Towards a European Welfare Policy? New politics and new forms of cooperation in the EU, SNS Förlag, 2001) and Real integration or just formal adaptation? On the implementation of the National Action Plans for Employment (with Herman Schmid, in *Building Social Europe through the Open Method of Coordination*, edited by Caroline de la Porte and Philippe Pochet, PIE Peter Lang, 2002).

Antony Lindgren is senior lecturer and associate professor of Sociology at Luleå University of Technology. His research interest is vocational education and training in Sweden. He also conducts research on regional policy and lectures on political and general sociology. Publications include: *Arbete, skola och familj i Sverige på 1900-talet* (Work, School and Family in Sweden in the 20th Century) and 'Lifelong learning in a changing world' (in Klaus Harney *et al.*, editors, *Lifelong Learning: On Focus, Different Systems*, 2002).

Margareta Oudhuis holds a PhD in Sociology. She is a senior lecturer at Borås University College. Her research interest concerns the individualization of work and its consequences for the individual, for team organization and for the workplace. She is the author of *Vägen till jämlikhet: En analys av den svenska arbetarrörelsens syn på effektivitet och emancipation i arbetslivet* (The Path to Equality: An Analysis of the View of the Swedish Labour Movement on Efficiency and Emancipation in Working Life, Atlas, 1999).

Åke Sandberg is senior researcher and associate professor at the Swedish National Institute for Working Life in Stockholm. His research focus is new technology and flexible forms of management and work organization and the outcome for employees in terms of competence and health, presently within the ICT and media sectors. Publications include *Technological Change and Co-determination in Sweden* (Temple University Press, 1992) and the edited volume *Enriching Production: Perspectives on Volvo's Uddevalla Plant as an Alternative to Lean Production* (Avebury, 1995).

Per Sederblad is researcher and senior lecturer at the School of Technology and Society, Malmö University. Publications include *Arbetsorganisation och grupper: Studier av svenska industriföretag* (Work Organization and Groups: Studies of Swedish Manufacturing Companies, Lund University 1993) and 'The Swedish model of work organization in transition' (with Paul Thompson, in *Global Japanization?: The Transnational Transformation of the Labour Process*, edited by Tony Elger and Chris Smith, Routledge, 1994). His current research focuses on teamworking in the service sector and in project organizations.

Lennart Svensson is a research leader at the National Institute for Working Life in Stockholm and visiting professor at Linköping University. His research focus is learning at work, organizational development, project work, teamwork, innovation systems, workplace democracy, and union activity. The research has an interactive approach: the idea is to organize joint learning with practitioners. He is the author or co-author of a number of books, including *Division of Labour, Specialization and Technical Change* (with Gunnar Törnqvist, Björn Gyllström and Jan-Evert Nilsson, Liber 1986) and *E-learning och arbetsplatslärande* (E-learning and Learning at Work, with Carina Åberg and Bilda Förlag 2001).

Renita Thedvall is a doctoral student of Social Anthropology at Stockholm University and a researcher at Score (Stockholm Center for Organizational Research), Stockholm University and Stockholm School of Economics. She is currently writing her dissertation on the European Employment Strategy, and the use of employment indicators to measure, audit, and compare member states. She has carried out fieldwork at the European Commission and followed the process of developing indicators of quality in work.

Linda Wedlin is a doctoral student at the Department of Business Studies at Uppsala University. Her research area is management education and knowledge, with special focus on issues of regulation, standardization, and classification in this field. Her thesis is about European business schools and the impact of media rankings of business schools on processes of creating and structuring social and cultural fields.

Preface

There is a story to this book as to every book – speaking of the joys of work as well as its strains. The joys are easily identified. They spring out of conceiving the very idea on a sunny day in May at a waterfront conference location just outside Stockholm, where ideas floated freely. They are embedded in the collegiality of the work, in the sharing and developing of ideas. And not least, they emerge in the moments of writing this note, towards the end of this particular journey. The pains on the other hand, loom in the complexities of orchestrating a complex project like this one, trying to grapple with an evasive and abstract generalized discourse. In retrospect, strains, too, are transformed into a sort of joys.

This volume is the result of a collective effort. We wish to thank all the contributors for working with us on this theme, for their enthusiasm and endurance. In particular, we are grateful to Michael Allvin for reading and providing constructive and inspiring comments upon several chapters. Tony Huzzard shared his ideas on the concept of discourse and commented on several chapters. We also wish to thank all authors who participated actively in our workshop discussions for taking the project further.

The volume also reflects the wider academic context within and across which we move. Colleagues at Score (Stockholm Center for Organizational Research) at Stockholm University and the Stockholm School of Economics have read and given valuable comments and criticisms on several chapters at a number of seminars. In particular, the research group of the Treo-project (Transnational Regulation and the Transformation of States, financially supported by the Swedish Research Council) and the project leaders Bengt Jacobsson and Kerstin Sahlin-Andersson have provided the kind of fruitful environment in which ideas and ventures like these may be conceptualized and delivered. Colleagues at the Department of Working Life Sciences at Karlstad University made an invaluable effort in reading and commenting on an earlier version of the volume which took us further ahead when the uphill slope seemed a bit too steep. At a later stage, we turned to Mats Börjesson, Rafael Lindqvist, Michael Power and Herman Schmid to test some of our ideas. Their generous engagement with our text provided a valuable check when we most needed it. Ann-Britt Hellmark has patiently edited the text with a sensitive eye, keen ear and professional attitude.

Our warmest thanks goes to all the people, in factories, public institutions, temp agencies, management consultancies, media companies or elsewhere who generously shared their everyday experiences and thoughts with us – and who told us stories of employability and beyond.

CHRISTINA GARSTEN
KERSTIN JACOBSSON

Stockholm

1

Learning To Be Employable:
An Introduction

Christina Garsten and Kerstin Jacobsson

In today's competitive labour markets, employability and learning have been placed at the centre of attention. In recruitment ads as well as in employment office documents; in corporate policies as well as in the policy recommendations of intergovernmental organizations, the significance of learning is underlined. Competence and skill are seen as perishable goods, of strategic value for individuals as well as organizations and even nations. Continuous learning is key to the successful navigation of individuals in labour markets. Learning is considered necessary in order to be *employable*.

Even if working and learning are not new companions, this message speaks of a transition from relatively stable patterns of work to more uncertain structural arrangements, with new demands placed on the individual. Many of these are posed by transnational organizations and with reference to market demands. A dominant idea is that getting a job, or being among the candidates for a job interview, is to a large degree dependent upon the power of initiative of the individual, upon one's own sense of responsibility for one's actions and decisions. The individual has to have certain characteristics: she must be 'employable', 'flexible' and be prepared to engage in 'lifelong learning'. A new conceptual topography is emerging (Stråth, 2000), prescribing a changed and arguably more limited role for the state and its authorities and greater space for market forces to operate, and, not least, greater pressure on the individual. This development has important implications for the way relations between employees and employers, unions and corporations, and politics and market forces are to be designed in labour markets, that is, for power relations.

The concept of *employability* has gained salience in the European labour market discourse, as an official policy category, during the last decade.

Employability as a concept captures well the current ideals for relationships between work, competence and learning. It illustrates the expectations and requirements of individuals to be and remain competitive in the labour market. Moreover, the shift of focus in labour market policy discourse from 'lack of employment' to 'lack of employability' illustrates a shift in problem perception and in policy from demand-oriented policies to promote full employment to supply-oriented policies to promote 'full employability' (Brown *et al.*, 2001; Serrano, 2000a; see also Jacobsson, Chapter 3 in this volume). It also illustrates a shift from a systemic view of the labour market to a focus on individuals and their qualities. We consider the discourse of employability as central to understanding contemporary changes in the workings of labour markets and in the logics of welfare states. It resonates with changes in ideas regarding responsibility and learning as well as with changes in ideas about the divisions of risk between the state, enterprises and individuals.

The aim of this book is to shed light on the powerful global discourse on employability in labour markets by providing insights from case studies of local work practices in Sweden. The key idea is to study the *global discourse and local practices of employability* in connection with each other. The meanings of the concepts of employability, competence and learning are partly contextual, as are the demands placed on individuals. Connecting global discourses – in the sense of being transnational and widespread (albeit unevenly!) – and local practices will allow us to see both how the discourse on employability and associated concepts may be operationalized and implemented in local practices; how the discourse may be translated and transformed into local practices, and how lack of correspondence between the discursive ideals and local practices may also be the result, due to such things as stable structures and strategies of resistance. It will allow us to assess to what extent and in what respects the global discourse on employability and learning is transforming actual practices, power relations and distribution of responsibilities.

The book addresses questions such as: What does the contemporary change towards more competitive labour markets mean for the individual employee? What demands are put on the individual in the discourse of powerful transnational organizations, such as the EU, the OECD and transnational enterprises? How is this interpreted and put into practice in and by actors at local workplaces? How are individuals regulated and governed in local contexts to meet the requirements set out in the discourse on employability? How do the individuals themselves learn to deal with these new demands? While our general hypothesis is that of increased demands placed on the individual, the character of these is open for empirical investigation in the various cases. We expect the discourse to have an impact on everyday working practices. However, we also expect resistance to discursive ideals to take shape and to 'talk back' to powerful actors.

In understanding the workings of the employability discourse and the practices of actors involved in shaping this discourse, diffusing it, putting it to use and resisting it, we have found the Swedish scene to be particularly interesting. Not just because most of the contributors happen to live in Sweden or have lived here for some time, but because the employability discourse resonates with a distinct set of established views and practices about how work and labour markets ought to be organized. While the book focuses primarily on work practices in Sweden, we will here provide a somewhat broader, albeit brief, back-ground context for changes in discursive ideals and practices.

Changes in working life: background and context

Learning has gained salience in the contemporary labour market debate – but it is far from a new issue. Working and learning have always walked hand in hand. Learning occurs as we solve problems at work, as we exchange information and engage in joint experimentation. It is in and through social interaction at work that we engage in learning activities. Learning is also a prerequisite for work. Before entering the job market, individuals spend a great number of years in the educational system. The complex division of labour in society requires specialized knowledge and expertise. The educational system is closely interlinked to the labour market, the matching of jobs and the skills of workers being a constant challenge.

The relationship between the two is, however, a complex one (Abrahamsson *et al.*, 2002; Tilly and Tilly, 1998). The supply of educated individuals does not always correspond to the demand in the labour market. In times of change, this relationship is often strained, and the matching of workers and jobs complicated by the inertia associated with the internal functioning of the respective field. The movement of individuals in labour markets across organizational and national bound-aries further accentuates the interdependency of work and learning. As individuals regroup into new teams in organizations, as they move between organizations, and as they re-educate themselves and shift career paths, they also engage in processes of learning. In open labour markets, that is, labour markets whose social networks transcend company and industry lines, and that blur the boundaries between the economy and community life, individuals and firms learn by continually recombining local knowledge, skills and technology (Saxenian, 1994: 36). The increase in temporary and project-based assignments further accentuates the need for continuous learning and the development of competencies and skills. With increased mobility in labour markets, acquiring transferable skills becomes a key issue (Grey and Garsten, 2001). What seems particularly characteristic of learning today is the development of generalized learning, developing skills that may be used in a variety of contexts. Likewise, the ability to engage in a sort of 'meta-learning', that is, learning to learn, has become critical.

As European governments experienced the recurrence of mass unemployment in the 1970s, the intimate relationship between working and learning was again stressed, accompanied by shifts in the allocation of responsibilities and risks between individuals, states, and other organizations. The state gradually stepped back from its position as caretaker, responsible for allocating job opportunities or compensation for unemployed individuals. Keynesian ideas about state intervention in the social question of unemployment and regulation of work lost credibility. While the role of the state has been partly redefined to support the employability of individuals (see Jacobsson in this volume), we have also witnessed a gradual shift of responsibility towards the individual, who, him- or herself, has to take initiative and to act accordingly.

The character of relation between working and learning is also to do with the organization of work. The Fordist production system was supported by a number of large institutions, such as dominant corporations, centrally governed labour unions, and collective agreements between parties. The welfare state, with a well developed social insurance system closely tied to the individual worker, played a significant role in integrating the practice of work with the identity of the worker (Allvin, 1997: 168f). During the Fordist era, the identity of the worker was established as a social norm. Work, and an occupation, became the axis of living in the industrial age (Beck, 1992: 139). The worker who fulfilled his duties in work could, in return, declare his rights as a working citizen. The relationship between the individual and the organization also structured what was to be known about work and organizing, how it would be known, and who would know it (Jacques, 1996: 96). The employee was 'made up' to a large extent by his or her relation to work and the organization. In a system with lifelong, full-time work organized in a single industrial location as the norm (but not the general practice), learning was expected to take place largely within the confines of the work organization.

Relations of work have over time become increasingly standardized and universal in character (Allvin, 1997: 178). The relation between employer and employed have changed from that of a relation between reciprocally identifiable parties to a strategic navigating of individuals in relation to a formal set of rules. This 'juridicalization' of the relation of work, characterized by a technical and formalized relation, was set in place by the regulatory activities of the welfare state, which paved the way for a standardization of employment contracts.

More recently, the system of standardized full employment has begun to soften and fray at the margins into flexibilization of labour law, work site, and working hours. Following de-regulation, boundaries between work and non-work are becoming fluid, employment contracts are more varied, and pluralist forms of underemployment and employment are spreading (Beck, 1992: 142). Work is in many ways becoming de-standardized and open to a variety of arrangements and patterns of organization. This de-standardization involves both temporal and spatial dimensions. Working together at the same time and at the same place is no longer to be taken for granted. And new demands on learning are being placed on the individual. We have seen an expansion of so-called 'atypical' jobs, for example in the growth of the temporary staffing sector, 'stand-by' jobs, 'project work', and various types of contingent work. The number of employees on fixed-term contracts has increased to reach almost 14 per cent of total employment in Sweden by 2002 (CEC, 2002: 26). Also, a larger proportion of individuals are now earning their income from 'self-employment'. This trend may be understood as part of a move towards increasing flexibilization of labour markets (Stråth, ed., 2000), of production systems, of work organization, working time arrangements (Atkinson and Meager, 1986; Harvey 1989, 1991; Hörning *et al.*, 1995), contracts, and even bodies (Martin, 1994).

Flexibilization in itself means an adaptation to market needs, hence a fostering of a certain 'culture of competitiveness'. Economic competition accentuates the requirements of individuals to adapt to new circumstances and the shifting needs of enterprises. Global economic competition also challenges the social contracts that have been negotiated in the welfare states as well as the social compromises negotiated in the industrial relations systems. It has been argued that competitiveness has become a hegemonic concept in labour relations and something that increasingly unites management and labour. In Streeck's (1998) formulation, a new 'peace formula' is replacing the postwar formula of full employment and income redistribution, namely the sharing of economic risk and responsibility in competitive markets: 'while in the past industrial relations was about negotiating a secure status for workers and unions, insulating these from economic fluctuations, in the national industrial relations systems of today ... it is about adjusting the governance of the employment relationship to the imperatives of joint competitive success' (Streeck, 1998: 439). To that extent, the national interest in maintained competitiveness replaces class interests. The concern for social security is redefined as a concern for maintained competitiveness (cf. the development of a new type of corporatism – competitive corporatism – and cross-class productivity coalitions or flexibility alliances (Rhodes, 1998).) The unions have had to, if not give up, at least shelve their earlier drive for a more egalitarian distribution of income (Ferrera *et al.*, 2000: 55) and redefine the notion of solidarity (see Huzzard, Chapter 6 in this volume).

Moreover, there is a relative consensus among welfare researchers that a policy shift has taken place in the West European welfare states from the previous emphasis on equity, freedom of choice and security of income towards various combinations of measures to increase the work incentive and to get and keep people in gainful employment (Heikkilä, 1999). This is seen as a strategy both to increase economic competitiveness and to avoid social exclusion. Jessop (1994) takes the argument furthest in speaking of a shift from a Fordist–Keynesian welfare state to a Schumpeterian workfare state, where social policy is subordinated to the key issue of how to strengthen structural competitiveness.

At the same time, with knowledge as an increasingly important factor in the accumulation of value – the (alleged) knowledge-based economy – human capabilities and resources are considered more important than ever to economic and social welfare. Learning is considered a strategic asset for individuals as well as for enterprises and nations. In this context, the concept of 'lifelong learning' takes on a partly different meaning than at the time it was launched in the 1960s and 1970s. Then part of an emancipatory discourse, where the ultimate purpose of learning was self-fulfilment (OECD, 1977: 23), the concept of lifelong learning now denotes the socio-economic need for mobilizing and adapting human resources in the struggle for economic growth, productivity and competition (Rubenson, 1996). Economic imperative, rather than the emancipatory project, is the dominating logic. Motives for learning are phrased in market language, such as that of increasing the power of attraction of a person in the labour market, and that of strategic value for business. Motives may also, of course, be phrased in alternative terminologies, but these tend to be overshadowed by economistic concerns.

Responsibility for learning has also partly shifted. In the discourse on lifelong learning in the 1960s and 1970s, this was mainly seen as a state responsibility and required public investment (for instance OECD, 1977). Today, responsibility is increasingly placed on the individual who, supposedly stimulated by the opportunities offered by the market, is expected to engage pro-actively in her own lifelong learning (Rubenson, 1996). The responsibility of enterprises for lifelong learning is also increasingly coming into focus, the argument being that investment in the human resources of the firm will lead to improved productivity and competitiveness. This is a view largely shared by the trade unions, who are now speaking of lifelong learning as something the individual worker needs to embrace and be prepared to assume some responsibility for (see Huzzard, Chapter 6 in this volume). This is not to say that the state has withdrawn its responsibility altogether. Rather, responsibility has been reformulated to support the employability of individuals. The supposition is that the enterprise, the individual and the state share a common interest in stimulating this.[1]

The concept of employability

The dominant conceptual framework for understanding the labour market and the employment situation has shifted over time. Stråth (2000) argues that the very concept of unemployment was invented in the 19th century to mediate experiences in rapidly changing labour markets. A distinction emerged between the deserving and the undeserving poor, indicating that the existence of poverty and unemployment was not necessarily the fault of individuals. Unemployment came to be seen as due to systemic problems (and not individual problems) and thus as a collective responsibility (Stråth, 2000: 12f; also Serrano, 2000a; Salais *et al.*, 1986). The handling of the 'social question' was a collective interest. This was later institutionalized in the welfare state, but only after struggles between different interests and social forces.

In many European countries, state responsibility for full employment was part of a general policy consensus in the 1950s and 1960s. This policy thinking was disrupted by the inflation and unemployment crisis of the 1970s. A supply-side economic theory with low inflation and structural reform as top priorities replaced the Keynesian consensus. Here came a shift from a focus on, and policies towards, full employment to a focus on unemployment (Stråth, 2000), combined with the understanding that unemployment was due to structural rather than cyclical causes. The lack of flexibility in labour markets and the need for regulatory reform became key concerns.

In the 1990s, we have witnessed another shift in the European policy discourse, now from the unemployed/employed to the *unemployable/employable*, with the properties of individuals in focus. In an edited volume on the flexibility discourse, Stråth (2000: 23) has raised the question of whether the concern for flexibility is the first sign of a new division between the just and the unjust unemployed. This may be even truer of the concern for employability. The categories of unemployable/employable can not only be used to classify and sort individuals but also, by implication, to legitimize their status in the labour market – unemployment is explained and to some extent legitimized with reference to lack of employability. The problem of unemployment is individualized both in the sense that the causes of unemployment are sought at an individual level (lack of employability), and in the sense that the responsibilities of individuals are underlined. While during the 20th century, unemployment came to be seen as a social risk and a collective responsibility, 'risk management' is now increasingly something expected from the individual (Crespo and Serrano, 2002).

Although the term employability itself has been in use since the early 20th century (Gazier, 1999), it was in the 1960s that it gained currency, then mostly understood in a static sense as a person's capacity to obtain and keep employment.[2] Since then, a more dynamic understanding of employability has developed. Employability now denotes the capacity of individuals to adapt to the demands of employment. This requires skills enhancement, continuous learning and also, according to one discourse, showing the 'right' attitudes (initiative, flexibility, availability). In its most market-oriented version, employability is simply a question of marketability of skills (cf. the human resource management discourse). Thus, while the terms unemployable/employable were initially used to categorize the unemployed and direct measures at them accordingly, more recent uses of the term also refer to the needs of currently employed individuals to live up to future labour market demands.

Lefresne (1999) contrasts two uses of the term employability back in the 1960s. First, it was used in the US with a primarily socio-medical focus. Employability then referred to individual ability as identified through functional tests of work capacity, an objective being rehabilitation. In contrast to this notion, there was the purely statistical definition, mainly used in France, referring to the probability for a given group at a given time to find a job, implying a more macro-economic perspective in the sense that fluctuations in the labour market were taken into account. Lefresne argues that with the increasing focus on supply, the idea of compensating for individual handicaps, and the parallel decline of macro-economic policies of full employment, the American notion is gradually gaining ascendancy in the European policy discourse. 'This notion involves a mainly neo-classical vision of the labour market: the fact that a person is unemployed is attributed above all to an inadequate "quality/price" ratio. In this context, according to behaviourist principles, employment policy consists of sending stimuli to companies by playing on this ratio (training/reducing labour costs) for the various people it is trying to place' (Lefresne, 1999: 466).

This pricing of productivity logic is highly prevalent in the OECD policy discourse, and is also present in the EU policy discourse (see Jacobsson, Chapter 3 in this volume). However, in the EU discourse, there are components both of this liberal Anglo-Saxon model and of the Scandinavian model, as Lefresne (1999) also acknowledges. In the latter, improved employability is not primarily an individual but a collective responsibility. Investment in the labour force is rational from the perspective of the collective. Moreover, a sufficient level and duration of unemployment benefit is considered necessary to ease the process of job matching, which in turn facilitates occupational mobility. At the same time, benefit systems should give incentives to take available jobs. Putting demanding requirements on the unemployed is seen as necessary both in order to motivate and to sustain high levels of benefit. The Scandinavian model is thus characterized by active labour market policies in combination with fairly generous benefit systems, however, shaped in such a way as to reinforce the 'work strategy'. The unemployment insurance schemes have been complemented with demanding qualification criteria. Skills enhancement, as part of the active labour market policies, is thus not new in the Scandinavian context, even if the term employability was not explicitly used in Sweden until the mid-1990s. But here focus has traditionally been less on the moral and social qualities of individuals and more on their skills so as to facilitate the process of job matching.

Today, employability is a key concept in European labour market policy discourse and is taken to include a number of different aspects. Improved employability is seen as a strategy for improving people's working capacity as well as their willingness to work and their access to the labour market. The policy agenda, as reflected for instance in the European Employment Strategy, includes both the reduction of non-wage labour costs, especially for low-skilled workers, *and* competence development and activation. Employability thus aims at both 'dynamic and updated competencies and a labour-market-oriented behavior' (Weinert *et al.*, 2001: xii.) for every person participating in the workforce. (For studies on the discourse of employability in the EU, see Bosco, 1998; Bosco and Chassard, 1999; Lefresne, 1999; Raveaud, 2001; Serrano, 2000a; Weinert *et al.*, 2001.) While different countries are to a varying extent influenced by the liberal model or the Scandinavian model (understood as ideal-types) in their enhancement of employability, all West European countries have moved in the direction of stronger pressures on unemployed individuals to accept jobs and/or training. This is also true in Scandinavia, where, as mentioned, active labour market policies and the work strategy as such are not new. Work incentives have been strengthened and work obligations made more explicit and stricter in all the Nordic countries in the 1990s (Johansson, 2001; Kautto *et al.*, 1999).[3] The work on reviewing the tax and social benefit system in order to increase job incentives and avoid poverty traps has continued in the 2000s. However, Swedish labour market legislation has not been subject to a great deal of flexibilization thus far.

The increased demands on the individual have been observed in the rich literature on activation and workfare (for instance Heikkilä, 1999; Lødemel and Trickey, 2001; Serrano, 2002b). Despite the differences in national social security systems (Esping-Andersen, 1990), which largely still remain (Ferrera *et al.*, 2000; Kleinman, 2001; Scharpf and Schmidt, 2000), there are currently converging trends in the West European countries, such as strengthened policies of activation, and easing of the transition from school to work by placing a great deal of emphasis on training and work experience schemes. Examples include the tightening of eligibility conditions for unemployment benefit; increasing the financial incentive to take up any available job; attempts to avoid 'welfare traps'; measures to deal with youth unemployment by early intervention and special youth training schemes (Johansson, 2001; Kautto *et al.*, 1999; Lefresne, 1999; Lødemel and Trickey, 2001). The research on activation and workfare points to a reformulation of rights and obligations for individuals along lines similar to the analysis in this book. However, our main focus is less on the attempts to increase the employability of the unemployed, that is on reform of labour market policy and social security systems, but, rather, on the demands placed on individuals in local arenas of work, that is in working life. While most previous studies of employability have focused on measures directed at the unemployed (Weinert *et al.*, 2001), we are additionally concerned to include individuals *in* employment (see also Bollérot, 2001). A key idea in the discourse on employability is precisely that in a rapidly changing world, employment today is no guarantee for employability tomorrow. As illustrated in the following chapters, employability can be achieved, *inter alia*, through adaptability, versatility, showing an entrepreneurial attitude, and through being service-minded and accepting continuous evaluation and ranking.

With changes in production systems and in the organization of work, the identity of the employee also undergoes changes. The employee of today is faced with new challenges, involving new expectations, rights and responsibilities. While we may not expect to spend our lives as full-time employees, we may expect to move between organizations, projects, and colleagues to a great extent. We may have to settle with the prospect of not having steady employment, but, rather, making sure we are employable when the opportunity arises. True, the degree to which these trends penetrate different nations and categories of employees varies. The nature of transformation may also be questioned in terms of its discursive or factual character. Nevertheless, there is reason to believe that, with employability on the agenda, what is to be known at work, how it is to be known, and who is to know it, is changing.

We are here concerned with norms of employability as well as with the techniques employed in the construction of an employable labour force in various local arenas of work in Sweden and in transnational policy-making organizations such as the EU and OECD. We thus take a broad view of employability, covering norms and measures directed not only at the unemployed but also, and more so, at employees in order for them to remain competitive in the labour market. Attention is placed not so much on what employability *is*, but on what it *does*.

Discursive dynamics and techniques

In this book, we explore the discursive shift towards employability, life-long learning and market orientation. We look more closely into how the growing power of transnational organizations to regulate individual and collective behaviour is expressed in a number of different arenas in and around the labour market. In so doing, we hope to shed light on the characteristics of the discursive field of employability and its shifting meanings in different contexts, and the contemporary forms of regulation in the labour market that are mobilized by way of this discourse. These new regulatory forms often supersede the state level and take on voluntary and subtle forms, but they may be extremely powerful and influential in character. The individual is facing new social techniques and discursive influences, which may function to fashion and control action and thinking in a particular direction.

We take a broad perspective on the discursive field, which means that we are interested in analysing how the concept of employability as well as related concepts, such as lifelong learning and flexibility, are played out in context. In Williams' (1976) view, such concepts may be seen as migrating keywords that, over time, acquire a range of contingent meanings. As they are used in new contexts, old meanings may gain new prominence or existing meanings may be stretched in novel and unpredictable directions. They are in this sense to be seen as multi-vocal concepts whose precise meanings depend on the user and the social-political arena in which he or she is situated. In Gallie's terms (1956), they are 'essentially contested concepts'. They have the capacity to be mobilized in a number of different processes, but may at the same time overshadow conflictual interpretations. This book looks closer at these concepts, their socio-political base and their concrete operation-alization in policy and practice. Accordingly, norms of employability may differ between countries as well as between local organizational contexts. The social structure of employability, as it were, is also stranded with unequal and conflicting relations.

Much recent work in the social sciences, including studies of organization and work, has focused on the language used by actors both as speech and writing. In what has been identified as a 'linguistic turn' in organizational research (Alvesson and Kärreman, 2000a), language has become central as researchers have sought textual and linguistic tools to reflect critically on subject positions. At the heart of such an approach is the view that language does a great deal more than simply communicate messages or represent perceived objects in an accurate way (Potter and Wetherell, 1987). Language also has the role of accomplishing things, a viewpoint that philosophers and linguists have long asserted (Austin, 1962; Searle, 1969). In such a view, language as an abstract system interacts intimately with social practice so as to become close or even inseparable from it: such interdependence whereby language is understood as social practice is usually denoted by the concept of 'discourse' (Fairclough, 2001). In our view, discourse, as a system of thought and meaning, is expressed in the language used but also finds material expression in social practice. Discourse presents a perspective from which reality can be described, phenomena classified, positions taken and actions justified. As such it is closely intertwined with specific social practice.[4] Hence our interest in what the discourse of employability actually *does*.

Still, what discourse really accomplishes is debated. Researchers from critical realist positions have questioned both the omnipotent properties usually ascribed to language in, for example, post-structuralist accounts as well as the associated implication that 'nothing exists outside the text' (see for instance Thompson, 1993; see also Alvesson and Kärreman 2000b on 'muscular discourse' as a sort of linguistic determinism whereby language is deemed to determine both subjects and objects). The usage of the concept of discourse is thus by no means restricted to post-structuralist work (Alvesson and Kärreman, 2000b). While we acknowledge the constitutive power of language – language-use does accomplish things for instance by providing classifications and justifi-cations – it is also important to acknowledge the scope for deviation and resistance. It is in defiance of the 'muscular' discourse that key social processes are played out, and this space is thus often the site of important research enquiry. Hence, it is important to acknowledge the possibility of resistance and discursive struggle. Discourse may come in plural forms and be associated with power as well as with resistance. Yet, there can be little doubt that language, seen as discourse, is of interest not least because of its close relationship with power. Power is central to discourse in that it is not 'simply that which translates struggles or systems of domination but the thing for which and by which there is a struggle, discourse is the power which is seized' (Foucault quoted in Thorne, 2001: 2).

Discourses as ways of thinking overlap or reinforce each other and function as to close off other possible ways of thinking. By its ability to rule out alternative ways of thinking a discourse can work to preserve a particular distribution of power. This view of discourse highlights the fact that language is socially constituted and not an autonomous domain, and, moreover, that our interest in discourse concerns the politics of discursive practice (Grillo, 1989). A common theoretical focus in this volume is the connection between discourse and social practice, in particular social techniques for the governing of individuals, that is, for 'the conduct of conduct' (Dean, 1999; Miller and Rose, 1995; Rose, 1999, drawing on Foucault). We are here interested in all endeavours of organizations to shape, guide and direct the conduct of individuals in the labour market. Such attempts may be formally rationalized in programmes, statements, policy documents and devices. But they may also be less formally articulated and existing in a variety of practical rationalities within particular types of practice, such as social work or labour market policy (Rose, 1999: 3f). We are, thus, interested in explicit documents and advice as well as implicit norms guiding and shaping individuals to meet the requirements of a competitive labour market.

The work of Miller and Rose (1995) on forms of government in the labour market provides a critical point of departure for analysing the strategies and techniques for acting, through indirect means, on the conduct of others in a range of different sites and under the aegis of a range of different authorities. The focus on the ensemble of norms and practices, ideas and devices that seek to regulate and shape the worker and his or her work experience is relevant here. Discourses provide norms for thought and action, norms that can be internalized and perceived as 'the normal'. Our way of labelling people and their acts have an impact on how they come to understand themselves and how they come to act. The most effective technique from a power point of view is the internalization of social control. Government as external control then becomes governance or self-regulation, a form of power that presupposes the agency of individuals rather than denying it (Shore, 2000: 30). According to what norms and by what means is 'the employable individual created in various local contexts?', we ask.

In other words, our approach combines a discursive analysis with close examination of social practices at the workplace. The perspective also situates such 'technologies' of regulation within a framework of transforming relations and alliances between diverse regulating authorities. Foucault's work on 'political technologies' provides a valuable theoretical approach for analysing how effective governance is achieved, or, as he put it 'regimes of truth' are established (1978, 1991). Political technologies work by taking what are essentially political issues, removing them from the realm of politics and recasting them in the neutral language of progress, science, and technology so that they appear as technical or managerial problems to be solved or managed rather than political issues. The evaluative practices and reward systems of corporations are examples of such political technologies, aimed at constructing the employable individual (see Garsten and Oudhuis in this volume). A key concern here is: who has the power to define? Dominant discourses work by setting up the terms of reference and by disallowing or marginalizing alternatives. Policies enable this to happen by setting a political agenda and giving institutional authority to one or a number of overlapping discourses. We believe that by taking a critical approach to concepts such as employability, lifelong learning and flexibility and to how they are 'operationalized' by different actors in different contexts, we will acquire deeper understanding of how and by what discursive and social practices the contemporary European labour market is being organized.

The following chapters explore the variety of ways in which a transnational discourse is translated into practice in ways that speak not only of the power of this particular discourse, but also of the power of local practices and structures.

In Chapter 2, Michael Allvin sets the stage for the chapters to come by giving an account of how labour emerges as a social category, and how our conception of labour is based on the rules regulating our participation in reproduction. With changes in production systems, rules regulating participation changes, from the very simple rules of spatiotemporal conduct required by small scale mechanized production, to a general commitment to furthering an agile business process. And, as the rules change, so does the conception of labour: from the shared capacity of 'labour power' to a functional and responsible cog in the great machinery of progress, to a self-efficient and self-reliant operator in a market.

In Chapter 3, Kerstin Jacobsson conducts an analysis of the discourse on employability of the EU and the OECD, as two transnational organizations with considerable ideational influence on the direction of national labour market reform in Europe. In this policy discourse the characteristics and responsibilities of individuals are accentuated. It reflects a changed role for welfare states from the redistribution of wealth to the support of individuals' adjustment to change by supply-side interventions. This chapter thus provides a look at the practice of power, and the kinds of ideas and perspectives that are distributed from these organizations.

Chapter 4 is concerned with EU social and labour market policy, as the social dimension of the European Union. Lotte Faurbæk discusses the relationship between this EU discourse and the national creation of meaning within the same policy area in one specific member state – Sweden. The chapter shows that, despite images of Sweden as being characterized by consensus and pragmatism between labour market parties, the Swedish translation of EU labour market policy is taking place in a discursive terrain that is ideologically polarized.

In Chapter 5, Lennart Svensson seeks to explain why lifelong learning so often fails in organizations. This chapter discusses the lack of correspondence between the strong discursive ideals at the official, discursive level and the weak practices at the local level. Why are strategies for lifelong learning so difficult to implement? Svensson seeks three types of explanations; at the societal level, looking at some important changes in contemporary labour markets; at the organizational level – the work practice, management and the role of learning; and in a current gap between the educational system and the production system.

In Chapter 6, Tony Huzzard focuses attention on the interaction between the discourse of the 'competent individual' with the discourses of trade union renewal in Sweden. Swedish unions retain a key role in regulating the labour process and are central actors in the social practices associated with work, as well as shapers of discourse. Three unions are examined as case studies. Following an examination of the everyday realities at three workplaces where these unions organize, the post-industrial discourse of the 'competent individual' is then discussed critically. The chapter concludes with an evaluation of the role of unions as discursive agents. It is suggested that the identity of unions has shifted from that of allocating wealth towards supporting the adaptation of the individual to labour market change, implying a widening of the concept of solidarity.

Chapter 7, by Renita Thedvall, gives an empirical account of how the ideological shift in Swedish labour market policy is connected to changes in the view of the individual. Thedvall describes how the Public Employment Service has shifted from mediating mainly regular employment positions to also promoting self-employment. Focus is placed on how the PES is 'constructing' the self-employed through a 'Self-Employment Project – Work Experience Scheme'. The PES project teaches the unemployed to feel confident in being entrepreneurs in the labour market and to perceive themselves as agents of change. It involves a gradual transformation of identity and consciousness by which they learn to view themselves as capable of 'doing it themselves', that is, creating jobs for themselves by being entrepreneurial, self-confident and responsible.

In Chapter 8, Christina Garsten continues the empirical description of changed expectations and demands on individuals, by giving an account of how flexible employees in the temporary staffing business in Sweden are taught to integrate these in their ways of thinking and acting. Focus is placed on the policies and everyday social practices through which flexibility, as a prerequisite for employability, is put to work among temporary employees through socialization, evaluation procedures and rewards. In the process, temps learn to integrate the perspectives of the agency in ways that make government as external constraint turn into self-regulation, or governance. The assumption of individualized agency, together with a great deal of discontinuity on the job, also challenges collective action, by undermining the very notion of 'colleague'.

The social and relational aspects of work in flexible environments exposed to market pressure are further discussed in Chapter 9, by Antony Lindgren and Per Sederblad. The chapter presents research on teamworking in new forms of service work in call centres. In call centre work, employability and flexibility come into play in that the externally oriented work tasks and the need to be service-oriented and customer-focused mean that the notion of 'team' is emptied of content. Personal and social relations in the workplace do, however, provide the employees with some degree of social and emotional support, even if their work tasks are seldom tightly interconnected. Managers often draw on this notion of 'team' and 'team spirit' ideologically to manage the employees, a strategy sometimes met with resistance at individual and collective levels.

Drawing on a case study at a Volvo Bus Plant, Margareta Oudhuis describes in Chapter 10 how discursive and organizational transition go hand with hand. The 'good worker' of the old team model organization gives way to the 'employable individual' of the new team model, with different ideals and expectations defining these notions, and different techniques being used to encourage and guide employees' ways of thinking and acting at the plant. Oudhuis also discusses the different consequences of these disciplinary techniques and strategies on the individual worker. What are the effects on mind, body and emotions? The shift in work organization and discourse may have positive as well as negative effects, with some individuals emphasizing the potentials and others experiencing threats to their position.

In Chapter 11, Fredrik Augustsson and Åke Sandberg take a closer look at a highly dynamic part of working life where technical innovations are frequent and presumed to call for constant competence development: the production of interactive media solutions. Their aim is to analyse the general discourse of competence development and employability in the context of the Swedish interactive media industry and its consequences for employees. Their empirical data shows that the promise of competence development at the firm level is a cost-effective tool to attract and keep employees, as well as securing their loyalty. On the other hand, even though most firms offer their employees substantial resources for competence development, very few employees take full advantage of these resources. An important reason for this, it is argued, is the way in which competence development is organized, and the one-sided responsibility for learning that this entails.

Chapter 12 explores management consulting as a business in which market-orientation is conspicuous, where employability as such is seldom talked about, but where competitiveness and the ability 'to sell' is a prerogative. Management consultants have a major impact on many parts of working life today and play an important role in the diffusion of a particular ideology. Staffan Furusten discusses the prerequisites for becoming employable as a management consultant and what they mean in practice; what types of knowledge and competence are viewed to constitute 'good' management consultation. To be employable as a management consultant depends to a great extent on the individual consultant's capacity to establish trust in the relationship with the potential customer, and 'to sell' oneself as well as the project.

In Chapter 13, Linda Wedlin elaborates on how the demands on institutions providing higher education in business and management to educate top-level, competitive, employable individuals are played out through media rankings. Media ranking tables of business education programmes, as provided by major international newspapers and magazines, provide an example of the heavy emphasis on education in society at large, and it is an arena where expectations and demands are expressed and formed. By looking at the criteria used in these rankings, a picture of the most valued features of graduates and the educational programmes provided emerges. It is argued that the rankings' focus on short-term values is almost contradictory to the concept of lifelong learning and employability in a more dynamic sense.

Finally, in Chapter 14 we sketch out some of the implications that may be drawn from our discussions. We suggest that the development may be conceived of as a *discursive transformation* reordering relations between actors (including power relations) and shifting the distribution of risks and responsibilities between them. The discourse on employability is indicative of a general market orientation in society, which has, in the case of the labour market, led to an emphasis on the labour market as *market*. This has, *inter alia*, reinforced pressures on individuals to be adaptable to market needs.

Discourses are performative. They give direction for daily practice, and they prescribe and encourage certain types of behaviour, sometimes supported by various types of practices, such as practices of evaluation and reward. The discourse on employability has established the 'employable individual' as a normative category. The category of employability, like other administrative categories, may function to legitimize measures directed – or not directed – at actors who fall under the category as well as their position in the labour market.

However, such generalized discourses are always *translated* into local contexts, where existing practices, traditions, and institutionalized ways of seeing and doing things, transform and reformulate ideas in specific ways. In this sense, local practice talks back at discourse. Moreover, discourses and their imperatives to action may also provoke resistance from actors. Discursive influence may not be a one-way street – a discursive transformation is also a dynamic process characterized by negotiations, resistance and ultimately power struggle. It is in this potential we place our trust.

Notes

1. In several European countries individual learning accounts have been introduced. This includes Sweden where the proposal has been launched that all employees will be offered the possibility to make savings for their own skills development in exchange for tax relief. It is also proposed to give employers tax incentives to contribute to these accounts, the idea being that economic responsibility is shared between the individual, the state and the employer. However, the stress on individual responsibility for lifelong learning is notable in the notion of individual learning accounts.

2. All in all, Gazier (1999, 2001) identifies seven uses of the concept during the 20th century. For an analysis of current meanings of the concept, see also Forrier and Sels (2002).

3. Swedish economic, labour market and social policy has long been characterized by a commitment to work, both in terms of a political commitment to full employment and the right to work *and* in the design of the social security system so as to reinforce the 'work strategy' (*arbetslinjen*) by giving incentives to work (Lindqvist and Marklund, 1995). The active labour market policy is an important instrument in the fulfilment of this commitment through training and the reallocation of labour. Demanding requirements have also been put on individuals historically, for instance moving to regions where there is work. The Swedish labour unions have accepted the need for structural rationalization in order to improve productivity and thereby enjoy rising living standards, and have therefore supported labour mobility across the country and across sectors. Industrial renewal and structural change have been considered to be in the long-term interests of the workers as a collective even if in the short term this may imply major difficulties and distribution problems between sectors. The active labour market policy was to take care of the 'islands of unemployment' that structural transformation gave rise to and reallocate the labour supply by different types of measures to facilitate adaptability and mobility (Jacobsson, 2002; Johansson and Magnusson, 1998).

4. We are grateful to Tony Huzzard for valuable contributions in elaborating our perspective on discourse.

References

Abrahamsson, Kenneth, Lena Abrahamsson, Torsten Björkman, Per-Erik Ellström, and Jan Johansson (eds). 2002. *Utbildning, kompetens och arbete*. Lund: Studentlitteratur.

Allvin, Michael. 1997. *Det individualiserade arbetet*. Stockholm: Symposion.

Alvesson, Mats and Dan Kärreman. 2000a. 'Taking the linguistic turn in organizational research: challenges, responses, consequences'. *Journal of Applied Behavioural Science*, 36(2): 136–58.

Alvesson, Mats and Dan Kärreman. 2000b. 'Varieties of discourse: on the study of organizations through discourse analysis'. *Human Relations* 53(9): 1125–49.

Atkinson, John and Nigel Meager. 1986. *Changing Working Patterns: How Companies Achieve Flexibility to Meet New Needs*. London: National Economic Development Office.

Austin, John L. 1962. *How To Do Things with Words*. Oxford: Oxford University Press.

Beck, Ulrich. 1992. *Risk Society*. London: Sage.

Bollérot, Patrick. 2001. 'Two actors in employability: the employer and the worker'. In *Employability: From Theory to Practice*, edited by P. Weinert *et al*. London: Transaction Publishers, 51–90.

Bosco, Alessandra. 1998. 'Putting Europe into the systems: a review of social protection issues'. In *European Trade Union Yearbook 1997*, edited by E. Gabaglio and R. Hoffmann. Brussels: ETUI, 305–34.

Bosco, Alessandra and Y. Chassard. 1999. 'A shift in the paradigm: surveying the European Union discourse on welfare and work'. In *Linking Welfare and Work*, edited by M. Heikkilä. Dublin: European Foundation, 43–58.

Brown, Phillip, Andy Green, and Hugh Lauder. 2001. *High Skills: Globalization, Competitiveness and Skill Formation*. Oxford: Oxford University Press.

Burton-Jones, Alan. 1999. *Knowledge Capitalism: Business, Work, and Learning in the New Economy*. Oxford: Oxford University Press.

CEC [Commission of the European Communities]. 2002. *Employment in Europe 2002. Recent Trends and Prospects*.

Crespo, Eduardo and Amparo Serrano. 2002. 'The EU's concept of activation for young people: towards a new social contract?'. In *Activation Policies for Young People in International Perspective*, edited by A. Serrano. Brussels: ETUI. Book manuscript.

Crompton, Rosemary, Duncan Gallie, and Kate Purcell. 1996. *Changing Forms of Employment*. London: Routledge.

Dean, Mitchell. 1999. *Governmentality: Power and Rule in Modern Society*. London: Sage.

Esping-Andersen, Gösta. 1990. *The Three Worlds of Welfare Capitalism*. London: Polity Press.

Fairclough, Norman. 2001. *Language and Power* (2nd edn). Harlow: Longmans.

Ferrera, Maurizio, Anton Hemerijck, and Martin Rhodes. 2000. *The Future of Social Europe: Recasting Work and Welfare in the New Economy*. Report to the Portuguese Presidency of the European Union.

Forrier, Anneleen and Luc Sels. 2002. 'Employability: the magic spell for a success-ful career'. Paper presented at the 18th EGOS Colloquium, Barcelona, 4–6 July.

Foucault, Michel. 1978. *The History of Sexuality*: Volume One. Harmondsworth: Penguin.

Foucault, Michel. 1991. 'Governmentality'. In *The Foucault Effect: Studies in Governmentality*, edited by G. Burcell, C. Gordon, and P. Miller. London: Harvester Wheatsheaf, 87–104.

Gallie, William B. 1956. 'Essentially contested concepts'. *Proceedings of the Aristotelian Society*, 56: 167–98.

Gazier, Bernard. 1999. 'Employabilité: concepts et politiques'. *InforMISEP*, no 67/68.

Gazier, Bernard. 2001. 'Employability: the complexity of a policy notion'. In *Employability: From Theory to Practice*, edited by P. Weinert *et al.* London: Trans-action Publishers, 3–23.

Grey, Chris and Christina Garsten. 2001. 'Trust, control and post-bureaucracy'. *Organization Studies* 22(2): 229–50.

Grillo, Ralph (ed.) 1989. *Social Anthropology and the Politics of Language*. London: Routledge.

Harvey, David. 1989. *The Condition of Postmodernity*. Oxford: Blackwell.

Harvey, David. 1991. 'Flexibility: threat or opportunity?'. *Socialist Review* 21(1): 65–7.

Heikkilä, Matti (ed.) 1999. *Linking Welfare and Work*, Dublin: European Foundation.

Hörning, Karl H., Anette Gerhard, and Matthias Michailow. 1995. *Time Pioneers: Flexible Working Time and New Lifestyles*. Cambridge: Polity Press.

Jacques, Roy. 1996. *Manufacturing the Employee*. London: Sage.

Jacobsson, Kerstin. 2002. 'The Cardiff process of structural reform in Sweden'. In *The Trade Unions and the Cardiff Process: Economic Reform in Europe*, edited by D. Foden and L. Magnusson. Brussels: ETUI, 101–48.

Jessop, Bob. 1994. 'The transition to post-fordism and the Schumpetarian workfare state'. In *Towards a Post-Fordist Welfare State?* edited by R. Burrows and B. Loader. London: Routledge, 13–37.

Johansson, Anders and Lars Magnusson. 1998. *LO andra halvseklet: Fackförenings-rörelsen och samhället*. Stockholm: Atlas.

Johansson, Håkan. 2001. 'Activation policies in the Nordic countries: social democratic universalism under pressure'. *Journal of European Area Studies* 9(1), 63–77.

Kautto, Mikko, Matti Heikkillä, Bjørn Hvinden, Staffan Marklund, and Niels Ploug (eds). 1999. *Nordic Social Policy: Changing Welfare States*. London and New York: Routledge.

Kleinman, Mark. 2002. *A European Welfare State?: European Union Social Policy in Context*. Basingstoke: Palgrave Macmillan.

Lefresne, Florence. 1999. 'Employability at the heart of the European employment strategy', *Transfer* 5(4): 460–80.

Lindqvist, Rafael and Staffan Marklund. 1995. 'Forced to work or liberated from work: a historic perspective on work and welfare'. *Scandinavian Journal of Social Welfare* 4: 224–37.

Lødemel, Ivor, and Heather Trickey (eds). 2001. *'An Offer You Can't Refuse'*: Workfare in an International Perspective, Bristol: Policy.

Martin, Emily. 1994. *Flexible Bodies*. Boston: Beacon Press.

Miller, Peter and Nikolas Rose. 1995. 'Production, identity and democracy'. *Theory and Society* 24: 427–67.

OECD. 1977 *Learning Opportunities for Adults. Vol. 1. General Report*. Paris: OECD.

Potter, Jonathan and Margaret Wetherell. 1987. *Discourse and Social Psychology: Beyond Attitudes and Behaviour*. London: Sage.

Power, Michael. 1997. *The Audit Society: Rituals of Verification*. Oxford: Oxford University Press.

Raveaud, Gilles. 2001. 'Dynamics of the welfare state regimes and employability'. In *Confidence and Changes: Managing Social Protection in the New Millennium*, edited by D. Pieters. Kluwer Law International, 5–26.

Rhodes, Martin. 1998. 'Globalization, labour markets and welfare states: a future of 'competitive corporatism'?'. In *The Future of European Welfare: A New Social Contract?* edited by M. Rhodes and Y. Mény. London: Macmillan – now Palgrave Macmillan, 178–203.

Rose, Nikolas. 1999. *Powers of Freedom: Reframing Political Thought*, Cambridge: Cambridge University Press.

Rose, Nikolas and Peter Miller. 1992. 'Political power beyond the state: problematics of government'. *British Journal of Sociology* 43(2): 173–205.

Rubenson, Kjell. 1996. 'Livslångt lärande: mellan utopi och ekonomi'. In *Livslångt lärande*, edited by P.-E. Ellström, B. Gustavsson, and S. Larsson. Lund: Studentlitteratur, 29–47.

Salais, Robert, Nicolas Baverez, and Bénédicte Reynaud. 1986. *L'invention du chomage: Histoire et transformations d'une catégorie en France des années 1890 aux années 1980*. Paris: Presses Universitaires de France.

Saxenian, Annalee. 1994. *Regional Advantage: Culture and Competition in Silicon Valley and Route 128*. Boston: Harvard University Press.

Scharpf, Fritz W. and Vivien A. Schmidt, (eds). 2000. *Welfare and Work in the Open Economy. Volume 1 + 2*, Oxford: Oxford University Press.

Searle, John R. 1969. *Speech Acts: An Essay in the Philosophy of Language*. Cambridge: Cambridge University Press.

Serrano Pascual, Amparo. 2000a. 'The concept of employability: a critical assessment of the fight against youth unemployment'. In *European Trade Union Yearbook 1999*, edited by E. Gabaglio and R. Hoffmann. Brussels: ETUI, 253–69.

Serrano Pascual, Amparo. 2000b. *Tackling Youth Unemployment in Europe*. Brussels: ETUI.

Shore, Cris. 2000. *Building Europe: The Cultural Politics of European Integration*. London: Routledge.

Stråth, Bo. 2000. 'After full employment and the breakdown of conventions of social responsibility'. In *After Full Employment. European Discourses on Work and Flexibility*, edited by B. Stråth. Brussels: PIE Peter Lang, 11–31.

Stråth, Bo (ed.) 2000. *After Full Employment: European Discourses on Work and Flexibility*. Brussels: Peter Lang.

Streeck, Wolfgang. 1998. 'The internationalization of industrial relations in Europe: prospects and Problems', *Politics & Society* 26(4): 429–59.

Tilly, Chris and Charles Tilly. 1998. *Work Under Capitalism*. Oxford: Westview Press.

Thompson, Paul 1993. 'Postmodernism: Fatal distraction'. In *Postmodernism and Organizations*, edited by J. Hassard and M. Parker. London: Sage, 183–203.

Thorne, Marie. 2001. 'Constituting change'. Paper presented at the 2nd Critical Management Studies Conference, UMIST, Manchester, July.

Weinert, Patricia, Michèle Baukens, Patrick Bollérot, Marina Pineschi–Gapènne and Ulrich Walwei 2001. *Employability: From Theory to Practice*. London: Transaction Publishers.

Williams, Raymond. 1976. *Keywords*. London: Fontana.

2
The Individualization of Labour

Michael Allvin

As elsewhere in Western countries, the labour market in Sweden is changing. The certitude and intimate relation between labour, progress and prosperity has been lost. The burden of efficiency, alterations, and adjustments has increased. Moreover, job security, continuous wage-increases and solidarity, things previously taken for granted, have acquired a much more precarious meaning. All in all, there is a widespread and inescapable awareness that the conditions of labour are no longer guaranteed by a benevolent welfare state, but are at the mercy of a capricious and callous global market. Following this is a mounting realization that since the immediate conditions of labour are not to be taken for granted, one is essentially adrift in a highly competitive labour market.

The Swedish labour market has been extensively regulated since the 1930s, first through negotiations between labour unions and employers and later through legislation instigated by the labour led government. Even though the Swedish labour market is still comparatively well regulated the changes are obvious. Labour *is* being deregulated and the individual is increasingly expected to initiate, plan, control and take responsibility for her own labour. As the individual is set loose on the market, she is also disconnected from her structural and traditional position within the institutional framework of labour. The impact of these developments may vary between industries, jobs, age groups, and regions. They are, nonetheless, affecting the entire Swedish labour market, and ultimately the very foundations of the welfare state.

To some this 'individualization' might seem outlandish, maybe even world shattering. Consequently, efforts have been made to explain it as merely a temporary setback in the circular, even dialectic, dynamic of opposing forces, or simply as a management trend. But it has also received serious attention as a qualitatively new development in industrial relations. Some have even referred to it as 'the third industrial revolution' (Magnusson, 1999). The term is illustrative in more than one way. On the one hand the current situation *is* a revolution in industrial relations, at least as far as these were established during most of the twentieth century.

On the other hand it is *merely* the third of a series of revolutions in industrial relations, each involving a structural transformation and a corresponding disconnection of the individual from the conditions from which she draws her living. As a consequence, workers have gradually been forced to operate in a more conscious way as self-reliant individuals. This chapter is about this historical process of social disconnection and increased self-awareness. I am not a historian by profession so I will be more concerned with the logic of progress than with the accumulation of concrete events. In other words, the purpose of this chapter is not to retell or rewrite the history of labour but to explain, in terms of rational development, the individualized conditions of today's labour market. The point I wish to make is that, far from being just a recent trend, these conditions are inherent in the very preconditions of labour. Although specific references will be made to the Swedish context, the narration refers to a more general Western (and perhaps protestant) experience.

The rise of labour

In pre-industrial times, most people drew their living from a household type of economy. The way people lived and the way they made their living were not separated from each other. Farmhands lived on the farm and craftsmen lived in, or on top of, their shops. Nature and tradition generally set their schedules. They usually inherited their position or trade and they expected to pass it on to their own children. They learned and practised their skills early in life and the necessities of their living shaped or disfigured their bodies. In other words, they were in almost every respect an inseparable part of the conditions from which they drew their living. Furthermore, the farm, local shop, or mill was an inseparable part of the local environment. What they did not produce themselves they acquired from the local community. Moreover, whatever they sold, they sold to an existing local market. Thus, the people, their bodies, and the economies of pre-industrial society were firmly rooted in the soil and traditions of the local community.

With the coming of industrial society all this changed, maybe not overnight, but rapidly enough to label such change as the industrial 'revolution'. During the nineteenth century there was a widespread rationalization of, what Jürgen Habermas (1981/1988) has called the material reproduction of society. Through this rationalization, material reproduction was subjected to a functional way of thinking that set it apart from the rest of life. As a consequence, people's lives were separated from the way they made their living. Life, however, was not totally expelled from its own preservation. It was allowed to take part in it on certain conditions. These conditions were devised as a set of rules regulating the relationship between life and its material reproduction. We have come to know these rules as 'labour'.

Labour, then, emerges with industrialization and the industrial revolution. Perhaps the most revolutionary aspect of the industrial revolution was the industrial system itself. The industrial system involved a functional division of labour tied to extensive mechanization. Compared to previous manufacturing, which was totally dependent on existing markets and restricted by established demands, the industrial system could operate on a much larger scale. It produced such a large quantity of goods at such a low cost that it became virtually independent of existing demands, and so generated its own markets.

The mechanization of the system not only enhanced the quantity of production; it also ensured the absolute regularity of it. As a consequence, it reduced the labour involved to a very simple and standardized procedure. The typical task was either self-evident with regard to the product or constrained by the operating procedures of the machinery. Labour, therefore, did not require much skill. Instead, the main issue of management was the disciplinary problem of 'how to get the human body to remain in one place, pay attention, and perform consistently over a fixed period of time' (Zuboff, 1988: 33). Or, to put it in more general terms, how to get people to abide by the absolute rules of time and space required by an industrially organized means of production. Several sources from this period testify to the fact that this was no easy matter. The trick was not just to induce people to turn up for work in the morning, but to keep them there, get them to stay in their assigned place, acknowledge the work periods, and to endure the tempo. Nor was it an easy matter to persuade workers to return to work once they had made enough money (Thompson, 1967).

The rules of work in the early days of industrialization were very plain and very explicit, often even posted on the wall. They dealt, not so much with the work itself, but with how to behave. Accompanying the rules was usually some sort of fine. There were fines for showing up late and there were fines for time lost at work. One work rule from around 1830, for example, stated that: 'Any person found from the usual place of work, except for necessary purposes, or talking to anyone out of their own alley, will be fined' (quoted from Zuboff, 1988: 33). There were also other rules that would seem very odd today, but that were specifically directed against any lack of concentration or proper behaviour. There were, for instance, punishable rules against singing, whistling, swearing, and yelling. There were rules for the fixation of gaze, paying attention, and opening a window. There were rules against being dirty, spitting, displaying aggressiveness, and sexuality. There were rules against throwing water, seducing women and, of course, being drunk (Zuboff, 1988).

At this early stage of industrialization, the rules of work were not codified to ensure efficiency, they existed to instil discipline. In order to fit the requirements of the mechanized division of labour in industry, people had to be transformed from farmhands, craftsmen, and whatever, into a consistently performing labour force. In short, they had to become machines themselves. The function of the rules was, therefore, to seal people off from their natural and traditional habits, and to block their physical and emotional impulses. The point was not to adapt the skills and experiences of people to the mechanized production, but to force them into giving up their skills and experiences altogether. Like in the army, they had to be washed clean of their previous life and turned into assessable objects (Foucault, 1977). People were essentially a crude force to be harnessed, sharpened, and put to use in the factories.

Once industrialization caught on and its new markets were established, industry forced other sectors of the economy out of business and absorbed their labour. As a result, the countryside was depopulated and traditional crafts, professions, functions, and chores diminished. People moved to the cities or to workmen's dwellings surrounding the large factories. Without any particular skills to protect or traditions to hold on to, they were free to take any job they could. They usually did not stay in one job for very long. Labour turnover was very high. It was not uncommon for workers to change their jobs every year. By the mid-nineteenth century, industrialization had created a large cadre of what Marx, not without irony, called 'free labour': people uprooted from their natural and traditional habitat and with all bonds to the past severed.

We are still not quite talking 'labour' though. Even though all the properties of exploitation were in place, it is not exploitation per se that gives birth to labour, it is people's reaction against it. During the first half of the nineteenth century, a dawning consciousness of the social consequences of industrialism started to emerge in the industrialized countries. Following this was an increased level of social engagement, political agitation, and even physical violence. The different reactions were generally instinctive, disparate, unplanned, offensive, and on the whole unsuccessful. In countries with strong liberal advocates the responses to these reactions were, at least to some extent, more benevolent and understanding. Welfare programmes aimed at the least fortunate were discussed and implemented. In countries lacking a liberal tradition, however, the initial response was largely repressive and irreconcilable. This eventually awakened a self-consciousness centred around the experiences of industrial labour. The key feature in this self-consciousness was a resistance towards the conditions of exploitation. It was through this self-consciousness that labour emerged as a categorically distinct condition of life. This means that both the provisions of and the conflict with industrial capitalism were built into the conception of labour from the start (Thompson, 1964). And, as a consequence, the labour movement emerged and grew rapidly in countries like Germany, Austria, and Scandinavia, countries without any significant liberal traditions (Therborn, 1994).

The institutionalization of labour

If the mechanized division of labour in production had been invented and developed in England during the eighteenth and most of the nineteenth century, it was taken to new heights in America in the late nineteenth and early twentieth century. The rationalization involved marks the beginning of a second industrial revolution (Piore and Sabel, 1984). This is also when the bulk of the Swedish industrial landscape established itself.

Up until then, labour had only been quantitatively regulated. It was performed in a certain place within a certain time frame. How to perform beyond that was largely in the hands of individual workers, their skills and habits. This way of organizing production had been enormously effective compared to any pre-industrial way, but in competition with itself it had its limits. The next step in regulating labour was formulated, above all, by Frederick Winslow Taylor. Taylor wanted to squeeze the air out of the labour process and create an optimal performance, or as Taylor himself put it: 'the one best way'. The idea was to systematically reduce labour to its most basic functional elements and then reorganize these elements into standardized *tasks*. Through this reorganization the labour process became almost entirely constituted as a functional resource, to be integrated with and consumed by the industrial system. As a consequence, the industrial system disentangled itself even further from its social, traditional, and corporeal ties, thus permitting it to evolve without having to compromise functional efficiency and systemic rigour (Littler, 1978).

Taylor's *The Principles of Scientific Management* was translated and published in Sweden with an appreciative preface as early as 1913, only two years after its publication in America, and in 1915 the first efforts to implement the methods of scientific management were made (De Geer, 1978). Although there was initial resistance, the reorganization of labour advocated by Taylor soon caught on. The separation of performance and planning, essential to the rationalization of work, generated a large cadre of specialized professionals to plan the work and administer the worker. Special offices for drawing, planning and personnel, inhabited by draughtsmen, engineers and administrators, were set up. Moreover, offices for marketing, sales, advertisement, accountancy and law were created. At the beginning of the First World War, the ratio between blue- and white-collar workers in Sweden was twelve to one. At the end of the Second World War the ratio was down to five to one. During these years the number of blue-collar workers had grown by 75 per cent while the number of white-collar workers had grown by more than 350 per cent (De Geer, 1985). Integrating all these different functions was a technique in itself.

Although there had been principles of administration employed within the armed forces since the Napoleonic wars, it was not until the beginning of the twentieth century that the principles of administration for industrial purposes were formulated. When Henri Fayol wrote his now classic book on administrative principles (1916/1988), and subsequently became something of a father figure for organization theory, he formulated a set of rules to regulate the relationships between the different functions and/or employees of a system. Together they formed the general principles behind the hierarchical organization. Along with the principles of rationalization, proposed by Taylor, the principles of administration extended the rules of labour in terms of performance and responsibility. Labour was no longer merely about being in the right place at the right time, it was about performing a specified task and fulfilling the responsibilities of an assignment. These additional regulations organized labour on a higher and more abstract level, as a functional resource. As a consequence, the main source for the generation of profit shifted from the mechanized labour process to the functionally integrated production process.

But the turn of the century not only saw the creation of rationalized labour but, it also saw the launching of *organized labour*. As industrialization spread so did the experience of exploitation. This experience was absorbed by the labour movement who realized that in order to gain an influence beyond the individual worker or workplace it had to get organized. Consequently, the second half of the nineteenth century witnessed a successive displacement of initiative from the morally justified resentment of individual workers to the tactical manoeuvrings of collective agents. By the turn of the century the Swedish labour movement had matured into a functional organization of its own. But its many and bitter conflicts with the forces of capital had shaped it into a mirror image of its opponent. It had learned that in order to stand up to capitalism it had to be its equal in strength and efficiency. Therefore, its organization was large, centralized, and with an internal division of responsibility that covered most areas of life. In Sweden the labour movement was divided into three nationwide branches involving labour, politics, and consumers' federations: the Swedish Trade Union Confederation (LO), the Swedish Social Democratic Party (SAP), and the Swedish Cooperative Wholesale Society (KF). There were subsidiary holdings like youth leagues, publishing firms, newspaper publishers and the Workers' Educational Association (ABF). Close ties were also kept with the sports federation and the temperance society.

In the 1920s the propagation of the techniques for mass production led to unprecedented rises in productivity in the industrialized countries. The productivity boom of the 1920s, however, gave way to 'a major crisis of overproduction' in the 1930s (Lipietz, 1987: 34). The crisis, and the ensuing world war, marks the beginning of a new expansion: an expansion characterized by the mutual recognition of capital and labour as organized agents. In Sweden this mutual recognition was ratified in the General Agreement of 1938 between LO and the Swedish Employers' Association (SAF), the two major parties on the labour market. In the agreement the labour representatives recognized the employers' right to command and allocate labour whereas the employers' representatives recognized the right of labour unions to organize, recruit, and represent the employees. With this mutual recognition the main focus of industrial relations shifted irrevocably from the concrete social relations of individual workers and their employer, to the structural relation between different collective agents. The main practice of industrial relations was now formed and institutionalized as 'collective bargaining'.

The deal proved advantageous to both parties. A general cease-fire was declared in the battle between work and capital. Antagonism gave way to a long and very profitable period of mutual back scratching, commonly referred to as 'the golden years'. The increased productivity of labour resulted in increased profits. The surplus could both be used to guarantee further investments and expansions, securing and multiplying the number of jobs, and be distributed among the workers as regularly increased wages. But the increased productivity also meant that the cost of the industrially produced products could be lowered considerably. When the wage earners did not have to fear for their jobs and, more importantly, were looking forward to regular raises, they boosted their levels of private consumption. This increased consumption, in turn, stepped up the demand for company products. The increased level of demand further boosted profits, which could be invested and distributed among workers, and so on. In the post-war period an unprecedented escalation of growth, involving such a symbiotic relationship of mass-production and mass-consumption, spread from America. This was what Michel Aglietta (1979) has called *a Fordist regime of accumulation*, and it dominated the Western world from the 1930s until the 1970s.

The Fordist regime of accumulation was guaranteed by a set of institutions, or 'modes of regulations'. We have already mentioned the large corporations dominating their trade as well as the large centrally organized labour unions, both bound together by collective treaties and collective bargaining. During the 1930s *the modern welfare state* emerged as another important institution. The amending benevolence of the modern welfare state had originated with the reform programmes of a liberal social policy. The Swedish Social Democratic Party, however, gave it a more communal and labour friendly profile. Through social transfers, legislation and insurances the Swedish welfare state not only reduced wage differentials, it also guaranteed its subjects uninterrupted private consumption in the case of sickness, unemployment, retirement and so on, thereby securing the continuous accumulation of capital (Lipietz, 1992). With the production of standardized housing and subsidized government loans to buy them, the welfare state, furthermore, contributed to the spiralling economy by forming 'the household' as an independent economic unit and 'the home of one's own' as an investment for the future. In the 1930s there were similar Fordist 'welfare contracts' signed all over the Western world, from America (Roosevelt's *New Deal*) to Germany (Hitler's programme for modernization), and, of course, in Sweden (Per Albin Hansson's *Folkhem*) (Hirdman, 1994; Roobeek, 1987). A whole pattern of consumption developed around the private home and the car, and it captivated people and made them dependent on a steady job and a regular income. In Sweden private consumption increased by 2–3 per cent every year between 1950 and 1970. Public consumption increased even more as a result of increased taxation (Magnusson, 1996: 432). The whole package was closely tied to the social role of 'labour'. As part of the 'labour force', it contributed to the generation of material welfare, and as 'organized labour' it was a living symbol of the equitable distribution of that welfare. Thus, labour was both a source and a precondition of the general increase in material welfare experienced during these years.

But, the self-consciousness of labour, originally tied to the concrete experiences of industrial exploitation, had been hollowed out by the rationalization and organization of labour, as well as by the extensive level of material welfare consumption. It was still central to the Fordist regime of accumulation though, and was supported by the mutual dependency of its institutions.

The crisis of labour

The Fordist regime of accumulation was mainly a compromise within the national framework. However, the extensive consumption, along with increased international competition and investments, resulted in a growing level of imports. To balance the mounting trade deficit, it was necessary to increase exports. This increased international competition even more, which made it even harder for companies to sell their products abroad. In order to compete on more favourable terms, the companies started making their investments overseas. During the 1980s Swedish investment in foreign production was twice as large as investment in domestic production. In the period 1984–91 Swedish companies invested more than £20 billion in industrial production abroad (Magnusson, 1996: 488). The escalating transnational investments interconnected the companies with each other in ways that were more extensive and intricate than ever before. Through mergers, acquisitions, divestments, joint ventures and strategic alliances, as well as licensing, franchising, subcontracting, and financial holdings the companies of the 1980s established relations with each other that allowed them to develop and grow beyond all national boundaries (Marginson and Sisson, 1994; Reich, 1992). In Sweden this development was facilitated by the traditional export dependency of its industry. So, rather than rebuilding and cultivating the relations with their native social institutions, the companies of the 1980s started to orient themselves more and more towards *the global network of commerce.*

Globalization, then, does not necessarily mean that companies relocate abroad, even if that of course is one option. It simply means that the companies are becoming increasingly dependent on other companies through relations of commerce while at the same time becoming increasingly independent of their social relations with the native cultural environment. Even small companies, operating in a local market, tend to be pulled into these networks of dependency as subcontractors or sub-subcontractors (Perrow, 1992). As a consequence, the logic behind their actions tends to refer more and more to the logic of the global network of commerce on which they depend. The strategies and loyalties of the companies, as well as the reasons behind them, are therefore becoming increasingly inaccessible and difficult to grasp from a nationally and culturally situated perspective. Furthermore, while the increased dependency of the global network of commerce has reduced the freedom of action for most companies, the relative independence of national conditions has made it possible for at least large and transnational corporations unilaterally to raise their demands for political concessions. So, while the autonomy, or power, of companies has decreased in one respect it has increased in another.

Unlike the techniques of mass production, utilized in production for large, stable markets characterized by uniform demands, the techniques employed when operating in the global network of commerce have to deal with specialized and highly unstable markets. One general technique emerging in the 1980s therefore involved an intense market and consumer orientation. This went beyond the mere employment of sophisticated market strategies. It advocated a change of perspective of the organization in accordance with the principles of *Service Management* (for example Normann, 1983). The immediate motive for this was the fact that the value produced by a company no longer restricted itself to the products of that company. Rather, the value was in the commerce of those products. Thus, rationalizing and organizing the company no longer meant rationalizing and organizing the labour process, or even the production process, but rationalizing and organizing the enterprise, that is the *business process* as such. As a consequence, the organizational focus had to be on the customer of the products rather than on the products themselves (Carlzon, 1987). Another general technique, also designed to tackle the problems of unstable market conditions, was the use of *Flexible Production* (Harrison, 1994; Piore and Sabel, 1984). This involved organizing the business process in such a way as to reduce its response time to market changes. The idea was to not just reduce, but to overcome any unnecessary time lag caused by detours or friction in the process, as reflected in the different management catchwords of the 1980s: *Just In Time* (Hutchins, 1988), *Lean Production* (Womack *et al.*, 1990), *Time Based*

Management (Stalk Jr and Hout, 1990), among others. The idea of flexibility, of course, is not restricted to production. It also involved administrating the labour force in such a way as to reduce the costs and risks of labour in general, and of long-term service contracts in particular (Atkinson, 1985).

When the global network of commerce grew, intensified, and became digitalized in the 1990s, operating in it also meant taking advantage of the network itself. This can be done in several ways. The general idea, though, is to use the network for the allocation of resources. To facilitate interaction and reduce transaction costs, different ways of ensuring the quality of products and services (involving the standardization and certification of their production procedure) were developed. These techniques, eventually subsumed under the general label of *Total Quality Management*, enable companies to distribute their resources throughout the network for economic and strategic purposes and still keep sufficient control to operate as a cohesive business process. So, instead of incorporating their resources – accepting economic and legal responsibilities, and getting stuck with long-term investments, plans, and obligations – companies can eject the resources and use techniques such as outsourcing, subcontracting, franchising, and joint venturing to integrate these resources on a market basis, thereby gaining maximum cost efficiency and interchangeability.

As the corporeality of companies disappears, their symbolic presence increases. One essential technique when it comes to enhancing the symbolic presence of a company is *branding*. Branding is about creating and preserving a distinctive and coherent image of the company through strategic display. It is about using matching staff appearance to project an image of a product, like Apple. Or, it is about using brand loyalty to padlock a share of the market, like Harley Davidson. Branding, however, is more than just advertising. It can also be used as a tool for integrating a distributed enterprise. The most striking example is perhaps Nike, which has outsourced the actual production process and now integrates all the tangible elements of the business process under the image of its highly distinctive brand name. Branding can also be used to maximize the advantages of co-ordination by producing one basic product, but marketing it throughout the network, using subsidiary companies and different brand names, like Volkswagen, Skoda, Seat and Audi.

Another way to take advantage of the network, popularly referred to as 'the New Economy' or 'e-Economy', is to charge for the *interactions* of the network, or for services in connection with these interactions. The economic logic of dealing in interactions is different than, and sometimes even inverted to, the economic logic of selling products. The values of products are subjected to the market law of supply and demand, which means that scarcity increases the value of the product while abundance decreases it. With services and products of interaction it is the other way around. A telegraph machine by itself is worthless. Two telegraph machines connected to each other, however, create an interaction. Each new machine that interconnects with that interaction raises the value of all the other machines within the network. With this logic in mind it makes perfect sense to give away £100 cellular phones for free, in exchange for a long-term commitment to a certain telephone network. The value of the material products as such, is of subordinate interest.

The extent and relative importance of these different techniques may well be debated. The important thing here, however, is the consequences they have on labour. I will limit myself in pointing out two general concerns. First, when operating in a global network of commerce, labour is a subsidiary resource. None of the techniques mentioned above depends on labour for generating profits. There are weak, or even non-existing, correlations between the amount of labour used in a given operation and the amount of profit generated by it. When business no longer depends on labour to evolve, the relationship between them disappears. If, for instance, a factory costs more money than it generates through its production, closing it down may be a blow to the workforce, but the argument that factory production shows no profit will confirm the interdependence between their labour and the reason for business, thereby providing a reason for labour as well. But, in the process of reallocating their resources within the global network of commerce, companies close down their factories despite the fact that the labour is skilled, work hard, and generate a profit (see for example Sandberg, 1995). In such cases the reason for business is clearly beyond the grasp of its labour force.

When companies adapted to the standards established through the global network of commerce in the 1980s, they consequently engaged in extensive structural rationalizations and closures all around Sweden, an early example being Volvo's brand new and innovative plant at Uddevalla. More recent examples of this transformation are the merging of the Swedish pharmaceutical company Pharmacia with the American company Upjohn, as well as the telecommunication company Ericsson outsourcing or selling off its production of cellular phones, making thousands of workers redundant.

The second concern worth taking note of is that when a company is organized as a business process rather than as a production process the rules of labour change. A business process, unlike a production process, cannot be clearly outlined in time. There is no definite beginning or end, and the process does not progress visibly or linearly through the corresponding accumulation of working hours. Placing £10 or one million on the stock exchange will take a stockbroker the same amount of time, but the profit of the former will be incomparable to the latter. The labour of a stockbroker is all about earning the trust of the client, being up to date with the market, and having the good sense to know where to invest. Neither of which may be clearly defined in terms of time, space, or task. Rather, the labour is defined in terms of the contribution made in promoting the business process. Whether this involves lying awake at night thinking about where to place an investment or merely forwarding a placement ordered through a 30-second phone call is irrelevant. As a consequence, the rules of labour change from the performance of a pre-determined task and fulfilling the responsibilities of a clearly defined assignment, to the obligations involved in promoting the business process, whenever, wherever, and however that may be done.

By insisting on a more personal and total commitment, these new rules break with the collective and limited commitment maintained by the traditional rules. Even if the majority of the Swedish workforce is still subjected to relatively traditional rules, the propagation and implications of the new rules represents a staggering blow to the predominant conception of labour in Sweden. If jobs are exclusive and personal rather than uniform and generally applicable, things such as vocational training programmes, common employment measures, even a general employment policy could become superfluous.

If capitalism has disconnected itself from labour, so, in a sense, has the labour union. In order to become an independent institutional actor, the labour union had, as we have already seen, organized itself in the image of its opponent. And like its opponent, its organized activities demand a certain discipline from its members. The individual worker or group of workers has to conform to the general and long-term demands of their organization. But, to surrender their decision-making power into the hands of an institutional agent, the workers have to regard that agent as legitimate. Moreover, in order to operate on an institutional level the agent will have to be regarded as legitimate by the other institutional actors as well. In other words, to successfully represent their members the unions require both an internal and an external legitimacy.

During the post-war compromise the labour unions in Sweden enjoyed such a multilateral legitimacy. The unions were legitimate in the eyes of the workers since they guaranteed job security, wage increase, and other benefits. The unions were also legitimate in the eyes of the employers since they guaranteed industrial peace and a regimented labour force. Finally, they were also legitimate in the eyes of the welfare state since they guaranteed social stability through the pursuit of a wage policy that showed solidarity with low-paid workers.

This equilibrium was disrupted by the breakdown of the post-war compromise. When profits decreased the companies had to reduce their activities as well as their personnel. This threatened both the job security and expected wage increases of the workers. As a consequence the union felt a need to put tougher demands on the employers, thereby endangering the industrial peace and discipline among the workforce. The heightened tension turned co-ordination and solidarity into a scramble, in which labour within more profitable industries could benefit at the expense of labour within less profitable industries. The tension was particularly evident between private and public labour. As a result, wage differences increased, which endangered the general welfare and social stability.

The disruption of the post-war equilibrium pushed the unions into a corner. Faced with intensified global competition and the internationalization of capital, the employers were pushing hard on a number of fronts: renegotiating or simply dropping many of the hard-earned rights of the employees; decentralizing bargaining, requiring more local-level involvement on the part of the union; and using more individualized payment systems, thereby eroding the traditional wage policy of solidarity. On the other side, faced with budget deficits and unemployment, the key actors in the welfare state were increasingly referring to the labour unions as just another pressure group craving money and social reforms but with no long-term commitment to the development of society as a whole. Nonetheless, in an effort to comply with these demands, the unions jeopardised the support of their members. To many of the workers, especially the younger generations, the union is increasingly perceived as a self-sufficient system whose usefulness is at best questionable (Allvin and Sverke, 2000).

Even the welfare state has withdrawn from its preoccupation with labour. The main function of a modern welfare state is to buffer the effects of the capitalist system on the individual. The particular brand of welfare state developed in Sweden interpreted this task as being a safeguard for labour. However, in the General Agreement of 1938 both unions and employers wanted to keep the labour market free from government interference in order to resolve their differences among themselves. This was a profitable strategy during the 'golden years' and as a result of this the Swedish labour market progressed with a minimum of government regulations. However, when mutual gains seized up and negotiations came to a standstill in the crises of the 1970s, the labour unions changed their attitude and urged their political wing (the Social Democratic Party) to keep furthering their demands through legislation.

During the 1970s the welfare state expanded into the labour market with legislation as its main tool. But, by generating new rights and obligations it not only ratified the demands of labour. It also sanctioned union motions for further demands. Through the use of labour law, the welfare state encouraged labour to penetrate and state its demands in order to have these confirmed as objective legal rights. As a result, the legal regulations of the labour market developed enormously from the 1970s onwards. Today it is almost impossible to act within the realm of labour relations without considering the legal consequences (Bruun, 1987).

Even though the legal regulations *have* made working life safer and in many ways a better place, they have done so at the cost of obscuring the labour relation as such. The idea of labour law is to mediate between the different parties. Instead the regulatory apparatus has taken over the relation altogether, thereby releasing both parties from their mutual concerns and obligations. Rather than allowing the different parties to meet as equals, labour law has become an institution that classifies the parties and imposes a specified course of action on them (Teubner, 1987). For example, in labour law the employee is constituted as a legal entity with affixed rights. To be eligible for these rights the worker must fit a certain profile with regard to age, physique, intellectual and linguistic abilities, training, service agreement, and so on. Also, the worker must have behaved in the proper manner: responsibly; following specified instructions and regulations; performing the designated task, in the right time, at the right place, and in the right manner. If an individual worker who meets these requirements, and thus qualifies as an 'employee' in the legal sense, is given notice, locked out, offended, injured, or in any way wronged, she may be compensated for this by being relocated, reassigned, re-educated, rehabilitated or paid off. So, in order to act as a legal entity within the labour relation, the individual worker must accept being reduced to a set of abstract categories and to behave in accordance with some elaborate criteria. Furthermore, the outcome of the process involves being subjected to any number of remedial administrative technologies.

As labour laws take charge of industrial relations they are, consequently, transformed into an incomprehensible and inhospitable system of rules and regulations, a legal minefield. In other words, industrial relations as a site of moral and social interaction – the very environment in which the self-consciousness of labour reproduces itself – is being 'colonized' by a technical language and standards (Habermas, 1986). So, by disqualifying the individual as a competent agent within industrial relations, labour law disconnects her from her traditional position within the institutional framework of labour.

Finally, one might even argue that the social role of labour has been abandoned, not only by capital, organized labour, and the welfare state, but by the individual worker as well. The heavy reliance on material mass consumption in the post-war compromise has shifted the focus of society from long-term economic gain through production to immediate personal satisfaction through consumption. As a consequence, the solidaristic work ethic acknowledged by labour is being subverted by an individual pursuit of life-style consumption (Bauman, 1998; Inglehart, 1990). However one wants to explain it, though, it is becoming increasingly clear that the social category of labour is being drained of its social and practical significance, and that all the previously interested parties are turning their back on it.

Disorganized labour

I have tried to show that labour emerges as a social category in the nineteenth century with life in society being separated from the material reproduction of it, and that our conception of labour is based on the rules regulating people's participation in that reproduction. As industrialization progressed, the rules regulating such participation changed, from the very simple rules of spatio-temporal conduct required by small scale mechanized production, to the more complex rules of task performance and responsibilities necessary to large, functionally integrated organizations, and finally to a general commitment in furthering an agile business process. And, as the rules changed so did the conception of labour: from the shared capacity of a 'labour power', to a functional and responsible part in the great machinery of progress, to a self-efficient and self-reliant operator on a market.

It is important to point out, however, that the material reproduction of society is not a uniform process that is subjected to uniform rules. That rules 'change' does not necessarily mean that old rules are disposed of while new ones are put into practice. Instead, new rules are implemented when new sectors and markets are developed. Some of these rules expand upon the old rules while others exist side by side with them. Other sectors and markets retain very traditional rules. This means that the rules as such do not change, they proliferate.

The diversity of working conditions caused by this proliferation is, arguably, the most striking feature of today's labour market. The diversity is giving rise to a new situation in itself. One important consequence of this is that the mixture of rules subjects people to very different conditions, sometimes even within the same workplace. This can be a cause of both social tension and stress. A person, for instance, having very flexible working conditions within an otherwise traditionally organized workplace may well be the focus of attention and envy. On the other hand, a person insisting on sticking to traditional working conditions in an otherwise flexible workplace may, likewise, be a source of irritation. In both of these cases problems of co-operation and even harassment may follow. Even subtler is the psychological conflict between a desire to adopt a more flexible approach to work without being capable of it, a conflict often resulting in insecurity and stress (Allvin, *et al.*, 1999).

Another, more ominous consequence of this new diversity is the inequality it promotes. The focus today in Sweden is on a minority of jobs with very flexible and individualized conditions while the majority of jobs that are still subjected to traditional conditions receive virtually no attention. In these jobs – common in large industries, fast food restaurants, call centres, and the public sector – the worker is still a replaceable part within the machinery. These differences leave very little linking of individual workers to each other. When there is no shared experience of labour, the communion of labour is disbanded. With this the individual worker, whether his or her job requires it or not, is driven out into a situation where it's every man, woman, and child for himself or herself. This means that although a majority of jobs are still subjected to traditional conditions, the minority working under newer conditions is sufficiently large to change the rules of the game for everybody. As a consequence, everybody is feeling the heat from an increasingly competitive labour market. In this situation the majority subjected to traditional conditions is doubly disadvantaged. As an exchangeable cog in the industrial machinery, these workers are not only subjected to more restraining conditions, they are also unable to take advantage of any collective resistance to change these conditions, since solidarity is only a feasible strategy when everybody collaborates.

In today's globalized and flexible situation nobody can be sure of their jobs or career plans. Instead, everybody is forced to fight for his or her future in a highly competitive labour market. In this respect everybody is exposed to the same conditions. Some, however, have the working conditions to match this fight – allowing them to further their competence, professional network, and competitive skills – while others have to rely on the responsibilities of the employer, the solidarity of fellow workers, and the benevolence of the welfare state. But, as I have argued, the responsibilities of the employers are facing towards the global network of commerce, the solidarity of fellow workers has evolved into an institutional agent in concord with other institutional agents, and the benevolence of the welfare state is concealed behind a technocratic system of rules and regulations. Having to rely on these is consequently a very unreliable and unattractive alternative. The inequalities of the present as well as the future, then, are not to be found between those who have a job and those who have not. Nor are they to be found between those who have good working conditions and those who have poor ones. They are to be found between those who are attractive to a labour market and are able to further their own career, and those who are not.

References

Aglietta, Michel. 1979. *A Theory of Capitalist Regulation: The US Experience.* London: NLB.

Allvin, Michael and Magnus Sverke. 2000. 'Do new generations imply the end of solidarity?: Swedish unionism in the era of individualization'. *Economic and Industrial Democracy* 21(1): 71–95.

Allvin, Michael, Per Wiklund, Annika Härenstam and Gunnar Aronsson. 1999. *Frikopplad eller frånkopplad: Om innebörder och konsekvenser av gränslösa arbeten* (Arbete och Hälsa 1999: 2). Stockholm: Arbetslivsinstitutet.

Atkinson, John. 1985. *Flexibility, Uncertainty and Manpower Management (89):* Institute of Manpower Studies.

Bauman, Zygmunt. 1998. *Work, Consumerism, and the New Poor.* Buckingham: Open University Press.

Bruun, Niklas. 1987. 'Arbetslivets juridifiering: perspektiv på den finska utvecklingen'. *Tidskrift, utgiven av Juridiska Föreningen i Finland* (2–3): 136–152.

Carlzon, Jan. 1987. *Moments of Truth.* Cambridge, Mass.: Ballinger Publishing Co.

De Geer, Hans. 1978. *Rationaliseringsrörelsen i Sverige: Effektivitetsidéer och socialt ansvar under mellankrigstiden.* Stockholm: Studieförbundet Näringsliv och Samhälle.

De Geer, Hans. 1985. 'Rationalisering och samhällsförändring'. *Daedalus: Tekniska museets årsbok.* Stockholm: Tekniska museet, 59–73.

Fayol, Henri. 1916/1988. *General and Industrial Management.* London: Pitman.

Foucault, Michel. 1977. *Discipline and Punish.* New York: Pantheon.

Habermas, Jürgen. 1981/1988. *The Theory of Communicative Action: Vol 2. Lifeworld and System: A Critic of Functionalist Reason.* Cambridge: Polity Press.

Habermas, Jürgen. 1986. 'Law as medium and law as institution'. In *Dilemmas of Law in the Welfare State,* edited by G. Teubner. Berlin: Walter de Gruyter.

Harrison, Bennett. 1994. *Lean and Mean: The Changing Landscape of Corporate Power in the Age of Flexibility.* New York: Basic Books.

Hirdman, Yvonne. 1994. 'Social engineering and the woman question: Sweden in the thirties'. In *Swedish Social Democracy: A Model in Transition,* edited by W. Clement and R. Mahon. Toronto: Canadian Scholars' Press, 65–81.

Hutchins, David. 1988. *Just in Time.* Aldershot: Gower.

Inglehart, Ronald. 1990. *Culture Shift In Advanced Industrial Society.* Princeton, NJ: Princeton University Press.

Lipietz, Alain. 1987. *Mirages and Miracles: The Crisis of Global Fordism.* London: Verso.

Lipietz, Alain. 1992. *Towards a New Economic Order.* Cambridge: Polity Press.

Littler, Craig R. 1978. 'Understanding taylorism'. *British Journal of Sociology* 29(2): 185–202.

Magnusson, Lars. 1996. *Sveriges ekonomiska historia.* Stockholm: Tiden Athena.

Magnusson, Lars. 1999. *Den tredje industriella revolutionen och den svenska arbetsmarknaden.* Stockholm: Prisma/Arbetslivsinstitutet.

Marginson, Paul and Keith Sisson. 1994. 'The structure of transnational capital in Europe: the emerging euro-company and its implications for industrial relations'. In *New Frontiers in European Industrial Relations,* edited by R. Hyman and A. Ferner. Oxford: Blackwell, 15–51.

Normann, Richard. 1983. *Service Management: Strategy and Leadership in Service Business.* Chichester: John Wiley.

Perrow, Charles. 1992. 'Small-firm networks'. In *Networks and Organizations: Structure, Form, and Action,* edited by N. Nohria and R. G. Eccles. Boston: Harvard Business School Press, 445–70.

Piore, Michael J. and Charles F. Sabel. 1984. *The Second Industrial Divide.* New York: Basic Books.

Reich, Robert B. 1992. *The Work of Nations.* New York: Vintage Books.

Roobeek, Annemieke J. M. 1987. 'The crisis in fordism and the rise of a new technological paradigm'. *Futures* 19(2): 129–54.

Sandberg, Åke (ed.). 1995. *Enriching Production: Perspectives on Volvo's Uddevalla Plant as an Alternative to Lean Production.* Aldershot: Avebury.

Teubner, Gunther (ed.). 1987. *Juridification of Social Spheres.* Berlin: Walter de Gruyter.

Stalk Jr, George and Thomas M. Hout. 1990. *Competing Against Time: How Time-Based Competition is Reshaping Global Markets.* London: Macmillan – now Palgrave Macmillan.

Therborn, Göran. 1994. 'Classes and states: welfare state developments, 1881–1981'. In *Swedish Social Democracy: A Model in Transition,* edited by W. Clement and R. Mahon. Toronto: Canadian Scholars' Press, 13–43.

Thompson, Edward P. 1964. *The Making of the English Working Class.* New York: Pantheon.

Thompson, Edward P. 1967. 'Time, work-discipline and industrial capitalism'. *Past and Present* 38: 56–97.

Womack, James P., Daniel T. Jones, and Daniel Roos. 1990. *The Machine that Changed the World.* New York: Rawson Associates.

Zuboff, Shoshana. 1988. *In the Age of the Smart Machine.* Oxford: Heinemann.

3

A European Politics for Employability: The Political Discourse on Employability of the EU and the OECD

Kerstin Jacobsson

Introduction: organizing politics for employability

Many organizations are competing with states in the formulation of rules and norms in labour markets. Corporations, international non-governmental organizations and governmental organizations try to set up and diffuse their ideas on how employees should operate in the labour market. Thus, while there are clear tendencies of increased individualization and de-standardization in work and labour markets, there are also significant tendencies towards increased regulatory activities in a variety of organizations and forms. Both these parallel tendencies are transnational in character, involving individuals and organizations across national boundaries, and entailing a flow of ideas, rules and norms across countries.

This chapter will focus on two powerful transnational organizations, the OECD and the EU, with the emphasis on the latter. Arguably their main source of influence on the labour market is their ideational and ideological influence on the reshaping of national social welfare systems. The OECD lacks and the EU has only limited legislative power in this policy field. Instead, they rely on various types of soft law instruments, such as recommendations and guidelines; the collection, standardization and diffusion of knowledge and ideas; benchmarking and identification of 'best practices', combined with peer review and political pressure (Jacobsson, 2001, 2002). Both organizations are important producers and diffusers of policy thinking and discourse. The EU also has a financial instrument, the European Social Fund (ESF), to support its labour market policy.

Based on key documents of the two organizations, this chapter will analyse the labour market policy discourse developed by the EU and the

OECD in the 1990s and onwards, with the main emphasis on *employability*. What expectations on the individual in terms of qualities and responsibilities can be traced in the discourse on employability? What ideals and norms for social behaviour are embodied in this discourse, and what social relations does it construct and legitimize? To what extent can shifts in the distribution of responsibilities be traced, indicating changes in social contracts such as those between the state and the individual, between employers and employees and between the state and enterprises?

Both the EU and the OECD have been important sources of inspiration and pressure for recent policy moves in most West European countries towards enforced activation policies and reform of social benefit systems (Drøpping *et al.*, 1999; Lødemel and Trickey, 2001). More subtly, both the OECD Jobs Strategy and the European Employment Strategy involve a discursive practice which suggests a perspective and a cognitive structure for understanding and describing the labour market, including concepts such as employability, adaptability, activation, entrepreneurship, social inclusion, gender mainstreaming (Jacobsson and Schmid, 2002). Although these concepts were not invented by these organizations, the EU in particular has made them into official terms and popularized them; they are increasingly used in national policy discourse. The key concepts guiding EU employment policy (employability; entrepreneurship; adaptability; equal opportunities) provide the structure for the National Action Plans which are worked out annually by the member states, and, moreover, they are guiding the ESF projects. Thus, as categories they provide a scheme for policy thinking and administrative practice nationally (Jacobsson, 2001, 2002).

Concepts such as employability, adaptability, flexibility may still have partly different meanings in different contexts. We can expect 'translation processes', where actors grant the core concepts a meaning that is acceptable in the local context. However, the European Commission has also tried to prevent national divergences in interpretation by introducing common definitions (CEC, 1999a). Interpretations and operationalizations of these concepts are inherently political and need to be 'managed'.

The employability discourse of the OECD

The main power of the OECD is in 'formulating, transferring, selling and teaching, not formal regulation, but principal and causal beliefs helping to constrain and enable certain types of social behaviour' (Marcussen,

2001: 2ff). The prescriptions offered have shifted over the years with shifts in the economic consensus of the OECD. The top priority of the OECD economic philosophy of the 1960s was to create favourable conditions for growth and employment which was best done by demand management, a Keynesian position. In the mid-1970s, the macro-economic policy advocated by the OECD shifted in a 'neo-liberal' direction with low inflation, budgetary discipline, and structural reform as top priorities (Marcussen, 2002), that is, supply-side economic theory. (Interestingly, while the OECD consensus shifted, the position of the European Commission at the time remained that inflation was not the primary problem but problems associated with economic distribution. In other words, the Commission and the OECD differed in their view of the problem in the mid-1970s.) The OECD came to advocate a medium-term policy strategy, which meant an acceptance of a less rapid reduction in unemployment in the short term in order to achieve lower levels of unemployment later on. Moreover, there was perceived to be a considerable need to increase flexibility in labour markets (OECD, 1977; Marcussen, 2002). Unemployment was due to structural, not cyclical, problems.

The OECD Jobs Strategy: avoiding rigidities and making work pay

In 1994, the OECD launched its Jobs Strategy. The methodology of the strategy includes general policy recommendations combined with multilateral surveillance of the performances of individual countries, and also identification of best practices. The member states are thus recurrently evaluated and advised. The main conclusion in the initial Jobs Study report was that the key to job creation and reduced unemployment was structural reform (OECD, 1994). Problems that needed to be dealt with included 'overly strict job protection, too generous benefit schemes, excessive minimum wages' (OECD, 1996: 19).

A key figure of thought underlying the OECD labour market discourse is the idea of global competition: 'In a world where trade in goods and services as well as international investment flows develop much faster than domestic economies, where technologies are developed and diffused extremely rapidly, and where domestic markets are being liberalized, competition is constantly increasing. To stay in the race, firms – and their staff – must continuously innovate and increase their efficiency. This objective is essential and is the basis for the general recommendations [of the Jobs Strategy]' (OECD, 1996: 5). The discourse brings about the impression of speed and irresistible force, which in turn constrains the options available and makes adaptation imperative. The globalization process 'requires economies to be more adaptable and workers more willing and able to change jobs or acquire new skills' (OECD, 1996: 13).

While the OECD discourse focuses on structural problems, demands on individuals are more or less implied. 'If work does not pay, people will be reluctant to work' is repeated as a mantra (for example, 1996: 7, 1997a: 7). Incentives to take up a job may be insufficient, particularly for low-wage earners. 'High benefits may also raise wage demands, and hence unemployment, by lowering the costs to workers of losing their jobs' (OECD, 1996: 7). Reviews of tax and benefit systems are therefore needed to avoid 'welfare traps' (unemployment trap, poverty trap). The lowering of labour taxes is expected to lead to the creation of more jobs. 'Low-wage work should not be over-taxed' (OECD, 1996: 10). Workers' prospects of being employed, and hence their employability, will be improved by a more adequate pricing of their productivity.

Partly in response to the criticism that the Jobs Strategy was too locked into neoclassical economics, the OECD has come to stress more the role of knowledge management and learning in the knowledge-based economy (Luque, 2001). Employability will also be improved by education and training. The OECD acknowledges the importance of lifelong learning, stressing that 'better-educated individuals have, on average, higher rates of labour force participation, lower unemployment and higher earnings than those with lower qualifications... education and training lifts individuals' productivity, and improves economic performance at the enterprise and national levels' (1997b: 6f). Education has to be rethought in the sense that 'preparation for work can no longer be thought of as a once-and-for-all process, and... further learning is required during working life in order to ensure that individuals remain productive and employable' (OECD, 1997b: 7). 'For young persons, the greatest emphasis should be on prevention. The key preventive strategy is to ensure that, when young people leave initial education and training, they have the skills, knowledge and attitudes necessary to be productive and employable workers.... The concept of employability, though, is broadening. Productive work habits, personal confidence, decision-making skills, and a commitment to learning are as important as specific vocational skills' (OECD, 1997b: 15).

Lifelong learning should be made 'a reality for all' (OECD, 1996: 16), by improved education but also by 'improving the pathways between education, learning and work'. Costs and benefits of lifelong learning should be shared equitably among individuals, employers and governments. It is acknowledged that: 'There are potentially strong financial incentives for enterprises as well as individuals to invest in training when it is undertaken in the context of organizational change and the introduction of technological innovation' (OECD, 1997b: 7).

The employability discourse of the EU

While the imagery of global competition is also present in the EU policy discourse, the key figure of thought is that of a knowledge-based society. In response to this, lifelong learning and employability have become catch-words on the policy agenda. The ability and preparedness of the individual to learn anew is considered a prerequisite for employability. The European Employment Strategy (EES) can be considered a policy framework for encouraging, among other things, these skills.

The European Employment Strategy

In the early 1990s, the European Round Table of Industrialists (ERT) called for an action plan to 'modernize Europe' and raise its competitiveness in world markets (ERT, 1992). The proposals included attempts to make the single market work to support the goal of industrial competitiveness by further deregulation; investment in infrastructure, technology and the environment; and investment in people: education, training and fuller employment. The latter included improved education of young people meeting the needs of employers; lifelong learning for people already in work; the development of flexible work hours and practices within the workplace, and effective measures to bring the unemployed back to work. To achieve this, economic, educational and social policies needed to work together to support one another (ERT, 1992).

The Commission White Paper from 1993 on the triad *Growth, Competitiveness, Employment* (CEC, 1993), which laid the ground for the European Employment Strategy, was largely a response to this call. It set out a growth-oriented strategy to come to terms with unemployment in Europe and a goal was a more competitive economy still within a framework of macro-economic stability. Equally important, the White Paper recognised unemployment to be a structural problem that could not be solved by economic growth alone, and it pointed, *inter alia*, to the lack of flexibility in labour markets. Despite welfare increases, the Community still had very high levels of unemployment. The background context was also one of new technologies and a more knowledge-based economy, increased competition and economic interdependence as well as demographic changes. Priorities set out were enhanced flexibility in enterprises; reduction of social costs of poorly qualified labour; a review of employment measures; and investments in lifelong learning. Social welfare systems needed to be reviewed in order to improve efficiency and reduce costs by introducing more 'responsibility' and 'selectivity'. The new 'European social model' needed 'less passive and more active solidarity' (CEC, 1993: 15). Active labour market measures were to replace passive payment support. Social exclusion was to be fought both by 'preventive' and 'supportive' measures.

The White Paper pointed to the need for 'double flexibility' – both internal and external – in the labour market, involving both an improvement in the match of supply and demand, for example by geographical mobility, and an improvement in the use of human resources, for example by the organization of work and working time in firms (CEC, 1993: 17).[1] Both 'the behavioural and structural lack of flexibility' needed to be addressed.

Part of the Commission's attempt to establish a rationale for EU action in the social field is to compare European competitiveness with that of the US and to stress the 'European social model' – however in need of modernization – as a 'productive factor' (CEC, 1997a, 2000a). Europe would not lose but gain competitiveness by investing in social security. This, however, required that social benefit systems are made compatible with competitiveness. Focus here is said to be on the system structures rather than levels of benefit, the latter being explicitly an issue for the OECD but in fact also for economic policy-makers in the EU (Ecofin, DG ECFIN). A key concern in the 'modernization of the European social model' is to make social policy and economic performance not perceived to be in opposition to each other as well as making them compatible in practice.

The European Council in Essen in 1994 established a number of common policy objectives. Member states committed themselves to promoting investments in vocational training; a more flexible work organization; a wage policy that favoured job creation; reduced indirect labour costs, particularly for non-qualified workers; improving the efficiency of employment policies by avoiding measures that negatively affect one's availability for work, and improving measures to assist groups that have been most affected by unemployment, such as the long-term unemployed, women and young people. A system for supervising the employment policies was established, where the member states were to make annual reports as to their progress along these lines. This was later developed and institutionalized in the Amsterdam treaty and its Employment Chapter (Art. 125–30). Based on the new treaty provisions, a cyclical procedure has developed consisting of common policy guidelines, decided by the Council on a qualified majority-vote; Council recommendations to individual member states to live up to previous commitments; national reporting mechanisms; evaluation, benchmarking and peer review. The guidelines are structured under four 'pillars': *improving employability; developing entrepreneurship; encouraging adaptability*; and *strengthening the policies for equal opportunities*. These correspond to four alleged 'gaps': a job gap, a skills gap, a participation gap and a gender gap.

Thus, a policy discourse in the EU on employment and social welfare developed in the 1990s, built on the key concepts of employability, adaptability, flexibility, lifelong learning and entrepreneurship but also on the concepts of social inclusion and social partnership. Connections were established, such as 'human resources as an investment' and social policy as a 'productive factor'; the need to strike 'a new balance between flexibility and security'; to modernize the 'European social model'; and to implement a 'preventive approach' with improved ability for actors to anticipate change instead of merely a 'curative' approach.

On the one hand, *continuity* with the past is stressed: The policy approach is presented as a defence of the European social model in contrast to the American one. The European social model is taken to be characterized 'by systems that offer a high level of social protection, by the importance of the social dialogue and by services of general interest covering activities vital for social cohesion'. It is perceived to be based on 'a common core of values' beyond the diversity of the member states' social systems (CEC, 2000a). On the other hand, there is a stress on *novelties* and the need to think anew: new technologies; new times with new demands; the need to order anew the economies and social systems; to 're-establish the links' between economic efficiency and external competitiveness and social rights and justice; to 'modernize social protection systems' and to 'update the social model'. There are new challenges but also changes and policy innovations are called for. Common European social values are seen to be the base for common responses to common challenges. 'Commonness' is emphasized in this rhetoric of mobilization. In reality, rather than one single 'European Social Model', there are diverse and historically contingent national solutions, shaped by the institutions, values, and established practices of various societies.

An ambition and achievement of the EES has been to establish at the Community level a more integrated approach with linkages between economic policy, social policy and labour market policy. A motivation has been to make welfare states more 'employment-friendly', that is, to make social security benefits more 'employment promoting' by providing incentives to work, and to make tax systems more 'employment promoting' by providing incentives to enterprise. Some changes in the discourse over time can be traced. Bosco (1998) has noted a 'gradual shift in the paradigm' since the 1993 White Paper and the Essen priorities compared to the first employment guidelines from 1997 and the policy papers thereafter. Initially, focus was on avoiding disincentives and improving the readiness to work (cf. the influence of the OECD view). More lately, 'employment-friendly' systems are interpreted not only in this way but more from the perspective of prevention and rehabilitation (Bosco, 1998). A complementarity of active policies and revisions of benefit systems has been sought. Another change in the late 1990s and in early 2000s has been a clearer focus on quality aspects, for example *better* and not just *more* jobs. The Social Agenda adopted in Nice 2000 emphasized 'the promotion of quality in all areas of social policy'. An interpretation of this can be that the neo-liberal problem description colours the discourse less today than it did at first (Bosco, 1998). However, the 'disincentive' argument is still highly prevalent in the broad economic policy guidelines and other documents relating to economic and structural reform, and reflects a certain discrepancy in the views of DG Employment and Social Affairs and DG Economic and Financial Affairs as well as between social and labour market ministries and finance ministries nationally. The labour market documents produced by the EU economic policy-makers reflect more the OECD view. It is still an open issue how the balance between the economic and social reform agendas will be struck.

Towards a new balance between flexibility and security

Thus, links between social policy and the economy were called for and established. The challenge was said to be to strike the 'right balance between competition and solidarity' (Larsson, 1996: 724) or to 'match equity and efficiency' (Ferrera *et al.*, 2000: 5). The former Director-General of the Commission Larsson called for a strategy for investment in human resources, improving both the skill supply and the flexibility of the labour market, which in turn required 'a new concept for the modernisation of the labour market... we need a new balance between flexibility and security, offering more security for personal development outside enterprises and more flexibility within enterprises' (1996: 732). A 'balance between the needs of companies for flexibility and the needs of employees for security' (CEC, 1999b: 8) was deemed necessary.

This in turn called for new definitions and the European Commission explicitly saw the redefinition of concepts as part of its strategy. Former Commissioner Flynn argued that old definitions of security and flexibility do not hold any longer and that: 'workforce flexibility and security *through skills* are the fuels which can transform the problem' (Flynn, 1999, emphasis added). Improved employability was perceived as 'positive flexibility' in contrast to the 'negative flexibility' of simple deregulation, a view basically shared by the trade unions. In their view, only workers who feel a basic security in the work contract will be flexible enough to be open to learning new skills and adapting to new circumstances.[2]

Thus, on the one hand social protection and economic performance are seen as compatible and indeed mutually supporting ('social protection as a productive factor'), on the other hand a new balance is required implying some kind of a trade-off situation. The challenge is to make them compatible or, as put by Ferrera *et al.* (2000: 3), the task 'is one of identifying new value combinations and institutional arrangements that are both mixed (in terms of solidarity and growth objectives) and virtuous (capable of producing simultaneous advances on all the affected fronts'. Positive-sum outcomes are perceived to be possible. Still, looking at the relation between social protection and economic performance and between flexibility and security in the discourse it is clear that 'it is on the systems of social protection that the burden of adaptation ultimately weighs' (Bosco, 1998: 326).

Becoming employable

Employability, as one of the four pillars of the EES, is understood as 'the capacity for people to be employed: it relates not only to the adequacy of their skills but also to incentives and opportunities offered to individuals to seek employment' (CEC, 1997b). Still, the preferred path to improved employability in the EU discourse is education and vocational training. It is said to play a double role: firstly, as an active labour market policy instrument, adapting skills to the need of the market thus being a key instrument in flexibilizing the labour market. It facilitates the entry of young people into the labour market as well as the re-entry of the long-term unemployed. Secondly, investments in human capital are also necessary to increase the competitiveness of enterprises, not least for assimilating the constantly new technology. The 1993 White Paper pointed to the need to improve the low level of education in the EU relative to Japan and the US, and also to the need to provide opportunity for continuous vocational training, to develop human resources throughout one's work career. More flexible and open training systems and the development of the individual's ability to adapt were expected to be ever more important, both for companies in order to better make use of technical innovations, and for individuals, who would increasingly have to change job four to five times in a lifetime. As regards youth, the challenge was to facilitate the step from education to work life (CEC, 1993).

Required from the individual was both basic knowledge and technical and social skills, including developing and acting in a complicated and technological environment, communicating and being able to establish contacts. The ability 'to learn how to learn' throughout life (CEC, 1993: 136) is key in this line of thought. One cannot be prepared for tomorrow once and for all, by acquiring skills and know-how. Instead the abilities to learn, to communicate, to co-operate and have social competence are required. That also includes being able to judge one's own situation, make diagnoses and propose changes. As put by a high-level group on 'Managing Change': 'The employability of a person is his or her ability to find a niche in the labour market. Employability encompasses more than just training: it also provides individuals with a better understanding of change, of the need for mobility and of the means to upgrade skills. In short, it means that individuals have confidence in their own ability to adapt to change' (CEC, 1998: 6). In the view of the Commission, the requirements of individuals in the knowledge-based society are not small: 'Workers in the digital age therefore need to be ICT literate, highly skilled, empowered, mobile and ready for training [lifelong learning]' (CEC, 2000b: 14).

Responsibility for lifelong learning is to be shared between the enterprises, individuals and states. As put by the high-level group: 'Companies have a duty to maintain the employability of their workers, while workers have a duty to participate fully in the training to maintain their own employability. For the unemployed, ensuring employability is a responsibility shared with government and local authorities' (CEC 1998: 6). It is implied that the interests of enterprises, individuals and states converge. For the enterprises, a well-equipped labour force will ensure that the company can make efficient use of new technology, improve its productivity, etc. For the state, employable persons will mean lower costs for unemployment benefit support. For the individual, it will mean an insurance against unemployment, *the concept of job security tending to be replaced by employability security*, that is the security to be derived from being employable (Bosco, 1998; CEC, 1997a; Chabbert and Kerschen, 2001). The enterprises should be more engaged in vocational training and states should develop fiscal and legal incentives to encourage that. Investment in public employment offices is deemed necessary to allow for more individual guidance. The unemployed should be offered training, but in exchange they must be prepared to 'make a personal investment in this training' (CEC, 1993). The employees are responsible for participating in training so as to retain their employability (CEC, 1998: 6). Still, the question of financing lifelong learning is not resolved at the EU level but left to be resolved nationally or locally.

The OECD and EU discourse in summary

Improved employability is a key concern on the agenda for labour market reform of both the OECD and EU. In both cases political programmes are combined with such practices as recurrent recommendations and evaluations of member state performance to encourage and support policy reform. In particular, the EU has developed a refined system of reporting and monitoring the EES and also has the ESF as a supporting financial instrument, encouraging local actors to seek support for local projects along the lines of the EES. A European politics for employability has indeed developed. There is a high degree of convergence in the labour market discourse of the EU and the OECD, albeit some differences in emphasis. The need for structural reforms, notably increased flexibility in labour markets, while present in the EU documents is more pronounced in those of the OECD. In the EU view, the problem of unemployment is not that of the labour market alone (cf. 'employment problems are not caused by excessive labour market regulations', Larsson, 2000: 35), and the EU employment strategy builds on a combination of growth-oriented policies and structural reforms.[3] The assumption of people's unwillingness to work is more dominating and the focus on 'disincentives' is stronger with the OECD. However, the economic policy actors in the EU tend to argue more along the lines of the OECD. While the OECD can rely on an expert – neoclassical economist – consensus, the EU has to moderate many other interests, including the two sides of industry and various national and political interests. Accordingly, its views are less one-sided.

The imperatives of globalization, competitiveness and the knowledge-based economy lay the foundation for both the EU and the OECD discourse, the EU emphasizing more the knowledge-based economy (and hence the dynamic aspects of employability as the need for constant learning) and the OECD more the level of global competition (and hence employability as a matter of adequate pricing of labour productivity and avoidance of welfare traps). Employability is a multivocal concept, which becomes forceful since different actors can give it an acceptable meaning.

Even within the EU documents, employability is talked of in several senses and covers a broad policy agenda. Serrano (2000: 24) identifies

Employability – a new or old ideal? *Photo: Christina Ottosson*

three problem definitions of employability in the EU policy debate:
(1) employability as a matter of *training*. With this concept, the perceived
need is one of technical and general skills that are to be acquired through
matching training to the needs of industry; (2) employability as a matter
of *prevention*. The perceived need here is social and procedural competencies (including attitudes of initiative and responsibility but also
methodological competencies related to effective job search) acquired
through individual guidance and career planning; and (3) employability
as a matter of *activation*. The perceived need here is moral competencies
(an improved work ethic, motivation and incentives to work) acquired
through steering devices towards work, for example, by the design of
social benefit systems. In the implementation of the employability
pillar of the EES, various countries lay the emphasis differently.

Both the OECD and the EU emphasize the need for attitudinal and
behavioural change besides changes in supporting systems and structures:
social skills (the ability to learn, cooperate and communicate), and
having the 'right' attitudes and social and moral qualities (activity,
responsibility, availability). The employability discourse, operationalized
in various labour market practices, also functions by *socializing* subjects
into a particular *ethos*. Depending on what concept of employability

one draws on, the emphasis of this ethos differs. However, in all cases, the focus is on the individual and his or her characteristics.

Shifting responsibilities

Certain structural demands on labour to be and remain a marketable commodity follow from processes of globalization and competition, transition to a knowledge-intensive economy, qualitative conversions of labour processes and a more unstable economic environment and labour market, as well as from the demographic challenges to the financing of social protection. However, by presenting these developments as *fait accompli*, the labour market discourse outlined above also functions to legitimize these developments as well as to legitimize changes in the distribution of responsibilities. The discourse must partly be understood against the background of ideological change including an increased 'marketization' of social democracies. The 'third way' under Blair and '*die neue Mitte*' under Schröder are strongly supply-side oriented much in line with the European Employment Strategy, and it was the coming into office of social democratic governments (however centre-left oriented) in a number of countries which made the EES come about. This supply-side policy covers both a deregulation and enforcement agenda *and* the more 'positive' agenda of investment in human resources. But it implies changed roles for states, enterprises and individuals. We will now turn to discuss shifts in responsibilities.

Supply-side politics

Alongside with the attempt to make economic policy, labour market policy and social policy work to support the same goals, we have seen in the EU and OECD countries a shift in the labour market and social policy paradigm. Two general tendencies are the activation of the jobless and the decentralisation of employment policy implementation. Demand-side policies have given way to tailor-made supply-side interventions, with the individual's employability being seen as the crucial objective and action thus being centred on the individual. Bonoli and Bonvin (2001) argue that this individualized approach has its most far-reaching consequences for social policy, entailing a shift from re-distribution to a production or supply-side approach and to an *ex ante* social policy concentrating on trying to equalize as much as possible the starting positions of individuals in the market, thus hoping to avoid *ex post* redistribution of cash benefits. Financial compensation is supplemented and sometimes partially substituted by individualized services.

Bonoli and Bonvin (2001) conclude that *servicing states* tend to replace welfare states, and that decommodification as the main goal of social policy is giving way to a recommodification. Jessop (1994) even speaks of a transition towards a 'Schumpetarian workfare state' where the main objective is to strengthen national competitiveness by intervention on the supply-side and where social policy is subordinated to the needs of labour market flexibility and/or to the constraints of international competition. However, the concrete implementation of this no doubt varies between countries according to welfare traditions and prevailing institutions.

Cash benefits are in any case seen as less legitimate. Instead investments in the individual in terms of education, training and individual guidance are encouraged. All EU member states have tightened their eligibility conditions for unemployment benefit and activated the search for employment. The activation policy is double-sided: 'On the one hand, activation measures are new opportunities offered to the unemployed, who receive support for re-entering the labour market. On the other, the burden of obligations placed on the unemployed could shed doubt on the quality of these opportunities' (Lefresne, 1999: 471), for example by a pressure to accept unskilled and unrewarding jobs. While improved competitiveness in the labour market can result from measures to improve human capital (qualifications, work experience and so on), it can also follow from a purely functional adaptation to the post to be occupied, reducing the worker's control over her professional value and consequently her power to claim her position, wage and a certain level of security (Lefresne, 1999). Employability policies thus can be empowering for individuals but can also be disciplinary and degrading.

The main policy instruments available for states are perceived to be supply-oriented structural reforms and to a much lesser extent, macroeconomic policy instruments. However, some researchers question the link between employability and employment and argue that there is no evidence to support a correlation between the skill level of a population and the level of employment or unemployment (Lefresne, 1999). Rather, improved employability may, at a given level of employment, alter the queue of job seekers. Moreover, Åberg (forthcoming) has argued that jobs with higher educational requirements have not grown fast enough to match the better-educated new age groups in a country like Sweden, and that an increasing proportion of the labour force is in fact overeducated (see also, Chapter 5 by Svensson in this volume). Rather than subsidizing jobs with low educational requirements, it would make sense to stimulate the economy to increase the total demand for labour in order to increase the chances of people with more education to get jobs at their educational level and leave job openings for the less educated. Thus, is the key problem the net creation of jobs by the economy or the individual characteristics of the employed? According to Lefresne, it 'seems that the employability rhetoric is aiming above all, in a context of mass unemployment, to shift the terms of the debate, moving away from a macro-economic approach to unemployment in order to focus attention on the individual characteristics of the unemployed, at the same time justifying their rate of unemployment' (Lefresne, 1999: 468). The rationale of improved employability, and the meaning of employability for individuals, of course differ depending on the labour market context. In the context of mass unemployment, employability does not necessarily mean employment but a promise to be a good candidate for a job – once there is one. To be employable in the context of labour shortages, on the other hand, is to have increased one's market value, i.e. an attractive position. One may argue that the EU employment strategy, even if initially devised to handle mass unemployment, is also aiming to respond to a situation of expected labour shortages.

The employability discourse in any case implies a stronger focus on the responsibility of the individual and it implies a changed role for the state, most notably the change from demand oriented to supply-side oriented politics and from the role of a redistributor to a service-provider or, as it is sometimes put, an 'enabling' state.

Redefining rights and obligations

The discursive shifts, including the salience of concepts such as employability, flexibility, adaptability and activation, imply a shifting of responsibilities. The increased emphasis on activation is a case in point. The activation measures tend to be based on a new definition of the relationship between rights and responsibilities, that is, a new social contract. This is not to deny that activation policies implemented in various countries differ in terms of the social contracts implied (cf. the Nordic versus the Anglo-Saxon models). However, they all imply greater pressure on individuals to take up jobs or training. In the activation discourse, the responsibilities of individuals are underlined.

That rights carry obligations is taken furthest in the political discourse of the 'third way', as promulgated by New Labour in Britain. To quote a typical statement by Blair: 'The Third Way needs a concept of modern civic society that is founded on opportunity and responsibility, rights and duties going together. Society has a duty to its citizens and its citizens have a duty to society' (quoted in Fairclough, 2000: 38).

How to 'combine obligations and opportunities' is also a key issue in the EES (CEC, 1997a, 1999c). Moreover, a key premise in the EU discourse is that it is possible to combine 'the twin objectives of competitiveness and cohesion...recognizing their complementarity' (Commissioner Diamantopoulou, in OECD, 2000: 8). Fairclough (2000) has characterized the discourse of New Labour as a 'rhetoric of reconciliation', which claims to reconcile what has by the 'old' politics misguidedly been seen as incompatible – 'economic dynamism and social justice'. This way of reasoning is also highly prevalent in the EU discourse. However, as pointed out by Fairclough, this 'not only this but also that' reasoning says nothing about the relationship between them. Do resources and energies go equally to achieving economic dynamism and social justice? Or does the one achieve the other?

Also the OECD has been forced to address the question of equity. Even if it is believed that 'improving the skills and competences of all workers can enhance, in the longer term, both labour market efficiency and equity', it is recognized that in the short term there may be problems of the trade-off between efficiency and equity (OECD, 1996: 18f). However, it is seen to be 'necessary to see the equity issue in a dynamic perspective' (OECD, 1996: 18f), where mobility of workers in and out of employment and across income scales means that groups are not confined to the same position throughout one's work career. This conception of 'equality through mobility and opportunity' (Ferrera *et al.*, 2000: 74) increasingly replaces equality in the sense of equality of outcome (which entails redistribution of wealth). As put by three prominent social researchers working as consultants for the Portuguese presidency of the EU: 'The European social model must place more emphasis within its normative framework on dynamic equality, being primarily attentive to the worst off, most hospitable to incentive-generating differentiation and flexibility, actively vigilant with regard to the "openness" of the opportunity structure and more interventionist on the mobility front' (Ferrera *et al.*, 2000: 75). While not giving up the equity ideal, Rhodes (1998: 179) argues that the nature of the social contract will change, 'involving greater centrality of the firm, both as an actor and model for socio-economic organization, and the tailoring of social intervention more closely with the demands of competition'. A reinterpretation of equality – from equality of outcomes to equality of opportunity – is part of this.

Conclusion: the politics of adjustment

Both the EU and the OECD have contributed to put the issue of people's employability in focus. Employability is understood in the context of a competitive and knowledge-based economy with increased demands on individuals both to acquire updated skills and the right attitudes towards work. Improved employability here covers a broad policy agenda including both improving people's working capacity, their access to the labour market and their willingness to work, and demanding a variety of measures such as basic and continuous training; individual guidance, and increased work incentives in tax, social and labour market policy. Stronger pressure through activation policies and reform of benefit systems is combined with 'positive' objectives for learning and competence development.

With global competition and a new knowledge-based model of production as an unquestioned point of departure, the space for action perceived to be available is mainly adjustment and adaptation, which in turn is considered key to prosper in the 'new' economy. These demands are put on the economy (calls for entrepreneurship), the 'European social model' (calls for 'modernization') and on individuals (calls for flexibility, the right attitudes, willingness to learn) (Crespo and Serrano, 2002). The policy discourse somewhat paradoxically combines calls for adjustment to functional imperatives with the belief in autonomous individuals able and willing to respond in a positive and open-minded way to change.

The role of the state is to support the adjustment process. The policy discourse reflects a changed role for the welfare state, from market-correction and wealth redistribution to the provision of opportunities by individually tailored supply-side interventions. Rather than protecting against social risks directly, the role of the welfare state is to support individuals' adjustment to change. The discourse also illustrates a shift from a demand- to a supply-oriented politics where the key problem is perceived to be lack of employability rather than lack of jobs.

The enterprise, the individual and the state are perceived to share a common interest in supporting the employability of individuals. The OECD and EU discourse on employability and lifelong learning is a consensual discourse which does not address conflicts of interests, thereby resonating with the typical 'third way' 'rhetoric of reconciliation' (Fairclough, 2000). Enterprises are expected to participate in the continuous training of employees to improve the enterprise performance, at the same time ensuring that employees keep their employability/ competitiveness – and can then manage without too much job security. However, from the employer side, enhanced profitability may be achieved through investments in the workforce but may also be achieved through costcutting and downsizing. Improved competitive capacity of enterprises may not at all coincide with either the national or the individual interest in skills and training (Brown *et al.*, 2001). The challenge remains: 'How to link training and employment in a contractual relationship which guarantees both life-long learning and security with mobility?' (Lefresne, 1999: 478).

If we see the contours of a new social contract with shared responsibility for individual mobility (mobility insurance, or 'adjustment insurance' as it is framed in the Swedish debate) between enterprises, public authorities and individuals, so far responsibility still ultimately lies with the individual. In the absence of legal rights or effective contractual agreements, 'turning unemployment insurance into an employability insurance' (CEC, 1997a: 10) will mean a relativization of the concept of insurance and ultimately of the concept of social right. For some unemployed workers, such as youth in Denmark and Sweden, training is really a right – besides being an obligation. However, for most workers it is not a right, even if negotiations are currently going on between unions and employers in Sweden on an 'adjustment insurance', which would give the right to a period of training before a dismissal and which would, unlike the present agreements, also cover blue-collar workers. Likewise, 'security through skills' is a relativization of the concept of security, such as when a Commission document speaks of skills enhancement and activation as 'a real employability insurance instead of a simple unemployment compensation' (CEC, 1997a: 6). As argued by Dahrendorf (1994: 12), entitlements and provisions are not the same thing and tend to be the concern of different and antagonistic parties. While the market can provide chances, it does not guarantee effective opportunities or rights. In the 'enabling' state, the provision of opportunities is the key priority, and equality of opportunities increasingly replace equality of income. The challenge remains: how to assure real, effective opportunities for all?

Moreover, while the concept of employability may serve to strengthen the chances of individuals, the other side of the coin is that employability as a category may function as an instrument for differentiation and sorting of individuals, and thus for potential exclusion, for instance at the workplace where the idea of employability may serve to establish the priorities for dismissal (Bollérot, 2001: 58). Moreover, the personal qualities and the right behaviour that are increasingly considered as important as are knowledge and know-how, are not as easy to document and are more open to personal judgements in the concrete employer-employee relation. As argued by Bollérot (2001: 60f) this trend towards individualization is in tune with the flexibility sought by enterprises and may lead to a personalization of contractual relations which would further endanger the status of the worker within the company. In the employability discourse generally, the problem of lack of employment tends to be personalized. In a longer term perspective, this may undermine the base for collective action and lead to divisions within the workers' collective rather than structuring conflicts along the division between capital and labour.

The adaptation to a competitive and knowledge-based economy has altered the balance between social rights and individual responsibilities. Stråth (2000: 24f) argues that an emerging convention of individual responsibility based on the concepts of flexibility – and we may add employability – is replacing the convention of full employment and state responsibility for employment. The redefinition of concepts such as security, flexibility, employability implies not only shifts of meaning but shifts of responsibilities and, ultimately, of power. While in the discourse studied, the state has the responsibility to 'enable' individuals to compete in labour markets and enterprises have a responsibility for supporting adjustment, the message is still clear: ultimately it is up to you!

Notes

1. A third type of flexibility, pay flexibility, is little mentioned in the EU policy documents. However, pay flexibility is a key issue for the OECD.
2. The new combination of security and flexibility is sometimes framed *flexicurity*. The concept originates from Holland where agreements have been struck which have meant, inter alia, a strengthening of rights for temporary workers in return for a loosening of dismissal protection for core workers. The normative argument being: 'it is morally fair to reduce the protection of the insiders and allow for more flexibility and greater earnings dispersion if this delivers greater opportunities to the worst off' (Ferrera *et al.*, 2000: 74).
3. According to EU research estimates, about 60 per cent of total unemployment is structural, rather than the 85 per cent reported by most other research, including the OECD (OECD, 2000: 8). It has been argued that the OECD Jobs Strategy is biased in favour of structural reform as against macro-economic policy, and also neglects the role of social partners and wage moderation (see for example Malinvaud, 2000). Moreover, the EU policy-makers are more favourable to the idea that it is possible to combine full employment and low inflation than are the OECD economists.

References

Åberg, Rune. Forthcoming. 'Unemployment persistency, overeducation and employment chances of the less educated'. *European Sociological Review*.
Bollérot, Patrick. 2001. 'Two actors in employability: the employer and the worker'. In *Employability: From Theory to Practice*, edited by P. Weinert *et al.* London: Transaction Publishers, 51–90.

Bonoli, Guiliano and Jean-Michel Bonvin. 2001. 'Rhetorics and reality of activation policies: national experiences compared'. Paper presented at ETUI seminar, 8–9 November, Brussels.

Bosco, Alessandra. 1998. 'Putting Europe into the systems: a review of social protection issues'. In *European Trade Union Yearbook 1997*, edited by E. Gabaglio and R. Hoffmann. Brussels: ETUI, 305–34.

Brown, Phillip, Andy Green and Hugh Lauder. 2001. *High Skills. Globalization, Competitiveness and Skills Formation*. Oxford: Oxford University Press.

CEC [Commission of the European Communities]. 1993. *Growth, Competitiveness, Employment, the Challenges and Ways Forward into the 21st Century*. COM (93)700.

CEC. 1994. *European Social Policy: A Way Forward for the Union*. COM(94)333.

CEC. 1997a. *Modernizing and Improving Social Protection in the European Union*. COM(97)102.

CEC. 1997b. *Proposal for Guidelines for Member States Employment Policies*. COM (97)497.

CEC. 1998. *Managing Change*. Final Report of the High level Group on Economic and Social Implications of Industrial Change.

CEC. 1999a. *Proposal for Guidelines for Member States' Employment Policies 2000*.

CEC. 1999b. *Community Policies in Support of Employment*. COM(99)127.

CEC. 1999c. *A Concerted Strategy for Modernizing Social Protection*. COM(99)347.

CEC. 2000a. *Social Policy Agenda*. COM(2000)379.

CEC. 2000b. *Strategies for Jobs in the Information Society*. COM(2000)48.

Chabbert, Isabelle and Nicole Kerschen. 2001. 'Towards a European model of employability insurance? Interaction between Europe and the member states'. In *Employability: From Theory to Practice*, edited by P. Weinert *et al.* London: Transaction Publishers, 91–112.

Crespo, Eduardo and Amparo Serrano Pascual. 2002. 'The EU's concept of activation for young people: towards a new social contract?'. In *Activation Policies for Young People in International Perspective*, edited by A. Serrano. Brussels: ETUI. Book manuscript.

Dahrendorf, Ralf. 1994. 'The changing quality of citizenship'. In *The Condition of Citizenship*, edited by B. Van Steenbergen. London: Sage, 10–19.

Drøpping , Jon Anders, Bjørn Hvinden and Kirsten Vik. 1999. 'Activation policies in the Nordic countries'. In *Nordic Social Policy: Changing Welfare States*, edited by M. Kauttu, M. Heikkilä, B. Hvinden, S. Marklund and N. Ploug. London and New York: Routledge, 133–58.

ERT. 1992. *Rebuilding Confidence: An Action Plan for Europe Proposed by the European Round Table of Industrialists*.

Fairclough, Norman. 2000. *New Labour, New Language?* London: Routledge.

Ferrera, Maurizio, Anton Hemerijck and Martin Rhodes. 2000. *The Future of Social Europe: Recasting Work and Welfare in the New Economy*. Report to the Portuguese Presidency of the European Union.

Flynn, Padraig. 1999. *Speech*. ISSA Regional Conference, Dublin, 5–7 May 1999.

Jacobsson, Kerstin. 2001. 'Employment and social policy coordination: a new system of EU governance'. Paper for the Scancor Workshop on Transnational Regulation and the Transformation of States. Stanford University, 22–23 June 2001.

Jacobsson, Kerstin. 2002. *Soft regulation and the subtle transformation of states: The case of EU employment policy*. Score research report 2002: 4.

Jacobsson, Kerstin and Herman Schmid. 2002. 'Real integration or just formal adaptation? On the implementation of the national action plans for employment'. In *Building Social Europe Through the Open Method of Co-ordination*, edited by C. de la Porte and P. Pochet. Brussels: PIE Peter Lang, 69–95.

Jessop, Bob. 1994. 'The transition to post-fordism and the schumpetarian workfare state'. In *Towards a Post-Fordist Welfare State?*, edited by R. Burrows and B. Loader. London: Routledge, 13–37.

Larsson, Allan. 1996. 'Social policy: past, present and future'. *Transfer* 2(4): 724–37.

Larsson, Allan. 2000. 'Putting Europe to work'. In *Policies Towards Full Employment*. Paris: OECD, 33–7.

Lefresne, Florence. 1999. 'Employability at the heart of the European employment strategy'. *Transfer* 5(4): 460–80.

Lødemel, Ivor and Heather Trickey (ed.) 2001. *'An Offer You Can't Refuse'*: *Workfare in an International Perspective*. Bristol: Policy.

Luque, Emilio. 2001. 'Whose knowledge (economy)?'. *Social Epistemology* 15(3): 187–200.

Malinvaud, Edmond. 2000. A comment. In *Policies Towards Full Employment*. Paris: OECD, 53–7.

Marcussen, Martin. 2001. 'The OECD: transnational regulation through the idea-game'. Paper Presented at the Scancor Workshop on Transnational Regulation and the Transformation of States. Stanford University, 22–23 June 2001.

Marcussen, Martin. 2002. *OECD og idéspillet – Game Over?* København: Hans Reitzels Forlag.

OECD. 1977. *Towards Full Employment and Price Stability*. Paris: OECD.

OECD. 1994. *The OECD Jobs Study*. Paris: OECD.

OECD. 1996. *Pushing Ahead with the Strategy*. Paris: OECD.

OECD. 1997a. *Making Work Pay. Taxation, Benefits, Employment and Unemployment*. Paris: OECD.

OECD. 1997b. 'Labour market policies. New challenges. Theme 3. Lifelong learning to maintain employability'. *OECD Working Papers* 88.

OECD. 2000. *Policies Towards Full Employment*. Paris: OECD.

Rhodes, Martin. 1998. 'Globalization, labour markets and welfare states: a future of "competitive corporatism"?'. In *The Future of European Welfare: A New Social Contract?* edited by M. Rhodes and Y. Mény. London: Macmillan – now Palgrave Macmillan, 178–203.

Serrano Pascual, Amparo. 2000. 'European strategies to fight youth unemployment: a comparative analysis and critical assessment'. In *Tackling Youth Unemployment in Europe*, edited by A. Serrano Pascual. Brussels: ETUI, 17–28.

Stråth, Bo. 2000. 'After full employment and the breakdown of conventions of social responsibility'. In *After Full Employment. European Discourses on Work and Flexibility*, edited by B. Stråth. Brussels: Peter Lang, 11–31.

4

Competition versus Regulation: Swedish Articulations of the EU Labour Market Discourse[1]

Lotte Faurbæk

Introduction: interpreting EU labour market discourse in Sweden

This chapter is concerned with EU social and labour market policy, sometimes referred to as the social dimension of the EU. This policy area has undergone a tremendous development over the last 15 years, from being tied to the internal market programme as a supporting policy, to being an important part of an integrated strategy to combat unemployment, increase economic growth, and enhance competitiveness in the EU. I will focus on the relationship between this EU discourse and the national creation of meaning within the same policy area in one specific member state – Sweden. When Sweden joined the EU in 1995, it became part of the EU decision-making process concerning EU social and labour market policy. This entailed being able to further national interests within this policy area, through the national EU decision-making process. This chapter focuses on the relationship between on the one hand an EU discourse on labour market policy, and on the other hand a national interpretation of EU labour market policy taking place in the Swedish EU decision-making process. It is a meeting between two different discursive contexts, in which EU labour market policy is being developed, articulated and negotiated, and where meaning is being ascribed to EU labour market policy.

Theoretically, the relationship can be interpreted as a question of how different ideas (or a collection of ideas) can influence political development and cause institutional or organizational change. Ideas are perceived as explanatory variables in connection with organizational change (Campbell, 1998). It is not the purpose of this chapter to study organizational change, but rather to discuss how we can understand the spreading of ideas from one area to another. It is tempting to understand this as a simple matter of diffusion: that ideas travel from one area to the other without being altered significantly, and the national perception of EU social and labour market policy will only differ a little from the EU discourse. In this way, diffusion presupposes the existence of fully developed and easily identified ideas and paradigms that are directly transferred from EU to national levels without alterations. I believe this to be a much too simple understanding of the spreading of ideas and discourses. The relationship between the EU discourse on labour market policy and the Swedish creation of meaning within the same policy area can best be understood as a complex process of translation (Latour, 1988; Czarniawska and Joerges, 1996). Translation is a continual process of meaning creation, where an idea (or a collection of ideas) is articulated and stabilised in the course of time (Kjær and Pedersen, 2001). Translation is a concrete process of meaning creation, where different distinctions are articulated and where meaning is ascribed to EU social and labour market policy. All meaning creation is thus local and context specific. There is no authoritative place 'outside' the discursive arrangement of a member state, from where meaning, status and validity can be ascribed to EU social and labour market policy. The creation of meaning is local, and thus highly dependent on the discursive and institutional arrangement of that specific country.

In this chapter, I focus on the institutionalized negotiations at the ministries concerned with articulating a Swedish position on EU labour market and social policy. I will thus present a concrete example of how a member state articulates EU social and labour market policy, and how meaning is created within the national EU decision-making process. First, I will briefly outline the EU discourse on social and labour market policy, articulated by the EU institutions in the period 1985–98. Then I will focus on the discursive arrangement and creation of meaning in the Swedish EU-related decision-making process today, with special emphasis on the Swedish articulations of unemployment, employability and lifelong learning. Finally, I will discuss the relationship between the two main articulations of EU labour market policy in Sweden and the relationship between the EU discourse and the national creation of meaning, and compare them to each other.

Two phases of EU discourse

In this section, I will outline some of the results of a discourse analysis of EU social and labour market policy. My approach to discourse analysis is mainly inspired by Foucault (1972) and the Danish tradition of institutional history (Pedersen, 1989, 1990, 1995; Andersen, 1994, 1995; Andersen and Kjær, 1996; Pedersen, 1997).[2] Here, I will focus mainly on the articulation of problems and solutions within the EU social and labour market discourse, and the change that happened around 1990.

My history of the EU discourse on social and labour market policy begins in 1985, but we can find traces of EU labour market policy in the Treaty of Rome with the establishment of the European Social Fund (ESF). Until the 1970s, most policy development focused on one of the so-called traditional areas of EU social and labour market policy – the free mobility of workers and anti-discrimination of workers, in the EU. The 1970s witnessed a new beginning within social and labour market policy, and the concept of 'the social dimension' was used for the first time. In 1974 the Council issued the first social action programme in the light of the beginning economic recession and the oil price crises. This resulted in policy developments in the areas of workers' rights, gender equality and health and safety at work. At the same time the Commission launched the social dialogue between the European labour market organizations (the European Trade Union Confederation (ETUC), the Union of Industrial and Employers' Confederations of Europe (UNICE) and European Centre of Public Enterprises (CEEP)), but with limited success, mainly because of the so-called Vredeling directive, which concerned information and consultation of workers in multinational firms. At the beginning of the 1980s, the social dialogue stopped; the Community suffered from serious budgetary problems and conflicts, and no new directives were issued on EU social and labour market policy (see CEC, 1989a). This was the background to the re-launch of EU social and labour market policy in 1985 with the new Chairman of the Commission – Jacques Delors.

The period 1985–98 may divided into two different phases of discourse: the social dimension of the internal market 1985–90, and the structural political frame of meaning about EU social and labour market policy 1990–98. The two phases entail two different ways of articulating EU social and labour market policy at the European level, that is, through the institutions of the EU. Unemployment is articulated as the most serious problem of the Community in both periods, but the rationality and the articulation of the problem are very different. The same applies to the articulation of solutions to the unemployment problem, and to the very definition of EU social and labour market policy. I date the change to just around the year 1990. This was an unusually quiet period in the articulation of the EU discourse. There were small signs of the beginning of a more structural understanding of EU social and labour market policy before 1990, but by 1992 we can see a much clearer structural articulation (see for example CEC, 1992). In 1993 with the Delors White Paper (see Jacobsson, Chapter 3 in this book) we can see a fully-blown structural understanding of problems and solutions within EU labour market policy.

In the first period (1985–90) unemployment was articulated as a technological and growth related problem. Unemployment was rising because of the recession and the substitution of workers by new technology (see for example CEC, 1988). Consequently, the ultimate measure to combat unemployment was growth. This was a period of optimism. The future looked bright, because the completion of the internal market was expected to generate the much-needed growth and create many new jobs throughout the Community. In the long run, the internal market was expected to solve the unemployment problem. The restructuring, resulting from the liberalization programme, was expected to enhance the competitive advantages of European firms *vis-à-vis* US and Japanese firms. This was the dominant picture of the future articulated in this period, and though it was generally an optimistic picture, some short-term concerns were also articulated. The process of restructuring within industry would possibly result in rising unemployment in the short run. Based on a scientific report (CEC, 1989b), the Commission expected that the development of employment, with the completion of the internal market, would resemble the shape of a 'J'. EU social and labour market policy was articulated as the remedy for this first decrease in employment. As such it was strongly tied to the internal market programme and the J-curve. EU social and labour market policy was expected to eliminate the short-term consequences of the liberalization programme, and this was the justification for re-launching the policy area.

While unemployment was articulated as the overall problem in Europe in this period, two related problems were identified – social dumping and regional inequality. Social dumping is a concept used to describe a situation, where firms can obtain a competitive advantage by moving to another EU country with lower standards of health and safety requirements, lower standards of workers' rights, etc. In this way firms can 'export' unemployment within the Community, and the overall result might not be a decrease in unemployment. This was the general argumentation used to articulate social dumping as a problem, and scientific studies confirmed that social dumping would most likely be a result of the internal market, especially where labour intensive industry was concerned. The EU institutions pointed to a Community charter of basic workers' rights as a solution to social dumping (see ECOSOC, 1987; CEC, 1990). The purpose of the charter was to establish a number of minimum rights for workers in Europe, so that social dumping would not be possible. The rights were established in the following areas: free mobility of labour, increases in living standards and work conditions, freedom of association and collective agreements, education and qualifications, equal rights of men and women at work, information, consultation and influence for workers, health and safety at work, protection of children at work, reasonable salary levels, reasonable social protection, reasonable pensions, and the integration of the disabled. This was eventually called the Community Charter, and was agreed upon in 1989, but without the participation of the UK. The Charter was, at the time, not legally binding, and the subsequent reports on the implementation of the Charter are rather depressing reading (see for example CEC, 1991).

Regional inequality was another related problem. It was expected because some regions were already lagging behind, and these were likely to deteriorate even further with the completion of the internal market. The solution to this problem was articulated as a reform of the structural funds (CEC, 1988). The financial support was ordered in accordance with six overall target areas, and there was a substantial increase in funding. This was completed with the ratification of two budget reforms (Delors I and II) in the beginning of the 1990s. In this period of the EU discourse the present was perceived as a time of crisis, and the future looked promising with the internal market and EU social and labour market policy to remedy the detrimental short-term effects. EU social and labour market policy was thus articulated as a supporting policy in relation to economic policy.

This way of articulating European social and labour market policy changed significantly after 1990. The development of the EU discourse in the 1990s is described in detail elsewhere in this book (see Jacobsson, Chapter 3 in this volume). I will therefore restrict myself to summarize some of the main developmental trends of this period. Unemployment was still articulated as the most important problem of the EU, but in a quite different way. Unemployment was now articulated as a structural problem. It was no longer just a question of growth and technology. The labour market was perceived as having a number of structural problems, and these had to be solved in order to raise employment. This meant that economic growth alone would not be able to create full employment and market clearing. As a consequence, attention was shifted to the supply-side of the labour market – the workers (CEC, 1993a,b). Two structural measures were pointed out as solutions: education and a more active employment policy. Education and qualifications had to correspond to the demands of industry. Education was increasingly articulated as lifelong learning. Workers would have to upgrade their skills, in order to be flexible and meet the demands of the labour market. This also applied to the unemployed. Because of changing conditions on the labour market, the unemployed had to upgrade their education and skills in order to be employable (CEC, 1994). The picture of the future changed in this period of the discourse. As we have seen in Chapter 3, the key figure in this period was the knowledge-based society. The future would bring the information society, and the employees would have to be ready for it. The unemployed needed new qualifications, partly to meet new demands on the labour market, and partly to become a part of the information society. Otherwise there was a risk that the population would be divided into two groups: those who were active participants in the information society, and those who were not.

Unemployment was perceived as resulting in social exclusion. Social exclusion was articulated as a complex structural problem that needed integrated and coherent solutions. Long-term structural unemployment was only one aspect of the problem, other aspects were housing, health, discrimination, poverty and abuse problems (CEC, 1993a). EU social and labour market policy was articulated as one part of a structural political strategy to combat unemployment and social exclusion. The present was perceived as a time of crisis with high levels of structural unemployment and rising poverty, while the past was an optimistic time characterized by job creation and general enthusiasm about the internal market. In this period of the EU discourse, solutions were seen as long-term integrated strategies where all the EU policy areas had to contribute. The structural discourse was penetrating the EU discourse, and the policy area was articulated as an integral part of a structural political initiative to increase growth, enhance competition and combat unemployment and social exclusion. It was no longer secondary to economic policy, it was one among many other policy areas integrated within a structural political frame of meaning. Since 1997, the European employment strategy and guidelines has been the most dominant policy area of EU social and labour market policy (see Jacobsson, Chapter 3 in this volume, for a closer examination of the EU employment discourse). This is the discourse that Sweden faced when joining the EU. In the next section of this chapter I examine how the Swedish translation of the EU discourse takes place through the local creation of meaning.

Opposing labour market articulations in Sweden

The Swedish EU-related decision-making process is a site for the struggle of the precise meaning of EU social and labour market policy. Different agents, such as civil servants and social partners, reproduce the institutional and discursive arrangements in Sweden, through discursive and institutional practices. Thus, a creation of meaning takes place through the ongoing articulation processes in Swedish governmental praxis. The Swedish EU decision-making process is characterized by highly informal relations and interactions between the different agents that take part in it. I have focused on the development of the national interest concentrated around the Ministry of Industry, Employment and Communications and the Ministry of Health and Social Affairs. They hold joint meetings with the Swedish labour market organizations (The Swedish Trade Union Confederation, the Swedish Confederation of Professional Associations, the Confederation of Swedish Enterprise, the Swedish Association of Local Authorities, the Federation of Swedish County Councils and the Swedish Agency for Government Employers), and through their institutional practice they institutionalize a Swedish translation of the EU discourse.

There is not only one single articulation of EU social and labour market policy in Sweden. There are a number of different articulations that are all in one way or another related to a basic discursive distinction between regulation and competition. Because it is possible to identify more than one articulation of EU social and labour market policy, I have chosen to use the term 'discursive terrain'. The ongoing articulation processes establish a discursive terrain in which articulations take place. I can identify at least five different articulations of EU social and labour market policy, but will concentrate on two articulations that have the entire policy area as their object.[3] The Swedish discursive terrain is characterized by these two articulations of EU social and labour market policy, which are in opposition to each other. I will call them 'the regulation articulation' and 'the competition articulation'. Even though the two articulations differ in many ways, they are both part of a structural political discourse. The rationality of the articulations is focused on the structures and the supply-side of the labour market – the workforce. The two articulations however point to different problems and solutions within EU social and labour market policy, and specifically in connection with EU employment policy.[4]

The regulation articulation

The regulation articulation is characterized by the articulation of regulation as the positive side of the basic discursive distinction regulation versus competition. The core argument is that regulation of the labour market is needed. This is the argumentation of the Swedish Social Democratic government (represented by the two ministries)[5] and the trade unions. These are the main agents within this articulation of EU social and labour market policy. It is characteristic of the regulation articulation that EU social and labour market policy in general is perceived as a counterbalance to the internal market. Business and industry got the internal market, and the workers got EU social and labour market policy to counterbalance the onset of free competition. The purpose of EU social and labour market policy is to counteract the detrimental aspects of the internal market. EU labour market policy is generally articulated as the social dimension of the internal market. It is considered important to regulate the labour market, so as to avoid 'unhealthy' competition on labour standards.

Unemployment is pointed out as the most important problem of Europe, and it is articulated both as structural unemployment and as a result of the recession. The trade unions would like the EU to lead a more expansive fiscal policy to generate more growth and create jobs. Social dumping is also articulated as a very serious danger, as part of the unhealthy competition within the internal market. One of the main purposes of EU social and labour market policy according to the two ministries and the trade unions is to prevent this kind of behaviour from arising in industry – the ravage of capital, as the Swedish Trade Union Confederation calls it. To prevent social dumping, the Swedish government and the unions have called for legally institutionalizing the basic workers' rights from the Community charter from 1989 in the treatises of the EU, which took place with the Amsterdam treaty. The unions also advocate transnational rights to strike within the EU. This is perceived as a necessary measure to counteract the free movement of capital. When capital can move freely in the internal market, it should also be possible to arrange strikes across borders or in sympathy with workers in other EU countries. This is articulated as a solution to social dumping, because it will make it easier to combat social dumping in the EU. The Swedish government supports this argument, and tried to place it on the agenda of the IGC in Amsterdam, but with little success.

The regulation articulation is heavily influenced by the structural political discourse. The unemployment problem and the problem of social exclusion are generally articulated as complex and structural problems. A director at the Ministry of Industry, Employment and Communication says in an interview in 2002 that within the last five years, they have focused heavily on the need for structural change in the labour market. There is a strong tendency to focus on the functioning of the labour market, and the supply-side – the workforce. The labour market is perceived as having mismatch problems, which prevent market clearing and hence full employment. The solutions to these problems are mainly articulated in connection with the employment guidelines and the National Action Plan. As we have seen in Jacobsson's chapter in this book, the guidelines consist of a range of common goals of employment policy. Every year member states write a report (a National Action Plan) on what they have done in the previous year to live up to their commitments and implement the employment guidelines in their national employment policies.

The Swedish government and the unions clearly stress education and lifelong learning as solutions to the employment problems. A well functioning labour market has a competent workforce with the necessary qualifications, demanded by the economy. The National Action Plan (Regeringskansliet, 2001) concentrates on the four pillars of the employment strategy: employability, entrepreneurship, adaptability, and equal opportunities. These areas consist of a mixture of both supply- and demand-side initiatives that must be implemented at national level and according to national traditions. However, within the regulation articulation there is a strong tendency to focus on the supply-side measures to combat unemployment: most importantly, education and the upgrading of skills. The employees must have the qualifications that are needed to be employable. The argumentation within the regulation articulation is that today the labour market is changing rapidly, and it is not enough to have a high level of education before entering the labour market. Employees must continually upgrade their skills and learn all through their working life, in order to meet the changes. This is captured in the concept of lifelong learning. If employees are not employable, the result will be an increase in mismatch problems, according to the Swedish government. Enterprises will have difficulties finding qualified workers, which will lead them to compete for employees. This, in turn, will lead to higher wages and higher inflation, increased unemployment and more long-term unemployed workers. At the same time, it is expressed in interviews at the Ministry of Industry, Employment and Communications, that the active employment policy in Sweden over the last ten years has been effective. Because of this policy it was possible to educate the unemployed, while waiting for the end of the recession, which made them employable when growth returned and new jobs were created. In a sense, the unemployed were 'on hold', until times got better.

Education and lifelong learning is a very important strategy within the regulation articulation, but it will only work if people are secure in their jobs. This is why both the two ministries and the trade unions talk about the quality of work. The vision of 'good work' consists of lifelong learning, high health and safety standards, variety in work, equal opportunities, a non-discriminatory climate, as well as being able to combine work and family and job security. Lifelong learning and education is all very well, according to the Swedish Trade Union Confederation, but employees have to dare to upgrade skills and engage in lifelong learning. According to the government and the trade unions, it is important to have a high level of social security, so that people feel secure, and dare to meet the changes through educational measures – they have to feel secure in order to be able to change and be employable, as a labour market expert from the Swedish Trade Union Confederation says. Every year the EU issues a recommendation to the Swedish government encouraging it to revise the tax and social security systems, lower tax on labour and thereby increase the willingness of the unemployed to work. Within the regulation articulation this is perceived as a much too detailed interference from the EU level. Recommendations are perceived as a useful instrument to obtain employment goals, but the method should be left to the member states, which ultimately have the competence on this area of EU social and labour market policy, according to the Swedish agents in the regulation articulation.

Rationality in the regulation articulation is thus based on the argument that free competition has to be regulated to prevent industry from competing on low levels of labour standards which will ultimately lead to regional inequality and the lowering of labour standards in the EU. The basic argument is that regulation of the labour market is necessary to prevent market failures. However, such regulation must be oriented towards common goals, and the methods of reaching these goals must be the competence of the member states.

The competition articulation

The competition articulation is obviously based on the articulation of competition as the positive side of the discursive distinction. The representatives of this articulation are the Swedish employers' organizations, both public and private. As the regulation articulation, the competition articulation has EU social and labour market policy as a whole as its object. It is defined as labour market policy and some social security measures. EU social and labour market policy is articulated as a policy supportive of the internal market. Its purpose is to make the internal market (the competition) work optimally, by increasing the free mobility of labour. According to the Swedish employers' organizations, EU social and labour market policy will at best increase the free mobility of workers, and at worst obstruct free competition.

Unemployment is articulated as the most important problem in Europe, as was the case in the regulation articulation. The problem is more specifically the lack of employers, and the lack of flexibility in the labour market. Unemployment is again articulated as structural unemployment, because of the rigid structures of the labour market, which prevent labour flexibility, and make it too expensive to be an employer. According to the employers' organizations this is the reason for the lack of job creation in the EU. Too much regulation of the labour market makes it too expensive to start new businesses, and creates lack of flexibility. According to the employers' organizations, there is a tendency to build more national regulation of the labour market at top of EU regulation. A senior advisor at the Confederation of Swedish Enterprise says that they do not see any need for more regulation on the EU level. Social dumping is not perceived as a serious problem in the EU, and is not considered widespread. Most labour market issues are already regulated at national level either through legal measures or through collective agreements between the labour market organizations. The need for regulation of labour market issues at EU level should be established with regard to actual transnational problems. According to the Swedish employers' organizations, the directives on posting of workers, works councils in multinational firms and the interaction of social security systems are relevant and needed, because these issues have truly transnational aspects. Swedish employers operate with an extreme interpretation of the principle of subsidiarity. The Confederation of Swedish Enterprise writes (Confederation of Swedish Enterprise, 2002b): 'All EU action in the social policy area should be guided by the principles of subsidiarity and proportionality. The EU should only take action on matters which are genuinely transnational in nature and for which it can add value.' The problem within the EU is that too much emphasis has been placed on social security regulation of the labour market, instead of increasing flexibility that, in turn, leads to more job creation and thus more job security. This is the basic argumentation within the competition articulation. As we can see, this is very different from the regulation articulation.

As a consequence, the competition articulation points to two additional problems: Over-regulation and subsidized job creation. Regulation of the labour market should only be used in relation to cross-border activities, such as labour mobility, and only if it is beneficial to market competition. The competition articulation points to de-regulation as the main solution to the unemployment problem. De-regulation of the labour market and simplicity of labour market regulation are the essential solutions to the unemployment problem in the competition articulation. The Confederation of Swedish Enterprise writes (Confederation of Swedish Enterprise, 2002a): 'Unnecessary barriers must be abolished and new barriers avoided . . . Rules must be simpler, fewer and more stable.'

The competition articulation is also heavily influenced by the structural political discourse. The perception of the structural problems of the labour market is almost identical in the two articulations. But although the diagnosis is almost the same, the weighting of the different solutions is different. Knowledge and skills are considered to be key factors for maintaining the competitive strength of the EU. The point of departure for the Swedish employers is the demands placed on employees in the future. Europe should not compete on the basis of low labour costs, but rather on high levels of education and competence. The lack of competencies demanded by firms creates mismatch problems in the labour market. Thus, it is in the interest of employers that the level of knowledge among employees is raised. This articulation focuses on a number of supply-side solutions to these problems. Swedish employers fully support the employment strategy and the call for lifelong learning. They write (Confederation of Swedish Enterprise, 2002b): 'Because Europe needs a workforce that is well-educated, competent and flexible, there is also a need to develop strategies for lifelong learning'. A high level of competencies and the right level of skills among employees are a prerequisite for a flexible labour market. According to the Swedish employers this will increase the geographical and job related mobility of workers in Europe. But lifelong learning should primarily be a national responsibility, and not be controlled at EU level.

However, other structural measures are considered equally important in order to create a flexible labour market. The Swedish employers criticize the attitude of the Swedish government on tax policy, specifically tax on labour. They fully support the recommendations of the Commission to lower the tax on labour by lowering the employers' tax and the income tax for low-income workers. It is considered unfair tax competition creating distortions in the EU, and the employers strongly criticize the

Swedish government for not living up to the recommendations. The same is true for the recommendation to increase the incentive structure in the social systems by lowering the levels of unemployment benefit. A senior advisor at the Confederation of Swedish Enterprise says that they could not have said it better themselves. Unfortunately, the Swedish government has neglected to implement these recommendations, and is not doing enough to promote lifelong learning, according to the Swedish employers. However, lifelong learning should not be the responsibility of the employer alone, the employees must also contribute by paying for their lifelong learning themselves. Generally, the Swedish employers are very sceptical towards the entire Swedish labour market policy. Until now the policy has only contributed to preserving an old industrial structure and keep people in unemployment. The ultimate goal within the competition articulation is to abolish national and EU labour market policies altogether.

The Swedish discursive terrain is dominated by these two articulations of EU social and labour market policy. Even though the two articulations have distinct similarities (the structural emphasis, unemployment as the main European problem, lifelong learning as a solution among others, etc.), they oppose each other on the basic discursive distinction between regulation and free competition. At the same time, the discursive terrain in Sweden, where meaning is ascribed to EU social and labour market policy, is characterized by an ideological boundary. The Social Democratic Swedish government and the unions establish the regulation articulation, while the right-wing opposition and the employers' organizations support the competition articulation. Thus, within EU social and labour market policy in Sweden, the ideological question is, does one attend to the workers' interests, or does one attend to the interests of industry? Does one endorse a 'socially acceptable' policy, or does one endorse 'the necessary and responsible' policy? The ideological boundary in the creation of meaning is the most important characteristic of the Swedish EU decision-making process studied. Not only is it an important discursive boundary, it is also strongly institutionalized, and reproduced through the institutional practices of the agents. It cuts across the whole decision-making process, and creates a core group of agents whose interactions are characterized by informal routines and personal relationships, and who are an integral part of each other's decision-making processes. It establishes a community of fate[6] in the Swedish decision-making process, between those who share the same understanding of EU social and labour market policy. The distinction between 'us' and 'them' in the Swedish EU decision-making process is thus a distinction between labour and capital.

However, although not unusual in an international perspective, the ideological boundary in the Swedish discursive terrain is not self-evident. We cannot find the same discursive boundary in Denmark, for example, within the same policy area. On the contrary, the Danish discursive terrain, related to EU policy, is characterized by consensus, even though the basic discursive distinction between regulation and competition is exactly the same. In Denmark regulation is always articulated as the positive side of the distinction, and this applies to all the core agents in the Danish EU decision-making process within EU social and labour market policy, regardless of national ideological differences. When it comes to EU social and labour market policy, Danish agents are characterized by a high level of pragmatism, which is almost unheard-of in the Swedish process. The Danish discursive and institutional arrangement and the creation of meaning concerning EU social and labour market policy are entirely different from that in Sweden (Faurbæk, 2001). In Denmark the distinction between 'us' and 'them' in EU labour market policy is a distinction between Denmark and the EU, not between labour and capital within Denmark. There is also an institutionalized separation between EU policy and Danish policy. In the latter, more ideological polarization is allowed, but in relation to the EU, consensus is the marked feature.

The Swedish creation of meaning in relation to EU labour market policy thus takes place in a highly ideologically divided discursive terrain. Traditionally, Sweden has been regarded a country characterized by pragmatism and consensus in labour market policy, but the 'Saltsjöbaden spirit' (see Allvin, Chapter 2 in this volume) had already started to wither away by the early 1970s. The ideological polarization has since then increased even further. For instance, in the early 1990s, the Swedish employers said 'farewell to corporatism' and decided to withdraw from all tripartite cooperation in Sweden (Bergström and Rothstein, 1999).

Articulating EU labour market discourse

Below I will first discuss the relationship between the two articulations of meaning in the Swedish EU decision-making process with special emphasis on the question of employability and lifelong learning. Secondly, I discuss the relationship between the Swedish discursive terrain and the EU discourse.

Comparing the two articulations

The two articulations of EU labour market policy in the Swedish discursive terrain have a range of similarities, even though they are in opposition to each other with regard to the question of regulation. At first glance, their 'diagnoses' of the problems of the labour market seem almost identical. Both articulations are clearly a part of the structural political discourse, and use structural arguments for their understanding of problems and solutions within EU social and labour market policy. The key term is mismatch problems on the labour market. The balance between demand and supply in the labour market has been disrupted, and this makes it impossible to achieve full employment. So far the two articulations are in almost complete agreement. At the same time, there is a tendency to emphasise the supply-side of the labour market rather than the demand-side. Both articulations agree that at least one of the problems is that the qualifications of employees do not meet company requirements. Employees are neither ready to meet future change in the labour market nor to adapt to the demands of firms.

The main difference between the two articulations of EU social and labour market policy is that the employability of workers is either considered to be a problem for society at large or simply an individual problem. One of the solutions pointed out by both articulations, as we have seen, is lifelong learning and the upgrading of skills. But the two articulations differ in their argumentation about this solution to the structural problems of the labour market. In the regulation articulation workers can only engage in lifelong learning if they feel secure. Job security is a key aspect of the strategy within the regulation articulation. This is why the Swedish government is sceptical towards some recommendations of the Commission. It is more important within the regulation articulation to develop the quality of work, than to strengthen the structure of incentives in the labour market by lowering unemployment benefits. Thus, being employable is not just an individual problem for employees, it is also a social problem for society. People will not dare to upgrade their skills (and thereby become more employable) if there is no safety net in the form of a relatively generous social system.

This is not the understanding of lifelong learning within the competition articulation. Lifelong learning and the upgrading of skills is obviously a societal problem, because it results in mismatch problems in the labour market. But it is ultimately an individual responsibility. Workers will have to meet the demands of industry in order to keep their jobs. The employers are very focused on the incentives to engage in lifelong learning and the incentive for unemployed workers to upgrade their skills in order to get jobs. With high levels of unemployment benefits, the unemployed do not have incentives to become employable. Lower levels of unemployment benefits will increase the willingness to adapt to the needs of the labour market, and thereby effectively reduce the mismatch problems. Job security is not the first element of the equation. Job security is the end product – the result – of increased flexibility in the labour market. At the same time, lifelong learning and education is only one part of the solution within the competition articulation. As we have seen, it is equally important to lower taxes on labour, both the employers' tax and the income tax. According to the employers, this will increase entrepreneurship and growth. The argumentation is that the differences in tax systems create unfair competition in Europe.

Within the regulation articulation, the tax issue is considered to be highly sensitive. The question of reducing unemployment benefits is not seen as a viable way of improving adaptability and upgrading qualifications. As for the de-regulation solution of the competition articulation, the regulation articulation is heavily sceptical. Its advocates warn that de-regulating the labour market will result in negative flexibility (lower labour standards, social dumping, lower health and safety standards, etc.), while positive flexibility will be the result of the development of the quality of work (lifelong learning, being able to combine work and family, non-discrimination, etc.). Hence, even though employability and lifelong learning are articulated as solutions in both articulations of EU social and labour market policy, the argumentation and the weight of the various elements are completely different between the two articulations. The Swedish discursive terrain is characterized by ideological opposition, as we have seen, and this is also true with specific regard to the question of employability.

Comparing the EU discourse and the national creation of meaning

What relationship between the EU discourse and the national creation of meaning can we identify, and how can we understand it? I use the term 'discursive couplings' to describe the relationship between the EU discourse and the national discursive terrain. A discursive coupling means that there is reference to an identical or at least overlapping understanding of problems and solutions on the EU and national levels. It is not enough to use the same words. The articulation of problems and solutions has to be identical or overlapping to identify a discursive coupling.

I can identify a number of discursive couplings between Swedish articulations and the EU discourse on social and labour market policy. There are strong couplings in the rationality of the creations of meaning. Unemployment is articulated as structural unemployment within both

Swedish articulations and in the EU discourse in the second period. The articulation of unemployment is almost identical, and is by and large shared by the two articulations in Sweden. Generally there are more couplings between the regulation articulation and the EU discourse, than between the competition articulation and the EU discourse. The problem of over-regulation cannot be found in the EU discourse connected to DGV in any of the two periods. Neither can the solution of de-regulation.[7]

On the subject of employability, there is a strong coupling between both articulations and the EU discourse on employability (which was described in Chapter 3). However, there is a difference between the couplings of the two articulations and the EU discourse. The solution of lifelong learning and education is articulated almost identically at EU and national levels, indicating a strong coupling between the two levels. This is true in the case of the regulation articulation in particular. But the competition articulation also advocates other structural solutions (the tax and social systems), and could thereby be said to have a stronger coupling to the EU discourse. In the light of Chapter 3, however, the question is whether the national creation of meaning represented by the competition articulation has more in common with the discourse of the OECD, rather than with the EU discourse. Couplings to the OECD discourse can be seen by its emphasis on the incentive structure and the tax and unemployment benefit systems.

Social dumping is being articulated identically at national (within the regulation articulation) and EU levels. But this is a strong coupling between the Swedish creation of meaning as it looks today and the EU discourse as it looked in the first period. If we look at the definition of EU social and labour market policy the picture is the same. There are strong couplings between the national and the EU level on this point, but again the Swedish articulations (both the regulation and the competition articulations) couple to the first phase of the EU discourse.

Conclusions: the Swedish EU decision-making process

The purpose of this chapter was to show how meaning is created through articulation within EU social and labour market policy, and that there is not a simple one-to-one relationship between the national creation of meaning and the EU discourse within the same policy area. As we have seen, the Swedish articulations of EU social and labour market policy are not a mere reflection of the EU discourse. Some aspects are the same, and some are quite different. If we were to compare the Swedish creation of meaning to that in another member state, it would also be different. The creation of meaning is local, and thus dependent on the local discursive arrangements and institutional context in the member state concerned.

The Swedish EU decision-making process is relatively informal. It is not a hierarchical process, with many formal levels and institutions as for example in Denmark. The Swedish process is characterized by relatively loose couplings between levels and processes. On the one hand, EU policy must be treated as ordinary national policy, but on the other hand there is a rather strong government prerogative within EU policy, because of the relatively weak position of the parliamentary EU committee. The national interest in EU labour market policy is developed through the local creation of meaning in relation to different policy areas (labour market and social policy). The creation of meaning is then co-ordinated through loose couplings primarily between expert government officials and transformed into instructions. These are then anchored around the senior civil servants and the Minister who is being prepared. In this way, a negotiated and coherent Swedish position is secured in spite of the oppositional discursive terrain in Sweden. This could lead to the conclusion that in Sweden there is room for different political visions about EU labour market policy, especially on employability, as we have seen. However, in reality, a selection of interests occurs at a very early stage in the process. The selection of the dominant articulation happens in accordance with the ideological boundary, and is thus a result of the political 'colour' of the Swedish government. The other articulation is more or less repressed from the EU decision-making process, and this is reflected in the interaction patterns of the agents. A group of core agents is established consisting of the Swedish government and the trade union organizations in Sweden.

In Denmark this behaviour by a government would be heavily sanctioned, because the distinction is not based on ideology but on different policy areas. As the Danish agents say, 'ideology is important, but we all have the same goals' (author's translation). This is not the case in Sweden, and thus the Swedish creation of meaning concerning EU social and labour market policy is likely to change if a right-wing government wins the next election.

Notes

1. The author would like to thank NorFA and Score for financial support.
2. By using institutional history as analytical strategy, I construct a history of the creation of meaning within EU social and labour market policy as it develops

from 1985 to 1998. I define discourse as a specific frame of meaning, regulated by specific ideals, and which through articulation of differences, similarities and relations orders social relations, interests and phenomena. Discourse is the establishment of a symbolic universe wherein a continual production of statements about objects, subjects, rationality, agents, past, present and future, and problems and solutions is going on. My definition of a discourse entails that I do not make a distinction between 'reality' and discourse. In my view, we can not perceive something as being outside of discourse and institutions. What is meant by reality is always and already created as meaningful within a specific discursive context. In this sense my definition of discourse is somewhat broader and more radical than the ones discussed in the introductory chapter of this book.

3. The other three have different aspects of EU social and labour market policy as their object, but all articulate regulation as the positive side of the basic discursive distinction.

4. This section is based on interviews with agents in the Swedish EU decision-making process on EU social and labour market policy conducted in 1998 and in 2002.

5. It would be wrong to assume that the Swedish government is a homogeneous entity in the regulation articulation. There is a distinct tension between the two ministries I focus on, and the Ministry of Finance. The responsibility for the employment guidelines is shared between the Ministry of Industry, Employment and Communications and the Ministry of Finance, but the Ministry of Finance does not adhere to the regulation articulation to the same degree as the two ministries discussed here.

6. A community of fate is established by the distinction between 'us' and 'them'. We, who share the same interests, and those who have other interests.

7. However, it is likely that we can find these problems and solutions in another area of the EU discourse, for example that connected to ECOFIN and the economic guidelines.

References

Andersen, Niels Åkerstrøm. 1994. *Institutionel Historie – en introduktion til diskurs-og institutionsanalyse*. COS-report 10/94.

Andersen, Niels Åkerstrøm. 1995. *Selvskabt Forvaltning, Forvaltningspolitikkens og centralforvaltningens udvikling i Danmark 1900–1994*. København: Nyt fra Samfundsvidenskaberne.

Andersen, Niels Åkerstrøm and Peter Kjær. 1996. *Institutional Construction and Change: An Analytical Strategy of Institutional History*. COS-report no. 5/1996.

Bergström, Jonas and Bo Rothstein. 1999. *Korporatismens fall och den svenska modellens kris*. Stockholm: SNS Förlag.

Campbell, John L. 1998. 'Institutional analysis and the role of ideas in political economy'. *Theory and Society*, 27: 377–409.

CEC [Commission of the European Communities]. 1988. *The Social Dimension of the Internal Market*. SEC(88)1148.

CEC. 1989a. *1992 – The Social Perspective*, by Patrick Venturini.

CEC. 1989b. *The Social Aspects of the Internal Market*, Volume 1, *Social Europe*, Supplement 7/88.

CEC. 1990. *Community Charter of Fundamental Social Rights.*

CEC. 1991. *First Report on the Application of the Community Charter of the Fundamental Social Rights of Workers.* COM(91)511.

CEC. 1992. *Communication from the Commission Towards a Europe of Solidarity.* COM(92)542.

CEC. 1993a. *Green Paper – European Social Policy – Options for the Union.* COM (93)551.

CEC. 1993b. *Growth, Competitiveness, Employment, the Challenges and Ways Forward into the 21st Century.* COM(93)700.

CEC. 1994. *European Social Policy. A Way Forward for the Union.* COM(94)333.

Confederation of Swedish Enterprise. 2002a. *Towards a More Entrepreneurial Europe.* February.

Confederation of Swedish Enterprise. 2002b. *A Swedish Business Agenda for Europe.*

Czarniawska, Barbara and Bernward Joerges. 1996. 'Travels of ideas'. In *Translating Organizational Change,* edited by B. Czarniawska and G. Sevón. Berlin and New York: Walter de Gruyter, 13–48.

ECOSOC. 1987. *Information Report from the Section on Social, Family, Educational and Cultural Questions on the Aspects of the Internal Market (a Social Europe).* Chairman: Danilo Beretta, CES(87)225.

Faurbæk, Lotte. 2001. *Europæisk social- og arbejdsmarkedspolitik: Nationale EU-beslutningsprocesser og politikudvikling i Danmark og Sverige.* PhD thesis 17/2001. Copenhagen: Copenhagen Business School.

Foucault, Michel. 1972/1995. *The Archeology of Knowledge.* London: Routledge.

Kjær, Peter and Ove Kaj Pedersen. 2001. 'Translation liberalization: neoliberalism in the Danish negotiated economy'. In *The Rise of Neoliberalism and Institutional Analysis,* edited by O. K. Pedersen and J. L. Campbell. New Jersey: Princeton University Press, 219–48.

Latour, Bruno. 1988. 'The politics of explanation: an alternative'. In *Knowledge and Reflexivity: New Frontiers in the Sociology of Knowledge,* edited by S. Woolgar. London: Sage Publications, 155–76.

Pedersen, Dorthe. 1997. *Forhandlet Forvaltning – en ny institutionel Orden for den statslige løn- og personalepolitik.* PhD thesis. København: COS and RUC.

Pedersen, Ove Kaj. 1989. *Nine Questions to the New-Institutionalism.* COS working paper 1/1989.

Pedersen, Ove Kaj. 1990. '…Og der var 10 og 11 og mange fler! Om ni grundlæggende problemer for en teori om institutionel forandring'. *GRUS,* årg. 11, vol. 30: 97–122.

Pedersen, Ove Kaj. 1995. 'Problemets anatomi: eller problemet, der er et problem'. *Tendens,* årg. 7, nr 1: 10–21.

Prop. 1999/2000: 98 *Förnyad arbetsmarknadspolitik för delaktighet och tillväxt.*

Regeringskansliet. 2001. *Sveriges Handlingsplan för Sysselsättning 2001.* Maj.

5
Lifelong Learning: A Clash Between a Production and a Learning Logic

Lennart Svensson

Introduction: lifelong learning – strong discourse and weak practice

This chapter discusses a puzzling contradiction of lifelong learning and employability – the lack of correspondence between the strong ideals at an official, discursive level and the weak practices at the local level.

A growing interest in learning has evolved simultaneously with a subtle change in political rhetoric – from promises of full employment to full employability. Full employability signals a shift from demand-side policies (to promote employment) to supply-side policies which emphasize individuals' education and skills (Brown *et al.*, 2001: ix; Jacobsson, Chapter 3 in this volume).

Sweden can be seen as an interesting case to test the reality of the idea of lifelong learning. We have a highly unionized workforce, a long tradition of partnership, an ongoing restructuring of the economy, a strong belief in lifelong learning as a way to promote growth and employability, and a variety of programmes for adult education and training.[1] Those politically responsible – both in Sweden and at the EU-level – have concluded that investment in training is the decisive factor behind the development of companies, regions and countries. In today's competitive labour market, learning is said to be the driving force both for company-innovation and individual development (Government Bill 2000/01: 04). Aside from national educational efforts, a series of different learning opportunities is also being launched at the initiative of trade and commerce as well as different local authorities and education providers. But in reality very little is happening. Why?

This chapter addresses the lack of correspondence between the strong discursive ideals of lifelong learning and the actual practices at the local level: Why are strategies for lifelong learning so difficult to implement? It seeks three types of explanation.

The first part of the analysis focuses on a societal level and looks at some important changes in contemporary labour markets. In particular, it focuses on the assumed *need* for competence in the knowledge-based economy. Human capital theory, which predicts a progression from low to high skilled work, is questioned. The knowledge-driven economies can instead be associated with polarization, imbalances and inequalities. There is evidence of both an under-qualification *and* an over-qualification of the workforce, where there will not be enough skilled jobs to meet the aspirations of better-educated students. The number of low skilled jobs in the service sector will continue to grow, as well as the number of part-time temporary jobs (Brown, 2001: 252; Nyström, 2000; Åberg, forthcoming). It is argued that such a polarized society makes a strategy for lifelong learning more difficult to implement.

The next part of the analysis focuses on the organizational level – work practices, management and the role of learning. A clash between a production and a learning logic at the level of enterprises is identified and discussed. It is argued that the persistence of Taylorism in Swedish workplaces and its consequences for the organization of work is a barrier to a strategy for lifelong learning.

The third part of the analysis focuses on the current gap between the educational system and the production system or between formal and informal learning. It is argued that the lack of co-ordination between the educational and the economic systems is a third barrier to a successful strategy for lifelong learning.

The chapter has a critical perspective, but the final section is more constructive wherein some general conclusions are discussed in a prescriptive way.

The alleged needs for competence and learning

It is generally considered that there is an increasing need for competence and learning in working life. The discourse on learning has been important both in the partnership and the political context since the mid-1980s, not only in Sweden but also in Europe. Since the mid-1990s, the interest in learning has increased substantially. Learning is seen as a way to reduce unemployment and as the driving force in the creation of the new knowledge-based society (AMV, 1999: 11). The belief in high skill levels is almost religious. It promises opportunities for the well educated to obtain rewarding and interesting work, high wages and so on. The creation of a highly skilled workforce will lead to economic prosperity and social justice, it is assumed (Brown, 2001: 235).

The discourse in Sweden rests on a central assumption – the *competence gap*, that is, the demand for competence in working life is higher than the actual level of competence possessed by its employees. It is assumed that globalization – in combination with technological change and organizational complexities – will result in an increased demand for qualifications. The establishment of EU Objective 4 funds was based on this assumption. This programme intended to promote growth, competition, new jobs in small and medium-sized companies by subsidies for training and organizational change (Växtkraft Mål 4, 1996; Hultman *et al.*, 2002). The 'new' Objective 3 is a continuation of this programme with similar objectives.

What is the validity of this idea of the competence gap? Is there really a lack of competence, which – when tackled by such programmes – will promote change and facilitate the restructuring of the economy?

The Swedish economy has undergone major restructuring since the 1960s, a process which has been intensified during the last few decades. Simple manufacturing firms have been replaced by more knowledge-intensive production. The number of high-tech companies is relatively high in Sweden. The effects of these structural changes have meant more skilled and qualified jobs. But there are simultaneous changes in the labour market in an opposite direction, namely the expansion of the service-sector with many unskilled jobs. These changes are reflected in the official statistics. These indicate an increased demand for qualified labour. In 1981, 65 per cent of all new (announced) jobs had specific demands for qualifications. In 1998 this figure was 92 per cent. During the same period the employers' demands for a university degree for new jobs had increased from 20 to 36 per cent. The actual demand for skilled workers did increase between 1975 and 1997, but only moderately and it still only consisted of a third of the labour market.

The figures presented above can be interpreted in different ways. They do not necessarily mean that higher skills are demanded to any substantial degree. There may be other explanations for the increased demand for qualified labour. In a new situation with high unemployment, managers probably increase their demands for formal training in order to get the best and most loyal workforce (LO, 2001). The discourse of learning and new management fashions are other explanations behind the increasing demand for qualified labour (SOU, 1994: 48; 1996: 64; Björkman, 2002).

The thesis of a need for increased qualifications can thus be questioned. During the period 1975–97 the level of education did actually increase. The result of this was an *over-qualification* of employees. The number of over-qualified employees (with at least an upper secondary school education), who were working in unqualified jobs increased – from a tenth to a third between 1975 and 1997. The increase in unemployment was similar for those with high and low qualifications, a finding that is contrary to the proposition put forward above. Surveys conducted by Sweden's main union confederation, The Swedish Trade Union Confederation, LO, (LO, 1995, 1999) showed that many members felt that their competencies were not being used in their jobs. Of the total number of workers 17 per cent felt that their competencies were not being drawn upon, while 19 per cent thought that they needed more competence in their job (LO, 2002: 37).

This finding – that there is both over-qualification and under-qualification – is an important explanation for the difficulties in implementing a successful strategy of lifelong learning in Sweden. The discrepancy between the rhetoric of a high skill society at an official level and the realities for large groups of employees in their daily work is obvious. Why should these groups be motivated to increase their skills in a lifelong perspective when they are not able to use their existing qualifications in their present jobs?

The statistics above strongly contradict human capital theory, which assumes a linear model of technological progression from low to high skilled work. They also falsify the idea that employers will upgrade the workers' skill base when qualified labour is available. The employer commitment to training is often low, especially in small and medium-sized companies. There are different explanations for the fallacy of human capital theory: the uneven development of technology; existing management practices based on Tayloristic principles (see below); the growing number of unskilled service jobs (in cleaning, fast food restaurants, call centres, retail stores, etc.); a process of social exclusion in which large groups – women, ethnic minorities, part-time workers, people with disabilities, relief workers, the young and the old – are discriminated against (Svensson, 1997; Brown *et al.*, 2001).

The development of a 'knowledge-based' economy is characterized by polarization, insecurity and inequality in the labour market (Nyström, 2000; Nyberg, 2002). These tendencies are not compatible with a high skilled society in which lifelong learning is a necessary component for all employees. Different demands on and unequal working conditions for employees will increase segmentation and marginalization in the labour market. Today more than one million people are outside the ordinary labour market in Sweden if the unemployed, the early retired, long-term absentees, etc. are all included. This exclusion of large groups is quite the opposite to a society characterized by high skills and equal opportunities for all groups of the population. In such a segmented and polarized society, learning can, instead, be seen as a way for an individual to strengthen his or her position in a lifelong career in relation to other groups. Learning can in this way function as a mechanism for inequality and increased differences in the labour market.

The above mentioned changes in the economy and the labour market can to a great extent explain the failure of lifelong learning in Sweden. Only the most important – that is the most profitable – employees will be selected for lifelong training and education. The rest will only get a very limited training of an instrumental character. Many companies compete through low prices and reduced costs, not through high quality. Investment in training will not pay, neither for the employer (in higher profits) nor for employees (in better jobs). In fact the amount of time spent on training has decreased for large groups of employees – the elderly, women in the private sector and part-time workers (LO, 2001). The amount of training granted to employees is also very uneven. Employees with a university degree in the public sector obtain most training, while privately employed female workers enjoy the least: only 1.2 per cent of their working time is used for training paid by the employer (LO, 2001).

The clash between a production and learning logic

The segmentation and marginalization of large groups in the labour market is the first explanation for the difficulties of implementing a successful strategy for lifelong learning. The second explanation focuses on the organization of work and its Tayloristic tradition.

Taylorism is intimately connected to the 'Swedish Model' and the partnership system. To develop the second explanation we have to understand some very important characteristics of Swedish working life – the strength of Taylorism, which was accepted by the unions at an early stage. Close co-operation between labour and capital is heart of the Model which, renowned worldwide, has the following characteristics (see also Korpi, 1978):

- strong labour unions, which organize a very high proportion of employees;

- close co-operation between the labour unions and the Social Democratic Party, which for most of the time has formed the government;
- union strength *vis-à-vis* the employer associations through the influence of the former as political actors;
- a long tradition of co-operation between the unions and the employer associations on different issues – wages, work-organization, rationalization of production, and so on;
- an acceptance among the unions of the rationalization of production based on Tayloristic principles.

We will develop our argument by focusing on the last point here and discussing its consequences in trying to explain the employers' lack of interest in lifelong learning. Partnership based on Taylorism – that is a scientific way to rationalize production by dividing planning ´and action – has a long tradition. The close co-operation between labour and capital started at the beginning of the twentieth century. The employers had already accepted the unions by 1906. But as a part of this agreement the unions officially accepted the right of the employer to 'lead and distribute' the work. In 1938 a very important national agreement (the Saltsjöbaden Agreement) was signed. It was the platform for an effective rationalization of production, peace in the labour market, high wages, low unemployment, and a welfare society.

The adoption of Taylorism in Sweden was exceptionally pervasive, especially after the Second World War, because of this agreement between the unions and the employer associations. A huge training programme was conducted to rationalize work. The measurement of time (with the help of the MTM-system: Method Time Measurement) was done on a large scale and supported by different research groups and development centres. Sweden was a leading country in the world in this rationalization of the production system based on Tayloristic principles (Björkman, 2002).

In the late 1960s this co-operation between the unions and the employers became increasingly strained. There were strong local protests against the negative effects of Taylorism: absenteeism, routine jobs, alienation, etc. The unions sought and obtained political support for radical changes in working life. Laws on co-determination and the work environment were enacted and the wage earner funds were introduced in the 1970s and 1980s. The effects of these laws and programmes were very limited, however, partly because of a changed political regime. The wage earner funds were abolished in the 1990s.

The period of radicalization and strong union opposition was short-lived. In 1982 a central agreement for joint development was signed between the Swedish Trade Union Confederation (LO), the Federation of Salaried Employees in Industry and Services (PTK) and the Swedish Employers' Association (SAF). The common values supporting effective production were stressed in the agreement, as were the importance of enriching jobs and the possibilities for learning. The Metalworkers Union presented an important policy document at its 1985 Congress: 'Good Work'. The idea propounded in this document was to combine learning, organizational change and a wage-policy. A great deal of experimentation then followed on a partnership basis to introduce new production systems which were more flexible and often based on autonomous teams (see contribution by Huzzard, Chapter 6 in this volume). The Volvo plants at Kalmar and, especially, that at Uddevalla attracted worldwide attention for their flexible organization of work, team autonomy, extended work-cycles, radical layout solutions and logistics (Sandberg, 1995; see also Oudhuis, Chapter 10 in this volume).

Many important changes in work organization were made, but the logic of the production system remained intact. Taylorism had a strong grip in both private and public sectors and still prevails in many sectors of the labour market – in call centres, cleaning jobs, hamburger bars, manufacturing firms etc. (see contribution by Lindgren and Sederblad, Chapter 9 in this volume). Taylorism is also a feature of the new management strategies – Total Quality Management, Time Based Management, Business Process Reengineering, Human Resource Management, Knowledge Management and the Balanced Scorecard (Björkman, 2002). The tradition of Taylorism – even if it is often draped in more modern clothes – will be a major obstacle to lifelong learning. Taylorism in this modern version includes the following:

- a strong vertical division of work and decision-making;
- a centralization of power, control and co-ordination at the top of the organization;
- a concentration of information in the hands of managers, which is facilitated by computer technology;
- an unequal gender structure and exclusion of women from central positions;
- a key role for science and the strengthening of the position of experts in organizational change and training;
- the idea of 'best practice', often applied by simplistic methods focused on measuring results (for example balanced scorecards, benchmarking, detailed quality instruments);
- reduced time for reflection in downsized and rationalized organizations.

Taylorism is an integrated feature of organizational structure, but it is also something in the minds of employers, managers, workers and union officials. It is part of their thinking and inherent in their values and attitudes as they are expressed in widely diffused management theories. We can illustrate this modern form of neo-Taylorism by pointing to some elements of the most popular management theories used during the last decade.

Lean Production, downsizing and outsourcing intend to reduce costs and increase profits in a short-term perspective. In these theories lifelong learning is often seen as a cost, not an investment. Other management theories – for example Total Quality Management (TQM), Time Based Management (TBM), Business Process Reengineering (BPR), the Boundaryless or the Learning Organization – advocate some autonomy and a broader degree of employee competence. A flat, flexible, decentralized and customer-oriented organization is in need of motivated, cooperative and innovative employees. But the opportunities for learning and development are often circumscribed and uncertain. Hard pressure from management and a lack of control over resources in combination with high involvement can result in stress and health problems (Karasek and Theorell, 1990). These 'modern' organizations can be seductive and greedy (Rasmussen, 1999).

In these new organizations, control over employees and their work has been intensified because of new methods and more sophisticated technologies. The new methods used (balanced scorecards, quality control, benchmarking) provide management with an opportunity to monitor different parts of the production flow more closely. Call centres are extreme examples of such Tayloristic practices entailing detailed supervision of individual employees.

The learning in these 'new' organizations is restricted in different ways and its objectives are carefully defined by Knowledge Management. Much of the learning has a single-loop character, which implies a restriction on the carrying out of tasks that are already given and defined by others. The learning is instrumental to the goals and values defined by management. Customer interests are stressed in TQM, TBM, BPR, and quality circles, but often from a calculative and short-sighted perspective.

In a situation with a focus on growth, competition and rationalization, the clash between the *learning logic* and the *production logic* is clear enough. The learning logic puts an emphasis on the following (Ellström, 2002):

- thought and reflection;
- alternative thinking, experimentation and risk taking;

- tolerance for ambiguity, variation, and mistakes;
- development oriented learning (or expansive, double-loop, creative learning).

The production logic, on the other hand, emphasizes:

- effective action on a routinized or rule-based level;
- problem-solving through application of given rules/instructions;
- consensus, standardization, stability and avoidance of uncertainty;
- adaptive learning oriented towards the mastering of procedures and routines.

The logic of production dominates in most organizations, which means that the logic of development and learning is often set aside. This dominance of the production logic is one important explanation for the lack of interest – both among employers and employees – in lifelong learning, especially in the existing downsized and anorectic organizations (Abrahamsson, 2000; Bengtsson and Berggren, 2001; Björkman, 2002). In these organizations there is little time for learning and reflection, which – in the circumstances – will create stress and strain, because learning will interfere with one's daily work.

In a Tayloristic organization, learning is not important, and when it occurs it is of a more adaptive, instrumental, and single-loop character. The clash between a production and a learning logic is becoming more obvious in an economy that is focusing on short-term profits in a very competitive and globalized market (cf. Hultman *et al.*, 2002). The increased rationalization during the 1990s illustrates this shortcoming – the lack of time for learning and reflection at work (Bengtsson and Berggren, 2001). The idea of lifelong learning cannot be fulfilled if it is based on the short-term interests of such a production system. It is deprived of all its essential elements – exploration, liberation, equality and humanity.

The role of the education system in lifelong learning

Many employers and employees are sceptical about the benefits of formal training for reasons other than those we have discussed above. They are sceptical because they do not think that the training will be of any practical use. The education and training packages are often too school-like and theoretical to be applied in a concrete situation. This mismatch between formal and informal learning can be analysed on a systems level – as a gap or division between the economic and educational systems. But a brief introduction to the theoretical aspects of learning and competence will be needed in the first instance.

What is learning and what is competence?

Learning is a process that is continuous (Dewey, 1989). The learning *process* can itself even be more important than its result since knowledge taken in can quickly become obsolete (Schön, 1983, 1987; Ellström, 1992, 1996; Svensson and Åberg, 2001). But learning processes can have different appearances. One common differentiation is between *formal* and *informal* learning, that is, between education and everyday learning (see Figure 5.1).

As used here, the concept of *formal* learning refers to planned, goal-oriented learning, which occurs within the boundaries of particular educational institutions (schools, universities, colleges, etc.). The concept of *informal* learning refers to learning that occurs in everyday life or at work. Everyday learning occurs spontaneously for the most part. Most learning in companies is of an informal character. Employees learn through practice – by problem-solving, helping each other, getting

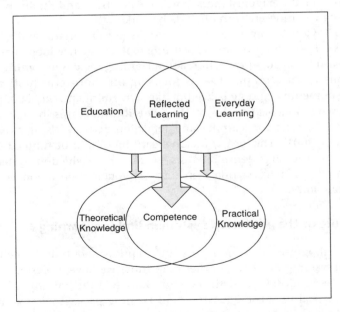

Figure 5.1   Competence as a result of reflective learning (Svensson and Åberg, 2001: 85)

advice and instructions. But learning can also be *non-formal*. It is organized, but not in a traditional way inside the educational institutions. Instead, the informal and much of the non-formal learning takes place at work – in the form of work rotation, exchange of experiences, group meetings, supervisory input, mentorship and so on (cf. Brown and Duguid, 1991). In modern working life neither formal education nor everyday learning alone is sufficient – both are needed and the two modes of learning should be viewed as complementary. Formal learning can be more effective if it is combined with informal and non-formal learning (Svensson and Åberg, 2001). Conversely, informal learning could be made more effective if non-formal and formal learning supports it. This is the case because informal learning presupposes conceptual tools and explicit knowledge about the task and the work process that cannot normally be acquired through experiential learning at work. Rather, the knowledge acquired through informal learning typically has a tacit character (Ellström, 1992). *Competence* is the outcome of a combination of education and everyday learning, that is, *reflected* learning (see Figure 5.1). The real challenge for a system of lifelong learning is to find methods for learning which can combine theoretical and practical knowledge.

The workplace, not the classroom, can be used to accomplish such integrated learning. There are many opportunities for learning at work. New groups can be included. The informal and formal learning can be combined. It is possible to use a pedagogy based on problem-solving, learning-by-doing and reflection (cf. Dewey, 1989). Social support from team-members can stimulate and motivate learning. Individual and organizational learning can be combined, which means that the participants can practise what they learn, thereby increasing their motivation for further learning (Argyris, 1977; Brown and Duguid, 1991; Argyris and Schön, 1996).

If the idea of lifelong learning is to be fulfilled the workplace is an important arena. Workplace learning is a new way to organize learning in a flexible and cost-effective way (Svensson and Åberg, 2001). But, as argued above, workplace learning has many limitations – the dominance of the production logic, the focus on instrumental learning, the short-term perspective, the lack of time for reflection and discussion, etc. Workplace learning must therefore be combined with learning based on other values, which are provided by the educational system.

The role of the educational system

What is the role of the educational system in lifelong learning? An educational system is a fundamental feature of a democratic society. Its objectives are wider than the short-term interests of the production system. Sweden has an ambition of creating a system for lifelong learning, where equal rights and the development of free and democratic individuals are the main objectives. This is a necessity if lifelong learning is to contribute to creating employability for groups with a weaker position in the labour market. In this section the education system for adult education is presented and analysed from this democratic and holistic perspective.

When we look at the Swedish system for lifelong learning from 'the outside' (see Figure 5.2) it looks very impressive.[2] 95 per cent of pupils pass through upper secondary schools, whereas 17 per cent continue thereafter to universities. This is not a high proportion, but many people start their university studies later in life. The recently established regional universities have dramatically increased the number of university students. 40 per cent (from upper secondary school) continue with their university studies within three years (SOU, 2000: 28).

One specific feature of the Swedish educational system is the alternatives to the traditional schools (see Figure 5.2). If students want to try a different pedagogy they can study at 'Folk High Schools' (35,000 students each year). Immigrants and overseas workers are obliged to take part in Swedish for Immigrants (20,500 students each year). Those wanting to finish upper secondary school later in life can study at the Municipal Schools for Adult Education (47,000 students each year). A special programme was introduced in 1996 for the unemployed and employees who lacked the basic upper secondary school competence (100,000 students each year). There is a special student grant and allowance attached to this programme that the students can apply for. In general, the results of the programme have been very positive (SOU, 2000: 28).

There are important supporting systems of different kinds (see Figure 5.2). Students can get loans and subsidies for taking part in education. There is a law providing the participants with the right to take a leave of absence for studies. In the school system – as well as in the job centres – pupils can obtain personal guidance that helps them to choose the right programme. Pupils can also get their theoretical and practical knowledge validated and in this way speed up their studies. Many municipalities have Learning Centres, which try to connect the educational system with the needs of individuals and workplaces (see Figure 5.2). At the Learning Centres learners can use different flexible systems for education – for example different forms of e-learning – but personal support from other students and a teacher can also be obtained. Sweden has also developed

Competence development – the way to security? (© *Hans Lindström*)

Educational system	Alternative system for education	Supporting systems	Economic and growth system
Universities Upper secondary school Lower secondary school Elementary school Pre-school	Folk high school Swedish for immigrants Municipal school for adults Government initiatives to promote adult education Free school	**Economic** Loans/subsidies **Institutional** Swedish model agreements Union programmes Rights to leave for studies **Organizational** Job centres Learning centres Research and development centres **Free associations** Informal adult education Study circles	Informal learning/ workplace learning Apprentice programmes Labour market courses EU Objective 3 programmes Qualified vocational training Private consultant agencies

Figure 5.2   Different components of a system of lifelong learning in Sweden (Randle and Svensson, 2002)

a few educational and training systems for working life, but these are rather limited – including qualified vocational training (12,000 students) and an apprentice programme. The labour market courses (38,000 students per year) focus on the unemployed (Randle and Svensson, 2002).

What general conclusions can be drawn from the Swedish system for lifelong learning? We would highlight the following positive aspects:

- the possibilities to continue one's studies later in life when one is more motivated or ready for (or forced into) a new occupation;
- different alternatives (Folk High Schools, Learning Centres, Net-Universities) which make learning more flexible – both for individuals and companies;

- the importance of different supporting systems – loans, subsidies, the right to leave for studies, job centres, learning centres, etc. A National Programme for learning accounts was put forward by the government in April 2002;
- the positive outcome of the practical programmes for training at the workplace (qualified vocational training and apprentice programmes), which could expand and be developed further.

However, a closer look at the system described for lifelong learning in Figure 5.1 indicates a number of problems. The participation rates in higher education are very unequal: it is thus a mirror of the class-system. There is a problem with integrating the different aspects (see Figure 5.2) from an individual and a company perspective. The system seldom functions in practice, neither for the individual worker nor for the small firm. It is too much a system developed 'from above', which is designed in a linear way and not adapted to the realities of everyday life and the dynamic of a rapidly changing society. The lack of a holistic perspective makes it difficult for an individual and a small firm to take advantage of all the opportunities that are available in the different systems. Most of all, it is not a system for lifelong learning in which work and learning are combined continuously (Svensson and Åberg, 2001).

There are, however, some changes on the way in which local and regional strategies are operating and thereby becoming more important. Municipalities are to be responsible for offering continuous career and study counselling to draw up individual study plans and to validate previous learning for all citizens who wish to carry on their studies at any level. The system of student allowances is to be improved so that more people can study to enhance their upper secondary qualifications. The number of places (in the educational programme for the government initiative to promote adult education) is to be increased (Government Bill, 2000/01: 72).

To summarize, the education system is Sweden is impressive in many respects. If it is used successfully it can be an important ingredient in a strategy for lifelong learning. A central focus has been put on adult education and on lifting people's formal educational levels to three years in upper secondary school.

A system fault – a gap between the educational and production systems

The real problem of fulfilling the idea of lifelong learning is not the basic training and education components, but making learning a continuous activity in working life for all employees. There are huge differences between firms when it comes to learning and training in different sectors of the labour market (see above). Small firms that try to compete through low prices in highly competitive markets are less interested in formal training and lifelong learning, especially if there is a surplus of labour. But there are also many companies for which continuous training of their employees is a necessity. Increased competition necessitates quick changes in how firms relate to markets and high quality products and services. These companies have to introduce a new, more flexible, decentralized, integrated and customer-oriented organization, which presupposes a high level of competence among employees. The growing problem of recruiting new personnel is putting additional pressure on the employers for more training and education.

Employers can gain a great deal from a comprehensive and well-functioning system of learning. A major study in Sweden points to a strong connection between training and profitability. The companies that did organize training in a more systematic way enjoyed profit levels that were more than 50 per cent higher than those that did not invest in any training (NUTEK, 2000: 52). This and other results indicate the significance of training in increasing competitiveness, profitability and productivity (NUTEK, 2000: 14).[3] What, then, holds employers back from investing in training and learning?

One fundamental problem with introducing lifelong learning is the division or gap between the educational and economic systems. This split between education and working life manifests itself in the conflict of interests between different departments in the government (the Education and Industry Departments) as well as those between organizations at the local level (see Figure 5.2). The education system is characterized by a high evaluation of theory, a long-term planning horizon, a discipline-based organization, a hierarchical structure and a traditional teacher-centred pedagogy. The pedagogy and organization of the Municipal Schools for Adult Education and Swedish for Immigrants are greatly influenced by these institutional characteristics of the educational system – with a traditional class-room pedagogy, an inflexible organization, supply-oriented courses etc. (Svensson and Åberg, 2001). The individual worker and the companies are more interested in a combination of practice and theory, a multidisciplinary approach, an equal communication structure, a flexible system, and a problem-based pedagogy (SOU, 1994: 48; 1996: 64; 2000: 28; Ellström, 2002).

This gap between the production and education systems is the third explanation for the failure of a successful strategy for lifelong learning in Sweden. The gap can be characterised by a lack of accessibility, flexibility, co-ordination, integration and supply-orientation. The latter is contrary to what the employers and employees demand (Svensson and Åberg, 2001).

The educational system works from a strong power position because of its tradition and its monopoly role in the certification of knowledge. What happens in a situation where the needs of individuals and companies are subordinated to an inflexible educational system? A very important effect is the lack of integration between informal and formal learning, as well as a split between individual and organizational learning. The lack of co-ordination between the economic and educational systems results in the outcomes of various training programmes being very limited. This can explain the low interest in education among many employers and workers. They have often adopted an instrumental attitude to learning. They want their investment in learning to have rapid, short-term pay-back periods.

In this situation the employers turn to private consultant agencies that are open to a dialogue to make the training more flexible and accessible. But their courses are often standardized, not tailor-made for the individual worker or the small firm. It is more profitable for the supplier to use a standard programme designed for the larger companies with a focus on general knowledge. If the market itself cannot produce lifelong learning and employability, the role of the educational system becomes central.

Conclusions: lifelong learning – limits and prospects

This chapter started by highlighting the contradiction in the current interest in lifelong learning and employability – the lack of correspondence between its strong discursive ideals and its weak actual practices. The concept of lifelong learning has not so far manifested itself in a system for training and education for large groups of employees. One explanation for the public interest in lifelong learning was sought on a societal level in the assumed need for skill formation in the knowledge-based and competitive economy. With globalization and rapid technological change, learning is said to be the driving force behind innovation and competitiveness. This may be true for some sectors in the economy, but not for others. A large part of the service sector consists of low-skilled jobs. An analysis of the level of available skills yielded astonishing results. The problem was as much that of over-qualification as under-qualification. A few hundred thousand workers are over-qualified for their jobs. As many are lacking qualifications

(LO, 2002). Upskilling and downskilling are occurring at the same time (Åberg, forthcoming).

The second explanation focused on the strong tradition of Taylorism and rationalization in the Swedish economy. Many employees cannot use their qualifications because of old-fashioned forms of work organization and routinized work practices. In a Tayloristic organization, learning is of minor importance, and when it occurs it is of a more adaptive, instrumental and single-loop character. The clash between a production and a learning logic is becoming more clear-cut in an economy that focuses on short-term profits in a very competitive and globalized market (Hultman *et al.*, 2002; Keep, 2002). The increased levels of rationalization during the 1990s indicated this shortcoming in a resultant lack of time for learning and reflection at work (Bengtsson and Berggren, 2001; see also the contribution by Augustsson and Sandberg, Chapter 11 in this volume).

Another explanation for the failure of lifelong learning focused on the conflict between the educational system and the production system. The former stresses stability, strict rules, and standardization, whereas the latter values flexibility, interactivity and accessibility in the organization of education and learning. The national projects adopted to implement new learning strategies are often too centralized, predetermined, isolated and short-sighted to be effective. 'Top down' initiated change-processes, which do not involve the people concerned, will not be successful. The failure of the educational system to create conditions for lifelong learning must be dealt with in a creative way based on broad participation and innovation.

What other explanations can be sought for this seemingly illogical interest in lifelong learning at the discursive level? One explanation – which I have not dealt with and which will not be developed at any length here (see Svensson, 1997) – is of an ideological and political nature. The concept of lifelong learning can be accepted both by the unions and the employers at a time of compromise and peaceful relations on the labour market. Who can be against learning and competence in a situation of globalization and innovation? Uncomfortable questions – about power relations, increased inequalities, the intensification of work and continuous high levels of unemployment for large groups in the labour market – are put aside.

Moreover, the content of learning is seldom open for critical discussion. The employers tend to include more and more personal attributes within the skill-concept such as discipline, motivation, responsibility, loyalty, punctuality and reliability. Is the objective of creating a subservient and committed workforce something that the educational system should accept and the state should subsidize?

It is important to develop a critical perspective because most of the literature on learning has a top-down, idealistic and conflict-free frame of reference (Svensson, 1997). Learning is supposed to be of a neutral kind that benefits all. Its values and alternatives are hidden in the strong consensus of the partnership model. But from a critical perspective, issues of learning and competence should be seen as part of an employment relationship which is based on difference of interests and conflict. A narrow focus of growth, competition and productivity shadow issues like inequality, powerlessness and discrimination in the labour market. The public debate on the 'new' (knowledge-based) working life seldom includes the situation faced by less qualified employees and the unemployed. Even within the world of work, not everyone will be a winner. A single-minded emphasis on learning *for* work can increase differences within the workforce (Boud and Garrick, 1999). The strategy for learning in the last few decades has focused on the 'elite', based on the idea that these groups will 'pull' the rest along on the road to individual success and national growth. Even the unions in Sweden seem to have accepted the idea of the elite as a motor for change and growth (Nyström, 2000).

A positive agenda for lifelong learning

Having pointed to a number of difficulties in implementing lifelong learning, the chapter will now turn to a more constructive perspective. The ambition is to discuss how a system for lifelong learning can be organized. It is important to promote education and training irrespective of all the restrictions and difficulties described above. There are different reasons for this conclusion. With a higher level of education, employees will be less dependent on employers, and with a higher competence the prospects for the individual in the labour market will improve. When employees can apply for new and better jobs, there is pressure on employers to change Tayloristic forms of work organization and improve the conditions for learning, especially if there is a labour shortage in some sectors. Society has a general interest in over-qualification, because the 'competence gap' will make the labour market more flexible and dynamic (LO, 2001).

A society can thus gain a great deal from investing in training and education. Strategies to promote learning can be organized in a number of ways. We can distinguish between the following three strategies: a state model, a market model and a social partnership model (see Brown,

2001: 259). The chapter advocates a combination of all strategies, but with a focus on the third model. The Swedish tradition of cooperation between the unions and the employers is a major strength and facilitator in introducing a strategy for lifelong learning. This tradition explains the ease with which the partnership system functions. The new agreements for training are a step further in the direction of lifelong learning, and a new union role as competence facilitators is being introduced in the Metalworkers Union.

But state initiatives are also important, especially when it comes to the less advantaged groups on the labour market. One successful government initiative to promote adult education is the Adult Education Initiative, directed mainly at the unemployed, which include 100,000 persons each year. The subsidies to the individuals taking part in the education packages are an important success factor of this programme. Such an education can provide individuals with more self-confidence and strengthen their *life-wide learning*, which takes place outside work.

A strategy to promote lifelong learning and employability must be comprehensive. The different components of the economic and educational systems must be integrated (see Figure 5.2). A system for lifelong learning must include a democratic work organization, better learning possibilities on the job, a flexible system for training and education, and equal opportunities for employees and the unemployed. Such innovative and complex solutions cannot be organized 'from above', but must be developed 'from below'. I do not have any ready-made proposals for a lifelong learning strategy, only some ideas on how to make progress with such efforts. As a summary I will – in a prescriptive way – focus on various key themes. The importance of learning must be stressed in an economy that changes very rapidly. In turn, this necessitates continuous learning for all groups in society. But we should not focus too much on instrumental learning. Instead, the focus must be on transferable skills and a lifelong approach. Learning must be an integral part of all work, especially in less skilled service jobs. The time for learning and reflection must be scheduled. The employers, the state, the unions and the workers must push for lifelong learning and employability. There have to be supporting systems for both individuals (loans, subsidies, guidance, validation, distance learning, e-learning, etc.) and companies (research and development centres, learning centres, job centres, project money). There has to be demand-based and democratic pressure on the educational system for change, and support for schools and universities that wish to experiment in order to create a flexible and problem-oriented pedagogy aimed at less qualified groups.

It is important to strengthen the rights of the individual and the prospects for small companies to develop methods for combining informal and formal learning. Workplace learning becomes important in this perspective. The workplace can be used as a central arena for learning, but the unemployed and excluded groups should be included in the training programmes. The support for education and training must be continuous, flexible, available and individualized, based on a combination of formal and informal learning. In this way problem-based learning can be used in combination with formal education, which equips the participants with more general skills. The workplace can create a more relaxed atmosphere for these groups, compared to the institutionalized school system. The Swedish tradition of joint learning in study circles is valuable for motivating new groups.[4]

Major national projects based on the idea of best practice should be avoided. Lifelong learning must, instead, be developed from 'below' and 'inside' the organizations in an innovative way. Local innovative systems for learning and employability with broad participation and strong partnership support should be created. New ways of cooperating between different workplaces based on learning examples should be developed. Networking is an effective way to stimulate learning and innovation. The unions have a central role to play in these local changes. They can for example support local changes, initiate projects, organize networks, cooperate with researchers, and negotiate with management. We have a long tradition of organizing projects in Sweden. It is important to learn from all these efforts.[5] Research on lifelong learning and employability should be strengthened, especially that which can combine an interactive and critical perspective in a multidisciplinary way.[6]

But more important than all these learning activities is a political and economic strategy that has an ambition to increase the general demand for labour and the employees' positions in the labour market. Otherwise, there is a risk that a higher level of qualifications will only have the effect of pushing the less educated out of employment.

Notes

1. Labour Force Surveys indicate a consistently high level of participation in education in Sweden compared to other countries in Western Europe. A recent survey (of 35,000 enterprises) on continuing vocational training gave a similar result (Heyes, 2002).
2. This section is based on a report which is part of an EU-project (Randle and Svensson, 2002).

3. There is always a problem of determining cause and effect in such a study.
4. Every year 1.8 million individuals take part in study circles in Sweden (Randle and Svensson, 2002).
5. The Working Life Funds (between 1992 and 1995) had a total budget of more than 30 billion SEK and initiated more than 20,000 projects. The EU Objective 4 programme (between 1995 and 2000) had less money but included as many projects.
6. The state official report (SOU, 2000: 28) recommends the government to take measures to bring about major and immediate investment in research on adult education and lifelong learning.

References

Åberg, Rune. (Forthcoming.) 'Unemployment persistency, overeducation and employment chances of the less educated'. *European Sociological Review*.

Abrahamsson, Lena. 2000. *Att återställa ordningen*. Umeå: Boreá.

AMV 1999: 11. *Om långtidsarbetslöshetens orsaker*. Stockholm: AMV.

Argyris, Chris. 1977. 'Double-loop learning in organisations'. *Harvard Business Review*, 55(5) (September–October): 115–25.

Argyris, Chris and Donald Schön. 1996. *Organisational Learning II: Theory, Method, and Practice*. Mass.: Addison-Wesley.

Boud, David and John Garrick (ed). 1999. *Understanding Learning at Work*. London: Routledge.

Bengtsson, Lars and Christian Berggren. 2001. 'Produktionens förändrade roll: mager klickfunktion eller kunskapsfabrik'. In *Lärdilemman i arbetslivet*, edited by T. Backlund, H. Hansson, and C. Thunborg. Lund: Studentlitteratur, 149–76.

Björkman, Torsten. 2002. 'Den långlivade taylorismen'. In *Kompetens, utbildning och arbetsliv: från överutbildning till underlärande*, edited by K. Abrahamsson, L. Abrahamsson, P-E. Ellström and J. Johansson. Lund: Studentlitteratur. Book manuscript.

Brown, John and Paul Duguid. 1991. 'Organisational learning and communities-of-practice: toward a unified view of working, learning, and innovation'. *Organization Science* 2(1): 40–57.

Brown, Phillip. 2001. 'Globalization and the political economy of high skills'. In *High Skills: Globalization, Competitiveness and Skill Formation*, edited by P. Brown, A. Green and H. Lauder. Oxford: Oxford University Press, 235–61.

Brown, Phillip, Andy Green and Hugh Lauder. 2001. *High Skills: Globalization, Competitiveness and Skill Formation*. Oxford: Oxford University Press.

Dewey, John. 1989. *Volume 8: 1933. The Later Works, 1925–1953. Essays and How We Think*. Carbondale, IU.: Southern Illinois University Press.

Ds 1999: 58. *Balansen mellan arbetskraftens utbildningsnivå och jobbens kvalifikationsgrad – ett struktur- eller konjunkturproblem*. (Bilaga)

Ellström, Per-Erik. 1992. *Kompetens, utbildning och lärande i arbetslivet*. Stockholm: Publica.

Ellström, Per-Erik. 1996. *Arbete och lärande: Förutsättningar och hinder för lärande i dagligt arbete*. Stockholm: Arbetslivsinstitutet.

Ellström, Per-Erik. 2002. *Workplace Learning, Reflection, and Time*. Centre for Studies of Humans, Technology, and Organisations. Linköping University.

Europeiska Gemenskapens Kommission. 2001. *Att förverkliga det europeiska området för livslångt lärande*.

Government Bill (Regeringens proposition) 2000/01: 72, *Vuxnas lärande och utvecklingen av vuxenutbildningen.*

Government Bill (Regeringens proposition) 2001/02: 4. *En politik för tillväxt och livskraft i hela landet.*

Heyes, Jason. 2002. 'Training, social dialogue and collective bargaining: issues for comparative research'. Paper presented at the Conference on Training, Employability and Employment. Monash University Centre, 11–12 July 2002.

Hultman, Glenn, Alger Klasson and Magnus Nilsson. 2002. *Organisationsövergångar och unika kulturer.* Stockholm: Vinnova 2002: 5.

Karasek, Robert and Töres Theorell. 1990. *Healthy Work: Stress, Productivity, and the Reconstruction of Working Life.* New York: Basic Books.

Keep, Ewart. 2002. *The Changing Meaning of Skill and the Shifting Balance of Responsibility for Vocational Education and Training: Are Employers Calling the Shots?* Warwick Business School. University of Warwick.

Korpi, Walter. 1978. *Arbetarklassen i välfärdskapitalismen.* Stockholm: Rabén and Sjögren.

Lave, Jean and Etienne Wenger. 1993. *Situated Learning: Legitimated Peripheral Participation.* Cambridge: Cambridge University Press.

LO (Report from the Labour Union). 1995. *Kompetens och internutbildning samt organisationsförändringar på arbetsplatserna.* Stockholm: LO.

LO (Report from the Labour Union). 1999. *Röster om facket och jobbet.*

LO (Report from the Labour Union). 2001. *Kompetensutveckling 2001.* LO-facken i Göteborg.

LO (Report from the Labour Union). 2002. *Utbildning – för tillväxten, jobben och rättvisan.* Stockholm: LO.

Metall (Report from the Metalworkers' Union). 1985. *Det goda arbetet.* Stockholm: Svenska Metallindustriarbetareförbundet.

Nyberg, Mikael. 2002. *Kapitalet.se.* Stockholm: Ordfront.

Nyström, Örjan. 2000. *Mellan anpassning och motstånd: Facket och det nya arbetslivet.* Stockholm: Atlas.

NUTEK 2000: 14. *Kompetens en bristvara? Företagarens syn på kompetensförsörjning?* Stockholm: Nutek förlag.

NUTEK 2000: 52. *Företag i förändring: Lärandestrategier för ökad konkurrenskraft.* Stockholm: Nutek förlag.

Randle, Hanne and Lennart Svensson. 2002. *Lifelong Learning: A Fiction or Reality?* EU-report. Learnpartner. University of Leeds.

Rasmussen, Bente. 1999. *Dehierarchization: Reorganizing Gender.* Trondheim: NNTU.

Sandberg, Åke (ed.). 1995. *Enriching Production.* Averbury: Aldershot.

Schön, Donald. 1983. *The Reflective Practitioner: How Professionals Think in Action.* London: Temple Smith.

Schön, Donald. 1987. *Educating the Reflecting Practitioner.* San Francisco: Jossey-Bass Publishers.

SOU 1994: 48. *Kunskap för utveckling.* Betänkande av utredningen om kunskapsbildning i arbetslivet. Stockholm: Allmänna Förlaget.

SOU 1996: 64. *Livslångt lärande i arbetslivet: steg på vägen mot kunskapssamhället.* Utbildningsdepartementet. Stockholm: Fritzes.

SOU 2000: 28. *Kunskapsbygget 2000: det livslånga lärandet.* Slutbetänkande från Kunskapslyftskommittén. Stockholm: Fritzes.

SOU 2001: 53. 'Har jobben blivit bättre?' In *Välfärd och arbete i arbetslöshetens årtionde.* Stockholm: Fritzes.

Svensson, Lennart. 1997. 'Lärande genom organisationsutveckling'. In *Ledning för alla?* edited by Å. Sandberg. Stockholm: SNS Förlag, 223–44.

Svensson, Lennart and Carina Åberg. 2001. *E-learning och arbetsplatslärande.* Stockholm: Bilda Förlag.

Växtkraft Mål 4. Svenska EU-programkontoret. 1996. *EU-stöd till kompetensutveckling i företag.* Stockholm: Publica.

6
Constructing the Competent Individual: Trade Union Roles, Responses and Rhetoric

Tony Huzzard

Introduction: trade unions and the competent individual

Some 30 years ago, Daniel Bell proclaimed the arrival of 'post-industrial society' (Bell, 1973). Since then, a wealth of claims have been made by scholars and practitioners that social relations at both organizational and societal levels have undergone some sort of fundamental transformation in what has frequently been called the epoch of 'postmodernism' (Harvey, 1989; Amin, 1994). Alternatively, the sociologist Anthony Giddens has alluded to some sort of change as being afoot by terming the recent era as that of 'late modernism' (Giddens, 1991). The extent of change and the issue of whether a new social and organizational 'paradigm' has superseded 'modernism' has, however, been hotly contested (Callinicos, 1989; Thompson, 1993; Amin, 1994; Smith and Thompson, 1998). Whatever one's position in such debates, the large volume of literature in the area suggests, however, that at the *level of discourse* some sort of change is undeniable.

This chapter explores these issues by focusing on the discourses through which the various claims to 'post-industrial', 'postmodern' or 'late modern' change are being constructed. Specifically, the intersection of two features of the discourse underpinning such 'change' is explored, firstly the claim that society and the labour process are becoming individualized and secondly the claim that the increasing focus on knowledge in society and at work are promoting a greater incidence of learning and 'knowledge work' (Prichard *et al.*, 2000). Together, such claims can be said to comprise a discourse of the 'competent individual' where workers are portrayed as being able to assume responsibility for their own employment – in other words to be employable. But how has such a discourse been constructed? How is it being reproduced?

The central argument of the chapter is thus that two themes appear to recur in the various claims and perspectives of the post-industrial discourse discussed here, namely the emphasis on the individual at work and a similar emphasis on the centrality of knowledge, learning and competence at work. Individuals are claimed no longer to be components in relatively stable work systems such as production lines or white-collar bureaucracies. Neither the state nor the capitalist firm can guarantee the right to work – the individual has the responsibility to make himself or herself employable to various employers over time by regularly updating competencies to comply with market requirements. Although workers previously required skills in traditional industry, these were cumulative, collectively provided on-the-job by the employer (see also Jacobsson, Chapter 3 in this volume). Today, I argue, we see a very different idea of skills and knowledge in the labour process.

In particular, the chapter focuses on the interaction between the discourse of the competent individual with the discourses of trade union renewal in Sweden. In contrast to countries elsewhere such as the US and the UK, Swedish unions retain a key role in regulating the labour process and are central actors in the social practices associated with work. Accordingly, a study is called for into not only how the unions are responding to discursive change, but also the role they play themselves as shapers of the discourse.

The chapter proceeds by looking in detail at various expressions of the post-industrial discourse both generally in the West and specifically in Sweden. Three unions are then examined as case studies, the Swedish Metalworkers Union (Metall), the Swedish Industrial Workers Union (IF), and the white-collar Swedish Union of Industrial and Technical Workers in Industry, Sif. Following an examination of the everyday realities at three workplaces where these unions are organized, the post-industrial discourse of the 'competent individual' is then discussed critically, and the chapter concludes with an evaluation of the role of unions as discursive agents.

The evidence suggests that the changes at the societal level being constructed by the discourse of post-industrialism are having a profound impact on the unions. In the case of the blue-collar unions studied there is clear evidence of an extension of union agendas to encompass both the perceived individualization of work and the perceived increase in the role of learning and knowledge. Such changes are, however, being contested and are augmenting traditional ideologies and praxis rather than superseding them. The white-collar union studied, however, has sought to respond in a more transformational though not uncontested way through discursively reconstructing its image and identity in the face of a diverse profile of members and potential members, often in knowledge-work occupations.

The discourse of post-industrialism

The concept of discourse has attracted considerable interest in the social sciences as post-modernist influences have foregrounded the role of language in social processes. In particular, discourse plays a central role in post-structuralist accounts. However, the usage of the concept is by no means restricted to such work (Alvesson and Kärreman, 2000). The view taken in this chapter is that views of discourse that collapse it into meaning, typical in work inspired by Michel Foucault, tend to overstate the constitutive power of language. The tendency in such efforts, termed by Alvesson and Kärreman 'muscular discourse', is towards a sort of linguistic determinism whereby language is deemed to determine both subjects and objects thereby arranging and normalizing the social world that gives little scope for deviation. While the likelihood of resistance is acknowledged in some Foucauldian studies, this is often an afterthought. Yet it is what happens in defiance of the muscular discourse that key social processes are played out and this space is thus often the site of important research enquiry.[1] The chapter's discussion of the discourse of the competent individual is thus conceived as not always determining, yet operating at both macro and micro levels – formerly the post-industrial discourse of the 'competent individual' and latterly in the specific context of discourses of union renewal.

The competent individual, reflexive projects and the new economy

The post-industrial discourse of work and employability is termed here the discourse of the 'competent individual'. This operates by a fore-grounding of the need for individuals to take responsibility for their own competence development rather than rely on the collective provision of skills updating by employers or the state. Moreover, an emphasis is also placed on the centrality of knowledge in the labour process as the core determinant of added value. Workers not only need to be knowledgeable, they must also take on responsibility for their own education. Such a view can be said to be a discursive construction in that it normalizes a particular view of the world of work. This highlights individualization rather than collectivism and sees learning and knowledge as the only true sources of competitive advantage for firms and are thereby the key to individual survival in the labour market. As stated by Senge (1990: 4, italics in original):

> The organizations that will truly excel in the future will be the organizations that discover how to tap people's commitment and capacity to learn at *all* levels in an organization.

The discourse of the competent individual is reproducing itself through a number of sources both internationally and in Sweden. Authors such as Giddens (1991) have argued that individual identities are based less on carriers of social identity such as class and, instead, are increasingly based on individual 'reflexive projects'. Such arguments appear to be lent support by attitudinal researchers. For example, Inglehart (1990, 1997) has concluded from cross-country studies that a slow and steady process of individualization can be discerned in the post-war Western world as physical and security needs, traditionally satisfied from the domain of collective provision, have largely been met. A key aspect of the post-industrial discourse is thus the alleged collapse of collectivism at the societal level in the increasing rejection of collectivist ideologies.

It has also been argued that as work is being increasingly rationalized and more effective in its execution, it is becoming more peripheral as a social condition that forms individual identities. In essence, work is becoming individualized and is facilitating increased employee autonomy (Allvin, 1997). Moreover, a process of individualization has been detected as occurring in terms of the employment relationship, a key theme in the so-called 'new economy' (Krugman, 1997; Atkinson and Court, 1998; Kelly, 1999). Authors proposing the idea that recent changes amount to something 'new' refer to a world in which people are working with their brains instead of their hands and where communications technology is creating global competition in goods and services. In such a world, innovation is more important than mass production and investment buys new concepts or the means to create them, rather than new machines. It no longer takes a production line to compete, just a good idea. The logic of industrialism – optimal efficiency from groups of workers in production processes – has given way to new logic of post-industrialism that highlights individuals as sources of new knowledge, innovation and competitive advantage (Pfeffer, 1994).

At the same time, a wealth of literature on the nature of work has foregrounded the centrality of learning and the importance of knowledge in the labour process (Drucker, 1993; Barley, 1996; Prichard *et al.*, 2000).

Warhurst and Thompson (1998: 2), for example, go so far as to state that work is 'no longer about the production of tangible goods but concerned with the centrality of knowledge and manipulation of symbols'. Although it may be argued that work has always been dependent on some degree of knowledge,[2] what is undoubtedly new is the extent to which knowledge bases are associated with electronically codified information (Zuboff, 1988; Blackler, 1995). As with the term 'post-industrialism', the new emphasis on knowledge finds a discursive echo at both the micro level ('knowledge work', 'knowledge intensive firms') and the macro level ('the knowledge based society'). The changes afoot have been heralded as the arrival of the 'post-industrial' organization and the end of bureaucracy (Heckscher and Donnellon, 1994). A lessening of bureaucratic tendencies, it is argued, has become associated with less *direct* control and thus scope for more individual autonomy at work.

The individual under a new business logic

A further development is that of a new business logic whereby the creation of new knowledge and innovative capacity have become the most robust sources of competitive advantage. The cost leadership and differentiation alternatives of Fordism cannot be sustained for any length of time as, in the information age, they are easily copiable. In terms of business strategy, responses to the current changes can be seen in terms of a contrast between two quite distinct options for the pursuit of competitiveness: the 'low road' and the 'high road'. Low road solutions focus on the traditional options in work organization of cost leadership, flexibility, speed and quality. In increasingly fierce global markets there is continuous pressure to deliver faster and better products and services at lower prices. But these are no longer seen as sufficient means for adding value; they are mere 'entrance factors' to the competitive game and offer no guarantee of winning it. Rather, winning organizations need to embrace high road solutions whereby organizational spaces are created that liberate human creativity in ways that achieve a dynamic balance between product and process innovation (Hague *et al.*, 2003).

As argued elsewhere in this volume, the post-industrial discourse envisages a policy switch from the *provision of employment* to the *provision of employability*. The latter questions the assumption of lifelong attachment to one or two employers or even occupations. Workers are more likely to pursue 'boundaryless careers' (Lindgren and Wåhlin, 2001) and work practices are more scattered, both spatially and temporally, as a greater proportion of employment becomes part-time, freelance and/or projectified. Writers such as Handy (1996), in his depiction of the 'portfolio worker', paint a rosy picture of this situation whereby workers happily go through life switching from one work experience to the next. In response, policy-makers have sought to stress individual learning accounts and promote the necessity for lifelong learning as well as inculcate workers with personal responsibility for such.

The discourse of the new economy not only finds its expression in the more scholarly texts of macroeconomics (for example Krugman, 1997) and business studies (for example Kelly, 1999; Burton-Jones, 2001). It is also reproduced through the genre of popular management. An illustrative example of this is a text *Funky Business* translated into some 20 different languages and readily available at airport bookstalls internationally. This claims that as knowledge in the new economy is the critical means of production, Karl Marx was finally proved right: the workers do actually own the major assets of society (Nordström and Ridderstråle, 2000). Knowledge is power, and, being in workers' heads, it is everywhere. 'Perfectly formed and individually owned, the human brain is over-powering the means of production... try to think of one major, successful contemporary business organization that is brawn based' (Nordström and Ridderstråle, 2000: 19). Renewal and agility are central to competitive survival – and speed in the generation of new knowledge is of importance to all, and thus everywhere. In stressing the macro implications of such claims, the authors state that 'Entire countries increasingly compete on the basis of knowledge.' At the individual level the claims of the new economy are just as brazen: 'No jobs but more power. We now own the major assets of society – our own minds. And power equals freedom. We are all potentially free to know, go, do and be whoever we want to be' (Nordström and Ridderstråle, 2000: 35).

The competent individual in the Swedish discourse

There can be little doubt, too, that the foregrounding of the competent individual has been infused into the discursive construction of society and working life in Sweden where authors such as Arvidsson *et al.* (1994) have concluded that individual values in Sweden are superseding those of collectivism. Such a development has also been identified as impacting on the workplace where the implication is likely to be 'a more individualized and direct relation between employer and management' (Boglind, 1997: 117). This inevitably calls into question the traditional division between blue- and white-collar work and poses a major challenge for trade union organization and ideologies. The text *Funky Business* referred to above, although incorporating many discursive features from the genre of American business gurus (Webster, 2002), was originally written in Swedish by academics working at the Stockholm School of Economics.

Bruhn (1999) provides evidence on the problems facing unions in an era of a perceived decline in attachment to collectivist values and an increase in individually based motives. In focus in this research was the changing attitudes and patterns of action of private sector white-collar workers in Gothenburg towards their union (in this case Sif). Bruhn's data revealed a significant generation gap in motives in relation to union membership and activity. Collectivist views about the union, often associated with solidarity and other traditional values, were more commonly held by older employees. Younger employees, on the other hand, displayed a greater tendency to adhere to instrumentalist views about the union that co-existed with what were identified as 'private post-materialistic' value patterns. For these employees, situationally bound activities are not shaped by any deep ideological convictions. Bruhn argues that the increasing relative significance of employees having 'private post-materialistic' values is indicative of increasing individualism – and such 'increasing individuality is the result of a long-term developmental process that springs from changes on a societal level' (Bruhn, 1999: 349).

Although expressing itself in various forms and being reproduced through various media and genres, there can thus be no doubt that the Western discourse of post-industrialism is permeating the contemporary discourse of working life in Sweden. *This seeks to normalize the view that business competitiveness and prosperity require knowledge work, flexible work forms, labour market deregulation and less secure work practices.*[3] Moreover, recurrent themes feature in such a discourse. Collectivist ideologies and bureaucratic organizing are allegedly on the wane; secondly there is an increasing focus on the role of knowledge as the crucial factor of production for ensuring competitiveness and survival at both the organizational and societal level. To encapsulate the intersection of these themes it accordingly seems apposite to discuss the discourse of post-industrialism in terms of the *discourse of the competent individual.* Yet how is this discourse responded to in localized settings? And how is the discourse actively reproduced in such settings? It is to these themes, in the empirical domain of unions in Sweden, that we now turn.

Trade unions and the post-industrial discourse

Data is presented here that represents discourses of renewal from national trade unions and, where appropriate, textual output from leaders of the local union organizations at three Swedish workplaces. Two blue-collar unions are considered – the Swedish Metalworkers Union (Metall) and the Swedish Industrial Workers Union (IF) together with one white-collar union – the Swedish Union of Industrial and Technical Workers in Industry, SIF, that has recently retitled itself as simply Sif to disassociate the union from the notion of 'industry' and 'white-collar workers' which are now seen as obsolete. The workplaces consist of Heatplates AB, a manufacturing plant employing some 700 staff in southern Sweden (data collected in May 1998), Frontloader AB, a manufacturer employing some 400 staff at its plant in northern Sweden (data collected in the first half of 2000) and Drugco AB, a knowledge intensive pharmaceutical multinational employing some 7,000 staff at its site in central Sweden (data collected in May to September 2001). All company names are pseudonyms. The data collected consists of interviews with union leaders as well as union documents. Contextual data was also obtained from company documents and/or interviews with managers. In the case of Frontloader, data was also collected from direct observation of union-management negotiation meetings.

The discursive ideal

Signs of a discursive shift are clearly evident in official texts being produced by the national trade unions. An example of this is the current action programme of the Swedish Metalworkers Union that was adopted at its 1999 Congress, convened under the slogan *Knowledge for Development*. In stressing the centrality of competence and learning, the union's president, in his first online chronicle of the new millennium, wrote as follows:[4]

> The second of Metall's goals concerns training and competence development to strengthen the metalworker in the labour market in line with the policy laid down by Congress.
>
> This issue is also relevant in wage negotiations. Metall wants all members to start their own learning accounts whereby money or hours can be set aside for strengthening one's competence and prospects for keeping up with new information.
>
> Locally and centrally we will train Metall's training officers whose tasks are to motivate their staff and members for continuing education, partly in basic computer skills, maths and English, and partly in more specific subjects such as operating new equipment at the workplace. (Metall, 2000)

Such views are not new, however, and can be traced back to the union's policy of 'Good Work' laid down in 1985 that explicitly sought to develop a qualitative union agenda promoting competence development and individual learning (Huzzard, 2000). Moreover, as the policy evolved into 'Solidaristic Work' (Metall 1989), the traditional collective notion of 'solidarity' was extended to encompass the equal individual right to skills upgrading, multi-skilling and solidaristic team working as integral aspects of 'Good Work'. In other words, the discursive construction of the policy implied an ideological shift to include equality of opportunity (for individuals) as well as the traditional (collective) goal of equality of outcomes. In attributing an increasing significance to skills and knowledge in manufacturing processes, the unions have engaged in a subtle shift in the 'solidarity' signifier away from collectivist distributional rights and towards individual rights to competence development and learning.

A similar policy, 'Developmental Work' (DUVA), was adopted by the Industrial Workers Union, IF, in 1995, although the implementation of this has been less extensive than in Metall. IF, at its website, explains the policy as follows:

> Employees' duties are changing in time with the rapid developments in technology. All must therefore have opportunities for continuing education... The training that is currently offered to employees takes little or no account of previous experience or knowledge. All training should take into account the existing practical and theoretical knowledge that individuals already have... We demand that salary developments run hand in hand with individual development on the job. (Industrifacket, 2001)

It can be seen that the IF, therefore, is accepting that individual learning is something that is of strategic significance in the context of a changed work organization and, in stressing its ongoing nature, an implicit link is being made to lifelong learning. However, although the union is clearly drawing on the discourse of the competent individual, the emphasis is more towards a linkage between this and its distributional agenda rather than a linkage to employability on the broader labour market.

As with Metall and the IF, the issues of learning and competence have been central in the recent activities of the main white-collar union organizing in Swedish industry, Sif. For example, it chose the slogan *It's high time for competence* to accompany the reporting of its 1998 salary agreement (Sif website, 14 October, 1997). Moreover, the union sees itself as the natural facilitator for the career and competence development of its members as exemplified by the extract below from the idea programme adopted by its 2000 Congress. This clearly signifies that Sif members should take on a degree of responsibility themselves for their employment trajectories:

> Sif considers that it is the responsibility of society and the employers to afford sound foundations for competence development. In various ways, Sif seeks to ensure that all members can raise their competencies so as to be sought after on the labour market. The individual also has a responsibility to take initiatives for the development of his or her competence. In order to motivate competence development, Sif shall create insights and preparative measures about the changes affecting firms and the labour market. Each member can then make rational choices in his or her working life.
>
> Sif shall actively support members and employers through offering tools and services that contribute to individual competence and career planning. The concept 'competence' can include the individual's theoretical knowledge, professional experiences and social skills. Competence implies the will and capacity to transform knowledge in practical action. By 'career' Sif means the choice of the individual, his or her opportunities and will to develop in a current or desired firm.
>
> Sif shall work for clear leadership that stimulates, engages and allows all people to develop. (Sif, 2000)

The foregrounding of learning and knowledge in official Sif texts has evolved over some time. By the late 1980s the perceived increase in the significance of organizational knowledge had been seen as an opportunity to develop the notion of employees as a developmental resource within the firm rather than a cost, an idea which required the union to promote competence development as a strategic issue. The explicitly stated tasks of Sif in its Action Programme, adopted by the 1987 Congress, were those of 'developing methods for union work with personal development and inventories of developmental needs'. It was time to 'strengthen the individual', and the promotion of competence development, in the context of changed work organization, had emerged as a central strategy in this respect (Sif, 1987).

The new emphasis on competence found its subsequent practical expression in the Competence Development Project that ran from 1989 until the 1993 Congress. The idea was presented as 'the development of the individual's knowledge and skills and his or her will and ability to use them to do a better job' (Sif, 1993a), and an opportunity to 'close the gap between those who are sought in the labour market and those who are not' (Sif, 1990b: 39–40). Moreover, the idea was also packaged to appeal to employers as meaning 'the organization's development with the aim of achieving some kind of sustainable competitive advantage' (Sif, 1993a). From being one of many elements in Sif's platform in 1987, competence development had accordingly been elevated by 1990 as a 'priority' (Sif, 1990a) and a 'heavy union issue' (Sif, 1990b: 39). The continuing significance of competence development as a strategic issue was underscored by its inclusion as the second of 15 points comprising goals in the union's Action Programme adopted by the 1996 Congress.

A subsequent campaign by Sif in 1997, designed to recruit graduate engineers, saw the issue of employability as a central union concern. Here the union marketed itself as a career development facilitator – and to reinforce this message the project coined a new phrase to signify the identity of the union, that of 'career coach'. Accordingly, the perceived trend of greater individualization has been responded to by Sif nationally through the discursive construction of a number of different identities in recognition of its diverse membership profile. Such reconstruction, which is also aimed at shaping new organizational images to appeal to potential members and employers, includes the 'professional service organization', 'insurance company', 'coach' and 'pressure group'. Sif's diversity, and the diversity in norms resulting therefrom, is illustrated in Table 6.1, an adaption from an internal Sif document.

Workplace reality

To what extent, then, have the new discourses being constructed nationally been internalized by union actors at the three workplaces? The Heatplates plant studied here encompasses three production units on two sites. The units are characterized by customer-oriented flow production which is fully automated and involves a number of stages: selecting metal sheets, coating, washing, centring, pressing, quality control, assembly (following manufacture of heat exchange stands), testing and despatch. The labour process consists of semi-autonomous groups working on all stages of an integrated production flow with the exception of final distribution. Requisite individual and group competencies are a key determinant of plant efficiency. Significantly, a payments system has been negotiated by the Metall club that recognizes and rewards individual competence development. The development of the labour process has required job enlargement, job enrichment and learning. A leader of the club stated:

> It's good, I think, that we develop the work organization and the company takes account of people's competence and knowledge in

Table 6.1 SIF – diverse identities, diverse images, divergent norms (Source: adapted from SIF, 1998: 29)

Issue	Old conception		New conception	
	Traditional representation	Insurance company identity	Coach	Competent partner
Context	Collective values; existing structures to remain; change can be planned	Individuals mainly 'look after number one'; unions in a competitive environment	Changing nature of work: atomization, increasing individual initiative	Innovative companies with climate of participation
Aims	Represent and defend the individual	Act as safety net; being present when needed	Act in lieu of an HRM department; career and professional consultant	Membership of the management team; defend jobs and create negotiating space
Main task	Conduct negotiations; defend employment laws	Issue packages for different needs; provide a service	Act as missionary in the labour market; identify needs; counsel; give support	Look after business needs of firms, especially locally
Norm (relation to/view of members)	Part of the union, sharer of collectivist ideology	Service consumer, customer	Competent, demanding client	Committed member, knowledgeable co-worker
Norm (relation to/view of employers)	Bargaining adversary	Potential risk	'Lessor' of labour	Colleague, co-partner
Internal relations	Anchorage system	Service producing organization	Professional consultancy	Management support

another way [than previously]...I see this as mostly positive...we get to do work with more enriched content and more responsibility. It's become more rewarding to work now. (Interview, May 1998)

The Sif club at the plant had seen its membership decline as a result of the changes in the labour process. Although the club was positively disposed towards the policies and practice of the plant management towards compensation, there was considerable hostility towards individualism in general and the discursive shifts of Sif nationally in response to it. The notion of 'jobs for life' was no longer seen as relevant. People now, in the words of one of the leaders, had to learn continuously and:

go back to school three times during their professional lives...and it's a must both for the company to survive and be developed and move forwards. At the same time, if our members are to have secure jobs, they need to keep up with the merry-go-round of development that just spins faster and faster. (Interview, May 1998)

Competence development was seen by one of the leaders as:

not just a question of pressing for more training resources from the company and distributing them to the employees, but also a question of kicking our members up the backside so that they understand they must learn, they must develop. (Interview, May 1998)

In general, respondents from both unions embraced the desirability of learning in the context of semi-autonomous group working and saw it as an essential aspect of work in a competitive global manufacturer. On the other hand, there was evidence in both clubs of a continued adherence to collectivist ideologies and a particular degree of scepticism in the Sif club to the discursive reconstruction being undertaken by their union leadership in Stockholm.

The plant at Frontloader consists of two separate factories approximately a mile apart. The labour process is specifically designed for the specialized production of frontloaders in terms of both machines and layout. The company claims that 'sound production flow control' is at the heart of its philosophy and relies on its own manufacture as far as possible. All components, including hydraulic cylinders, are manufactured in one factory and the welding, assembly, painting and despatch in the second factory have been undertaken by a form of teamworking since

1990/91. The company in its presentational brochure in English states that the work of its employees in 'independent production groups allows for each individual to assume responsibility for his (sic) input into the process'. On the other hand, the union representatives stated that the groups had no responsibility for planning, purchasing, customer relations or problem solving. These tasks were carried out by production supervisors whose role was seen by the club leadership as increasing, despite the switch to groupworking. Apart from the cylinder line, the labour process in the first factory is characterized by specialized individual tasks with high-cycle times.

The leadership of the local union (Metall) were strongly in favour of greater competence development but saw this as being resisted by management. The union felt that there were no stimuli for change or development at the plant and that the company was only interested in higher production levels. One leader expressed the view that:

> Competence is a bigger concept than knowledge. The pressure for rationalization is real in our industry – we recognize this and want to be rewarded for contributing positively towards it through having the capacity to come up with new solutions. We want to drive the company forward. (Negotiation meeting, April 2000)

The plant management, however, saw learning differently. Whilst in favour of competence development, their view was that there had to be bottom-line advantages in terms of production gains for it to be justified. The following quote is illustrative:

> Where we've been in disagreement is assessing work performed. How do your proposals increase productivity? This isn't just a matter of learning. I accept that learning helps the breadth of capabilities, but it doesn't help on the issue of 'how much'. (Negotiation meeting, April 2000)

Although an espoused theory of learning was at times discernible in the utterances of the plant management, the actual theory in use was that of a bottom-line, productionist view, that is, Taylorism. The competencies required in the groups were far less than, say, at Heatplates; moreover, management strongly defended specialization, even within the groups.

Drugco, a global pharmaceuticals multinational, has a Swedish subsidiary where around 7000 staff are employed in marketing, production and R & D facilities. The firm has a central business concept of being 'first for innovation and value', seeing the latter from a diverse stakeholder perspective. The centrality of research in the business renders it a definitive knowledge-based firm having strategic partnerships with academics and commercial partners. The largest union is Sif and the centrality of the R&D function is such that much of the work undertaken by white-collar employees can be termed knowledge work. The production activities undertaken by the blue-collar workforce are located at six separate units in which the labour process is largely based on teams working on machine-controlled production lines. Compared with Heatplates, however, the work organization was less developed; for example production supervisors remained in charge of planning. The chair of the IF club described the blue-collar labour process as follows:

> We have a lot of routines that have to be carried out and it's awfully conservative the way we work here... We have to make some changes so that the employees get more into their work... Most of the factories are production lines. The machines control all the production – there are quality aspects and you have to dress up in a certain way and follow all your protocols and it's awfully strict – you're not allowed to do this and you're not allowed to do that – it's rigid in a way. (Interview, September 2001)

And:

> We have [as a company] been growing too fast and the easy way to expand as a company is to do it the Tayloristic way – but it's not good. (Interview, September 2001)

Ordering was undertaken in some of the teams, but in others this remained a management task. But overall the club leadership was of the view that more responsibility could and should be granted to the teams. This required a greater focus on individual competencies, not just on the immediate skills required in the labour process, but also strategic thinking related to the future of the business.

On the white-collar side, however, individual knowledge was a key site of added value for the company. This was recognized by both the Sif club and management and the consensus on its importance was such that it was not a contentious issue. The Sif club chair explained matters thus:

> Drugco is a very knowledge intensive firm and training is not especially difficult to obtain. If one can motivate a need to attend courses it's

rare that the answer [from management] is 'no'. I have never heard it talked about as a union issue to take up. It's never been a really hot potato. (Interview, May, 2001)

As to individualization, it is noteworthy that Drugco introduced a new rewards system in 1999 that included bonus payments for all employees at the individual level. This is partly based on assessments of individual performances in relation to expectations and individual salary discussions between line managers and individual employees. The significance of individualization is greater on the white-collar side in that there is no basic (collective) element in the agreement allowing for uprating in line with cost of living increases. Clearly, then, the discourse of the competent individual has been most clearly internalized among the local white-collar representatives at Drugco.

Discussion

The diversity of learning

Overall, competence development is seen in discourses of union renewal to be of central importance for individuals to enjoy greater job security and better prospects of progressive development on the job both in terms of wages and in terms of job content. Collectivist aspirations as expressed in the 'solidaristic wages' policy remain, but the well being of members individually is seen as needing to be buttressed by personalized competence development. Although envisaged as being voluntary, this is nevertheless to be encouraged by the unions. The desirability of competence development is being linked to the question of company competitiveness, and arguments are thus being developed for companies to take on competence development as an integral part of their strategic HRM. It is also accepted that in the exposed sectors, in the context of international competition, both employers and employees increasingly had many areas of common interest in training, competence development and flexible specialization of work tasks. As stated in an interview with one national Metall official:

We wanted this flexibility to be on our terms, that it would strengthen the metalworker at the workplace. So the strategy became one of strengthening the metalworker at the workplace through [acquiring] wider knowledge and that this was also self-evidently rational for companies. (Interview, November 1997)

Although union policies have not evolved in a perceived context of increasingly scattered work practices, they can nevertheless be seen as at least partially resonant with the post-industrial discourse of the 'competent individual'.

The data presented here suggest that the desirability of individual learning is widespread at the workplace. The point should be made, however, that actors, when talking about 'learning' are talking about three different things. First, there is uniform agreement on the need for training to perform routine tasks in the production process, often involving technology. This is generally learning of a single-loop nature. However, even F. W. Taylor (1911/1947) acknowledged the need for each 'workman' to be studied by management:

> with a view to finding out his [sic] limitations on the one hand, but even more important, his possibilities of development on the other hand; and then, as deliberately and systematically to train and help teach this workman. (quoted in Pugh, 1971: 126)

This being so, individual learning equated with training in this way can hardly be said to constitute a new discursive formation – it is a feature of the discourse of Taylorism. Such learning was clearly a feature of the labour process at Frontloader and of the blue-collar labour process at Drugco. At Heatplates, however, learning was understood in more reflective terms (Schön, 1983) involving individuals in experimentation and innovation in the context of extended teamworking (Hague *et al.*, 2003). Here, blue-collar staff in the teams are involved in all activities in continuous flow production, including customer contact but excluding distribution. The company's policy is that its workplaces '...should flow with ideas and thoughts. Such openness lays the basis for flexibility and new thinking from all the company's co-workers'. This suggests learning of a more double-loop nature through an involvement of production workers in the value-adding activities of the firm both in the marketplace and the labour process as well as reflection on the latter from insights derived in the former.

However, while both types of learning here clearly entail a role for competent individuals, they are not the same as the third type of learning referred to in the 'competent individual' discourse. This is that of the cumulative learning of the individual over the life cycle without any direct connection with any employer or set of duties. This type of learning emphasizes employability and is associated with knowledge work. Such work is typified by the R&D activities that are a central site of added value at Drugco. However, at Drugco, the blue-collar labour process is relatively undeveloped: although it is a knowledge intensive firm relying on research and development staff with high degrees of knowledge, it is far from the case that all work in the firm is knowledge work.

The limits of knowledge work

It is thus mistaken to describe work in the companies studied here as 'knowledge work'; as in the blue-collar labour process at Drugco, the form of teamworking at Frontloader merely involves multi-skilling and job enlargement on an assembly line. Under this low road approach, functional flexibility is achieved through job rotation – and union attempts to bring more knowledgeability into the work organization have been resisted by management (Huzzard, 2001). Such resistance may have a sound logic from a shareholder value perspective – if entry barriers remain robust then low road, cost leadership strategies make good business sense and there is little immediate requirement for costly experimentation and the innovation supplied by knowledge workers. In such situations there are dangers to firms in unnecessarily boosting employability – to do so could well make it easier for employees to leave the business for betterment elsewhere.

The data here suggest some difference between the meaning of the 'competent individual' between blue-and white-collar workers, or to be more precise between knowledge workers and non-knowledge workers. Whilst a discourse emphasizing lifelong learning and employability may resonate with the workplace experience of the former, it is more difficult to see that it accurately depicts the situation faced by the latter. As argued by researchers elsewhere, while it may be the case that manu-facturing employment is on the decline, it does not follow that workers in production processes are being replaced by knowledge workers (Thompson *et al.*, 2000). Knowledge workers, also termed 'symbolic analysts' (Reich, 1991), remain a minority of the workforce: the most noteworthy trend, rather, is the growth of services and retail workers in Tayloristic labour processes (Thompson *et al.*, 2000).

A changing role for the unions?

There is also clear evidence that the new discourses being constructed by the unions are leading to changes in the forms of joint regulation of the labour market: changing union agendas and an increased human resource focus on learning and knowledge have altered the backdrop against which industrial relations processes are being played out (Huzzard and Nilsson, 2002). A series of agreements were introduced in various sectors in the 1990s where both unions and employers sought a more co-operative relationship. Typical of this was the Industry Agreement, signed in 1997, that sought to introduce mechanisms for more coherent dialogue on pay bargaining in the context of the competitiveness of Swedish industry. This included joint discussion on issues such as training and can be seen as an attempt by both sides at creating clearer, agreed linkages than hitherto between distributional and developmental issues at the sector level. Increasingly, the unions have seen the need to build their arguments in partnership arenas around a sound business case on the need for the positive development of human resources. Competence development has become a central union issue and in some cases this has resulted in individualized elements in blue-collar payments systems at the sector and local levels.

However, competence development and job redesign are not new issues for the unions: these matters first surfaced as being central to union agendas in the 1980s. Yet there is evidence that certain assumptions made at that time are no longer appropriate. For example, it was believed that Swedish firms operated in relatively static markets and that employment patterns would accordingly be reasonably stable. This was thought to provide a promising backdrop for the progressive implementation of 'Good Work'. But as we enter the new millennium, restructuring and redundancies have arguably become the norm rather than the exception, and in many respects the solidaristic development of workplaces has stalled. 'Good Work' and its equivalents have been conceptualized on static assumptions that do not take into account the nature of contemporary business dynamics. Unions such as Metall are accordingly promoting learning and employability as key issues because 'Good Work' has turned out to offer no guarantees of job security.

Conclusions: union discourses of continuity and change

The evidence at the workplace thus indicates that there is some divergence between the discursive ideal being articulated nationally and the everyday reality locally. For both Metall and the IF the meaning of solidarity was extended in the early 1990s to encompass the equal right to skills upgrading, multi-skilling and solidaristic team working as integral aspects of 'Good Work'. However, although the near-iconic status of the 'solidarity' signifier has remained centre stage in the new strategies, this has now taken on meaning in the context of rights to (individual) development as well as rights to (collective) inclusion within fair rewards. In other words the policy implies an ideological shift to include equality of opportunity as well as equality of outcomes.

As to Sif, a perceived increase in the significance of organizational knowledge has been seen as an opportunity to develop employees as a developmental resource within the firm rather than a cost, an idea which has required the union to promote individual competence development as a strategic issue. This foregrounding of the individual member in Sif has also been evident in the discursive reconstruction of the union's identity and image around the 'coach' metaphor that sees a new role for the union as an individual career development facilitator (Huzzard, 2000). Clearly both identity and image are of significance here – the former as a means of constructing subjectivities of existing members and the latter as a means of constructing subjectivities of potential members and employers in the context of social partnership.

The discourse of individualization clearly threatens the traditional collectivist ideologies that have historically been a foundation for union organizing (Allvin and Sverke, 2000). In response, unions have sought discursive forms that accommodate the changes constructed as being afoot and are thereby partially colluding in their discursive reproduction. Yet the unions' role is ambivalent: they appear to be both recipient and promulgator of the new discursive formation yet are simultaneously constructing discourses both of change *and continuity*. Unions, therefore, are colluding in the construction of learning discourse, but this is less clear-cut in the case of individualization. Despite the new discourse, collective union support remains a prerequisite of individual protection and development at work. Accordingly, there is some enduring attachment to *collectivist means* evident in the discourses of the unions studied here. Complicity in discursive forms centring on the notion of employability and lifelong learning are clearer in Sif than its blue-collar counterparts, yet all three unions are seeking to make a link between various forms of personal development through learning and their respective distributional agendas aimed at pursuing *individual ends*.

Whilst there have certainly been recent changes in the labour process, I remain to be convinced that such developments amount to a historical rupture of any significance. Contemporary macro and micro economies are characterized by both change and continuity. Such a state of affairs has always prevailed, thus claims to a 'paradigm shift' are decidedly tenuous (Smith and Thompson, 1998). Some elements of 'knowledge' have always existed in the labour process; it can be plausibly argued, too, that the betterment of the individual (in the context of the unequal employment relationship) has always been a traditional union objective. Moreover, although blue-collar unions have often had a collectivist, socialist ideology as an espoused theory, the theories in use of their day-to-day activities have historically had little connection with such an ideology (cf. Allvin and Sverke, 2000). Normatively, given the co-existence of both continuity and change, unions would thus appear to be well advised to take heed of the views of a respondent from the Sif Negotiating Department:

> Both traditionalism and renewal are needed. We need to preserve the traditionalists and strengthen the new. (Interview, September 1998)

Texts containing statements such as '... we now own the major assets of society – our own minds. And power equals freedom. We are all potentially free to know, go, do and be whoever we want to be' (Nordström and Ridderstråle, 2000: 35), may construct a world that serves certain commercial interests. But it is profoundly premature to claim that such views accurately represent the everyday reality of Swedish workplaces. The incidence of the empowered, knowledgeable individual, free to sell his or her scarce labour to Swedish employers on his or her terms, is by no means pervasive. For this reason the institutionalization of the competent individual within the discourse of Swedish unions remains far from complete. But change is afoot: the discourse of the competent individual is increasingly being linked to discussions in the unions on employability and individual learning accounts rather than discussions on solidaristic workplace development. But will this new emphasis inevitably mean the abandonment of 'Good Work'? Time will tell.

Notes

1. This debate and its metatheoretical underpinnings will not be entered into here.
2. Indeed, this was a central premise on which Braverman (1974) based *Labor and Monopoly Capital*.
3. This is not to say, however, that such a view has universal acceptance. Some working life researchers, for example, have argued for workplace reform along alternative lines by developing a discourse of sustainable work systems (see for example Docherty *et al.*, 2002).
4. All extracts in the chapter from union texts and interview transcripts are the author's translation from Swedish.

References

Allvin, Michael. 1997. *Det individualiserade arbetet: Om modernitetens skilda praktiker.* Eslöv: Symposium.

Allvin, Michael and Magnus Sverke. 2000. 'Do new generations imply the end of solidarity? Swedish unionism in the era of individualization'. *Economic and Industrial Democracy* 21(1): 71–95.

Alvesson, Mats and Dan Kärreman. 2000. 'Varieties of discourse: on the study of organizations through discourse analysis'. *Human Relations* 53(9): 1125–49.

Amin, Ash, (ed.). 1994. *Post-Fordism: A Reader.* Oxford: Blackwell.

Arvidsson, Håkan, Lennart Berntson and Lars Dencik. 1994. *Modernisering och välfärd – om stat, individ och civilt samhälle i Sverige.* Gothenburg: City University Press.

Atkinson, Robert D. and Randolph D. Court. 1998. *The New Economy Index.* Washington: Progressive Policy Institute.

Barley, Stephen. 1996. *The New World of Work.* London: British–North America Committee.

Bell, Daniel. 1973. *The Coming of Post-Industrial Society: A Venture in Social Forecasting.* New York: Basic Books.

Blackler, Frank. 1995. 'Knowledge, knowledge work and organizations: an overview and interpretation'. *Organization Studies* 16(5): 1021–46.

Boglind, Anders. 1997. 'Facket och de magra åren'. In *Ledning för alla? Om perspektivbrytningar i företagsledning,* (3rd edn), edited by Å. Sandberg. Stockholm: SNS, 107–26.

Braverman, Harry. 1974. *Labor and Monopoly Capital: The Degradation of Work in the Twentieth Century.* New York: Monthly Review Press.

Bruhn, Anders. 1999. *Individualiseringen och det fackliga kollektivet.* Örebro University: Department of Social Science (Doctoral Dissertation).

Burton-Jones, Alan. 2001. *Knowledge Capitalism: Business, Work and Learning in the New Economy.* Oxford: Oxford University Press.

Callinicos, Alex. 1989. *Against Postmodernism: A Marxist Critique.* Cambridge: Polity.

Docherty, Peter, Jan Forslin and Rami Shani, (eds). 2002. *Creating Sustainable Work Systems.* London: Routledge.

Drucker, Peter. 1993. *Post-Capitalist Society.* Oxford: Butterworth Heinemann.

Giddens, Anthony. 1991. *Modernity and Self-Identity: Self and Society in the Late Modern Age.* Cambridge: Polity Press.

Hague, Jeremy, Friso den Hertog, Tony Huzzard and Peter Totterdill. 2003. *The Convergence of QWL and Competitiveness in Europe.* Report for the EU Commission (EU Innoflex Project).

Handy, Charles. 1996. *Beyond Certainty.* London: Arrow.

Harvey, David. 1989. *The Condition of Postmodernity.* Oxford: Basil Blackwell.

Heckscher, Charles C. and Anne Donnellon (eds). 1994. *The Post-Bureaucratic Organization.* Thousand Oaks, Ca: Sage.

Huzzard, Tony. 2000. *Labouring to Learn: Union Renewal in Swedish Manufacturing.* Umeå: Boréa.

Huzzard, Tony. 2001. 'Discourse for normalizing what? The learning organization and the workplace trade union response'. *Economic and Industrial Democracy* 22(3): 407–31.

Huzzard, Tony and Tommy Nilsson. 2002. 'Social partnership at the contemporary Swedish workplace'. Paper presented at the 20th International Labour Process Conference, Strathclyde Business School, Glasgow, 2–4 April.

Industrifacket. 2001. Internet www.industrifacket.se/10.9.01.

Inglehart, Ronald. 1990. Culture Shift in Advanced Industrial Society. Princeton, NJ: Princeton University Press.

Inglehart, Ronald. 1997. Modernization and Postmodernization: Culture, Economic and Political Change in 43 Societies. Princeton, NJ: Princeton University Press.

Kelly, Kevin. 1999. Den nya ekonomin. Stockholm: Timbro.

Krugman, Paul. 1997. 'How fast can the US economy grow?'. Harvard Business Review July/August: 123–32.

Lindgren, Monica and Nils Wåhlin. 2001. 'Identity construction among boundary crossing individuals'. Scandinavian Journal of Management 17: 357–77.

Metall. 1989. Solidarisk arbetspolitik för det goda arbetet. Stockholm: Metall.

Metall. 2000. Internet www.metall.se/23.11.01.

Nordström, Kjell A. and Jonas Ridderstråle. 2000. Funky Business. Harlow: Pearson Education.

Pfeffer, Jeffrey. 1994. Competitive Advantage Through People. Boston: Harvard Business School Press.

Prichard Craig, Richard Hull, Mike Chumer and Hugh Willmott (eds). 2000. Managing Knowledge: Critical Investigations of Work and Learning. Basingstoke: Macmillan – now Palgrave Macmillan.

Pugh, Derek S. 1971. Organization Theory. Harmondsworth: Penguin.

Reich, Robert B. 1991. The Work of Nations: Capitalism in the 21st Century. New York: A. A. Knopf.

Schön, Donald. 1983. The Reflective Practitioner: How Professionals Think in Action. New York: Basic Books.

Senge, Peter. 1990. The Fifth Discipline: The Art and Practice of the Learning Organization. New York: Doubleday.

Sif. 1987. Handlingsprogram för kongressperioden 1988–1990. Stockholm: Sif.

Sif. 1990a. Handlingsprogram för kongressperioden 1991–1993. Stockholm: Sif.

Sif. 1990b. SIF på 90-talet. Stockholm: Sif.

Sif. 1993a. Nine Starting Points for Competence Development. Stockholm: Sif.

Sif. 1993b. Handlingsprogram för kongressperioden 1993–1997. Stockholm: Sif.

Sif. 2000. Internet www.sif.se/23.11.01.

Smith, Chris and Paul Thompson. 1998. 'Re-evaluating the labour process debate'. Economic and Industrial Democracy 19(4): 551–77.

Taylor, Frederick W. 1911/1947. Principles of Scientific Management. Harper and Row: New York.

Thompson, Paul. 1993. 'Postmodernism: fatal distraction'. In Postmodernism and Organizations, edited by J. Hassard and M. Parker. London: Sage, 183–203.

Thompson, Paul, Chris Warhurst, and George Callaghan. 2000. 'Human capital or capitalizing on humanity? Knowledge, skills and competencies in interactive service work'. In Managing Knowledge: Critical Investigations of Work and Learning, edited by C. Prichard, R. Hull, M. Chumer and H. Willmott. Basingstoke: Macmillan – now Palgrave Macmillan, 122–40.

Warhurst, Chris and Paul Thompson. 1998. 'Shadowland: the real story of knowledge work and knowledge workers'. Paper Presented at the 16th International Labour Process Conference, UMIST, April.

Webster, Graham. 2002. 'Corporate knowledge/Contestable spaces/Funky business'. Working Paper No 1, American Studies Project. Skellefteå: Skeria Utveckling.

Zuboff, Shoshana. 1988. *In the Age of the Smart Machine: The Future of Work and Power*. New York: Basic Books.

Interviews

Club committee members, Swedish Metalworkers Union, Alfa Laval Thermal, Lund 1998.

Club committee members, Sif, Alfa Laval Thermal, Lund 1998.

Club committee members, Swedish Industrial Workers Union, Astra Zeneca, Södertälje, 2001.

Club committee members, Sif, Astra Zeneca, Södertälje, 2001.

National official, Swedish Metalworkers Union, Stockholm, 1997.

National official, Sif, Stockholm, 1998.

7

'Do it Yourself': Making Up the Self-Employed Individual in the Swedish Public Employment Service

Renita Thedvall

For many commentators this is the era of the entrepreneur. After years of neglect, those who start and manage their own businesses are viewed as popular heroes. They are seen as risk-takers and innovators who reject the relative security of employment in large organizations to create wealth and accumulate capital. Indeed, according to many, the economic recovery of the European economies is largely dependent upon their efforts. (Scase and Goffee, 1987: 1)

Introduction: entrepreneurship in vogue

Swedish labour market policy has traditionally focused on helping people to get a full-time permanent position. During the last two decades, however, policy has gradually been opened up to different forms of employment. New forms of employment such as fixed-term work and temporary work are becoming political tools to lower unemployment and infuse dynamism into the labour market. In this context more attention has been drawn to self-employment as a way to increase employment and growth in industry. Self-employed individuals are depicted in the media as 'heroes' of a transformed economy. Both left- and right-wing parties in Sweden are now putting the importance of the small business owner at the top of the agenda and the Public Employment Service (PES) organizes projects and courses for the unemployed to learn how to become self-employed. This is an ideological shift in traditional Swedish labour market policy.

This chapter discusses how the PES has shifted from mediating primarily full-time permanent positions to also promoting self-employment. Focus is placed on how the PES is constructing the self-employed through a Self-Employment Project – Work Experience Scheme (in Swedish: starta eget projekt arbetslivsutveckling (ALU).[1] The PES teaches individuals to feel confident in being entrepreneurs in the labour market. They are taught to prepare themselves for their new career in self-employment, to appreciate themselves and their competencies, to be self-reliant and confident. Case material is provided by participant observation at a Self-Employment Project and interviews both with unemployed participants in the Project and with administrative staff at the PES.

On a more general level the chapter discusses how the ideological shift in Swedish labour market policy is connected to changes in the view on the individual. Responsibility for employment has gradually shifted from the state to the individual. This shift may be described as moving from the right to employment to the 'duty' to be employable. This means that individuals are taught to perceive themselves as agents of change, or as imbued with agency. It involves a gradual transformation of identity and consciousness by which individuals learn to view themselves as capable of 'doing it themselves'; of creating jobs for themselves by being entrepreneurial self-employers.

The idea of the 'entrepreneur' has become more and more influential at the turn of the millennium both in Sweden and the rest of Europe. One of the four pillars of the European Employment Strategy is devoted to entrepreneurship. The word 'entrepreneur' originates from French and came to have the meaning 'undertaker'. It was the entrepreneur who handled the risks attached to organizing labour, material and machines (Landström, 2000). In the eighteenth century Richard Cantillon, François Quesnay and Nicholas Badeau all contributed to the definition of the concept by stressing the risk-taking and innovative aspect (Landström, 2000). In the nineteenth century Jean Baptiste Say added the meaning 'catalyst' to the definition (Landström, 2000). In English the word entrepreneur originally had the meaning 'to be a manager of a musical institution' (Gough, 1969). British theorists such as Adam Smith did not make a distinction between the 'capitalist' and the 'entrepreneur' (Swedberg, 1994). It was not until the twentieth century that the word became associated with something other than entertainment, such as the undertaking of enterprises (Gough, 1969).

Of later years the word entrepreneur has become more associated with certain personal characteristics, than with a function in the economic system. Schumpeter stressed the innovative side of the individual who acts as an entrepreneur (Swedberg, 1994). During the last two decades there have been continuous attempts to define the terms 'entrepreneur' and 'entrepreneurship'. The entrepreneur has been associated with risk-taking, creativity, innovation, hard work, flexibility, creating wealth, independence, and decisiveness (Davidsson, 1989; Johannisson, 1996; Hjorth and Johannisson, 1997; Granfelt and Hjort af Ornäs, 1999). The entrepreneur, as described in the written material at the Self-Employment Project, is an individual with visionary abilities, who is curious, future oriented, and self-confident. He or she is focused on possibilities, not problems, dares to break traditions and rules, and thinks in unorthodox ways. Miller and Rose critically discuss this ideational shift in terms of the 'enterprising self'. The enterprising self is creative, autonomous and her or his own agent (Miller and Rose, 1995). The idea of the enterprising self very much resembles the idea of the entrepreneur. The concept blurs the boundaries of the employee and the self-employed. The entrepreneur becomes the model both for the employee and the self-employed. Individuals have the responsibility to make themselves 'employable' or 'self-employable'.

These ideas of the entrepreneurial, employable individual spring out of a neo-liberal political discourse. Rose and Miller, with inspiration from Foucault, discuss them in terms of *political rationalities* and *governmental technologies*. Political rationalities are the changing discursive fields in which problems of government are formulated (Rose and Miller, 1992). Political rationalities are expressed through different governmental technologies, that is, programmes, documents, statistics, calculations, what Foucault (1991) defined as *governmentality*. The political rationality of neo-liberalism in the 1980s and 1990s has influenced and changed the ideas of government and the view of the individual. It has also had practical consequences in how labour market policy is formulated. Moreover, it has opened up more flexible types of employment as well as the idea of the self-employed or small business owner as the answer to all prayers. This is particularly evident in the political direction of the PES in Sweden. The PES has by tradition been an ideological instrument in the service of the wage-earner. During the 1980s something changed, however. In 1984 the 'self-employment grant' was introduced and the PES thereby became a party in the process of creating new potential employers.

When the PES began to educate the unemployed in how to be and think as self-employers, it became connected to 'new' ideas on how individual identity and change should be created. Martin (1997) argues that there has been a shift in the view of the individual and how change is perceived in individuals. The 'truth' of the individual resides '... neither in the subject, made up of inner memory, childhood, a single history, nor will it be made up of Marxism's forces that bear down on subjects from outside' (Martin, 1997: 245). The individual is viewed as being 'constructed' in her or his engagement with the environment. Martin (1997) proposes the idea of an *interface zone*. The interface zone is a space where the possibilities and capacities of individuals are endless, since the surrounding environment changes in different contexts. 'Individuals come to consist of potentials to be realised and capacities to be fulfilled' (Martin, 1997: 247). This perspective influences the way individuals view themselves. It makes it possible for individuals to see themselves as a project to be constructed by themselves. It is connected to the neo-liberal idea of the independent individual taking responsibility for her or his future. Individuals become their own agents and, in some sense, their own creators.

The idea of the individual as a potential to be realized also makes the individual a potential object of management. The idea of managing individuals is nothing new, but there are new ways of managing. It is in the meeting between the individual and the environment, the interface zone, that a potential to manage individuals emerges (Martin, 1997). This stands in contrast to what Martin calls an *edge*. She elaborates on Goffman's idea that '...all management takes place inside, and the finished product is shown on the person's outside surface' (Martin, 1997: 249). Martin, in line with Donzelot, describes the new individual as '...always changing, scanning the environment, and dealing with all aspects of the interface with the outside in creative and innovative ways' (Martin, 1997: 252). As Rose and Miller argue, power is not a question of the state building walls or the creation of prohibitions, but of 'constructing' citizens who can handle a kind of regulated freedom (1992). The idea is that individuals should be managed to become self-managed individuals.

In a society where entrepreneurial skills become more important and are sought after, ideas regarding what constitutes the 'normal' or 'good' individual change. The individuals who take part in the Self-Employment Project are being managed into becoming self-employed entrepreneurs. The PES is trying to 'make up' the self-employed. In Hacking's (1986) view the *making up of people* involves categories that need to be filled with content. Once a category is filled with content it is possible for individuals to identify themselves with the category. The category is not clear-cut, however, but continuously negotiated (Martin, 1997). This dynamic becomes evident in the Self-Employment Project. The participants believe that they can become self-employed, in the sense that 'it is only a question of changing identity'. At the same time there is a belief that to be self-employed is to be born with the right personality.

This is expressed both in the views of participants and by the Project Manager (in the Self-Employment Project). The idea of the individual being born with the right personality, of a self that is inside and expressed on the outside, is confronted with ideas of the individual as her or his own agent.

Before going further into how this is done I now turn to the ideological shift in Swedish labour market policy. This change can be studied through the policy shifts in the PES.

The Public Employment Service: part of the supportive stratum

The history of the PES in Sweden is usually divided into two time periods. In 1902–40 the municipalities were responsible for the organization of the PES. From 1940 until today the PES has been organized by the state, even if the municipalities have gained more responsibility during the second half of the 1990s (Wadensjö, 1998). The PES then became a tool, a governmental technology, for the state. The state uses the PES as a channel for cultural engineering, influencing the construction of citizens (Hannerz, 1992). The state thus is introduced as a third party between the employee and the employer (Rose and Miller, 1992), and is connected to the political rationality of welfarism (Rose and Miller, 1992).

Swedish modern active labour market policy was mainly formulated during the 1950s and 1960s (Trygged, 1996; Johansson, 1998; Unell, 1999). Prior to that period labour market policy upheld the idea of keeping people active, but more in terms of their duty to work. During the nineteenth century it was regarded as immoral and sinful, even illegal, not to work. It was not until 1914 that unemployment was perceived as a social problem for the first time. Relief work was provided for the unemployed, but the underlying principle was still that it was immoral not to work (Trygged, 1996). In the late 1940s and especially during the 1950s and 1960s the idea of the 'activation principle' was transformed into the responsibility of the social state (Trygged, 1996; Johansson, 1998). The PES became a central tool for realizing labour market politics (SOU, 1990: 31). During this period unemployment benefits and social security also became more and more tightly connected to income. Benefits were paid in proportion to prior income (Trygged, 1996). The PES became part of what Lyttkens labels *the supportive stratum* (1985, 1989). The supportive stratum: the PES, the Social Insurance Office, the school, the hospitals, and the prisons helped individuals to become employable through education, training and nursing. Those who could not work also needed to be controlled and monitored. The salaried employee constituted the norm. Those who were not included in the norm were, according to Lyttkens, in 'social quarantine'. The supportive stratum was thus the authorities helping and controlling individuals in 'social quarantine' (Lyttkens, 1985). The self-employed were partly outside this regulatory system since they were neither part of the norm of the salaried employee nor helped and controlled by the supportive stratum (Lyttkens, 1985).

In the 1980s there was an ideological shift in Swedish labour market policy and the tasks of the PES. In 1984 the PES began to administer the 'self-employment grant',[2] which meant that the unemployed could obtain a grant, equivalent to their unemployment benefit, to start their own company (SFS, 1984: 523). The ideological shift was not deep-rooted, though. In the same year, the Swedish government started five collective wage-earner funds that were financed by excess company profits and a system of employees' contributions (Johannisson, 1987). The idea of the 'self-employment grant' was a response to new ideas where small businesses were seen as the driving force of economic recovery in Europe. During the 1960s and 1970s small entrepreneurial businesses were normally seen as inefficient and unproductive, but in the 1980s this view slowly changed (Scase and Goffee, 1987).

It was not until the 1990s, though, that self-employment grants became, in any real sense, part of Swedish labour market politics. At the beginning of the 1990s, Sweden was hit by an economic down-turn and unemployment rose to 10 per cent. The government sought to keep people active in different labour market programmes. One of the programmes was the 'self-employment grant'. In 1992 the self-employment grant became part of the 'work experience schemes' programmes. An unemployed worker, or someone at risk of becoming unemployed, could take part in a Self-Employment Project where the PES educated individuals in how to become self-employed. In 1993[3] the Self-Employment Project gained the same priority as any other work experience scheme[4] (Okeke, 1999). There was a time limit of 1 January 1998 imposed on the work experience schemes (SFS, 1992: 1333). In 1998 new programmes were introduced called 'active labour market policy measures' which included self-employment grants and self-employment courses. Their regulations were the same as those of the work experience schemes. The individual had to be unemployed, or at risk of becoming unemployed, to become eligible for the grant and/or the course (SFS, 1998: 1784). In 2000 the possibility of obtaining self-employment grants was expanded to people in employment as well (SFS, 2000: 634). The argument was that the unemployed were not alone in being suited to self-employment. The idea of the importance of having 'entrepreneurs' and 'entrepreneurship' had exceeded the idea of the self-employment grant being an active measure for the unemployed. This new emphasis is also connected to the idea that individuals are, at the core, entrepreneurial. Hence, their entrepreneurial identity would in this way be developed.

I discuss below how these ideas of the new entrepreneurial individual are expressed in a Self-Employment Project at the PES. I describe how a small business owner and entrepreneur is constructed at the PES. The empirical material is based on participant observation at a Self-Employment Project in autumn 1996 in Stockholm. When the Project was coming to an end I interviewed six of 16 participants who belonged to the group of ten individuals who had been present at almost every meeting. The Project lasted two months and we met every Tuesday for a half or full day at a Public Employment Office in Stockholm.

A self-employment project at a public employment office

The first day

There were 16 participants in the room when I entered. They were in discussions with each other while we waited for the Deputy Director of the Public Employment Office and the Project Manager of the Self-Employment Project. Most of them were women (12) and between 40 and 50 years old. When I became acquainted with them, I learned that several of them had an academic degree, and more than half of them had worked in the public sector or in large-scale corporations. Almost half of them wanted to become consultants in the area where they had worked before. Several of them wanted to sell products, through their own shop or otherwise, and some wanted to start service companies.

When the Deputy Director and the Project Manager entered the room the conversations stopped and the attention was turned to the Deputy Director, who opened the course by describing the purpose of a Self-Employment Project. She stressed that people often want to start their companies too soon. It is important to prepare oneself thoroughly. A Self-Employment Project makes it possible to evaluate a business concept properly. She also pointed out that while participating in the Project the participants did not have to look actively for work in order to get their unemployment benefit.

The Project Manager continued to explain what they were going to discuss during the next two months. The participants began to ask questions about financing. The Project Manager underlined that the best way is to have money of one's own or borrow from friends and family. The last resort is the bank. My understanding was that the participants expected that they would get help with financing from the PES. During the break, one of the women revealed that she thought the self-employment grant was a form of financing that one disposed of as one liked. Several heads nodded. Four of the participants also almost immediately dropped out of the Project after the first day.

The Project Manager said that he would discuss the issue of financing later on and then distributed a paper with the heading 'Our Roles in the Project'. He saw himself as a leader and a coach. He was the coordinator, the stimulator, and the critic. The participants needed to be creative and self-reliant. Most of the participants had not thought of becoming a business owner until they became unemployed. The Project Manager needed to support and motivate the participants to see themselves as 'entrepreneurs'. The participants were interested in a life of self-employment, but they had problems identifying with the personal characteristics and the way of thinking they associated with a business owner. We will now follow how the Project Manager used different techniques to socialize the participants into thinking and acting as a self-employed entrepreneur.

What was mediated in the project?

Certain personal characteristics and certain aspects of knowledge were both portrayed in the Project as important in making up a self-employed person. A self-employed individual is: prepared, wants to make money, is self-reliant and self-assured. The self-employed may differ in terms of personality, but there are certain personal qualities, such as being an 'entrepreneur', that are more suited than others in order to be a 'good' self-employed person. As discussed above, the concept of the entrepreneur is defined as someone who is innovative, decisive, responsible, risk taking, welcomes change, is a creator of wealth, and hardworking. This was also the definition used in the Project. The techniques used by the Project Manager to motivate and support the participants to become self-employed entrepreneurs were a personality test, pedagogical techniques such as asking the participants to suggest and think for themselves and then tell them how they should think, and articles from magazines addressed to business owners to help support his argument.

The personality test

The Project Manager carried out a personality test with the group. The test was designed by the Swedish Industrial Development Fund to be used in self-employment courses (Gyllenstierna, 1993). The test portrays seven different personality types that are connected to the idea of a self-employed person: the 'entrepreneur', the 'worker bee', the 'administrator', the 'economist', the 'risk taker', the 'salesperson', and the 'networker'. The 'entrepreneur' is, on the positive side, a starter: creative, enthusiastic and energetic, but on the negative side interested in everything and never finishes projects. The 'worker bee' is a hard worker and never gives up. He or she is persistent and productive. The 'administrator' is, on the positive side, methodical, orderly and is able to keep several projects going at the same time. On the negative side he or she is a perfectionist that never reaches her or his goal. The 'administrator' is good at formulating plans, but has difficulties realizing them. The 'economist' is careful and economical. He or she has an understanding for numbers and does not like to take uncalculated risks. Being economical on the border to thrifty may result in the 'economist' not taking any risks. The 'risk taker' is, contrary to the 'economist', willing to take risks, but might take inordinate risks. The 'salesperson' has the ability to reach people, to persuade, is a good listener, and is a person who likes to compete. The 'networker' has a good existing network, has the ability to develop it and enjoys doing it. On the negative side the 'networker' might just talk and never get anything done. The personality types that are preferable in making up a 'good' successful self-employed person are the 'entrepreneur', the 'worker bee', the 'salesperson', and the 'networker'. The 'worker bee', the 'salesperson', and the 'networker' all share characteristics associated with the definition of the 'entrepreneur', as discussed above.

The test consists of 41 questions on a scale from 1 to 5 where the participants answer if a statement fits well or not, with her or his view of the self. The questions are meant to capture what it means to be an 'entrepreneur'. Some of the statements are: 'It is important to keep regular hours so that the body gets to rest'; 'I have several relatives who are self-employed'; 'I hardly ever pay my bills on time'; 'No one would call me stubborn'; 'I have always liked to sell things'; 'I like both theatre and literature'. It is easy to understand that it is 'good' not to care about keeping regular hours, to have relatives that are self-employed, be stubborn, like to sell things, be self-assured enough to enjoy making speeches, and curious enough to like both theatre and literature. It fits the idea of the entrepreneur as hard working, self-assured, curious, and a creator of wealth.

The answers are analysed and the participants get to know if their selves have 'little', 'moderate' or 'much' of the different personality types. Only one person in the Project had 'much' under the heading 'entrepreneur'. All of the participants were more or less 'worker bees', but few of them were 'salespersons' and about half of them were networkers'. There was only one 'risk taker' in the group, but she left the Project because she did not have enough capital to start her business. Most of the people in the group were 'administrators' and 'economists'. According to the test and the Project Manager it is good to be an 'administrator' and 'economist', but it is not necessary. These qualities and competences may easily be obtained from someone else. They are not entrepreneurial qualities.

According to the test most of the participants did not fit in the category of a successful self-employed entrepreneur. The test could have successfully asserted the participants' decision to become self-employed by confirming that their personality fitted the category of the self-employed, but as it turned out it almost had the opposite effect. One woman became downhearted and wondered if she had what it took to become self-employed.

The categorising of the participants through the test came to be viewed by some as objective (see Hacking, 1986). The test in itself was regarded as objective knowledge. It was based on the idea that everything is measurable. The idea of the personality test also invited the view that entrepreneurship is something to be discovered within the participants. The test was then used as help for the Project Manager to identify potential entrepreneurs in the group. At the same time the Project was based on the idea that entrepreneurship is something the individuals may learn. There are shifting perspectives on the individual at work.

Pedagogical techniques

One of the Project Manager's techniques was to encourage the participants to find their own answers to questions and then tell them how they should think if they did not yet think in a self-employed manner. The technique helps support the participants to become self-employers they were told. The Project Manager then discussed competition, profit, and personal characteristics.

The Project Manager asked how one of the participants, who wanted to start a pet shop for dogs, should conduct her market research. One woman suggested that she should do a survey at the underground station. Another woman thought she should contact the kennel club in the area. A third suggested finding out whether there were any statistics on how many dogs there were in the area and a fourth proposed contacting a veterinarian. The Project Manager advised her to begin by examining the competition. To be an entrepreneur means to be prepared to compete, she was told.

On another day, the Project Manager discussed profit with the group. Striving for profit was viewed by some in the group as negative since they associated it with someone only interested in money. One of the participants believed that the ambition had to be to make a profit. Another participant did not think it was important to make a profit. She did not want to be rich. A third participant did not want to make a profit at all. If she made a profit then she would give it to charity. A fourth participant did not think that one should start a business if one did not want a profit. A profit was a condition for the company to survive. A fifth participant thought that one should make money. She wondered why it was considered bad to make money. A sixth participant believed that it was not the profit that was the most important, but that she was working for herself. She said that she would rather work 60–70 hours for herself than for someone else. That was more important than money. A seventh participant did not think of making a profit. She said that she had never been interested in money. The fourth participant believed that it was demanding to be a business owner. She said that you had to make money to survive. If you had a bad conscience about making money people would take advantage of you.

The Project Manager emphasized that making money is good for all parties involved in a company. It is good for potential employees, customers, and lenders, because it makes it more likely that the company will survive. It is good for the company's image. Other companies prefer to do business with well-off companies, since the company is then considered to conduct well thought through business deals. It is good for future investment, since a profit might be reinvested in the company. The Project Manager educated the participants on the importance of profit. He used arguments that the participants might be able to sympathize with. Profit is not only good for the individual; it is also good for the surrounding environment. By using words such as 'a solid company', 'company image', and 'well thought through business deals', the Project Manager was mediating a sense of solidarity into the word 'profit'. Profit, then, was no longer only connected to money loving, greedy employers. An image of the responsible business owner was projected; it is someone, who by taking care of herself or himself also takes care of others. This fits well with the neo-liberal idea of the self-reliant, 'active citizen' that takes responsibility for herself or himself, thus not burdening others, that is, the state (see Heelas, 1991).

The idea of the entrepreneur as someone who is self-confident was viewed by the participants as a typical trait of the self-employed. Some of the participants had difficulties in taking the step to contact potential clients. The Project Manager pointed out that one cannot be too cowardly if one is self-employed. You have to be sure of yourself. One participant said that a self-employed person is someone who can make decisions and knows exactly what to do. It is a self-confident person. She could not identify with that. The Project Manager tried to build the participants' self-confidence. The participants were asked to tell what personal characteristics one woman in the group had which would support her in her life of self-employment. Traits such as spontaneity, openness, cockiness, outgoingness and fearlessness were mentioned. These were traits that all supported the idea of the entrepreneurial individual.

The articles

The Project Manager also used articles from magazines addressed to the self-employed to socialize the participants into thinking as a self-employer. The articles in the magazines explained the difficulties of becoming self-employed and the importance of being well prepared (see Biggert, 1994; Helmersson, 1996). The message in the articles was to learn the rules and the self-employed way of thinking by taking part in a self-employment course. The number of entrepreneurship courses has, accordingly, increased during the last decade in Sweden. At the turn of the millennium entrepreneurship is being encouraged in schools, and introduced as a topic of university courses. It supports the idea that it is possible to teach someone how to be an entrepreneur. It upholds the idea of the individual as manageable by connecting to the interface zone where individuals are socialized and formed.

To be an entrepreneur is seen as being part of the future labour market (Lönnqvist, 1995). The future labour market will be more fun, according to the articles. Individuals will be able to choose how and when they want to work, and being self-employed makes this possible. The articles describe entrepreneurs as autonomous, independent individuals. They focus on the 'new' ideas of the labour market where everyone works as a consultant (also see Reich, 1992). It is a labour market that is more flexible and where being self-employed is the ultimate goal of the individual. But the articles also emphasize that the world of the entrepreneur is essentially different from the world of the employee. 'The difference between being an employee and an employer is not a difference in scale. It is a difference in nature. It is like the difference of living in a safe enclosure and living in a cruel wilderness' (Kullstedt and Melin, 1993: 6; author's translation). The world of the self-employer is all about risk, but according to the articles, one gains freedom. The employee might be safe, but he or she is not free. To be free means to be self-reliant. If one wants to be 'free' one has to take care of oneself. The articles are trying to convince the reader that it is worth the risk. 'No one who has survived as an entrepreneur can think of a better life' (Kullstedt and Melin, 1993: 6; author's translation).

The Project Manager sought to manage the interface zone of the participants into thinking and being entrepreneurs through the discussions in the group and the articles. At the same time the participants in the interface zone negotiated the characteristics of the entrepreneur into something they could identify with. Below I discuss how the participants dealt with these negotiations and how they viewed the role of the self-employed and whether their attitudes towards self-employment changed because of the Project. Before going further into that, however, I discuss the participants' reasons for wanting to become self-employed.

The role of the self-employed: expectations and perspectives

The reason for becoming self-employed stated by most participants was to gain freedom. Equality in the work situation was important and that was regarded as impossible to obtain as an employee. One woman said:

> I'm tired of being an employee, having someone who decides and tells me what to do and having to do things I don't feel like doing at the moment; that I'm not allowed to take responsibility. (all quotes have been translated into English by the author)

The aspect of making one's own decisions was especially important:

> One simply makes one's own decisions. I don't like it anymore . . . to have to go and ask someone if I may go to the dentist . . . regular employees, damn, they have to ask for everything. At the workplace they aren't allowed to buy a pen or pad without asking someone higher up in the hierarchy.

It's positive to be able to decide for oneself, what one wants to do, how one wants to do it and how much one wants to do it. But in a company [working as an employee] it isn't like that... you have to adjust. Being a self-employer you're not controlled... in that sense.

The participants also emphasized freedom as meaning being self-reliant. Self-reliance was, as in the articles referred to above, defined as independence from the social security system of the state, but in a different sense. In the entrepreneurial culture advocated by a neo-liberal discourse the individual should be independent and responsible, not dependent on the state (see Keat and Abercrombie, 1991). The participants discussed independence from the state from a different perspective. They wanted to be self-reliant because they did not trust the state social security system to take care of them anymore. They have to 'For the sake of economic survival... make themselves the centre of their own life plans and conducts'. (Beck, 1992: 92) One woman was very worried about the future. She said:

Everything is getting worse, people living on the street, and I, I'm worried about the future...I also feel, uh, now I have to try... for the children...to try to find a job, to make some money and put some money away if they can't get a job.

Another reason for becoming self-employed was that the participants believed this to be the future. They pointed out that the labour market has to be more flexible. The participants were interested in futurology and tomorrow's labour market. Many of them believed that the labour market of the future would grant more opportunities to do different things. They believed that the future labour market would be more fun. This is also how it is portrayed in some of the articles (see for example Biggert, 1994: 3). They considered that the society of today still cherishes old values that would not survive in the future. One man said:

the unions and society...they still work with...the old ideas from Industrialism, with the ideas that all have the right to have a permanent position. Not everyone wants that. They haven't understood that. They still discuss 8 hours a day, 40 hours a week and a permanent position. I don't believe in that anymore or it doesn't feel like that for me. Not everyone need have it like that. One has to be more flexible.

The participant believed that by becoming self-employed, he would be part of tomorrow's labour market.

The self-employed is the symbol of the employable, autonomous, and self-reliant individual. Miller and Rose (1995) argue that concepts and practices of the enterprise and the 'enterprising self' became a central mentality of politics in the 1980s and 1990s. In Sweden this became especially evident in the 1990s when politicians and the media discussed matters in terms of flexibility and focused on the importance of entrepreneurship. (See also Augustsson and Sandberg's discussion in this book, Chapter 11, on the discourse of the inevitable future labour market of the new economy, flexibility and entrepreneurship.) The Project participants were willing to try the world of the self-employed. They saw it as being part of the future. However, many of them were worried about the risks involved. When asked, most of them preferred a full-time permanent position. They knew the language of the labour market of the future, but in practice they might not be willing to trade social security for the risks they associated with becoming self-employed.

Identification with the role of the self-employed?

When we discussed how the participants identified with being self-employed, they talked about looks, gender and personality. They associated the business owner with a man in a suit. One woman said that even if she knew that a business owner could be anyone she still saw a man in a suit:

> I see that 'suit' in front of me with a tie and so on, who makes decisions. That is the way I see it.

She pointed out that in the media and in the articles the participants read during the Project the illustration was almost always of an older man in a suit. The participants also associated the business owner with a certain personality that they could not identify themselves with. A recurrent image of the business owner was a person who only wanted money. One woman said:

> the labour market is constituted by people who need to make money by taking a job and then the employer is the other party that tries to keep costs down and make a profit. That's not how I see myself. I'm not one of the small business owners.

Another woman said that the self-employed are those who were the best at selling Christmas magazines[5] when they were children:

> He's always been very keen on money since childhood. I think that's often...the perception of a small business owner...the negative traits.

Several of the participants believed that the self-employed are not like employees, but the participants had a different perspective than the one expressed in the articles discussed above. One woman said that business owners are seen as strange and suspicious people. They do not have the ability to cooperate and that is why they become self-employed:

> small time fiddler, hard working, yes, all these sorts of things, a bit of an obstinate person.

One woman did not consider consultants as business owners. Consultants offer a service to another company. She was of the opinion that a consultant is a wage-earner who decides over her or his own time and is her or his own boss. Another participant stressed the difficulty in trying to think as a self-employer; to start to think that you have to be self-reliant:

> And I still think it is difficult to judge if it's possible to learn that...that other way of thinking...or if I will feel a loss of security that will be difficult to cope with.

She was worried about the loss of security she would suffer if she became self-employed. One participant pointed out that most of the participants had been employed in large organizations and were used to a certain security:

> Many of us...have worked a very long time in large organizations. There's more of security in that way, than in having to risk everything by yourself.

The participants continually returned to the question of trading security for the risks of being self-employed. The articles in the magazines all proclaimed that it is worth it in the end, but the participants were not sure. The participants also had difficulties in identifying with the idea of being a self-employed. The Project Manager sought to motivate and support the participants.

'The project has taught me to be and think like a self-employed'

The participants attempted to identify with the role of the self-employed, while at the same time negotiating the personal characteristics of the self-employed. In the interface zone of defining the self-employed, the idea of the self-employed was transformed into something the participants were able to identify with. Still, they discussed typical entrepreneurial traits such as self-reliance, autonomy and the future labour market as reasons for starting their own business. The discourse of the entrepreneur and entrepreneurship was made familiar to them through the Project, but their perceptions of themselves as self-employed were different. One woman elaborated on the idea of starting to think like a self-employed:

> I think, somehow, that if one hasn't thought of oneself as a self-employer, seen oneself in that role, then one has to try to change identity a little. It's as when you smoke and you stop, then you have to change attitude to a whole lot of things in life and begin to see yourself as a non-smoker and that's a sort of step by step process ... and I think I have to think that through. What's my relation to other business owners? What should the relationship with the customer be? And things like that.

The Project has helped her to begin to think like a self-employed. She always had a negative view of being self-employed. In her view, the employer takes all the money and is self-centred. Now she saw the self-employed as part of a context where all business owners are dependent on each other. In this context the business owner has to make money so that other companies are not hit. She could put herself in that context. She was able to see solidarity in making money, which made it easier for her to think in terms of profit.

The participants' views of a business owner were based on their identification with the wage-earner and the image of the self-employed that was portrayed in the media and by the self-employed themselves. One woman said that after the Project she could identify herself with the role of a business owner even though she was neither a man nor wore a suit. Now she felt that there were different types of business owners. She used to believe that all business owners were self-confident and knew what they wanted. She could not identify with that, but now she believed that she could become self-employed on her own terms.

Concluding discussion: negotiated identities

The change in the perception of the individual from being employed to employable is not something that is produced by itself. It is a process actively constructed in the state discourse where individuals are portrayed as being their own agents, as being 'enterprising selves'. The process of individuals being confronted with and reconstructing the discourse of the enterprising self is made visible in a Self-Employment Project at the PES. The PES, as an institution, has become a tool for implementing labour market policy tuned to ideas of the importance of the entrepreneur. The participants were confronted with an ideal of what it means to be and think like an entrepreneur. They tried to adapt to the concept while at the same time negotiating the meaning of being a self-employed entrepreneur. On the individual level this is an example of 'creolization' (Hannerz, 1992). The participants adapted to the discourse but at the same time transformed the meaning of the self-employed into something they could identify with. Through negotiations over the concept of the entrepreneur, the participants created their own perception of the entrepreneur in the interface zone of their own ideals and the Project Manager's perception of how they should be or what they should become.

Not all participants expressed the same view, but they had all been confronted with the ideas in the Project and all had to negotiate their own perspectives into what they believed a self-employed was like. They had their preconceptions of the self-employed, which most of them described when the Project started as money-loving, self-absorbent individuals. The Project, however, made them reflect on their opinion of the self-employed. The personality test, the Project Manager, and the articles advocated the idea of the risk-taking, autonomous, self-reliant entrepreneur with whom the participants should identify. However, because of their own identification with the wage-earner they transformed and negotiated the self-employed individual into someone who does not necessarily need to be self-confident, who needs to make a profit but possibly for solidarity reasons, and who risks loosing social security by becoming self-employed not because he or she wants to be independent from the state, but because he or she fears that the social security system will fail in the future. The risks are still there, and freedom and independence are still sought for, but the motives of the actors involved differ.

Notes

1. In 1996, the PES offered self-employment courses and self-employment projects work experience scheme. The self-employment course is a three-week course teaching the basics in business administration. The ALU Project is a regular work experience scheme. The ALU Project is a two to six months project where the participants are taught for example how to present their business concept, do market research, and the basics in business administration. When the participants take part in the ALU Project they are, as in other work experience schemes, entitled to unemployment benefit. The unemployment benefit is based on the former wage level. The courses and the project are a complement to the 'self-employment grant' administrated by the PES. The self-employment grant corresponds to unemployment benefit and is paid every month for six months. It is possible to get the grant extended because of unforeseen incidents, if the business is started in a sparsely populated area, if you are a woman, or if you are an immigrant. To be able to apply for the grant you have to be 20 years old, be unemployed or at risk of becoming unemployed. Applicants have to make a budget and have a business proposal that is reviewed by consultants. The consultants make a recommendation and the PES decides on eligibility for the grant.
2. In 2002 this is called a 'start-up grant' or 'support for entrepreneurial start-ups' (Swedish National Labour Market Board, AMS, 2001; Regeringskansliet, 2002).
3. In 1993 and 1994 there was also a drastic increase in newly registered businesses.
4. In the 1992/93 budget 9,000 individuals received the self-employment grant, but in 1994 the figure increased to 20,600 (Okeke, 1999). In 1996 29,000 received the self-employment grant (Okeke, 2000).
5. During Christmas time in Sweden children sell Christmas magazines by going door to door in their neighbourhood. To earn any money they have to sell a lot of magazines, which means that most children do not earn anything.

References

AMS. 2001. *Support for Entrepreneurial Start Ups*. http://www.ams.se/RDFS.asp?L=241.
Beck, Ulrich. 1992. *Risk Society. Towards a New Modernity*. London: Sage Publications.
Biggert, Magnus. 1994. 'Man kan visst lära sig till entreprenör' ('It is possible to learn how to become an entrepreneur'; author's translation). *Eget Företag* (2): 3.
Davidsson, Per. 1989. *Continued Entrepreneurship and Small Firm Growth*. Stockholm: EFI, Stockholm School of Economics.
Foucault, Michel. 1991. 'Governmentality'. In *The Foucault Effect*, edited by G. Burchell, C. Gordon and P. Miller. London: Harvester Wheatsheat, 87–104.
Gough, J. W. 1969. *The Rise of the Entrepreneur*. New York: Schocken Books.
Granfelt, TiiaRiitta and Anders Hjort af Ornäs. 1999. *Småföretagandets kultur: det saknade sammanhanget*. Centrum för kommunstrategiska studier, Linköpings Universitet, rapport 1999: 3.
Gyllenstierna, Tove. 1993. 'Har du rätt personlighet för att bli egenföretagare... Svaren får du här. ('Do you have the right personality to become self- employed... You get the answers here'; author's translation). *Eget Företag* (1): 18–21.

Hacking, Ian. 1986. 'Making up people'. In *Reconstructing Individualism. Autonomy, Individuality, and the Self in Western Thought*, edited by T. C. Heller, M. Sosna and D. E. Wellbery. Stanford: Stanford University Press, 222–36.

Hannerz, Ulf. 1992. *Cultural Complexity: Studies in the Social Organization of Meaning*. New York: Columbia University Press.

Heelas, Paul. 1991. 'Reforming the self: enterprise and the characters of Thatcherism'. In *Enterprise Culture*, edited by R. Keat and N. Abercrombie. London: Routledge, 72–90.

Helmersson, Stina. 1996. 'Varför vissa lyckas och andra misslyckas'. ('Why some succeed and others fail'; author's translation). *Du & Co* (2): 10–14.

Hjorth, Daniel and Bengt Johannisson. 1997. *Entreprenörskap som skapelseprocess och ideologi*. SIRE-Working Paper 1997: 2.

Johannisson, Bengt. 1987. 'Entrepreneurship in a corporatist state: the case of Sweden'. In *Entrepreneurship in Europe: The Social Process*, edited by R. Goffee and R. Scase. London: Croom Helm, 131–43.

Johannisson, Bengt. 1996. *Entrepreneurship: Exploiting Ambiguity and Paradox*. SIRE-Working Paper 1996: 1.

Johansson, Kjell. 1998. 'Från fattigvård till arbetsmarknadspolitik'. In *Visioner och Vardagar*. Stockholm: Arbetsmarknadsstyrelsen, 139–64.

Keat, Russell and Nicholas Abercrombie, (eds). 1991. *Enterprise Culture*. London: Routledge.

Kullstedt, Mats and Lars Melin. 1993. 'Företagarens spelplan' ('The business owner's arena'; author's translation). *Eget Företag* (1): 6.

Landström, Hans. 2000. *Entreprenörskapets rötter*. Lund: Studentlitteratur.

Lönnqvist, Stefan. 1995. 'Hem till kunden finns det inga genvägar'. ('On the way to the customer there are no shortcuts'; author's translation). *Sälj* (3): 40–1.

Lyttkens, Lorentz. 1985. *Den disciplinerade människan. Om social kontroll och långsiktiga värderingsförskjutningar*. Stockholm: Liber Förlag.

Lyttkens, Lorentz. 1989. *Of Human Discipline*. Stockholm: Almquist & Wiksell International.

Martin, Emily. 1997. 'Managing Americans: policy and changes in the meanings of work and the self'. In *Anthropology of Policy: Critical Perspectives on Governance and Power*, edited by C. Shore and S. Wright. London: Routledge, 239–57.

Miller, Peter and Nikolas Rose. 1995. 'Production, identity, and democracy'. *Theory & Society* 24: 427–67.

Okeke, Susanna. 1999. 'Starta eget-bidragets effekter: utvärdering av företag tre år efter start'. Gnesta: AMS Närservice, report Ura 1999: 12.

Okeke, Susanna. 2000. 'Hur går det för arbetslösa som får bidrag för start av näringsverksamhet?'. Gnesta: AMS Närservice, report Ura 2000: 4.

Regeringskansliet. 2002. *Basic Information Report. Sweden 2002*. http://naring. regeringen.se/inenglish/areas_of/labour_market.htm.

Reich, Robert B. 1992. *The Work of Nations*. New York: Vintage Books.

Rose, Nikolas and Peter Miller. 1992. 'Political power beyond the state: problematics of government'. *British Journal of Sociology* 43(2): 173–205.

Scase, Richard and Robert Goffee. 1987. Introduction. In *Entrepreneurship in Europe: the Social Process*, edited by R. Goffee and R. Scase. London: Croom Helm, 1–11.

SFS (Svensk Författningssamling) 1984: 523. *Förordningen om bidrag till arbetslösa m.fl. som startar egen näringsverksamhet.* www.rixlex.riksdagen.se.

SFS 1992: 1333. *Förordningen om arbetslivsutveckling.* www.rixlex.riksdagen.se.

SFS 1998: 1784. *Förordningen om arbetsmarknadspolitiska aktiviteter.* www.rixlex. riksdagen.se.

SFS 2000: 634. *Förordningen om arbetsmarknadspolitiska program.* www.rixlex. riksdagen.se.

SOU (Statens offentliga utredningar) 1990: 31. *Perspektiv på arbetsförmedlingen.* Stockholm: Allmänna förlaget.

Swedberg, Richard. 1994. Inledning. In *Schumpeter: Om skapande förstörelse och entreprenörskap. I urval av Richard Swedberg.* Stockholm: Ratio, IX–XXXII.

Trygged, Sven. 1996. *Arbetslös och medellös. En studie av beredskapsarbetare i Stockholm.* Stockholm: Stockholms universitet, Institutionen för Socialt arbete, Rapport i socialt arbete nr 78.

Unell, Elisabeth. 1999. *Arbetslös: möjligheter på arbetsförmedlingen i Norberg.* Eskilstuna: Centrum för välfärdsforskning.

Wadensjö, Eskil. 1998. Arbetsmarknadspolitiken under AMS första halvsekel. In *Visioner och vardagar.* Stockholm: Arbetsmarknadsstyrelsen, 51–78.

Abbreviations

ALU (in Swedish: Arbetslivsutveckling) Work experience schemes.

AMP (in Swedish: Arbetsmarknadspolitiska aktiviteter) Active labour market policy measures.

AMV (in Swedish: Arbetsmarknadsverket) The Swedish Labour Market Administration.

PES – Public Employment Service.

8
'Be a Gumby'*: The Political Technologies of Employability in the Temporary Staffing Business

Christina Garsten

Introduction: flexibilizing employment

The growth of the temporary staffing business signals a move towards a destandardization of employment contracts and greater variety of contracts between employer and employee. Employability and flexibility are the buzzwords of the business, auguring an end to the contract as we know it, announcing instead the advent of work on short-term contracts, rolling contracts, at unknown locations, and with different expectations attached to work. The temporary staffing business in Sweden, as well as in Europe as a whole, is dominated by large transnational corporations that have their own particular policies and practices for running their business and that have as well to adjust to the national legislative and cultural context in which they operate. Despite strivings for harmonization of the temporary staffing business in Europe, there is still a great deal of national and sectoral variation.

Moreover, the 'temp agencies,' as it were, work to fulfil the demands for flexibility in client organizations. By making use of the services of temp agencies, client organizations can maintain a degree of flexibility in numbers as well as functionality. This requires that temporary employees learn to adapt to the needs of the client – that they can be flexible. Being flexible is in turn a requirement for staying on the books of the agency, and hence for being employable.

Focus will here be placed on the policies and social practices through which flexibility, as a prerequisite for employability, is taught and regulated among temporary employees. The chapter takes a close look at what ideas and norms the temp agency teaches its temporary employees as part of the socialization process; how temps are being evaluated and rewarded as 'good' temps; and what their own views on working in the temping sector are. It is argued that temps learn to integrate the perspectives of the agency in ways that make government as external constraint turn into self-regulation, or governance, and that this is a form of power that presupposes the agency of individuals. Hence, the making up of flexible temporary agency workers relies on the establishment of new norms and 'technologies of self,' by which normative categories and categories of subjectivity are established and internalized (cf. Shore and Strathern, 2000: 30). It will be important therefore to examine those processes or 'political technologies' by which certain discourses of flexibility and employability are rendered powerful and authoritative while others are marginalized. The term political technologies here refers to the configurations of knowledge and power that are mobilized in particular ways to shape the way individuals perceive of and conduct themselves (Foucault, 1978, 1991). The discourse on employability and flexibility is, it will be argued, a powerful individualizing force. While the discourse itself speaks to structural conditions of a new governmentality of labour markets, its effects are individualizing in their consequences, leading people to perceive of themselves as the primary source of agency responsible for their position in the labour market. The discourse of employability and flexibility has a double edge to it; while it is understood to mean the loosening of rules and adaptation to unique, local conditions, it also entails the putting into place of new, alternative rules to govern the individual, with universalistic claims. It entails the capacity to bend, to adapt, to be attentive to manners and attitudes, in order to be employable. While certain aspects of individual ideas, attitudes and actions are rendered normal and indeed wanted, others are muted.

The case material provided builds primarily on around 30 interviews with temps and staff at Olsten Personalkraft in Sweden during the period 1996–99, complemented with some degree of participant observation.[1] As part of the research process, internal documents, such as policy documents, information leaflets, administrative forms and promotional material have also been studied and analysed. The interviewed temps were predominantly administrative personnel, employed as receptionists, administrative support personnel, financial assistants, switchboard operators and the like. Most of them, with a handful of exceptions, were female in ages ranging from 19 to 50.

The temporary staffing sector in Sweden may easily be understood as an entirely new phenomenon. But in fact, the state monopoly over the allocation of job opportunities was only operative during a period of some fifty years, from 1935 until the early 1990s. Previously, job placement was undertaken by municipal agencies, branch agencies as well as private corporations. The centralization of job allocation into the hands of state agencies that took place in the 1930s was an important step in the realization of the Swedish Welfare State in which regular, salaried employment functioned as an ideological tool and cornerstone. During the state monopoly period, the Labour Market Board could grant permission to private firms to mediate employment on a licence. An increasing number of lawsuits testified to the increasing demand for temporary workers and to the tendency of temporary staffing agencies to test the limits of state control. The subsequent abandonment of ILO conventions and changes in Swedish legislation signalled a deregulation of the Swedish labour market, allowing private firms to recruit and lease workforces for profit as well as an opening for transnational staffing agencies to start their operations in Sweden. (For a more detailed account of the Swedish legislative structure in relation to temporary agency work, see Friberg *et al.*, 1999.) When temporary staffing agencies were allowed to operate freely without licence, the number of temporary agencies as well as temporary employees rose quickly. Today, approximately 0.87 per cent of the Swedish workforce, or 38,000 people, work through temp agencies. As a comparison, the EU ratio is somewhat higher, 1.5 per cent of the workforce (www.spur.se, 24.9.2002). Approximately 58 per cent of temp workers in Sweden are women (Fridén *et al.*, 2000: 61).

The legacy of Swedish employment security is reflected in the working conditions of employees in the temporary staffing sector. Employees are to a large extent closely tied to agencies in varied forms of long-term employment contracts, with a guaranteed salary of between 75 and 85 per cent of the full-time rate. Other benefits, such as insurance, pension rights, parental pay etc. are often the same as for employees on regular, stationary employment contracts. Sector based collective agreements regarding pay and general conditions exist for most areas. Consequently, average turnover time is longer than for many other European countries: approximately 38 months in the administrative sector and 12 months across sectors.[2]

Such agreements did not come effortlessly, however. They were the result of prolonged and heated discussions between unions and employers, in which the Salaried Employees' Union, HTF, played a significant role in pushing the discussions forwards. Unions have also been pushing for the right of employees to use working time for educational purposes. Continuous learning is a necessity in a competitive labour market and temps are regularly reminded by agency staff of the need to upgrade their skills and pass tests to check on their progress on, for example, using software. To date, most of this upskilling has taken place outside office hours, though.[3]

Hence, despite the global spread of temporary staffing agencies, the local working conditions and employment contracts may thus vary a great deal across countries. The variability of employment conditions makes international comparisons hazardous.

The transnational regulation of the temporary staffing sector has also been an issue for the EU. During 2000 and early 2001 the social partners were negotiating a framework agreement on standards for temporary agency work. The negotiations failed in May 2001 (see Harvey, 2002). After consulting the relevant European-level associations representing this sector, the Commission proposed a directive in March 2002 (CEC, 2002). The proposed directive aimed to improve the working conditions of temporary employees, whilst providing a step in the harmonization of the European labour market. The directive makes it clear that temporary employees shall receive at least as favourable treatment, in terms of basic working and employment conditions, as a comparable worker in the user enterprise, unless the difference in treatment is justified by objective reasons (CEC, 2002: 21). At the same time, the directive aims to establish a suitable framework for the use of temporary work to contribute to the smooth functioning of the labour and employment market (CEC, 2002: 19).

The relation of the staffing sector to the public job centres in Sweden has also changed from one of mutual mistrust and competition to one characterized by relatively close relations and co-operation. For the job centres, the staffing agencies are important clients. While the most employable individuals often find their own routes to employment, the more vulnerable job seekers rely on job centres to guide them. For the staffing agencies, the job centres perform vital functions in finding potential job candidates, informing about work in the temporary staffing sector, and the like. What used to be a polarization of interests between public and private has become increasingly blurred. Accordingly, the discourse of employability spreads across organizations, and may now be evinced in the staffing business as well as in the public job centres (see chapter by Thedvall, Chapter 7 in this volume). Employability captures what the EU, the Swedish labour market authorities as well as the temp agencies see as the qualities needed to adapt to the requirements of future employment – continuous skills enhancement, continuous learning, but perhaps most of all, an attitude of flexibility, availability, and reliability.

Staying on the books: expectations of temping

'Ask a temp, or anyone associated with the temporary worker industry, what the three most important qualities for successful temping are and that person will tell you flexibility, flexibility, flexibility.' (Rogers, 1996: 94)

To describe somebody as being flexible, or talk about a group of people as being flexible makes a difference. Our ways of labelling people and their acts have an impact on how they come to understand themselves and how they come to act. Labelling is part and parcel of the process by which people are constituted in social interaction. It is a way of 'making up people', as Hacking (1986) describes it. To a large extent, human beings and human acts come into being hand in hand with our invention of the categories with which we label them. This means that as new labels are placed onto individuals, as we learn to think about ourselves with a new inventory of labels at hand, we will, to some extent, be transformed as part of the process.

The business of temping is one with a great deal of movement. Temps themselves move between job assignments, clients and locations, and often between temporary staffing agencies. It is also a business in which time frames tend to be rather short. Individuals seek temporary assignments in between regular employment contracts, or careers, for a number of reasons, for example to change business sectors, to avoid becoming unemployed in a process of downsizing, before embarking on a long-distance journey, to avoid long-term commitment to a single employer, or because of a lack of other options. Space and time are, in other words, rather discontinuous. This places a great deal of pressure on agencies and temps alike to learn the ropes quickly, and to be clear about expectations, competences and job requirements. Hence, temp agencies put a great deal of effort into making sure that temps are given the right information and are socialized quickly into the world of temping.

Temp agencies provide their employees with a number of written documents to help them learn quickly what is expected of them. In many of these documents, the need for flexibility is stressed. In *Temping: The Insider's Guide* (Rogers, 1996), a self-help manual for temporary employees, it is argued that flexibility is the key to success in the temping business. Whilst it is recognized that people often look for jobs in this business because they wish to have a job that provides a degree of personal freedom, the reader is reminded that flexibility works both ways:

> People looking at temping from the outside often associate flexibility from the temp's point of view and, to some extent, that's true. The

temp lifestyle can enable you to gain as much control over your schedule as you need. But flexibility works both ways. If you want to remain on your service's 'A' list, you won't say no too often. Turning down a few jobs in a row will definitely place you at the end of the list. (Rogers, 1996: 95)

This passage makes it clear that it is the flexibility of the temp agency and the client that matters the most. Flexibility for the temporary employee has its limits. These are dependent on the needs of the agency and the client. To work as a temp and stay on the 'A' list, you need to recognize this fact and be adaptable. It is the market for temporary services that provides the context of flexibility for the individual temporary employee. As Rogers puts it:

Flexibility + Good Attitude = Success

Although the above citations are written with the US labour market in view, they are equally valid in Europe. The fact that many of the large staffing services, such as Manpower and Olsten, are US-based and operate through local agencies has contributed to the shaping of a transnational temping business with a clear American key signature. The idea of the self-reliant, competitive individual, taking on responsibility for his or her employability, is one that has gained a strong foothold in the European context, in which Sweden, despite its history of collective bargaining and organized interests, is no exception.

Working as a temp entails adhering to certain expectations from the temp agency, as well as from the client organization. To a large degree, being flexible is about being able to accommodate different clients. A good temp, in the view of Olsten, is one who can be sent anywhere, to whatever client needs his or her services, and who can adapt to different tasks. It also entails adopting a friendly attitude and avoiding involvement in company gossip or conflicts. Temps are advised to avoid potentially conflict-laden behaviours or topics. As noted by Henson (1996: 124), 'Looking submissive or adopting a suitable demeanour with the appropriate mix of cooperation, deference, and cheer was essential for the successful performance of the temporary role and was expected and demanded by temporary agencies'. While looking submissive would be too strong a recommendation of appropriate behaviour for Olsten temps in Sweden, they were advised not to 'burden the client with your views on their routines' and 'what you think of their managers' (in the folder *Att tänka på när jag arbetar i Olsten* ['To remember while working with Olsten']), and 'If you have a complaint tell US [Olsten] not someone else working in the company'. Temporaries then, learn that they must avoid displaying too much of their personal views and emotions, that they must engage in 'emotional labour', to disguise or manage their personal attitudes and feelings to be successful at work. Following Hochschild (1983: 7), 'This labor requires one to induce or suppress feeling in order to sustain the outward countenance that produces the proper state of mind in others.' Performing emotional labour is understood to be more than situational adjustment; it is a skill you acquire through having done temping for a while and having learnt how to be socially flexible with the right attitude.

The value of being flexible is also often referred to among temporary employees themselves. In interviews, it comes across as the most common response to questions about what it takes to be successful in the temp labour market. To be flexible, employees need to show a willingness to adapt to the expectations of the client regarding manners, task fulfilment, dress code, and professionalism, as well as to the client's social environment. In return, temping may offer the employee a relative degree of freedom; freedom to decide when and where to work, how many hours to put in, and in what kind of business to work. This is often referred to as the greatest advantage of temping. On the other, more negative side, flexibility is often said to be the hardest part, involving difficulties such as defining the parameters of the task, maintaining a sense of integrity, and being under constant scrutiny by the agency as well as the client. For temps, flexibility is a double-edged sword. Birgitta, who is 27 years old and works for Olsten in Sweden as a financial assistant, reflects upon the different aspects of flexibility in this way:

> You absolutely have to be flexible all the time ... I define flexibility as being able to re-prioritize your tasks. You have to check continuously to see if something more important comes up. The most ideal situation is to work on one task at a time, finish it, and then proceed to the next. That way you are in control. But ... that does not work here. If the sales manager says – Shit! In ten minutes I have a very important meeting with a customer. Could you please help me with the contract? Then you have to shift immediately ... and be service minded. I can't find a better word for it. You have to like it, to give it your best. And take on tasks that aren't really yours. But it's also important that you don't lose yourself to them. You actually have to say no if they ask you ... to polish their shoes. It may be very hard, since it's not in the

papers what's part of your tasks. The boundary is unclear. So it's up to your own judgement...When you start to know people, then you may start to say no. Cause you do get used. You do. Cause they know... you are in a very delicate position. If you do it wrong you may have to go. And in such a position, it's clear that I give more than I would otherwise have done. I would have been a lot more cocky on my former job than I am here...And you know it's a very important client for Olsten. So pride can be tough, sometimes.[4]

For Birgitta, defining the limits of flexibility is difficult. Being flexible, switching tasks and being service-minded, is important to her chances of staying on the books. It is a way of being employable. To her, it relates to integrity and pride, which may be hard to uphold in the face of client expectations and of loyalty to the temp agency. For Lotta, 33 years old, and working as a secretary with Olsten, the experience of flexibility is a bit different. She likes her job with Olsten and finds it relatively easy to accommodate with the expectations of her clients:

> To me, flexibility is simply being able to do many things simultaneously. And being in control of things. I think that's mostly it. To have a lot of things going and still be in control. That's flexibility. Flexibility is basically a good thing...in life in general. To be flexible and to foresee things and...But then you can't always plan this job. Three people may suddenly appear through the door for whom we don't have any office space. And we have not received the information. Then we have to know what to do with them. You can't plan everything, but then you can always ask. For example about this meeting or that. How many are coming? You have to be almost a detective. Check things up and...ask. Simply in order to create as few disturbances as possible.

Beginning at registration, temporaries are advised and socialized, formally and informally, to be attentive to and to conform to the agency's standards (Henson, 1996: 144). Dresscode is one of these. Temps at Olsten Personalkraft are given written as well as oral guidelines as to how to dress:

> Dresscode
> When you are on an assignment you are Olsten's face outwards. Therefore it is important that you dress professionally and that you use Olsten's PIN. Dress up a little for your first day on the assignment.

We use neither jeans nor tights at Olsten. (In the folder *Ett jobb att älska* ['A job to love'])

Olsten Personalkraft temps are sometimes provided with a business suit to facilitate dressing appropriately for a new assignment. While the suit sometimes comes in handy since you do not have to reflect upon what to wear for a new assignment, few of the interviewed temps report to wear it regularly. It does, however, provide them with a degree of comfort to know that it is there, should they need it. One temp told me she always had hers ready on a coat hanger at her client's office.

Learning to be flexible is also the acquisition of a specific sort of female reflexivity. It involves being attentive to the needs of the client, in terms of what tasks are to be performed, but also an attentiveness to appropriate dresscode, manners and the like that are not only professional but also gender-appropriate. The gendering of flexibility reveals itself in the subtle forms through which a 'feminine' code of conduct is fostered; one marked by social versatility, sensitivity and responsiveness to other's expectations and needs. Temps are generally well dressed and well-behaved, with a ready smile on their lips. Many of them emphasize the need to 'fit in' in terms of dresscode and manners as part of performing well. Generally, they say, it is better to dress professionally the first day. When you have taken a cue from the others in the office, you can adapt your dress accordingly (Garsten and Turtinen, 2000: 188–91). Birgitta expressed with a degree of irritability the anxieties of dressing:

> Tiresome story, I must say [dressing, my remark]. Because you are poorly paid in this business. Well, I myself am well paid, but there are many girls who earn very little. And they have great demands on you at the client's. It's OK here, we are rather sloppy here. It's great [laughing] . . . But I was on four, five assignments before this one and on two of them they were really strict . . . snobbish, sort of. So it's like they check out what brands you wear. How are you supposed to meet those demands? It's impossible! To me, it was really hard to feel that . . . you are examined . . . Olsten lend you a suit costume. Thank heavens. I liked that, to have it just in case. A marine blue suit you may not feel like buying yourself. Not everyone has that as his or her style. And it costs a great deal. So it's a great idea.

Flexibility then, embraces attitudes, behaviours, expectations, as well as dresscodes. In a transformed European labour market, and more specifically here in the temping business, flexibility has emerged as a preferred point of direction, with normative implications for practice. Notions of flexible temps navigating in flexible labour markets, and adapting to the expectations of clients and temp agencies imply the putting in place of particular mindsets and practices among employees. We are led to understand that these are significantly different from the mindsets, behavioural dispositions, and the regulated collective structures to which we are accustomed. The discourse of flexibilization may, to quote Schneider (1993: 2), be seen as 'an enchanted milieu', with conceptual invocations as yet not fully explored. The notion of flexibility invokes notions of a different, alternative kind of labour market and individual disposition. Its performative power resides in the difficulties of clarification. It may embrace a variety of meanings and frame mutual on-the-surface understandings. It acquires meaning only in the context in which it is used, and in reference to the position and interest of the actor. Its multivocal character also makes it a convenient shorthand in the encouragement of certain modes of thought and action. Hence, its inherent political dimension, raising issues of power and responsibility, should not be underestimated.

The audited temp: practices of evaluation

In the sense that the concept of flexibility may be seen as a political, normative tool, we may also ask how it is put to work in the context of evaluation of performance. The rise of what has been called the 'audit culture' and the associated techniques of accountability are clearly evinced in the temporary staffing business. Seemingly mundane, dull and routine practices of evaluation may have profound effects on the future assignments, salary levels and career development of temps. Such practices may be understood as 'audit technologies' that function as instruments for new forms of governance and power (Shore and Strathern, 2000: 57). As Shore and Strathern put it with reference to higher education, 'They embody a new rationality and morality and are designed to engender amongst academic staff new norms of conduct and professional behaviour. In short, they are agents for the creation of new kinds of subjectivity: self-managing individuals who render themselves auditable'. As noted by Shore and Strathern (2000: 58), ideas and practices of auditing are but one expression of a global process of neo-liberal economic and political transformation that have migrated not only across sectors but through various transnational connections (Hannerz, 1996), and taken on particular local forms in specific local contexts. For the temporary staffing sector,

Children in the age of flexibility (© *Robert Nyberg*)

the practices of evaluation can in large part be traced back to management strategies of their American headquarters.

Characteristic of temping is a 'manufactured uncertainty' (Giddens, 1994: 184). Many aspects of working life, such as if and when there will be a next assignment and where one will go for the next one, are undecided until shortly before the current assignment is terminated. The continuity of work is organized only in terms of 'scenario thinking', in the way of an as-if construction of possible future outcomes. And since transience has become a more or less permanent condition, the temps 'have no choice but to choose how to be and how to act', to borrow Giddens' phrasing (1994: 75). The individual temp is made to reflect upon her own, individual role in influencing its outcomes (Garsten and Turtinen, 2000: 187).

One way of doing this is to pay attention to continuous learning in order to stay 'employable', as labour market rhetoric has it. In the folder 'A job to love', Olsten Personalkraft emphasizes the importance of:

Continuous development
  We know that it is important to develop one's competence within one's professional area. We can offer you that. We can also offer you more. During 1997 we are enlarging our learning departments to modern, comfortable and easily accessible knowledge centres. These are open for you, as much as you want. Come on in during day- or evening time, practise on a switchboard or surf the Internet. Test your knowledge of Excel or learn PowerPoint from the basics, everything is possible! The knowledge and competence you have when you start working with us, we'd like you to maintain and develop. The centres are serviceable both for you and our customers. Your chances of varied assignments increase with the breadth of your competence. Take advantage of the chance you get through Olsten to learn something new.

As highlighted in other chapters in this volume, becoming employable does not just involve training – it involves a great deal more. What is needed is an ability to learn, to communicate, to cooperate, to judge one's own situation, to make diagnoses, to understand and embrace change, as well as mobility. Moreover, responsibility for employability is shared. Enterprises, governments, local authorities and individuals alike are encouraged to take on responsibility for employability. As we have seen, employability in the temping business is largely to do with flexibility. Flexibility in turn requires continuous learning and upgrading of skills. Most of this is done by the individual him- or herself outside office hours and is unpaid. The agency provides the computers and software they consider appropriate as well as testing routines that may help temps qualify for higher pay. But it is in the hands of the individual to make the time actually to practise and learn, something many of them find difficult to do after a full day's work. Educational interests outside of these are not particularly supported, nor discouraged, but looked upon as a sideline.

  Another important aspect of employability is evaluation. The practices of evaluation are intended to make temps aware of the necessity for development and improvement as well as keeping track of the performance of their dispersed workforce. The practices of evaluation are an integral part of the political technologies of governance in temping.

Temps at Olsten are always evaluated after a completed assignment. The manner in which the evaluation takes place is highly standardized. While the testing that a new candidate has to go through concentrates on the skills of the candidate, the evaluation concentrates on the perceived traits of character and behaviour of the temp. An 'Evaluation Form' (*Utvärderingsblankett*) is used on which details of the performance including punctuality, attitude and skill level are rated. Furthermore, the individual temp is evaluated by Olsten Personalkraft once a year. During this performance review, the temp may also share his or her experiences from temping, for example regarding what assignments have been most and least appreciated, and why. However, the temp does not make an evaluation of his or her experiences with clients in any routinized way. Depending on the character of the temporary employee – assignment coordinator relationship, the temp may informally make some sort of an evaluation, but this is not archived or kept, as are client evaluations of temps. Client evaluations are considered to be very valuable to the agency, and as they are received they are attached to the bundle of papers that together make up the record of the individual temp.

Temps are generally aware of the fact that they are being evaluated, and consider it 'good' and 'reasonable'. There is a general understanding as to the competitive character of the labour market, and the normality of being evaluated. A good evaluation helps them in getting a good assignment, they tend to say. By taking this attitude, they contribute to the governance of temp work and to a particular understanding of the attitudinal and behavioural characteristics of the flexible temp. Mary, who is 25 years old and has been working with Olsten for three years, expresses well a common view among temps:

We have, like, little performance reviews or whatever you call them with our contact persons at Olsten, and then we talk. At that time, they have had this evaluation with the client so they will know what the client says, and then they talk to us, and we will know what the client thinks about us. We get to know what they have said about us ... And then we may reply to that ... We may not write anything, but we do have these talks with our contact persons so that's good.
Interviewer: Do you think this works well or are you nervous about being evaluated? No, don't think I am [nervous, my remark]. I mean, I can only do my best ... There has not been any problem yet, so. No, I haven't [been nervous, my remark], 'cause then it wouldn't work ... You can't work well with everyone. You don't fit in with every

company...You can only do your best. If they want something different you can't really do anything about it. Or, you can always improve, but, well, that's the way it is. So it's not something I go around thinking about, that it could be unpleasant or something like that.

Like Mary, most temps interviewed regard the evaluation as a normality, something they have not thought could be questioned. Rather, they subject themselves to the routines of the temp agency. And if reflecting about them, they tend to accept the necessity of evaluations. How would it otherwise work? It would seem here that the 'normalizing gaze' has conferred upon evaluations a taken-for-granted status. Not only have they been made into routines the temps comply with, but into routines they tend to take for granted, contribute to, and even welcome. What would the alternatives be?

To enhance and reward professional competence and appropriate behaviour, the temp agencies regularly announce awards that are made public among the temps and staff. Olsten offers the recognition of 'Golden Ant' *Guldmyran* on a yearly basis to temps in different categories. There are, for example, the categories of the 'Receptionist of the Year', the 'Accountant of the Year', the 'Olsten Employee of the Year', and the 'Newcomer of the Year'. The winners are made public in the newsletter *Bullen*, and rewarded with a diploma and an ant coloured in gold and presented at the yearly customer- and employee party. These awards work to encourage identification with agency expectations and to foster acceptance of the company's claims on their performance. Shortly before my interview with Lotta, she had been awarded the Golden Ant for her outstanding contributions, together with a colleague of hers. As she told me about it, she glowed with excitement and joy about the attention and confirmation she was given:

It's so much fun when they are to nominate ... We were all sitting at a table in the Concert Hall when they [one of the managers at Olsten] announced the name of my colleague. And we looked at each other, she and I, and then they read my name. But that's me! [laughing]. You get completely.... Then one doesn't hear a word. You float into some sort of [laughing] dream world.... We got a diploma, with an ant. And then we received a large golden ant made of cellophane paper or something. It was such a lot of fun [laughing] ... Cause then you get an official recognition. That's really great. And then everybody is sitting there watching and you walk up to the stage and ... You get really nervous. It really is fun. And it's so much fun because so many of my colleagues have also received these awards.

Awards, like the public announcement of the Golden Ant, gives visibility to the good and desired performance of temporary workers. Individuals become conscious of themselves as 'performers', seemingly 'in control' of their performance (cf. Munro, 1999). On occasions like this, what constitutes good performance and a good temp is made explicit and visible. The codified expectations of pamphlets and introductory courses are given content and concrete expression, and the individual temp stands out as the performing agent. Good practice is here related to individual conduct (cf. Shore and Strathern, 2000: 292).

Apart from developing and evaluating individual skills and competence, the temp is also made to reflect more consciously on the kind of impression he or she gives in front of the client, and on how to manage and improve these. Elsewhere, I have described how the enhanced reflexivity and the increased concern about individual appearance and manners are a significant aspect of the construction and maintenance of the categorical temp identity (Garsten, 1999; Garsten and Turtinen, 2000). The need for 'emotional labour', that is the management of feeling to create a publicly observable facial and bodily display, relates strongly to the intermediary role that temps perform between client and temp agency. As Rogers (1995: 152) rightly spells out; 'The agency relationship creates a stronger need for emotional labor in two ways. First, the temporary worker actually has two jobs: one as a clerical worker at the hiring company and another as a representative of the temporary employment agency'. Even though her material builds on interviews with temporaries in the US, the basic condition of the agency relationship is valid in the UK and Sweden as well. Like the temps interviewed by Rogers in southern California, the temps at Olsten Personalkraft are highly aware that they are considered as representatives of the temporary employment agency and that their future assignments may depend upon their accommodation of the clients.

The self-evaluative gaze is learnt by temps as part of the job, so to speak. It is a way of adapting to existing structures and normative demands, and a response to the rhetoric of the flexible labour market as freedom from hindering structures and with increased opportunities of constructing one's own life-narrative and work-biography. Lash (1994: 120) emphasizes the need to address what he refers to as 'the structural conditions of reflexivity'. What underpins the reflexivity of temps is a web of global networks of corporate structures, in which the conditions for temporary work are to a large extent a question of the place of temps in these structures.

Collective individualization: the making of individual performers

The agency's claim to influence over a temp's physical appearance, manners, and emotional display is backed by the continuous reference to the need to represent the agency professionally and to accommodate to the client's expectations. It is a market demand to which individuals have to adapt flexibly. Showing the right attitude and dressing properly is part of what it takes to be flexible. However contradictory it may seem, being flexible thus involves accepting the rules of standardization (cf. Hochschild, 1983: 103).

By linking flexibility to standardization of patterns of thought and action, the agency can control aspects of the temps' behaviour that they would otherwise not be able to, given their spatial dispersal and mobility. The more precarious the temp – agency relationship, the larger the scope for control of the temporary agency worker's display of attitude, appearance and manners. Looking smart and behaving professionally in a somewhat subdued manner increases one's chances on the market for temping, which is indeed a market as we commonly understand the term (Garsten and Turtinen, 2000: 187–91).

The temp is thus led to take on a reflexive attitude towards him- or (more commonly) herself, to constantly keep an eye on her employability as a flexible worker. This means working on one's power of attraction for clients and assignment coordinators at the temp agency, accepting continuous monitoring and, not least, learning to monitor oneself. The temp is led to understand that responsibility for continuous learning and upgrading of skills, for getting a next assignment and for being employable in the long run, is placed onto herself. The political technologies for putting this into practice show a striking degree of similarity across the temporary employee workforce, across corporations, and across nations. The collective, collegial basis for discussing the demands of temporary work, common or varying experiences, or potential joint interests is, due to the discontinuous and scattered character of the job, very weak.

In this process, the discontinuous character of the job plays a significant role. The social aspect of work is undermined by continuous movement across client organizations as well as by the fact that assignments are by nature temporary. Temps experience a lack of collegial community. Concepts such as colleague, competitor and client are often vague and interchangeable. To begin with, a temp's interest in getting to know her temp colleagues is scant, since they will rarely end up working within the same client organization anyway. Interest in participating in social events organized by the temp agency is low, since one hardly knows anyone of those who might attend. At the workplace, most temps prefer to keep a distance from their workmates, since they prefer to focus on the task at hand and not to get too involved. Moreover, they are recommended by the agency not to take part in gossiping or talking behind people's back at the client's. Nevertheless, most temps regard their workmates at the client's as their colleagues, as exemplified by Vera:

> My colleagues . . . [hesitating], well that's the people I work with on a daily basis at the client's. But, wait a minute, they are not really my colleagues. They're my clients. So my colleagues have to be the other temps at Olsten . . . But I hardly know what they look like to begin with, or what their names are.

There is also the sense that temp colleagues are simultaneously competitors, competing for the appreciation of agency staff and for wages. Temps at Office Angels and Olsten Personalkraft share, however, the concern for developing and maintaining good relations with the coordinators at the office during assignments, since being known and appreciated helps them get a next, and perhaps more fulfilling, assignment. These shared interests never coalesce into concerted action of any kind, however. The fact that union membership among Olsten Personalkraft temps is relatively high does not seem to have any impact on the formation of interest groupings, either. There is a striking lack of ideas regarding what the backing of a union or collective bargaining might bring about for them as individuals, and even less on what it might entail for them as a collectivity. With lack of recognition of union membership, the place of the temporary agency worker in the community of workers is unclear at best, evinced in the lack of formation of interest groups along these lines. 'The union. . . . I don't really know what it could do for me . . . ' is a common expression when asked about the role of the union in the temporary staffing business.

To sum up, the discourse of employability and flexibility has been seen as involving new ways of controlling the individual. It points to a tension between individual control of the work situation and the self on the one hand and the framework provided by the temporary employment agency and the client organization on the other. The discourse entails, in other words, a tension between existing and emerging regulatory patterns in the construction of social identity. While flexibilization would at first glance appear to strike a contrast to anything that leads in the direction of rigidity, structure, standardization, and the like, the case is not as simple as that. We see then, how the individualization of risk in the labour market goes hand in hand with a social construction of a category of workers – the flexible temps – where the procedures of being employed, assigned and evaluated involve new patterns of regulation and governance. The workplace is a pre-eminent site for contestations about the nature of social identity, and one that speaks to larger structures of interdependence. I suggest that work, as evinced among temps, is being collectively individualized. The political technologies of auditing work collectively to standardize certain aspects of the temp identity. At the same time, the temp is taught to perceive of herself as the primary source of agency for ensuring her employability.

Conclusion: employability and the audit gaze

In this chapter, focus was placed on the policies and social practices through which flexibility, as a prerequisite for employability, is taught and regulated among temporary employees. Learning to be employable as a temp builds on acquiring a sense of agency by identifying with a particular category of subjectivity. Temps learn to integrate the expectations of the agency in ways that make government as external constraint turn into self-regulation, or governance. In the discourse of flexibility and employability, notions of the reliable, versatile, and independent individual are rendered powerful and authoritative while notions of the self-monitoring and 'bending' self are just as significant, but rarely talked about. The everyday social technologies of work practice are mobilized in particular ways to shape the way individuals perceive of and conduct themselves.

Both agency staff and temps see flexibility as a necessary trait for the full engagement of individual aspirations in the pursuit of employability in the labour market. Standardized evaluation procedures by which the individual is put to test are part and parcel of the schemes of government that regulate work performance to be experienced as an individual affair. Here, I would agree with Bauman in that '[the] present-day anxiety is a powerful individualizing force' (Bauman, 2000: 148). It divides instead of uniting and the idea of 'common interests' grows ever more nebulous and loses all pragmatic value. While the discourse and practices of employability and flexibility affect employees at a structural, organizational level, the effects are experienced and dealt with individually.

Together, they constitute a powerful individualizing force. While the discourse itself addresses structural conditions of smoothly functioning, dynamic labour markets, its effects are individualizing in their consequences, leading people to perceive of themselves as the primary source of agency and responsibility.

The work on fostering the worker as a 'disciplinary subject' that took hold with the establishment of wage-labour as an ideological tool thus continues, albeit in different organizational forms and with somewhat different content (cf. Jacques, 1996: Chapter 6). The temporary staffing sector has its own ways of developing its employees in the preferred direction. The political technologies of employability and flexibility are important instruments in the attainment of this goal. They entail accepting, and embracing, the audit gaze.

The fact that these technologies stretch across sectors, organizations, and nations, gives us all the more reason to believe that they express not just 'market demand', but an ideology in its own right: an ideology that is transnational and expansive in character.

Notes

* 'Gumby' is the name of the little green plasticine boy from the toy-land world of Gumbasia. Gumby could walk into storybooks and through mirrors, blast off to the moon and travel back to the dinosaur age, and roll himself into any shape he chose. What kid didn't want to be Gumby?!

1. As reflecting the ongoing change in this business, a large part of Olsten was acquired by Swiss Adecco during spring 2001 and hence abandoned its brand name. After the fusion, Adecco had 4,500 employees in Sweden. I will, however, use the name the company had at the time of my research throughout the chapter.
2. Personal communication with the The Salaried Employees' Union, HTF, and the Swedish Association of Temporary Work Businesses and Staffing Services, SPUR, September 2002.
3. It may be interesting to note here that the educational level of temporary workers in Sweden is somewhat higher than the workforce average. 48 per cent have completed upper secondary school, while 37 per cent have a post-upper secondary school education. The equivalent numbers for the workforce as a whole are 50 and 29 per cent (Fridén et al., 2000: 61).
4. All informants' quotations have been translated from Swedish to English by myself, as have Olsten documents in Swedish.

References

Bauman, Zygmunt. 2000. *Liquid Modernity*. Cambridge: Polity Press.
CEC [Commission of the European Communities]. 2002. *Proposal for a Directive of the European Parliament and the Council on Working Conditions for Temporary Workers*. COM(2002)149 final.

Foucault, Michel. 1978. *The History of Sexuality*: Volume One. Harmondsworth: Penguin.

Foucault, Michel. 1991. 'Governmentality'. In *The Foucault Effect: Studies in Governmentality*, edited by G. Burchell, C. Gordon and P. Miller. London: Harvester Wheatsheaf, 87–104.

Friberg, Kent, Åsa Olli and Eskil Wadensjö. 1999. *Privat förmedling av arbete i Sverige*. Stockholm: Swedish Institute for Social Research (SOFI), Stockholm University.

Fridén, Lennart, Ylva Hedén and Eskil Wadensjö. 2000. *Personaluthyrningsföretag: en bro till arbetsmarknaden?* Bilaga 2 till Mångfaldsprojektet. Stockholm: Ministry of Industry, Employment and Communications.

Garsten, Christina. 1999. 'Betwixt and between: temporary employees as liminal subjects in flexible organizations'. *Organization Studies* 20(4): 601–17.

Garsten, Christina and Jan Turtinen. 2000. '"Angels" and "chameleons": the cultural construction of the flexible temporary employee in Sweden and the UK'. In *After Full Employment: European Discourses on Work and Flexibility*, edited by B. Stråth. Brussels: Peter Lang, 161–206.

Giddens, Anthony. 1994. 'Living in a post-traditional society'. In *Reflexive Modernization: Politics, Tradition and Aesthetics in the Modern Social Order*, edited by U. Beck, A. Giddens and S. Lash. Stanford: Stanford University Press, 56–109.

Hacking, Ian. 1986. 'Making up people'. In *Reconstructing Individualism*, edited by T. Heller, M. Sosna and D. E. Wellbury. Stanford: Stanford University Press, 222–36.

Hannerz, Ulf. 1996. *Transnational Connections*. London: Routledge.

Harvey, Michael, W. F. 2002. 'The Social Dialogue as a case of network governance: lessons from the failure of the framework agreement on temporary agency work'. University of Toronto: Department of Political Science. Paper presented to the First Annual Pan-European Conference on European Union Politics, Bordeaux, 26–28 September 2002.

Henson, Kevin. 1996. *Just a Temp*. Philadelphia: Temple University Press.

Hochschild, Arlie Russell. 1983. *The Managed Heart: Commercialization of Human Feeling*. Berkeley: University of California Press.

Jacques, Roy. 1996. *Manufacturing the Employee: Management Knowledge from the 19th to 21st Centuries*. London: Sage.

Lash, Scott. 1994. 'Reflexivity and its doubles: structure, aesthetics, community'. In *Reflexive Modernization: Politics, Tradition and Aesthetics in the Modern Social Order*, edited by U. Beck, A. Giddens and S. Lash. Stanford: Stanford University Press, 110–73.

Miller, Peter and Nikolas Rose. 1995. 'Production, identity and democracy'. *Theory and Society* 24: 427–67.

Munro, Roland. 1999. 'The cultural performance of control'. *Organization Studies* 20: 619–40.

Rogers, Jackie Krasas. 1995. 'Just a temp: experience and structure of alienation in temporary clerical work'. *Work and Occupations* 22(2): 137–66.

Rogers, Richard. 1996. *Temping: The Insider's Guide*. New York: Macmillan – now Palgrave Macmillan.

Schneider, Mark A. 1993. *Culture and Enchantment*. Chicago: University of Chicago Press.

Shore, Cris and Marilyn Strathern. 2000. 'Coercive accountability: the rise of audit culture in higher education'. In *Audit Cultures: Anthropological Studies in Accountability, Ethics and the Academy*, edited by M. Strathern. London: Routledge, 57–89. (www.spur.se, 24.9.2002).

9
Teamworking and Emotional Labour in Call Centres

Antony Lindgren and Per Sederblad

Introduction: teamworking as a way of organizing work in call centres

Service work is today one of the cornerstones of the capitalist economy. The impact of the discourse on employability is discernible not least in the practices, power relations and social contracts at work in call centres. Call centres are expressions of the contemporary change towards more competitive labour markets. Even though call centres have existed for a long time, since the 1960s at least, they became during the 1990s the most striking phenomenon in service work internationally (Bain *et al.*, 2001). This expansion is due, we believe, to the spread of organizational ideals and models advocating concentration of core competencies and lean production models, and to processes of globalization. The rapid growth of call centres is also related to the development and spread of new information and communication technology (ICT), which is a prerequisite for the development of call centres and their use of the Internet and intranet.

Even though ICT is a prerequisite for the transformation of labour markets, social change is more decisive. Call centres are often viewed with reference to 'outsourcing', involving the setting up of new contracts between employees, employers and clients. These contracts are being elaborated in a global neo-liberal discourse and involve adjustment to market demands, customer needs and other externalities. Thus, it is in the tension between marketization and customization on the one hand, and the need for organizational commitment in new forms of service work on the other that the driving force towards increased reliance on call centres is to be found. Teamworking is a managerial strategy for creating commitment in a work environment

172

often characterized by intensive work and surveillance. In organizations with a relatively high degree of flexibility, with increased mobility of employees, and high customer focus, organizational commitment is an essential prerequisite for management. Employability in the service sector reflects the use of normative expectations and organizational commitment as managerial tools.

The point of departure for this chapter is teamworking and its changing form and meaning in Western societies. The teamwork concept used to refer to small units of employees with technically and functionally interdependent relations in industry (Berggren, 1992; Sederblad, 1993; Ahlstrand, 1999). Today, teamworking is often used in reference to larger units, or even to whole organizations. According to Procter and Mueller (2000) this shift is attributable to several factors: the spread of teamwork into the service sector; the dominance of employer-driven initiatives; and a more strategic use of teamworking. The new use of the concept resembles the use some Japanese companies make of 'teams'. According to Benders and Van Hootegem (2000: 54) 'team' here '...refers to a collective spirit'. In this sense, a 'team' may be said to constitute something of an 'imagined community' (Anderson, 1983). One consequence of this shift is a focus on new competencies geared to new forms of teamworking in service work, which speak to the demands of employability.

For employees in call centres, certain competencies are particularly important for their employability, such as being able to work intensively and, in a proper manner, handle customer contacts by telephone. Arlie Hochschild (1983) made a considerable contribution to the understanding of service work when she elaborated the concept 'emotional labour' to analyse how service workers deal with Tayloristic organizational structures but also must be able to handle customer relations. Work at call centres introduces new dimensions of emotional labour, such as having to deal with a continual technical registration and surveillance of work as well as demands for handling a variety of different customers. Hochschild makes an important distinction between 'emotional labour', based on the management of feelings of the employees, and 'emotion work', referring to more genuine relations between individuals.

The chapter presents research on teamworking in new forms of service work, primarily in call centres.[1] It focuses on teamworking and emotional labour and deals with the issue of flexibility. The research presented here builds on case studies in Sweden at three plants: two call centres and one travel agency with a work organization similar to call centres. The call centre plants studied are a call centre with about 30 employees offering switchboard services of different ranges to other companies, and another larger call centre with more than 70 employees with a variety of services offered. Both these call centres are located in municipalities in rural districts in northern Sweden and are owned by the same company. The company is Swedish and was founded in the early 1990s. Its customers are primarily to be found in the Stockholm area.[2]

The travel agency studied, also with around 70 employees, had recently changed its work organization according to a call centre concept for frontline work. It is located in a larger town in southern Sweden and it is the local office of an international company. One reason for including a travel agency in our study is that call centres are increasingly being established in this sector. We are also interested in studying the change towards call centre models in existing offices. Moreover, before we started the research in the agency presented here, we conducted an exploratory study of a small local office working in traditional ways but increasingly using ICT.

Several methods were used in the research. First, around 20 interviews with managers and employees were conducted. Secondly, a short questionnaire was distributed to employees at the workplaces, including questions on personal backgrounds, education and training and attitudes to work. Thirdly, we also made observations for several days at the plants and at the call centres we were allowed to listen in on conversations in some of the incoming calls.

The argument in this chapter aims at integrating a discussion around teamworking and emotional labour analysis in call centres. We will argue that organizing work in teams can be a way to ideologically control employees and contribute to the establishment and maintenance of tighter social relations between them. These relations can be useful for the employees, and indirectly for the employers, since they facilitate their endurance of a work situation characterized by intense forms of emotional labour. In the call centres studied we have found examples of teams consciously organized by employers to support a 'team spirit' at the plant and to increase the feeling of wellbeing of the employees in the workplace. The chapter gives examples of successful attempts to establish this control as well as examples of resistance and conflict at individual and collective levels.

Teamworking in call centres: cooperation and relations

One source for the theoretical background to Hochschild's analysis of emotional labour is labour process theory, emanating from the work of

Braverman (1974) on how Taylorism in capitalist society leads to deskilling and increased control of workers. This analysis was further developed by Friedman (1977) by introducing the idea that there are different forms of control strategies: 'direct control' based on Taylorism, but also an alternative strategy termed 'responsible autonomy'. This latter strategy includes an organization of teams with functional cooperation and a considerable degree of autonomy in the conduct of work. Both types of control can be found in call centres.

While cooperation in teams in industry has been described in a great deal of research (see Sederblad, 1993), the crucial question today seems to be cooperation in teams in the service sector. It is important to be aware that work in the service sector shows a great deal of variation, for example in the skills necessary to conduct the work. The kind of work conducted in particular call centres can also be very different, and even in the same call centre, work practices can vary a great deal (Mulholland, 1999).

In similar vein, we have in our case studies identified two forms of teamworking in call centres. These can be described as 'functional cooperation' and the establishment of 'personal and social relations'. This distinction recognizes Friedman's categorization, but is more related to the specific social conditions at call centres.

In the two call centres we have studied, the degree of functional cooperation is low. Reporting on her case study of a broadcasting company call centre in Northern Ireland, Mulholland (1999) paints a similar picture for the day shift. The night shift, on the other hand, is less pressured and some time is available for collaboration between employees answering customers with specific knowledge and demands.

What comes out of our research is that under 'normal' working conditions in a call centre, with hard workloads and calls waiting to be handled under strictly regulated time periods, a mass-production kind of work organization is utilized. Opportunities for cooperating are very limited: employees can seldom leave their communication with the customers. To be sure, there are breaks during the day, even though they are often very brief. However, and more importantly, employees are supposed to share their experiences and knowledge with workmates and the management. This is done through a continual updating of the databases used in the call centre.

The operators in the call centres studied updated their information when performing their work tasks, even though the customer service department had the main responsibility for this and for maintaining relationships with the customer companies in the form of signing the contracts, specifying the service, the instructions, and so on. The customer service department alone would not have been able to update the database – including in our small call centre some 4,500 customer-companies and their employees – without the support of the operators. The degree of dependence of the client companies on the operators for database quality was testified by the lively discussion taking place at one of our call centres. The discussion concerned the changed instructions on how to handle a customer question of a difficult technological kind. The expert system – the instruction manual – was not sufficiently clear to make this understandable to the layman. The IT-support department was consulted, but this did not result in a better understanding. Since none of the operators wanted to 'look stupid' in the eyes of the callers the end of the discussion was a joint agreement on how to reply.

Thus, to make things work, the company depends on the loyal cooperation of all employees. The example shows how dependent companies in this kind of service work are on their employees – those in 'the frontline' (Carlzon, 1985). The new aspect, in our view, is that the cooperation of the employees is not only decisive in 'the moment of truth' of the service encounter but also in the routines of keeping the database updated – this is the precondition of the service they are performing. The employees cooperate by keeping the knowledge needed alive, at the same time as supporting the combination of information handling and managerial control. Moreover, the work is very intense. There is a great deal of information to keep in mind while processing a call.

In our studies of teamworking, we have found that real, or functional, cooperation is rare in the service sector. In all probability it is becoming even rarer with changed working conditions and the increase in the number of call centres. Given the background of the mass production organization of the labour process and the individual element of communication between the employee and the customer, this should be no surprise.

Nevertheless, teamworking is often claimed to be practised in the service sector. A more thorough investigation into what teamworking actually is in this environment is, however, necessary. Our interpretation is that the second aspect, establishing social and personal relations, comprises basic elements of teamworking in the service sector. These relations have more in common with what Hochschild calls 'emotion work', the creation of more genuine relations between employees. Personal relations are here understood to involve two individuals while social relations can be established between a varying number of employees. Informal kinds of relations are quite an appropriate basis for building teams, especially since the workload creates a strong need for personal and social support among the members in the team. At the same time, as we will show later, these kinds of relations open up forms of strong normative, ideological control.

In our case studies, it was obvious that the whole workplace was regarded as a team, sometimes even the whole company. Thus, the team concept is in transition: from small work groups to larger units as the whole subsidiary or the whole company. What we are left with is 'empty' teams, in the sense that there is limited functional cooperation but strong personal and social relations between employees that may be integrated into normative structures. Thus, employees often report that they belong to a team when no formal team structure is applied; they say 'we are all a team', an expression often used by employers. We come quite close to what Procter and Mueller (2000), relying on Benders and Van Hootegem (2000), have identified as the first form of Japanese teamworking, namely that the whole company or organization constitutes a team. In our opinion, however, it is important to draw a distinction between the local subsidiary and the whole firm. In the call centres we have studied the strongest identification is with the local level. Below, we will provide examples of strong identification with smaller teams at workplaces using a call centre concept.

The praxis of emotional labour in call centres

In this section, we present some empirical observations from our case studies, illuminating the specific form of emotional labour at call centres. The smaller call centre offers switchboard services to other companies. Here, it is essential that the operators are customer-oriented, friendly and accommodating. In principle, all the information one needs as a telephone operator to perform one's work task is on the computer screen. Here instructions are given regarding in what manner to answer the call and in what way the call should be processed. The manner in which one is supposed to answer the call is specified on the screen with an instruction as a 'phrase of greeting': 'welcome to...' or 'good-morning ...' followed by the name of the company. Sometimes there is a phonetic instruction on to how to pronounce the company name, for example, 'English pronunciation' or 'ko-fee', etc. This is followed by one's own name, for example, 'It is Anna!' or 'the telephone attendance' or 'the telephone service'. The result may be something like this: 'Welcome to

Coffee Break! This is Anna! You called NN. She is not in at the moment, can I ask her to call you back?' alternatively: 'Can I take a message?'

The instruction also informs about the way in which the telephone operator should process the call. Generally staff are supposed to take a message and say that the person being asked for will call back. The charge for every call taken care of is 6 SEK (approximately 50p or $0.60); every message costs an extra 6 SEK and there are also smaller extra charges for messages via fax, SMS-texts, mini-call messages and emails. There is also a regular fee per month or year. Since salaries have a small piece rate element (paid when surpassing the norm for calls and messages) the telephone operator also has an interest in taking a message.

In addition to the written instructions, there are many graphic symbols on the computer screen. An example of the kinds of symbols the instructions may contain is the so called 'smileys' – a minimalist face in the form of a circle with a line for the mouth indicating three different states of mind: very kind, kind, and neutral. Smileys are not a complement to a text, but contain meaning in themselves. There are other symbols of the same self-referential kind: one is a 'blip' on the screen telling the operator has received an internal message, not yet opened. There are other 'marks' (*asterisk*, etc.) indicating that the customer has not yet read a message, that the operator has charged the customer for the message, that the operator is allowed to state the mobile-telephone number and the like. One such symbol is a 'flash' – showing the names on the client company's list of employees and who the caller has been asking for. There is also a 'signature' attached to the messages making it possible to identify which operator has written the message.

A few of the graphic symbols function as a complement to the written instruction, such as a traffic light showing a red, yellow and green light indicating the degree of availability of the client company. Thus, a red light indicates very restricted availability, no messages or only messages of a very private nature to be noted. The traffic light is, thus, a complement to a more detailed written instruction describing how to process the telephone call in regards to noticing, dumping and taking messages.

The travel agency studied operates in the business-travel sector. This travel agency has, since a few years ago, been divided into two departments, where the 'frontline' employees are separated and others work with administration in the back office. Here a call centre concept is introduced with the aim to work 'open gate', this means that all operators should be able to work with all customers. However, some of the larger companies have specific teams of operators to communicate with. The interest in these arrangements is increasing even though they are costly for the companies. It could be mentioned that the employees in this travel agency are obliged to write newsletters on the subjects they are responsible for, according to the division of labour in the agency.

The use of ICT tends to blur the distinction between a call centre and a travel agency. In one of the call centres, we found a group of employees working only with booking tickets for one airline company, thus acting as a sort of travel agency, although specialized. When the booking of a journey takes place via the use of the telephone or the Internet, the distinction between the 'real' travel agent and the call centre operator is basically a difference in their individual competence. Here we have found a marked contrast. By using a questionnaire, we found that in the traditional travel agency, the competence is higher in the sense that the employees are given more continuous training – in the call centres practically no one gets this type of training. These observations indicate that the competence of the call centre workers at first sight could be evaluated as quite low.

In a call centre with intense work and elaborate surveillance techniques, emotional labour is a dominant phenomenon. The space for emotion work might, at first glance, be very restricted. However, our interpretation of the case studies is that a more detailed analysis would reveal that the work situation can vary considerably both between call centres, and within one specific call centre. The existence and need for tight personal and social relations suggest that there is an acceptance of emotion work by managers. Less developed social relations would mean the risk of customer dissatisfaction being considerable. The social and personal relations between employees are also an important source of control at the workplace where teams are an important element. However, the system of using teams as a basis for control might be somewhat fragile as the teams could also be a basis for resistance. While call centre work demands emotional labour on the part of employees, employees also turn to each other for emotion work and to develop support structures. Emotion work may provide a social base for the formation of collective sentiments and interests.

In our view, neo-liberal politics has led to increased marketization. The discourse of employability has been implemented in this social context. The strategy of direct control has given way to a strategy of management by learning including a changed meaning of teams. In this new strategy, normative elements are combined in a discursive practice blurring the distinction between those managing and those being managed. The structural demands of the market turn this into a necessity.

The energy required for intense emotional labour creates the need for support and the establishment of tight personal and social relations. To 'be social' thus becomes a necessity in all call centres.

Control and resistance

Control of the employees in call centres is rigorous. Performance is 'directed' by the expert system, that is primarily by the software, which makes flexibility in performance of the work task very restricted. The labour process is registered and controlled in numerous ways by using the capacity of 'electronic surveillance' inherent in the new technology: time being logged on/off; number of calls handled per day or hour; SMS-messages delivered per day; number of coffee/tea breaks, longitude of breaks and other information. These historical data are registered both on the individual level and on the plant level. The control system at call centres is thus based on technical control (Bain *et al.*, 2001; Lindgren and Sederblad, 2001).

From a labour process perspective, it is obvious that the call centre provides management with advanced possibilities for technological control. This control mainly concerns the intensity of work; the length of the calls is, for example, continuously registered. The content of communication is, at least in the call centres we have studied, only rarely controlled. Operators have some freedom to communicate with customers in their individual way. There are examples of a substantial degree of motivation on the part of employees to contribute to the smooth working of the call centre. These observations go beyond the control perspective as they illustrate that workers in the service sector perform important tasks in communicating with customers, tasks that cannot be completely controlled.

The individual and externally oriented character of the work task – communication with customers – makes control a difficult task for management (Mulholland, 1999). This means there is a limit to the extent of bureaucratic, direct or technical control that can be exercised in call centre work (Lindgren and Sederblad, 2000a). The performance of the work task must, ideally, be controlled in other, indirect, ways – for example, through establishing norms favourable for the company and for the work tasks (Lindgren and Sederblad, 1999). Shared meanings are created, making human resource management important to management and a management strategy of 'learning' is thus recommended (Zuboff, 1988). Due to this generic restriction on traditional forms of control and the consequent necessity of relying on other forms of control, there is, potentially, both 'freedom' in work and 'resistance' to control and to management in call centre work.

At call centres there are also elements of traditional bureaucratic control such as instructions and rules. Control is exercised by scripting, telling the operators by written instructions or graphic symbols (or both ways) how he or – most often – she should perform her work task. In addition to these forms of control, there is also direct surveillance, through the team leader 'listening in' to the operators' calls, allegedly making it possible to help the single operator improve his or her handling of calls. Thus, there are a number of ways in which management – generally 'team-leaders' – try to 'direct' the performance of the work of the operators. In addition to this control, there are 'test-calls' made by the customer-companies using the service, an activity that may indirectly influence the performance of the work task of the individual operator (Callaghan and Thompson, 2001).

Thompson and Wallace (1996) have distinguished three dimensions of control in teamworking: technical, governmental and normative dimensions. The technical and governmental dimensions of control at call centres are mainly exercised directly in relation to the employee. Yet we have also found the normative aspect of teamworking to be very important in call centres. The normative control is based on personal and social relations that are, as shown above, characterized by frequent interaction. A Swedish union report based on an investigation of 15 call centres stresses that employees often show a high degree of loyalty to the employer (HTF, 2000). Research in the UK also indicates that ideological control in call centres can be quite strong and also involve life outside the workplace (Knights and McCabe, 1999). The relational ties between employees and loyalty to the employer make normative control an important managerial tool.

The new management strategy and work organization assumes that employees, to an increasing extent, 'offer themselves' while carrying out their duties. At the same time – due to the decisive importance of the customer – operator relationship – individual as well as team-based regulation of emotional labour has become important. To the individual, this is a matter of escaping the risk of burning out; to the organization this is a question of maximizing profits.

In her analysis, Hochschild (1983) touches upon the meanings that flight attendants confer upon their job. Here group cohesiveness and identification plays an important role. The flight crew may stimulate each other in carrying out genuine emotion work by manipulating the cabin atmosphere into being cosy and intimate. In this case the employees themselves manipulate the passengers, while the management exercises a profit maximizing pressure. At the call centres we have studied, there were examples of conscious attempts to foster identification between the parties involved, between employees and customers as well as between operators and client organizations. In many cases, this occurred in smaller client companies. The call centre took care of their telephone service when they were out of office for some reason. One of these clients, a very satisfied one, repeatedly told the operators that when asked how many employees there were at his company, he used to tell his customers: 'We are two people in the field and two hundred ladies at the office!' This referred to the whole call centre company. The operators were proud of this and obviously felt a responsibility for representing the company well.

When we were listening in on conversations, we noticed that people calling in often thought that the operators of the call centre were actually employed by the company they were calling. The operators generally let them believe this and presumably this is the reason why they found it so embarrassing not being able to answer questions like: 'What is your address? Is that around the corner from the petrol station?' The 'fraud' was then discovered!

The team was thus there – in their minds – as one source of identification, the other being the client company. The clients called in regularly to inform about their whereabouts the next day, at the same time updating information about their future whereabouts. They seemed to know each other, in the sense of having had 'this conversation' many times before. It is hard to tell, but this familiarity may also be a part of the business idea of the telephone service offered by this call centre company and is thus 'forced', or managed, in some way.

Work at travel agencies has traditionally been socially intense due to its basic face-to-face character. The social interaction between the travel agent and the customer or traveller has always been crucial and the expert systems – such as booking computer programmes, as well as the traditional printed colour catalogues, have only been auxiliaries in the performance of the work tasks. In terms of control, we can say that it has traditionally been, and still is, characterized by autonomy – responsible autonomy in Friedman's terminology (Friedman, 1977).

With the diffusion of new ICTs, this situation has started to change. Today the customer can book his or her own air tickets, hotels and so on 'on-line' without the interference of the travel agent. Thus, new ICT is changing the market conditions of the travel agencies by introducing new competitors, including call centres specialized in booking travel for single airlines and 'virtual' Internet competitors. In spite of technology, the face-to-face interaction still seems to be important to customers when booking a journey. Nevertheless, the new information technology is affecting work practices and work relations at travel agencies, including the establishing of in-house call centres.

Where management relies on traditional forms of control, 'alienation' appears, for example as a lack of responsibility for the quality of the service (Houlihan, 2000). Traditional forms of resistance occur, for example by 'dropping unpleasant customers' (Taylor and Bain, 1999). Organizing and acting in trade unions have at the call centres in Sweden during the late 1990s increased, indicating a recognition of conflicting interests.[3] The forms of resistance to other types of control, such as norms, are less obvious, but in line with Foucault we can expect that where there is power, there is also resistance (Beronius, 1986). Thus, resistance is generically an important issue in call centre work, and the question of the new forms it takes in response to new forms of management is something which has to be studied alongside other aspects of call centre work, for example in relation to the way 'teams' are used in call centres.

We have observed that the introduction of new time schedules and increased control of the disposal of working hours in relation to leisure time is often met with resistance from employees. This refers to individual discontent expressed in our interviews. Control of how work is conducted and even the often detailed control of the intensity of work is mostly accepted, but when the span of control also influences the whole life situation for the individual, spontaneous and organized resistance arises. During our interview periods, both at the call centres and at the travel agency, there was discontent with short-sighted work schemes, sometimes causing conflict.

The union (The Salaried Employees' Union, HTF) has now reached an agreement with the employer organization for call centres (HTF, 2001). The agreement is specific on employment conditions and working hours; employment shall be permanent if the employee works more than 832 hours during a period of six months. As to working hours, no more than 48 hours of work per week are accepted and in a six-month period 40 hours on average is the limit. On other working conditions, the agreement is more general: wages are stipulated for work in excess of ordinary hours, but the agreement can be substituted by individual or local agreements between employers and employees or unions.

We interpret this agreement as a first attempt from the union to regulate Sweden's now rapidly growing call centre sector. Union strategy in the sector can also be found in a report by HTF titled 'The "new" labour market', based on visits to 15 call centres and questionnaires to union representatives and 244 members (HTF, 2001). The report concludes that employees at call centres are not homogeneous and can broadly be divided into two categories: young people who have little experience of other work and regard the work at the call centre as a temporary job, and employees with the ambition to stay longer and to acquire more qualified work tasks and managerial positions. The union has to try to represent both these groups although their interests sometimes differ.

Flexibility in call centres

In public debate and managerial discourse, call centres are often used as examples of 'the flexible firm'. The degree of flexibility in call centres is, however, as shown by Bain and Taylor (2002), often exaggerated. For example, most employees work full-time at call centres and extra hours are relatively rare. We find employers at call centres attempting to increase flexibility, but these attempts are often met with resistance from employees. In this section, we will discuss call centre flexibility by giving examples of different forms of flexibility (Thompson and McHugh, 1995).

The demands on employees at a call centre to be *functionally* flexible are often high, as they are supposed to be able to handle many different customers as well as serving several companies with different kinds of business. The skill of the employee to be able to handle this in a decent and even pleasant manner could be seen as a central aspect of employability at call centres.

Sofia Beckman reports on a study based on interviews with 'communicators' and managers at an outsourced call centre facility. The competencies demanded are not only functionally specific or task related, but are seen as necessary to handle the specific work situation at a call centre and to endure emotional labour: 'being flexible, having a sensitive ear, being a strong personality and having a go-ahead spirit, being service-minded and having a natural talent for communication with people' (Beckman, 2002: 97).

There is a common division between call centres with in-bound and out-bound calls respectively. The in-bound call centre is the most common form and our cases belong to this category. The out-bound call centre includes, for example, telemarketing and sales. Currently, there is a tendency in Sweden to mix these forms of call centres and let employees at in-bound call centres work with, say, telemarketing when the workload from in-bound calls is low. However, as the work tasks as well as the wage systems at the two forms of call centres are quite different, these attempts have been followed by some problems in planning the workflow as well as resistance from employees defending their work situations and earnings.

The second form of flexibility, *numerical flexibility*, refers to the ability of a firm to adjust the number of employees according to need. The degree of numerical flexibility in call centres in Sweden has been exaggerated (see Malmö stad, 2002). There is a strong tendency today to use temporary employment agencies at new call centres, for example, at the telenursing centre started in Malmö at the end of 2001. The use of agencies increases the flexibility for the call centre company as well as the demands for flexibility on the part of the employee, who will find herself involved in quite a complex organizational structure with relations to the temporary employment agency, the call centre company, several customer companies – and many customers!

The idea behind outsourcing and call centre companies could be seen as a way to increase *financial flexibility*, the third aspect of 'the flexible firm'. The outsourced call centre is supposed to cut costs by specialization and large-scale advantages and to diminish the financial risk of the customer company. Here we find a clear example of the impact of the 'marketization' at call centres discussed in the introduction of this chapter. In the flexible firm model, marketization is followed by segmentation and we now see obvious trends in this direction in the Swedish call centre sector.

The consequences of the segmentation of the labour market are that there are both winners and losers in the labour market. The increased prevalence of numerical and financial flexibility is followed by large groups of employees with more unstable employment conditions. Functional flexibility, though, may be favourable for employees in the core sector of the labour market. The widespread view of call centres as 'low-end' workplaces in the IT sector needs qualification, since there are tendencies indicating that call centre work may also be 'core' and involve key organizational aspects.

Conclusion: call centre work and employability

We have argued that the concepts of 'team' and 'teamworking' are in transition. Whilst teams, as in traditional industry work, could be defined in a functional manner, this is no longer the case. The new teams, rather, have the purpose of providing employees with personal and social support, especially when work is of the emotional labour kind. Teams are increasingly defined subjectively – by identification – rather than in an objective sense.

The new forms of teamworking fit in with the prevalence of emotional labour in a society with an increased share of service work. Call centres illustrate this development neatly. Call centre work is characterized by intensive work under strong surveillance, with a large amount of customer contact. This creates a need for 'emotional support' to be able to endure the work situation. This can most easily be solved by establishing personal and social relations among the employees.

Employees create various types of formal, or more often, informal work teams to provide the support needed. Hochschild (1983) described this for flight attendants working in pairs, but in the call centre larger teams may serve similar functions. The team may be a smaller work group, as in the travel agency studied, but more often at call centres the team refers to the whole work organization.

There are also instrumental reasons underpinning the changed ways in which the team concept is used. The employee – customer relationships, which are at the core of the new service work, sometimes make strict technical or traditional bureaucratic control difficult, especially if the strategy is to focus on quality rather than quantity. Hence, employers may try to use the team concept for normative and ideological control purposes. The existing personal and social relations in work teams are a convenient basis for pursuing management strategy.

The growth in the number of call centres in several societies, among them Britain and Sweden, can be expected to be followed by increased demands for specific forms of employability. This includes the competencies necessary to work in new kinds of teams in call centres as well as capacities to work intensively under strict control and to communicate with customers of different kinds by telephone and by using computers. We can see, from an employability perspective, how new forms of teamworking go hand in hand with new forms of emotional labour in call centres.

Notes

1. The research is part of our project 'Working conditions at call centres and travel agencies', 2001–2003, sponsored by AFA (formerly AMF insurance), Stockholm.
2. The ownership has now been restructured and the Swedish company has been taken over by an international company.
3. In a union investigation of 15 call centres, the degree of unionization varied between 30 per cent and 100 per cent. The degree was, at 7 of the call centres, 50 per cent (HTF, 2000: 9).

References

Ahlstrand, Roland. 1999. *Förändring av deltagande i produktionen: Exempel från slutmonteringsfabriker i Volvo.* Lund dissertations in Sociology 31. Lund: University of Lund.

Anderson, Benedict. 1983. *Imagined Communities.* London: Verso.

Bain, Peter and Phil Taylor. 2002. 'Workforce flexibility in call centres: stretching to the breaking point'. Paper presented at the 20th Annual International Labour Process Conference. Glasgow: University of Strathclyde.

Bain, Peter, Aileen Watson, Gareth Mulvey, Phil Taylor and Gregor Fall. 2001. 'Taylorism, targets and the quantity-quality dichotomy in call centres'. Paper to the Annual International Labour Process Conference. Royal Holloway. London: University of London.

Beckman, Sofia. 2002. *Kulturens inflytande över möjligheterna till lärande: en fallstudie om call center.* Master's thesis. Department of Economics. Stockholm: Stockholm University.

Benders, Jos and Geert Van Hootegem. 2000. 'How the Japanese got teams'. In *Teamworking,* edited by S. Procter and F. Mueller. London: Macmillan Business.

Berggren, Christian. 1992. *The Volvo Experience: Alternatives to Lean Production in the Swedish Auto Industry.* Ho: Basingstore Macmillan – now Palgrave Macmillan.

Beronius, Mats. 1986. *Den disciplinära maktens organisering.* Lund: Arkiv.

Braverman, Harry. 1974. *Labour and Monopoly Capital.* New York: Monthly Review Press.

Callaghan, George and Paul Thompson. 2001. 'Edwards revisited: technical control and call centres'. *Economic and Industrial Democracy* 22(1): 13–37.

Carlzon, Jan. 1985. *Riv pyramiderna!* Stockholm: Bonniers.

Friedman, Andrew. 1977. *Industry and Labour: Class Struggle at Work and Monopoly Capitalism.* London: Macmillan – now Palgrave Macmillan.

Hochschild, Arlie Russell. 1983. *The Managed Heart: Commercialisation of Human Feeling.* Berkeley: University of California Press.

Houlihan, Maeve. 2000. '"Where is management?": Power and knowledge in call centres: views from the middle'. Paper at the conference 'Working Together?' Knowledge and Management in the Information society. Keele: Keele University.

HTF, 2000. *Den 'nya' arbetsmarknaden: HTF's projekt om förhållanden inom Telemarketing – Callcenter – Telefonintervjuföretag.* Stockholm: Tjänstemannaförbundet HTF.

HTF, 2001. *Avtal för call/contactcenter – och marknadsundersökningsföretag.* Stockholm: Tjänsteföretagens arbetsgivarförbund och Tjänstemannaförbundet HTF.

Knights, David and Darren McCabe. 1999. 'Team drives and private lives: gendered tensions in teambuilding at work'. Paper at the 3rd International Workshop on Teamworking. School of Management. Royal Holloway. London: University of London.

Lindgren, Antony and Per Sederblad. 1999. 'Post-fordist regulation in the service sector: emotional labour in Sweden and England'. Paper presented at the 17th Annual Labour Process Conference. School of Management. Royal Holloway. London: University of London.

Lindgren, Antony and Per Sederblad. 2000a. 'Teamworking, control and information in a travel agency and a call centre'. Paper presented at the conference 'Working

Together?': Knowledge and Management in the Information society. Keele: Keele University.

Lindgren, Antony and Per Sederblad. 2000b. 'Inside or outside? Relations and borders of the new work teams'. Paper at the 4th International Workshop on Teamworking, Nijmegen Business School. Nijmegen: Katholieke Universiteit Nijmegen.

Lindgren, Antony and Per Sederblad. 2001. 'Work organization, control and qualifications in a travel agency and in a call centre'. Paper presented at the 19th Annual International Labour Process Conference. Royal Holloway. London: University of London.

Malmö stad. 2002. *Callcenter i Malmö 2002*. Malmö: Utvärderingsgruppen i Malmö stad på uppdrag av Näringslivskontoret.

Mulholland, Kate. 1999. 'Gender, emotional labour and teamworking in a call centre'. Paper presented at the 3rd International Workshop on Teamworking. School of Management, Royal Holloway. London: University of London.

Procter, Stephen and Frank Mueller. 2000. 'Teamworking: strategy, structure, systems and culture'. In *Teamworking*, edited by S. Procter and F. Mueller. London: Macmillan Business.

Sederblad, Per. 1993. *Arbetsorganisation och grupper: Studier av svenska industriföretag*. Dissertation. Department of Sociology Lund: Lund University.

Silverman, David. 1979. *The Theory of Organizations: A Sociological Framework*. London: Heinemann.

Taylor, Phil and Peter Bain. 1999. '"An assembly line in the head": work and employee relations in the call centre'. *Industrial Relations Journal* 30(2): 101–17.

Thompson, Paul and David McHugh. 1995. *Work Organization: A Critical Introduction*. 2nd edn. London: Macmillan – now Palgrave Macmillan.

Thompson, Paul and Terry Wallace. 1996. 'Redesigning production through teamworking'. *International Journal of Operations and Production Management*. 16(2): 103–18.

Zuboff, Shoshana. 1988. *In the Age of the Smart Machine. The Future of Work and Power*. London: Heinemann.

10
Work as an Arena for Disciplining Mind, Body and Emotions: The Volvo Bus Plant Case

Margareta Oudhuis

Introduction: a change of discourse

Traditionally, obedience was a significant and important trait in order to be looked upon as 'a good worker'.[1] One was supposed to work hard and consistently and do what one was told to do without questioning the boss or the given order. Today, being employable means being able to make one's own decisions, to be creative and independent or at least to act on one's own behalf without being told what to do. It also means wanting to learn more, to be flexible, multifunctional and thereby able to rotate between different tasks on different levels of assignments as well as between different units within workplaces. Being employable also suggests that the responsibility to learn skills general enough to be put to use across companies and in different jobs, lies in the hands of the individual. In summary, this shift of discourse implies that one can no longer rely on simply doing a good job, to obey and subordinate one-self, as in 'the old days'. This is just not good enough anymore.

The change of discourse also has consequences for the organization of work and leadership style. Traditionally, even though less pro-nounced in Sweden than elsewhere, organizational leaders were characterized by being responsible for making all decisions, for knowing all the answers, for being in control, while the new form of leadership means being more of a coach. This in turn suggests someone with the capacity to delegate responsibilities and control, someone who listens to his or her employees, giving them the right to make decisions on their own. Their main purpose is to make sure everyone is developing, one might even say creating the right attitude – making individuals eager to learn more and to be self-acting (Ekwall, 2000). As the new head of the Volvo Bus Plant at Borås, Sweden, put it: 'My job is to make sure the individuals and the teams in the organization are developing. To make sure everyone gets the chance to grow. My job is not to be a problem-solver, but to ensure conditions that enable the personnel to solve the problems themselves'.[2]

Drawing on a case study of the Volvo Bus Plant, this chapter sets out to deal with the issue of how this transition has been possible, what different techniques *were* and *are* being used when trying to make up or construct 'the good worker' as compared to 'the employable individual'. I also intend to discuss the different effects or consequences on the individual worker when being subjected to these different kinds of disciplinary techniques and strategies. What are the effects on mind, body and emotions? In which ways do these effects differ? I will argue that even though the outcome might be similar at specific times there are significant differences as to people's reactions and deep emotional responses.

It is important to note that this transition is far from an overall phe-nomenon. Instead, a polarized development regarding the organization of work seems to be at hand in current working life. On the one hand there is a development towards more varied and qualified tasks demanding well-educated and self-acting employees, while on the other hand a backlash towards more Tayloristic ways of organizing work is evident.

As mentioned above, the chapter draws on findings from a study of the Volvo Bus Plant at Borås, Sweden. Volvo is a well-known forerunner on work organization issues – with its Kalmar car factory and, even more famously its Uddevalla Plant, as key examples. The latter entailed a model described as 'enriching production' that was introduced as an alternative to lean production (Sandberg, 1995). Even though the plant was closed down at the beginning of the 1990s, the overall concept is still valid as a guideline according to Volvo's official publication *The Volvo Way*. Volvo therefore remains an interesting case to study.

I participated at five seminars led by the head of the plant with people from the shop floor, four of them by the end of 2001 (October and November) and one of them, a follow-up seminar, in May 2002. The seminars were part of the so-called staff member seminars, occurring every six months, in which all workers participate. The purpose of the seminars was to make sure everyone got the chance to take part in discussing the goal of the plant and how to 'translate' that goal into their own daily job-situation. I also conducted participant observation, lasting four days, at one of the lines in the factory. Finally, seven of the workers together with the leader of that specific line were interviewed. The workers were all male, aged 23–58, with different periods of employment, from two years up to 25. The leader of the line was interviewed twice, in the autumn of 2001 and in May 2002. Moreover, the study builds on informal conversations with people, working in that specific line, but also in other lines.

The Volvo Bus Plant case: a change in work organization and leadership style

In this section, I will describe the transition from one discourse to another as regards the organization of work and leadership. First I will give a short background of the plant. Then I will describe the present situation regarding the organization of work using some comparisons with how it was organized previously. The plant was founded in 1977 and is one of the largest bus-chassis assembly plants in the world with a capacity of about 20 built-up and 12 knocked-down (material kits to other assembly factories) chassis per day. The plant functions as a hub for Volvo Buses' global chassis production and apart from supplying material kits also provides technical knowledge and support to local factories around the globe. At present, about 470 people are employed of whom about 400 are in production and 70 in white-collar positions.

The plant, situated a short distance outside the centre of Borås, consists of three buildings connected to one large main assembly hall, plus one separate building for test-driving. When approaching the plant one first sees a small separate entrance building that has to be passed before entering the plant itself. The main office is situated to the right of the reception while the assembly lines are placed to the left after passing through a long passage. When entering the workshop one is met by bustling activity and equipment is universally visible. From the roof conveyers hang for transportation of the 8–13 metre long greyish chassis frames and material racks are placed all along the lines. People move about or are busy mounting brackets and other details to the frame with the use of whistling pneumatic hand tools and fork lifts. Special towing vehicles continuously pick up or deliver material to the racks.

The assembly-division was until recently divided into three different departments – the pre-assembly department, the chassis assembly department and the final assembly/test-driving/adjustment department. The teams were in turn divided into six different docks, A–F, each consisting of three different assembly stations and one quality-assurance-station, situated very closely together.[3] The pre-assembly department was divided into six stations, situated at a distance from the docks, serving all of them (Christmansson *et al.*, 2000: 10; Bennehall, 1999). Moreover, the plant has from the start used a team-model with rather long assignment cycles and a relatively strong decentralization of responsibilities to the teams. The leadership style seems, however, to have been of a more traditional kind. In effect, according to a presentation of the FLiSa-project (2001), different kinds of problems were detected during the 1990s, such as a reduction of the commitment among the workers, that everyone's competence was not fully used, and that an increase in the dependency between the workers had occurred (Christmansson *et al.*, 1998: 10).[4] Another problem was that the material needed to build the chassis was placed some distance from the docks. Ideas of a new team model therefore took form. Making use of the competence and capacity of every worker was to be one of the guidelines of the new model. Moreover, its starting-point was the employees' wish and capacity to take on new assignments and increased responsibilities as long as the right prerequisites were given (Christmansson *et al.*, 2001: 3). Accordingly, multi-skilled, flexible and customer-focused workers should be rewarded (Bennehall, 1999: 4–6). This in turn would demand a flatter organization as well as increased learning possibilities.

The change of team model was decided in June 1998 and gradually effected from November 1998 until the summer of 2000. At first there had been plans for introducing another team model consisting of just two or three stations, a model which was not possible to carry through. The old team model was, however, broken down and replaced by five different lines. Each line consists of five different stations. Four of them have each three to four different groups of tasks or 'balances', whereas the fifth is a quality assurance station. Three people usually work on each of the four stations (not counting the quality assurance station). In addition, five employees have the role of a 'substitute' – someone who knows all the different tasks or balances belonging to one or two specific stations (often more). The pre-assembly stations are situated alongside the line (thus the pre-assembly department has been broken up). Everyone is supposed to rotate, both between the different tasks at the station itself and between the pre-assembly stations and the line-stations. As we shall see later, this difference in placement of the stations has had some rather radical consequences. Furthermore, some tasks which used to be carried out at the office-level, have now been delegated to the lines, creating different support functions such as technique-support, personnel-support, 'improvement'-leader etc. These roles are supposed to be held by different workers for a year or two and then passed on to someone else. The same idea applies to the two team leaders of the line.

Each station (and therefore each person) has about one hour and twenty minutes to build their part of the bus. There are quite a few different models to build and therefore many learning opportunities are in-built, especially if everyone rotates between the different jobs. In addition, the plant is and has been aiming at using a just-in-time model to avoid tying up capital, ensuring that goods come in when needed instead of keeping a stock at the factory as well as building for more or less immediate delivery. This, however, makes the organization vulnerable to disturbances. Every now and then the lines therefore stand still waiting for parts or equipment from outdoor- or indoor-suppliers.

A new head of the plant was appointed in early spring 2001. She came from another Volvo plant where she had very successfully adopted a leadership style with emancipatory overtones. Her arrival gradually resulted in the replacement of some of the previous line leaders to others with a more distinct coaching leadership style. Consequently, the change of management coincided with a change of leadership more in accordance with the employability discourse.

The plant is still in the middle of such a transition process. One might say – even though the term employability has seldom been used – the elements inherent in the discourse have to a great extent come to the fore in the new team model. This becomes evident after listening to the new head at one of the seminars:

> There is no security today, anywhere. There is only one person to turn to and that person is you, yourself. Only you can make yourself employable. Being employable makes us attractive. In order to achieve that you will need non-company specific competence. It is in fact this non-company specific competence that makes us employable. It's our only security.

As is shown by this quotation, the responsibility is put on the individual. It is up to him- or herself to make sure to gain the right kind of knowledge, to uphold the competence needed to be viable in the labour market. This point was stressed at another seminar. A line leader present at the seminar showed an overhead with the following words:

> I actively take responsibility for my own competence development.

He went on to describe his satisfaction with the fact that one of his men had done just that – had taken care of his competence development all by himself. To make this possible it is however, according to the discourse of employability, necessary to introduce a leadership style characterized by management by objectives, trust, and a continuous development of the workers.

The shift of team model

In terms of the actual layout of the stations the line has undergone some radical changes. Previously, the four stations formed one united team; today every station is more or less a team in itself, with not as much contact with the other stations as before, therefore creating difficulties to see the whole line as one team. As Peter, one of the persons interviewed, put it: 'It's as if the line consists of five small factories'. The stations themselves differ greatly in the way they function. Interestingly, quite a change occurred between November 2001 and May 2002, that is within the period following the shift of model and discourse. Before making a comparison between the old and new team model I will try to describe the present model while also comparing the situation at the two points in time (November 2001 and May 2002). The main reason it differs is due to the plant being in the middle of this time-consuming transition process of accommodation at the time of the study.

While three of five stations in this specific line function quite well, two have at times had rather severe problems. The people working there do not always get along. At one of the stations they used to shout frequently at each other while silence has been a more dominant feature of the other. The problems are to a great extent traceable to one of the station-members at each station. One of these stations previously functioned more as one team with everyone trying to help each other get the job done. This changed after the arrival of a newcomer. 'That is not my balance' became a prevailing attitude. 'If he notices that one of us has a "slow" day he goes off somewhere else instead of helping out. If he himself has problems he shouts for help', as another informant, Michael, commented the behaviour of his co-worker. They also have problems getting everyone to rotate. Even if only one person refuses to leave his balance it affects everyone else. Apart from creating difficulties for the others to rotate, an unpleasant and irritable atmosphere and a feeling of discouragement is created. The situation at the other station can be described as both similar and different. As mentioned above silence prevails here to a greater extent. Once again one of the workers has had problems fitting in, again someone who does not want to help the others while demanding help for himself. At times he creates severe disturbances and frustrations, 'pretending' to have finished his part of the job, when in fact he is just taking a break, or simply refuses to do his share. People from other stations stopped trying to help out. At certain times the whole line has been standing still, waiting for this station to finish its part of the job. As one informant put it:

> They have been arguing and nagging at each other ... it simply has not worked out. Sometimes the rest of the line has to wait for half an hour/45 minutes for them to get the work done. If one tries to help, they simply stop working.

As mentioned above, some of these difficulties have been handled successfully since November 2001. This has mainly been achieved through dialogue between the line leader and the people at the stations. Another technique has been increased joint decision-making and encouragement. By the end of May 2002 one of the two stations functioned more effectively. The people working there had jointly decided to start rotating, which in turn had resulted in more positive attitudes towards one another, as well as fewer disturbances in the production process. The situation at the other station is also starting to sort itself out; the person in question is voluntarily moving to one of the pre-assembly stations where he will be working by himself.

The other two assembly stations, on the other hand, function quite well. The members of each station try to help each other; they regard themselves as one team with a mutual responsibility for the station and the work to be done. They try to rotate as much as possible. One difference between these two stations is that one consists of younger people wanting to have fun (making practical jokes), while somewhat more 'mature' people work at the other. The fifth station, the quality assurance station, is in turn run by two people who seem to get along very well.

What experiences are traceable to the change of team model?

Experiences related to the old and new team model

As noted above, the pre-assembly stations have been moved to the lines and different support-roles have been delegated to the stations on the line. These changes have created more learning possibilities for all, but some individuals in particular have been able to take advantage of them. Moreover, some of these learning possibilities, such as the delegated support-roles, have in turn contributed to skills enhancement in accordance with the employability discourse. At the same time, the role of the individual worker has changed. As shown above, it is today to a greater extent up to the individual to take steps to enhance his or her competence. This is to the disadvantage of some who cannot, or are not given the chance, to live up to what the discourse demands from them, and is for the better for others – as the following quotation from one of the workers with supporting roles shows:

> My tasks are much more qualified. I got the role as personnel support as well as the finance support role. I got training to handle these new tasks; I can thank Volvo for it all.

Even though he obviously is one of the winners from the team model and discourse change, he feels that competence development and possibilities to rotate to a greater extent must be a more central part of work itself than is the case today.

John, another informant, has been offered to go to one of the Volvo factories abroad for a few weeks to show them how to build a new bus model. Also, two of the other informants, Peter and David, have been given a chance to move on in their careers. Both of them will succeed today's team-leaders, positions for which they partly have been and will keep getting education. Both are very skilled, dedicated workers willing to develop in their jobs. They seem to be a perfect fit with the employability discourse, taking initiatives of their own, always wanting to learn more, not satisfied with staying in one place. In particular, one of them is very popular among his fellow workers. His name came up quite a few times when the informants were asked to mention a role model. He is regarded as being *both* skilled and helpful. To be a role model one very clearly has to be helpful. It is not enough to be skilled.

Both workers and management feel the different support roles are too 'wide' and 'deep' requiring too much time to fulfil support roles as well as to learn. The persons upholding these functions often do not participate in the line anymore, which, in turn, creates dissatisfaction among other workers. They also tend to keep the functions over far too long time periods, making it difficult for their fellow workers to take over. Thus, there has been a discussion about making the roles 'narrower' and easier to learn, and thereby possible to combine with routine assembly tasks. To make an individual willing to take on one of these support-roles can be regarded as a normative trait of the employability discourse. On the other hand frustrated and irritated employees – counterproductive to the discourse – are a result when denied the possibility to perform support duties when feeling ready for them.

Problematic aspects of the new team model

Some problematic aspects of the new team model are a loss of community and a decrease of certain kinds of learning possibilities.

According to Peter, the people working in the line did not know each other as well as they used to. Previously, they were more closely united, functioning more as one group. They also used to see more of each other outside work: 'We used to go fishing every year. Not anymore'. People working in one of the pre-assembly stations, in turn, used to spend a considerable amount of free time together, often including their families. Since the break-up of their previous pre-assembly department they have not been able to keep such contact up. Apparently the basis of their friendship and solidarity was the organization of work (its actual setting enabling them to have more personal contact as well as to share the same work content).

All in all, it seems that apart from the constant flow of new people into the line, the breakdown of the old community has been due to the actual layout of the line. With the further distance between the stations there are simply fewer opportunities to get to know each other well enough for friendships to evolve. The loss of community at times has the effect that when people at one station have finished their part of the bus, they feel they have finished even if the line as a whole has not. The solidarity between the fellow workers seems to be related to people sharing the same station rather than to the line as a whole.

As to the reduced learning possibilities, John described the situation as it used to be at one of the previous pre-assembly-stations, which served all the lines, and consisted of 17 people. Everybody knew all the different models that were built which meant 'it's a hell of a difference, there were a lot more [models] before', even if he felt there are plenty as it is. Moreover, the possibilities of learning from each other in the actual work setting have at least partly been reduced – today there is too long a distance between the stations to enable employees to actually see what their colleagues are doing. As Michael put it:

Before, everybody could see each other, we were all only 3–4 metres away. There was a greater sense of solidarity between us all and the work flowed so much better. One could also see what the others were doing, which made it easier to rotate. Moving the bus from one station to another was also easier and much faster. Of course, most of us had been working for four or five years, we had so much experience...

everyone helped each other, you just needed to give a shout. If someone didn't function, everybody would try to affect that person, but today every station is on its own ... the others don't seem to bother; they have enough of their own problems.

The possibility to give feedback regarding mistakes has also been reduced – it takes too long a time for the fifth quality-assurance station to contact the stations at the beginning of the line, asking the person responsible for the mistake to come and correct it. This is therefore done to a lesser degree than before.

In summary, even though the learning possibilities as a whole have greatly increased, in some respects they have also diminished.

Experiences of the change of leadership style

The new leadership style as brought in by the head of the plant as well as the leader of the line has, according to the informants, had many positive effects on the people working in the line. Means such as increased influence through delegation of tasks as well as responsibilities and decision-making, positive feedback and being listened to, have for many resulted in an increased sense of self-worth as well as well-being. However, for those not willing or wanting to take on more responsibilities or tasks the effects are less positive. Feelings of distress and frustration have also been created for those who want, but are not given the opportunities to take on more advanced assignments. Moreover, the increased responsibilities create disruptions and conflicts between individual workers, as well as between groups of workers. As regards the positive experiences, John remarked that the new head 'has meant very much ... she has the right values: It's not "I decide" but "all of us 300 here decide"'.

Comments at one of the seminars from other workers to the new head underlined the positive feelings towards her: 'Thank you for the meeting we were called to. That has never happened before'.

According to the informants, the assembly workers are also favourably disposed towards their new line-leader. He takes an active interest in them and their ideas, delegates more, asks them for possible solutions to problems, encourages them to take initiatives on their own, walks around among them etc. This was done less frequently before. John said that the new coach 'is the best'. He went on to say:

He is at the same level as us. He tells us if we don't do a good day's work, we shouldn't be there. Together we make up a team he says.

The contrast with the previous leadership could not be greater as we listen to Sven, who has worked at the plant since its opening, when controllers were in charge:

> Before there were complaints all the time, no matter how hard one worked. No encouragement. Only demands: 'do this and do that', 'you're no good'... It was horrible.

The leadership was characterized by demands, negative feedback and scolding. Peter described the way it used to be compared to today's leadership:

> We were treated very badly. We were scolded at, never any positive words; finally one feels depressed and pushed down. 'You are only building shit the whole time'. Today it's really excellent. Even when things aren't perfect we are told we are doing a good job... that gives us motivation to keep working.

Peter went on to say:

> Before, a person making a mistake was called up to the boss to explain why things had gone wrong (even if the mistake was not found until much later). She kept this little black book. But... we aren't machines... things can go wrong... one more or less ends up not giving a damn about the job.

Another noticeable difference has to do with solving conflicts. According to the informants, one technique was to send people off to other departments. Michael put it this way, regarding one of the previous line leaders: 'She just sent them away when they refused to work overtime. They were sent to another department.' According to John, others acted the same way: 'If he [a previous coach] doesn't get along with someone, he just moves that person. Somewhere else. Instead of trying to resolve it.'

Today, however, conflicts in this line are solved differently. As was pointed out above, other ways are tried out such as using dialogue, encouragement and increased responsibilities. What needs to be underlined, however, is that this has been and still is an ongoing process where some of the people in the line have had to put up with many stressful situations for quite some time before a solution has been found.

Disciplining mind, body and emotions

The disciplining techniques and ways of constructing 'the good worker' as compared to 'the employable individual' differ greatly. At the same time, techniques belonging to both discourses were used during the transition period studied here. Trying to construct these different kinds of individuals can be understood in a Foucauldian sense as using governance techniques or attempting to 'conduct the conduct': to shape, guide and affect the conduct of others, in this case the workers (Burchell *et al.*, 1991; Miller and Rose, 1995). Another useful perspective is to look at the technologies of creating or authoring one's own self (Miller and Rose, 1995; Danaher *et al.*, 2000). Moreover, with Foucault we can ask ourselves if within the discourse of employability it is possible to become an autonomous, self-determining agent, able to resist existing power structures and thereby able to make the choices as to whom we want to be and become (Danaher *et al.*, 2000: 150). Alternatively, is it possible to simply become a self-steering individual who have internalized the ideals and norms of what it takes to be 'successful' in a society striving for a rationality based on efficiency and economic success?

Techniques used to construct 'the good worker' may be regarded as a form of hierarchical steering, aimed at creating and upholding an order of hierarchy, obedience and 'knowing one's place'. On the other hand, techniques such as delegation of tasks and responsibilities, increased learning possibilities, encouragement, praise and positive feedback are in use when constructing the employable, self-steering individual.

Constructing 'the good worker'

As has been shown above, the hierarchical techniques used to create the obedient worker can be categorized as humiliation, subordination, oppression and punishment. Some of these have meant that workers were not asked before decisions were taken, only told what to do, and not able to take initiatives on their own. Other expressions of these techniques are frequent negative feedback and seldom praise, as well as feigning that hundreds of workers are standing outside the factory waiting to get in. The consequences were described at a seminar:

> Many of us don't dare to express what we feel for fear of reprisals. People who have been critical have been pushed down while the opportunist is supported.

To be removed from the department as a consequence of not 'following the rules' of the coach was also a mode in use. Losing one's position was also a technique – as happened to John on his return from vacation, when he found he was no longer a team leader. The reason, according to John, was some kind of misunderstanding and difference of opinion between him and the coach.

Humiliation through repression, affecting self-worth and confidence, was achieved by letting individuals know they were not good enough and could do nothing right, by scolding and by writing their names in the 'black book'. Yet another way used to push people down came to the fore at one of the seminars:

> The blue-collar-workers are regarded as a cost. 'Remember you are an expense', I was told when I was hired. And I thought I was an asset.

Some comments from the seminars uncovered the problematic situation, in the eyes of management, of being right in the middle of a transition from one discourse to another. When management sets out to use techniques belonging to the employability discourse but – for different reasons – are not able to carry them through, frustration is easily created. The process of fully grasping and carrying through the new discourse, making sure people on the floor are given the right prerequisites to meet the new demands, seemed to be a rather delicate matter. As a voice from a seminar stated:

> We must be important to you. Do you see us as a faceless crowd? In such a case we won't bother about anything.

The above quotation highlights the need and wish to be seen as individuals and not 'as a crowd', as belonging to a faceless collective. This, in turn, suggests the process of adapting to the employability discourse is in progress.

Constructing the employable individual

Techniques to construct an individual who is self-steering, committed, creative and eager to learn more take the form of encouragement, praise and joint decision making. To be praised in front of fellow workers for displaying what it takes to act according to the demands of the employability discourse, such as taking initiatives on one's own for one's further training, is one example. One might add the existence of individualized payment systems as another important factor – the more one learns, the more one earns. This is a prerequisite for making up the individual worker – which in turn may be regarded as necessary for making the workers embody the discourse of employability. Moreover, talking about the importance of being employable, may have a strong disciplinary effect. These are the words of a manager as expressed at a seminar:

It's all about your market value, about being employable. Make sure you use the gaps between assignments to learn more.

Comments like these probably help create individualized workers striving to continuously improve themselves, while at the same time, as Miller and Rose (1995) point out, giving praise and encouragement are excellent ways of making use of everyone's desire to perform well and thereby be seen as successful in one's own eyes as well as others'.

A conclusion from this study is, however, that there are some problems connected with these techniques in relation to their purpose or aim. One has to do with the gap between the responsibilities given for one's own continuous learning and the means and conditions for making it come true. To be promised further training and learning possibilities at work, and then to be denied them, at times results in a great sense of frustration, disappointment, bitterness, low-spiritedness and finally indifference – quite the opposite to the desirable engagement in accordance with the employability discourse.

One factor explaining why continuous learning at work does not always function to its fullest is the lean organization model. Another reason has to do with the fact that some people do not want to take part in rotation, which in turn decreases learning possibilities for team members at other stations.

In fact, one might say the new model of leadership and way of organizing work have contributed to weakening the workers as a collective while strengthening their loyalty towards management. This has been achieved by the individualization of work which includes individualized salaries, a new team model, new techniques to conduct the control of the workers and delegating responsibilities and learning possibilities to individual workers.

Consequences on mind, body and emotions

The consequences on mind, body and emotions of being subjected to the above mentioned techniques of making up 'the good worker' and the employable individual differ greatly – but do actually bear some resemblance in specific cases.

In November 2001 some of the people threw tools at the wall when building a new bus model, feeling they did not learn their balances fast enough. The degree of frustration was very high. Some also expressed a doubt that the balances of their fellow workers were easier to build than theirs. This indicates the fear of regarding oneself and/or being seen by others as a failure. A similar attitude was shown when someone at one of the stations was not able to learn a balance as fast as his fellow workers when being asked to rotate. The person in question became highly upset, simply refused to go on trying to learn the new balance forcing himself back to 'his' old balance. Apart from feelings of failure on his own part, he was regarded as a hindrance for others wanting to rotate and thereby learn more. John expressed a similar experience when talking about the reaction from some of his fellow workers as they noticed he wanted to learn more: 'One hears sometimes from the others that "there is no reason for you to learn more stuff". That's what they say. Usually people who stand at one place and maybe don't know so many balances . . . maybe they get stressed "since he is learning more and more and I' don't". . . . ' Apparently some feel they are not really good enough if they do not want to rotate, or are able to learn new balances fast enough. This in turn suggests, again in line with Miller and Rose (1995), that success and failure at work are today to a great extent linked to one's self-evaluation and self-judgement. Moreover, our self-worth is measured not only according to how well we perform the job at hand – as would be the case during the 'good-worker' discourse – but also based on our eagerness and ability constantly to learn more, to take on still more responsibilities, showing the right attitude, and the desire to 'get ahead'.

Consequences on mind, body and emotions during the obedient-worker discourse are clearly visible when listening to Sven's reaction when being subjected to techniques like scolding and humiliation:

> I wanted to leave immediately, but since I had a family to support . . . what else could I do? I had to have an income . . . I made myself into a robot. I had to make myself into a robot.

This behaviour coincided with a period when he was working at a pre-assembly station with only one other person, a very strong-minded individual, with a work capacity beyond the normal. Since he did not get any support from anyone else, Sven felt he had to embody a robotized way of being. He embodied that notion to such a degree, that the new coach (without knowing) commented on his performance with the words: 'He actually works like a robot'. Sven put it this way:

> I didn't allow myself to feel... I let my body work and do what was needed. I tried to think of other things. When things are that hard one often comes home feeling sore and blunt.

The way he was treated, together with the actual job in itself, had further physical consequences: 'I could hardly stand on my two legs'. But what weakened him most 'was that I felt mentally bad'. Today, however, he has 'only a bit of pain in arms and legs' and once again, he 'feels human', as he puts it. While getting positive feedback, being treated as someone who knows what he is doing, his life once more has become worth living.

John, having been at the plant for seven years, described his feelings when he lost his position as team leader a year and a half ago (before the arrival of the new line leader):

> I didn't care about anything... I became one of those I never thought I would, one of those I had heard about. One just waits for four o'clock. I never wanted to be one of those people. I just want to do a good job. I was like that for a year, for God's sake, just waiting and hoping for the clock to turn four so I could go home.

According to John it influenced him outside work as well: 'I could do nothing at home. ... Only the very necessary stuff ...'. He felt tired and 'got to bed early sometimes. If she [the wife] sees I'm not feeling well she leaves me alone. Nothing makes you happy and ... it takes some understanding from your family.'

At the same time it affected his work performance. John mentioned that 'at such times one is not a good worker at all. One doesn't care. If you do a bad job, you don't give a damn. It doesn't matter. That's how you get ...'. Low spirits and indifference involving work and work performance are thus created.

Since the arrival of the new line leader, John had felt so much better. This affected his well being both at work and home, so much so that he no longer wished to leave the line. Moreover, being asked to go abroad to help out at other Volvo plants meant some kind of redress for the grievance to which he feels he was previously subjected.

However, a strong feeling of discomfort in heart, body and mind still hits him today. Michael expressed his feelings in this way when he was not able to carry out his plans to take over one of the support roles he was promised: 'They tell me it's up to me, but since I'm not given the means to carry out my plans...'. Not to be given the prerequisites to live up to the demands according to the employability discourse when one feels ready to do so, has clear disciplining effects on the individual. Michael went on to say:

> If things are nice and pleasant at work, then I have that state of mind, too. But if things are troublesome and don't go right, then that too affects me. I have been tired the whole autumn and can only relate that to work. I have been exhausted when coming home, not wanting to do anything...and with the kids, you tend to get unnecessarily irritated at small things...the same with the wife... When you are in a bad mood you can't just let go of that feeling.

Finally he added:

> I have noticed that I have become much more negative...it's no fun.

Another indication of him becoming negative can be traced back to the fact that he works at a station where one of his fellow workers has made life difficult at times. The same applies to another informant, Lenny, who at times got so upset at the behaviour of his fellow worker that he – shivering with anger – simply had to leave the place.

However, the opposite is more often the case: well-being has increased for most people on the line. Opportunities to develop at work, being encouraged and praised, being asked before decisions are taken, are examples from informants as to the difference that has occurred. Peter described his feelings after being asked to become a team-leader:

> One gets a vision of not having to stand here to build buses until I'm 65...I feel that I develop and get to learn more.

In summary, the disciplining techniques of making up the 'good worker' as compared to the employable individual differ greatly, but at times still have similar outcomes of frustration, low-spirits and irritation. Conversely, it is important to underline the most prominent difference: the move from making up obedient repressed workers to the construction of individuals feeling good about themselves and their achievement. With Miller and Rose (1995) one might say quite a few have been managed in a such a way – through encouragement, praise and increased learning possibilities as well as responsibilities – that a desire to be creative, self-steering, willing to improve oneself, has been achieved.

Conclusion: winners and losers?

As stated in the introductory chapter, this anthology sets out to show how the global discourse of employability and lifelong learning is operationalized and implemented in local practices. From this study the shift from one discourse to another seems to have brought with it both winners and losers. We seem to find ourselves in a polarized situation. Some individuals have become multi-skilled, flexible, task-oriented, self-steering and involved in continuous learning; these are individuals in demand in the prevailing information society as pointed out in the introduction to this volume. The opposite, however, is true for other individuals and groups of individuals. Even though we are dealing with the same discourse on a structural level, it is expressed differently and has different outcomes on an individual level. In fact, its structural logic may also differ in that it has emancipatory as well as more pronounced economic imperatives. It is, however, not possible to detect from this study whether such a difference in logic creates various outcomes at the individual level.

As pointed out in earlier chapters, an important part of the discourse concerns creating the right attitude towards work and one's performance, that is, making people act in a way that increases their market value. This in turn includes a certain instrumentality in the eyes of the agent. John's strategy when losing his team-leader position is an excellent example of a person embodying the employability discourse along these lines:

> But ... as soon as it happened I thought 'I will learn as much as I can' ... I decided to learn everything on the line and then move on to another one; that's what I had in mind.

John's strategy evidently was to make himself more or less indispensable in contrast to someone who builds only one balance and who is thus rather easy to replace. John, stressing the equal value of everyone as human beings, still recognized that someone who is multi-functional is more valuable to his company (and to other companies) than those who are not.

Noticeably, competition is embedded in the prevailing perspective. In Peter's own words: 'When I start something I have never built before and build it faster than the others – at higher quality – then I feel satisfied'. Also Lenny weighed up himself and his performance in relation to his fellow-workers: 'When I started here, I was looking at those who were good at building. Then I competed to finish my part before the people in the station next to mine.' Together with John, these are examples of individuals embodying what it takes to be 'employable', following the advice of management to increase their market value. This also suggests that embedded in the perspective is the possibility for individuals to act as their own agents. At the same time, this could result in greater manageability. An effective way of regulating people is to make them internalize the desired norms, thereby contributing to a self-regulated conduct in accordance with the dominant discourse of employability (see Jacobsson, Chapter 3 in this volume). Furthermore, alienation may occur when individuals become – as well as see and treat themselves as well as others – as goods that need to be made as attractive as possible on the market.

Consequences of another kind follow for those who do not want to or are unable to appropriate the discourse. Some individuals at times appear to doubt themselves and their capacity, scared of being regarded as a failure in the eyes of others. Besides, as John put it, some workers want to keep doing what they always have been doing since 'they need to feel secure at work. To know you know the job well and...they've got theirs and they know what they will be doing during the day...and then they just go home feeling great.' In turn John recognizes his own attempts to 'move ahead' might make them 'feel threatened'. Furthermore, Michael pointed to the fact that some people who had been standing for a long time doing the same job 'don't really take any initiatives, they don't argue, they don't interfere...they do their job and that's it'. To understand oneself along these lines, in turn, affects how one comes to act – or not act.

In conclusion, positive as well as negative sides to these different ways of disciplining and constructing self-employed individuals have been detected. For some this has had clear positive effects, while the opposite is true for others. Some of those who do not live up to the demands of the discourse feel they have failed in life – which was not necessarily the case before. To perform and achieve thus have different meanings. In the 'good-worker' discourse, to perform well meant a job well done. It also included reliability and efficiency about work without having to worry about issues like lifelong learning and social skills. Today the prevailing attitude implies a desire to achieve something beyond what one already knows. What traditionally gave a worker high prestige is not enough anymore. To lose prestige and reputation could therefore be one of the consequences for those who cannot or do not want to take part in the race towards being employable.

Some final questions need to be asked: are we able to become independent, autonomous individuals or merely self-steering, doing whatever is expected to be successful in the eyes of the prevailing discourse? Conversely: do we actually stand a chance of becoming autonomous and independent, or is this in fact just another way of disciplining and constructing self-steering individuals to fit the traditional discourse of economy, rationality and efficiency in the information society? Are we being manipulated or are we actually independent? Are we autonomous or simply functionally adaptable following the ideals of the discourse of rationality and economy in disguise? The difference between the two may be subtle and the only people to tell the difference may be the individuals themselves.

Notes

1. The concept 'the good worker' is constructed by me, but has a reference to F. W. Taylor and his concepts 'competent man' and 'first class man'; concepts he used in his famous work *The Principles of Scientific Management* (1911/ 1942), to describe workers with similar characteristics as 'the good worker'.
2. This and all other quotations are my translations from Swedish to English.
3. There was yet another station belonging to each dock which, however, was placed at a long distance from the other stations creating problems getting material to the docks.
4. FLiSa – Flexible Teamwork in Co-operation – is the name of the chosen team model. Within the framework of the FLiSa-project, consisting of a steering-group, a project group and three work-groups, all in all 20 members, the FLiSa-team model was effected to its completion involving all employees at the plant.

References

Bennehall, Jerker. 1999. *FliSa: Flexibelt Lagarbete i Samverkan.* Borås: Volvo.

Burchell, Graham, Colin Gordon and Peter Miller (eds). 1991. *The Foucault Effect: Studies in Governmentality with Two Lectures by and an Interview with Michel Foucault.* Hertfordshire: Harvester Wheatsheaf.

Christmansson, Marita, Anders Edström, Lars Medbo, Per Medbo and Johan Wass. 2000. *Kompetens och lärande i arbete: ett projekt vid Volvo Bussar AB, Boråsfabriken.* Göteborg: ALI Väst, CORE, Chalmers Tekniska högskola, institutionen för Transportteknik, Chalmers tekniska högskola.

Danaher, Geoff, Tony Schirato and Jen Webb. 2000. *Understanding Foucault.* St Leonards NSW: Allen & Unwin.

Ekwall, Göran (ed.). 2000. *Navigatör och inspiratör: Om chefer, ledarskap och förändringar*. Lund: Studentlitteratur.

Foucault, Michel. 2001. *Övervakning och straff*. Lund: Arkiv förlag.

Miller, Peter and Nikolas Rose. 1995. 'Production, identity and democracy'. *Theory and Society* 24: 427–67.

Sandberg, Åke (ed.). 1995. *Enriching Production: Perspectives on Volvo's Uddevalla Plant as an Alternative to Lean Production*. Aldershot: Avebury.

Taylor, F. W. 1911/1942. *The Principles of Scientific Management*. New York and London: Harper & Brothers Publishers.

Vitbok: FliSa – Flexibelt Lagarbete i Samverkan. 2001. Borås: Volvo.

Volvo Way, The. 2000. Volvo.

11
Time for Competence?: Competence Development Among Interactive Media Workers

Fredrik Augustsson and Åke Sandberg

Introduction: seductive discourses in a dynamic industry

The discourse of knowledge is both dominant and seductive: who in their right mind can be against knowledge when the opposite is presented as ignorance? Employees of today are not only expected to have high levels of education from formal institutions when entering the labour market, they should also continuously develop their own competence to maintain their employability. Thus, learning has become the responsibility of the individual, should be lifelong and take place at work and outside working hours. This chapter focuses on a highly dynamic part of working life where technical innovations are frequent and presumed to call for constant competence development (Rosenqvist, 2000): the production of interactive media solutions. Our purpose is to analyse the general discourse of competence development and employability in the context of the Swedish interactive media industry and its consequences for employees. The empirical material is based on findings from the authors' recent survey directed at managers in Swedish firms producing interactive media solutions (Sandberg and Augustsson, 2002). Areas dealt with are: the types of competencies managers view as important for different groups of employees; the sources seen as important for employees' current state of competence; the amount of resources employees are offered for competence development; the proportion of employees having the possibility to use the resources put at their disposal; and the organization of competence development in different firms.

Empirical results from roughly 350 companies show that most firms offer their employees substantial resources for competence development, but in most firms very few employees take full advantage of these resources. The ways in which firms choose to organize competence development is an important reason for this. Most firms leave the responsibility to individual employees who seldom have the opportunity to use the resources handed to them, since the way work is organized leaves little room for reflection and learning. A reason why on-the-job learning is seen as more important than off-the-job learning in this industry (Johansson, 2000; Aneesh, 2001) might therefore not be something inherent in the learning process, but a pragmatic result of the way work is organized. It is further argued that the use of stock-options and other 'golden chains' to tie employees to firms is not as common as sometimes stated and that the promise of competence development may have taken their place. The attractiveness of the latter promise may be built on interactive media workers' fear of getting behind and losing their jobs (Batt *et al.*, 2001), irrespective of whether that fear is justified or not.

The chapter continues with a discussion of the discourse on competence development and employability and how it is translated in the context of the Swedish industry for interactive media production, that is, how competence development is organized at the firm level. This is followed by the empirical results from our survey showing the extent and organization of competence development. The chapter concludes with a discussion of promises of competence development as a cost-effective tool to attract and keep employees, as well as securing their loyalty.

The discourse of competence development and employability in the IT industry

Discussions about the importance of constant competence development to maintain employability for workers in the interactive media industry have to be understood as part of a broader discourse about the specific nature of the IT industry as a fast moving high-tech field where innovations are recurrent, work demands high, industrial dynamics extreme and current knowledge rapidly becoming obsolete (Rosenqvist, 2000; Johansson, 2001). The IT industry is constructed as something partially different from working life in general (Strannegård and Friberg, 2001; Holmberg *et al.*, 2002), which is best summed up in the idea of a new economy (Tapscott, 1996). Although this discourse rests upon the idea of globalization and the death of distance, there are processes of translation occurring. The Swedish and American discourses, for instance, are not identical (*Ekonomisk Debatt*, 2000). Still, the inherent fluidity of concepts and discussions enables most actors to embrace the new economy as something positive. In Sweden, the idea of the new economy has been linked to both a discussion of a changing or disappearing Swedish model, the restructuring of industries and the idea that old knowledge is constantly losing value and in fact is being destroyed by new practices (Holmberg *et al.*, 2002). And if 'we' (which might mean anything from single companies to Sweden and the EU) do not speed up, we are going to fall behind in the ever-increasing competition and lose out to 'them'. Who 'they' really are is often not specified, but they are not 'us'.

An interesting aspect to note in this *first* line of argumentation above is its determinism: The change is happening, and there is nothing we can do about it, except to go along (Bell, 1976; Castells, 1996). The *second* important part of the argument is the claim that this is happening fast. It is stated in media and public debate that we are already behind, even if we believe that we are not (cf. Jacobsson, Chapter 3 in this volume). The *third*, and most important line of argument, is the displacement of responsibility for competence development. It is you, as an individual worker, who are responsible for acquiring the necessary competence development to be employable! The result is a discourse which identifies competence development as the most crucial factor for working life, places the responsibility for it upon individual workers, and legitimizes employers' right to get rid of workers that do not have the competence required by the current occupation or job (whether employees have been given a realistic opportunity to acquire that competence or not).

The first, deterministic argument is most obviously open to critique. Research on both technology (Rosenberg, 1994), technical systems (Bijker *et al.*, 1987; Bijker and Law, 1992; Bijker, 1995; Latour, 1996), and industries (Chandler, 1962/1998; Aldrich and Fiol, 1994; Hollingsworth and Boyer, 1997; Granovetter and McGuire, 1998; Helgesson, 1999; Fligstein, 2001; White, 2002) clearly show that processes do not develop deterministically. There are always options, different paths and fluxes that might lead to alternative outcomes, although we are not always aware of them. Yet, the idea of a single possible (and often identified as best) state of reality and future path is seductive. It is practically the basis of any current, dominant discourse (Calhoun, 1995).

The second argument, that everything moves faster, is often coupled with the idea that changes are so great or rapid that we are moving into a new societal stage (Bell, 1976; Castells, 1996; Ritzer, 1998; Magnusson, 2000), which seems to be an everlasting truth of every generation (Block, 1990). Trying to empirically test the extent of changes on a societal level between time periods is difficult (Hansen, 2001). A basic problem is that of finding out what constitutes change (Ahrne and Papakostas, 2002). With regard to the interactive media industry, there are indications that the amount or speed of changes is actually decreasing, or at least altering in kind. Innovations and technical developments are still occurring, no doubt, but probably not as rapidly as during the mid and late 1990s.

Related to the idea of accelerating speed is the idea of jobs becoming increasingly specialized (Ransome, 1999), advanced and requiring constant competence development (Bell, 1976), an idea formulated already by Marx, Durkheim, Simmel and Weber. It is true that general levels of formal education are increasing, although not evenly, among the population. But whether this reflects actual increases in job demands on the general labour market is less certain (le Grand *et al.*, 2001). One has to distinguish what workers actually do, from how their jobs are labelled and the demands for education put on them by employers (Thompson and Warhurst, 1998; Augustsson, 2001). Still, even if job demands are not higher, they may be different, necessitating competence development, or rather competence alteration. The current discourse states that the demand for learning does not end when one finishes school (which has probably never been the case for any group of workers). More importance is given to competence development as a natural and integrated part of working life. A number of important issues arise from such a standpoint. Are employers supposed to give employees the opportunity and resources to learn not only what is absolutely necessary for carrying out current projects, but also the more general competence required to be employable and attractive on the labour market? Or, are employees supposed to use non-working hours for their competence development? A situation putting the main responsibility for acquiring competence on individual employees may support and legitimize a system of hire and fire based on the current competence needs of the firm.

The discourse on competence development in Sweden

Having personal networks and competencies in great demand has increasingly become viewed by many as the foundation of security in the interactive media industry, perhaps even more so than having a permanent employment contract (Batt *et al.*, 2001). Firms might disappear, but individual competencies are still in need. This does not mean that the form of employment has lost all importance. Surveys show that an overwhelming majority of Swedish workers prefer to have a permanent employment contract, and this holds true also for the young and the well educated in sectors similar to the IT industry (Kjellberg, 2001).

To speak of competence development in relation to employability assumes there is a risk of unemployment. Previously, the case was rather the opposite within interactive media production in Sweden: there was a shortage of skilled workers and practically anyone with at least rudimentary skills in interactive media could find a job. After the so-called dotcom crisis in 2000 (see more below), unemployment risks rapidly increased. Accurate numbers of layoffs and unemployment for Swedish interactive media workers are not available since they cannot be distinguished in official labour market statistics, but in general they are growing within the IT-sector.

Nevertheless, most actors related to the field seem to be in agreement that continuous competence development is crucial in order to sustain the employability of interactive media workers (both those employed and those currently out of work), although the reasons for this partially differ. Unions and workers view it as crucial for sustaining the employability of workers and possibilities of development at work. The argument is that with higher levels of competence, workers will have an easier time finding jobs, or simply keeping the job they currently have and securing future advancement. A reason why workers and their unions should be aware of the potential risk of becoming unemployed through lay-offs, are the difficulties in getting back into the industry. Results presented below show that managers view on-the-job learning as the most important source of workers' current, as well as future, competence development. In an industry as rapidly moving as interactive media, employers are suspicious of the freshness of the competence of workers who have been out of work for longer periods of time due to the assumed rapid destruction of knowledge.

The unions' emphasis on competence is nothing new, it has been part of a union strategy for development of work organization to ensure 'good work' for all members (The Swedish Metalworkers' Union, 1985, 1989; The Swedish Trade Union Confederation, 1991). During the last few years, however, unions seem to have weakened their ambitions to influence work organization and increased their emphasis on members' competence development in order to get the jobs offered by the market (cf. Huzzard, Chapter 6, and Svensson, Chapter 5, in this volume).

Corporate managers tend to view competence development as a way of securing the possibility to meet customer demand by having relevant knowledge to offer to the market (Holmqvist, 2000). Competence development is also seen as crucial for further development and innovation within the firm (Rosenqvist, 2000). Thus, managers focus on the functioning of the firm, rather than on the individual workers or workers as a collective. The total competence stock of a firm and its organization determines what functions and assignments it is capable of handling (Powell, 1990; Holmqvist, 2000; Fligstein, 2001). One cannot deliver what one does not know how to accomplish, even if one can fake a bit – and some did so in the heyday of the Internet hype in the late 1990s: customers did not really know what was possible to build and what they wanted, and producers did not always know how to build it (Mattsson and Carrwik, 1998; Uvell, 1999). Interactive media is a dynamic field, both in terms of technology and industrial organization. Companies have little possibility of knowing exactly what competence mix to aim for. The payoffs of any investment are uncertain and hard to predict in advance (Rosenqvist, 2000). In a situation like this, it might be easier for employers to use a system of 'hire and fire', especially in periods where the supply of competent personnel is good.

We have seen recent examples of this. Several of the largest layoffs among interactive media companies during the last couple of years (Framfab, Icon Medialab, Cell Network) have been made with explicit reference to the need to 'adjust the competence mix within the company' (cf. articles in journals like *Vision, Computer Sweden* and *Industry Standard*). Managers attempt to lay off employees with the lowest or 'wrong' competence (which is not necessarily those with the shortest formal education). These may be employees whose competence development has been lagging behind during the last few years due to an extensive workload. In other words: companies who are faced with the wrong competence mix have the possibility of offering their employees competence development to 'correct' or improve the situation. Yet this is not always done. Instead, some firms have launched recruitment campaigns only weeks after, or even simultaneously with, laying off a large proportion of employees.

Against this background, it becomes fruitful to understand managers' promise of resources for competence development partially as a way of attracting and keeping competent workers (besides high wages, promises of rapid advancement, perks, etc.). A tight financial situation for firms and greater supply of interactive media workers might make competence development both less possible, and less necessary in order to tie employees to firms. This highlights the need to study questions of competence development and its organization in relation to the current competence levels of different employees within firms, the overall labour market situation, and strategies to attract workers with the desired competencies.

Interactive media producers in Sweden

As part of the wider IT industry, the field of interactive media production has been at the centre of discussions about the restructuring of the labour market and business life. Interactive media production technically means the production of design and programmes for digital, interactive media like the Internet, intranets and for off-line media like CD-ROMs and DVDs.[1] This is an area where visions of new innovations in technologies and digital design (Negroponte, 1995; Pavlik, 1998) are coupled with hopes and fears of a new economy (Tapscott, 1996) and eventually an informational or network society (Castells, 1996; van Dijk, 1999), brought about by bold entrepreneurs in fast growing high-tech and knowledge intensive companies with new (or no) structural features (Davidow and Malone, 1993; Dosi *et al.*, 1998). In the mid 1990s, some managers had the ambition that their companies should become global business leaders within a few years, based on the principle of first mover advantage (Stael von Holstein, 1999). Workers in the industry have been portrayed as anything from computer nerds to IT gurus, creative geniuses and flexible multi-taskers with both generalist and specialist skills (Kidder, 1981; Rogers and Larsen, 1984; Mattsson and Carrwik, 1998; Uvell, 1999; Rehn, 2001; Himanen *et al.*, 2001; Strannegård and Friberg, 2001).

The so called 'dotcom crisis' in 2000, which was more a stock market bubble and e-business failure than an actual economic collapse of the IT and Internet industry, has given the initial hype a little perspective. The hype was simultaneously created by entrepreneurs who sought customers and investors through the media, IT gurus searching for fame and the media itself on the lookout for a good story (Pettersson and Leigard, 2002). Much of what was said and written is now commonly believed to have been mere fads and visions with little substance (Lennstrand, 2001).

However, regardless of the discrepancy between what has been written about interactive media producers and the reality (Lennstrand, 2001; Rössler, 2001), there are still in Sweden a large number of firms active in the business. If anything, the number of firms has grown during the last few years (although there has been a continuous negative trend in 2002), which can be shown by comparing the results of our two national surveys directed at interactive media managers (Sandberg, 1998; Sandberg and Augustsson, 2002). In 2001, there were an estimated 700–1000 interactive media firms in Sweden, of which the majority were placed in larger cities, with roughly one third in Stockholm. The vast majority of firms are small, with a mean of 16 and a median of five employees, although there are a few considerably larger firms. The industry is young, the mean firm was founded in 1992 and started producing interactive media in 1996 (the median was 1996 and 1997, respectively). The field is constituted by both old firms from other sectors (advertising, printing, traditional media, etc.) that move into the field and new start-ups focused specifically on interactive media production (Augustsson, 2002).

Interactive media production is organized in short-time projects based on teamwork, tight inter-firm collaborations and production networks aided by information technology (Rosenqvist, 2000). The industry has, to date, been highly dynamic, characterized by constant mergers, acquisitions, consolidation and restructuring (Johansson, 2001), which has led to a state of complex dynamics, fluidity and uncertainty. Knowledge of which firms exist, in what firms workers may be employed, which other actors they might collaborate with (and compete against), the sort of projects they may work on and the skills needed in the nearby future is truly scarce.

Sources of skills and competence development in interactive media

Although sources of competence can be distinguished in great detail, it is sufficient for our purpose here to distinguish between three sources: formal education (secondary and post-secondary education); private training institutions offering courses to anyone willing and able to pay; and learning on-the-job. These are described below, with an emphasis on learning on-the-job that managers in our study perceive as the most important.

Formal education

The emergence of new work activities has a tendency to precede formal educational programmes. Given that interactive media production as a commercial activity of some scope has only been in existence for about five years in Sweden, there is little wonder that advanced formal educational programmes directed specifically at interactive media are of recent date. Some early schools and courses for multimedia production and web-design were rather basic to begin with, giving a broad but rather superficial training in several aspects of interactive media development: programming, design, project management etc. This was to a certain extent the competence asked for by employers during the first years of hype. Later, demands grew for more in-depth knowledge of different aspects of the interactive media production that these schools could not provide. As a result, some training programmes were not well thought of among employers within the business.[2]

Nevertheless, schools managed to prevail due to a general demand from young people who wanted to work 'in the media'. Due to the rapid growth of the market for interactive media, these courses were initially not able to supply the amount of personnel needed. As a result, many workers active in the field of interactive media do not have an education specifically tailored for the kind of work they are supposed to do. There are, however, several other formal education packages containing parts suitable for the kind of tasks inherent in interactive media production. According to our findings, a majority of interactive media workers do have some form of post-secondary school education, usually meaning three years or more at a university (Sandberg and Augustsson, 2002).

Now, the supply of education has improved at universities and higher schools of technology. The government has granted these schools more funds to increase the number of students within IT. However, following the media attention surrounding layoffs in the IT-sector, the dotcom crisis and the pessimistic view of the future labour market for IT-workers, several universities now have problems filling their places. A large number of students with a specialized interactive media education will probably enter the labour market in a period of weakened demand for workers.

Private training institutions

Sudden demands for competence development within the Swedish interactive media industry, retraining of workers from other parts of the labour market, training of employees in firms who produce and/or maintain their own interactive media in-house, etc. have created a market for private training and educational firms. Some of these training institutions are directly linked to, or certified by, specific software developers (Microsoft, Sun, Adobe), while other firms offer general interactive media related training programmes. Some interactive media producing firms themselves offer education as an additional service. This is unusual, however (Sandberg and Augustsson, 2002).

On-the-job learning

As shown, there are several forms of organized competence development off-the-job, but the major part of competence development for interactive media workers takes place through on-the-job learning. The separation between work and competence development (and play!: Himanen *et al.*, 2001) is not always possible, or fruitful, to make within interactive media production. To learn new skills in order to solve technical problems is as much part of the job as actually producing the solutions (Kidder, 1981; Johansson, 2000; Aneesh, 2001). Here, on-the-job learning is defined as learning in close or approximate relation to carrying out specific tasks involved in interactive media production. This is contrasted to off-the-job learning which takes place outside work, for instance through formal education and at courses offered by private training institutions.

The most basic *form* of on-the-job competence development is individual or collective learning by trial and error. Workers are asked to perform certain tasks for which they initially have insufficient or limited knowledge, and are expected to obtain necessary knowledge during the process of production. The actual learning is not at the centre here, it is, rather, learning as a necessary element in the employees' completion of a task. How they accomplish this (getting past tricky parts, bugs, faults, etc.) is usually up to themselves: it is the responsibility of the individual. They can ask friends and co-workers, pose questions on professional mailing-lists, read manuals or text books, search the Internet, call support-lines, work their way around the problem, etc. The important point is that the problem is solved. Thus, the specific learning that comes out of the process is uncertain, and largely specific for that and similar contexts. But depending on the type of problem that has to be solved, and the preconditions for a narrow or wide search for solutions, the contribution to long-term employability may vary.

Another version of on-the-job competence development is the method of 'following Joe around' (Batt *et al.*, 2001), which basically means that a less skilled employee works with someone a bit more experienced and learns by watching and asking questions. A more organized form of this is mentorship, which is common in labour markets where practical experience and tacit knowledge are seen as especially important (Aspers, 2001).

Learning and competence development also takes place within the teams that make up specific projects. Here, different workers meet and learn from each other while working on specific solutions through group-based problem solving. For this to be possible, however, the task logically needs to include elements that all workers do not already know, and there must be sufficient time for sharing knowledge and learning to take place. However, a problem repeatedly talked about in the interactive media industry is the shortage of time for reflection and learning. As soon as one project finishes, the team is split up and new formations are built up in other teams. Thereby, the potential learning that could have taken place is sometimes lost.

The constant reformation of teams with different workers, some of them from different firms, seems to be less frequent in Sweden than in the USA, where some companies are mere shells that replace a majority of workers on every project (Batt *et al.*, 2001). In Sweden, workers are more closely attached to firms, which is illustrated by the fact that 85 per cent of all workers in interactive media firms are permanent employees.[3] Swedish firms achieve flexibility through outsourcing and collaboration in production networks. With increased supply of interactive media workers, the Swedish situation might change to be more in line with the American. However, one should keep in mind that labour market and working life institutions, including traditions and legislation, differ significantly between Sweden and the USA. Institutions are not automatically implemented, they are transformed to fit their context (Fligstein, 2001).

Discourse in practice: any competence development left for workers?

According to the discourse presented here, competence levels and continuous competence development are of vital importance for the survival of firms as well as for the employability of individual workers. Here, we analyse this general discourse in the Swedish interactive media industry.[4] First, we draw a comparative picture of the importance of specific competencies for various groups of workers directly involved in interactive media production: design and content developers; IT and programmers, and project managers. We describe the importance of different types of competencies: deep knowledge within one's own area of specialization, broad knowledge of the whole process of interactive media production, social and network competencies, and initiative. This is followed by a discussion of the importance of the sources of competencies described above: formal education, private training institutions (off-the-job) and learning on-the-job. After that, we turn to the central question of the promise of competence development, the actual occurrence of competence development, and how competence development is organized within firms.

Desired competencies and how to obtain them

As argued, many interactive media workers have not attended specialized interactive media courses, neither at university nor elsewhere. As a result, the backgrounds and learning processes leading to present levels of competence differ widely among workers. It is interesting therefore to find out what competence sources the *managers* that responded to our survey view as most important for the different groups of employees since they hire (and fire) workers, as well as control and distribute resources for competence development. In our survey, respondents were asked to rank the relative importance of four different sources: formal education (secondary school, university, etc.); experience from other companies (including training); education packages paid for by the current employer (for example courses), and individual learning and experience from the current company and workplace (including practical experience and guidance). In relation to the three sources of learning described above, experience from other companies and learning at the current company are viewed as on-the-job learning. Formal education and training paid by the current employer (which refers to private training institutions) are viewed as off-the-job learning. All sources were ranked from 'of crucial importance' to 'less important'.

For project managers, initiative, social and networking competencies are seen as the most important competencies. These results are not surprising, these are competencies traditionally required from managers. Knowledge of one's own areas of expertise, or the interactive media process as a whole, is not as important. The most important sources for the competencies of project managers are individual learning, followed by experience from other firms. Thus, various aspects of leadership and knowledge of 'how to get the job done' are viewed as the most important competencies for project managers and these are viewed as personality traits or tacit competencies that cannot be acquired through formal education.

The most important competencies for workers focused on design and content production are in-depth knowledge of their own field, and initiative. This indicates that creative personnel are not only expected to deliver on demand, but actually take an active part in the planning of the production and direct the development of the content. Individual learning and experiences from the current employer are seen as the most important sources of competence. This reflects the image of content production as being a somewhat artistic activity dependent on the creativity of individual workers, and their ability to experiment with different techniques. It is also a result of the fact that there have been few formal educational programmes focusing on digital and interactive design as well as content production.

Workers focused on IT and programming are quite naturally expected to centre on their specific area of expertise: programming and other technical aspects of making interactive media solutions operate as intended. However, the ability to take the initiative is not seen as quite as important for this group as for workers focused on design and content production. Just as for the other groups, individual learning and experiences retrieved from the current company are the most important sources of relevant competencies within interactive media production.

The overall picture given by managers is that formal education is the least important factor for all groups of employees, followed by training paid by the current employer. Although the mean age of employees is low, the levels of formal education generally are high, and their knowledge thus is rather recent, it is still practical working experience, not formal education, which is seen as the most important aspect of employees' competence. The situation is further highlighted by respondents' view that, on average, 75 per cent of the learning takes place on-the-job, and only 25 off-the-job. Although courses for interactive media workers given by private training companies are often expensive, managers tend to view them as a rather insignificant source of competence within interactive media production.

Resources for competence development: promises and realities

Results indicate that practical working experience is the main source of both current skills and further competence development. Of crucial importance to firms and employees is the amount of time and resources devoted to competence development, and how it is organized at the company level. Our findings show that 72 per cent of the companies offer their employees a specified amount of time annually, intended for competence development (Figure 11.1). Only 19 per cent of these firms (14 per cent of all firms, respectively) give equal time to all employees in interactive media production, and 81 per cent of them (58 per cent of all) decide the amount of resources based on individual competence plans. The amount of time offered to employees differs between companies, although roughly two thirds (65 per cent) obtain between one and ten days a year.

The numbers in Figure 11.1 show the amount of time employees are offered, not the actual time spent on competence development. To get a picture of time spent, respondents were asked to estimate the proportion of employees actually fully using the time offered during the year 2000. The results are quite striking. In 44 per cent of the firms in the study, fewer than 60 per cent of employees used their opportunities for competence development maximally. Only 23 per cent of the firms reported that at least 80 per cent of employees used all the time to which they were entitled (see Figure 11.2). Furthermore, managers seemed to have

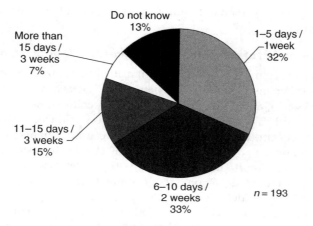

Figure 11.1 Annual time designated for competence development among employees of Swedish interactive media firms

little knowledge of the extent to which their employees actually use the time given to them, one fifth of respondents answered that they did not know. Keeping in mind the size of the average firm (a mean of 16 and median of five employees) which makes it possible for managers to have close contact with most employees on a regular basis, this is somewhat surprising. It shows that firms lack routines for systematic control

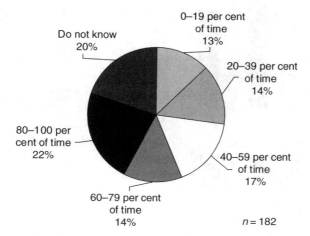

Figure 11.2 Proportion of employees of Swedish firms producing interactive media using the full time offered for competence development in 2000

of competence development, indicating that it has a low priority within these firms.

The organization of competence development: *ad hoc* planning

How, then, is competence development actually organized in interactive media producing companies? When asked how firms ensure that employees are granted sufficient time for competence development, the answers reveal that it is mostly an *ad hoc* or unorganized activity. Less than ten per cent of firms have specified time arrangements for competence development, or have set limits to time charged to customers lower than total working hours (Figure 11.3): 30 per cent use *ad hoc* planning of competence development, meaning that time is taken when perceived to be needed. The figure is actually higher since a large proportion of those who claim to use 'other methods' to secure time for competence development say that time is taken when a project or customer demands certain skills. From the perspective of firms, *ad hoc* organization might be rational and cost-effective, at least in the short run, because it limits the competence development to the employees directly involved in a particular project and the skills currently needed. But for employees it is uncertain and unpredictable since they do not know if, when and to what extent they will receive competence development. The competence development they do receive is mainly within

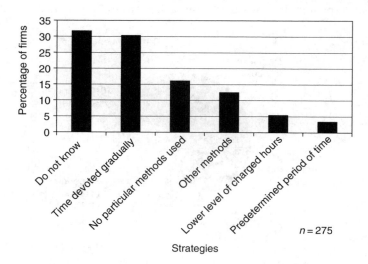

Figure 11.3 Strategies to secure necessary time for competence development among employees of Swedish firms producing interactive media

the frames of the current project. General competence development extending the time limits and needs of projects becomes harder to attain.

A further indication that competence development has low priority among interactive media firms is the fact that 16 per cent claim to use no specific method at all, and 32 per cent – nearly one-third – of respondents do not know how competence development is organized within their company. This corresponds to the findings reported above that 20 per cent of managers do not know the actual extent of competence development within their firm. The overall picture is that, in spite of the discourse on quick transformations and rapid technological developments, many firms in this sector lack a consistent strategy to secure time for competence development. Hence, safeguarding the knowledge capital of the firm and the employability of all workers is jeopardised. Currently, the solution to this dilemma seems to be that workers use non-working hours to secure their competence development, and thereby their employability, individually.

Conclusion: the promise of competence development as a means of securing loyalty

As argued here and in other contributions to this volume, there is a strong discourse linking competence development to individual employability. In this chapter, we have highlighted this discourse in the context of the Swedish interactive media industry. Our findings show that managers view on-the-job learning as the most important type of competence development and that employees are offered quite extensive resources for competence development in terms of money and time. However, few firms are able to secure sufficient time for competence development. It is argued that the way production is organized – in short-time projects based on teamwork, tight inter-firm collaborations and production networks – is a reason for this. This, in combination with an *ad hoc* or no formal organization of competence development, makes competence development largely the responsibility of individual workers.

This individualization of competence development is not necessarily a problem in itself. It brings with it the potentials for greater freedom of choice for workers, making it possible for them to focus on their own areas of interest. It might be seen as an individually chosen specialization that moves beyond the division of labour traditionally determined by management. Nevertheless, since current skill levels and future competence development is directly linked to the employability of the individual, the actual freedom of choice is greatly limited. Employees are forced to choose competencies perceived to be seen as vital by employers, rather than those they are interested in. Furthermore, since employees in practice are not given sufficient time to take advantage of the resources for competence development offered to them, they might be in a particularly risky situation. Interactive media workers not only lack the necessary competence development needed to keep up with future demands in the industry, their competencies also quickly become obsolete. Paradoxically, they may work themselves towards decreased employability. Currently, the solution to this paradox for many workers seems to be to use their free time for competence development.

Employers' promises of extensive resources for competence development becomes a cost-effective alternative to the use of stock-options and other 'golden chains' to tie employees to firms and secure their loyalty. But the new promise might prove to be of just as little value to workers as the stock-options turned out to be, due to the incapacity of employers to secure enough time to realize it.

This chapter shows the ways in which general discourses of competence development and employability are manifested in the Swedish industry for interactive media production. It further shows the importance of understanding the practical outcomes of competence development in relation to current competence levels of workers, employers' strategies to secure the supply of workers and the overall labour market situation. When the responsibility to secure competence development and employability is placed upon individual workers, there is a risk of employers using a system of hire and fire when there is a labour surplus, especially in an industry characterized by high dynamics where benefits of investing in competence development are uncertain.

The interactive media industry has sometimes been presented as the core of the new economy and the future of working life. Does this industry give a picture of the future of competence development? Or will the interactive media producing companies left after the shake-out and dotcom crisis build more formal and permanent organizational forms, and develop routines for and organize competence development? Levels of union membership among Swedish interactive media workers have increased rapidly since the dotcom crisis (although from low levels) and industrial relations have in this respect been somewhat normalized (according to Swedish traditions). How will this effect the organization of competence and its relation to employability? In short, will the new industries become similar to the old ones, or will the old move towards the new?

Notes

1. Multimedia, digital media, web-production and Internet-consulting are other names for these and similar activities.
2. An example is the media programmes started at some secondary schools in the middle of the 1990s. Critics claimed the schools gave students the false impression that the courses were sufficient for getting a job within the media sector, while in reality being too rudimentary.
3. Permanent employment does not necessarily mean that employees work for a long time in the same firm. We are currently planning a survey of employees to find out the actual *lengths* of each period of employment. Neither do the figures include consultants and freelancers working within interactive media firms.
4. The complete results and a description of the research-design are available in Sandberg and Augustsson (2002).

References

Ahrne, Göran and Apostolis Papakostas. 2002. *Organisationer, samhälle och globalisering: Tröghetens mekanismer och förnyelsens förutsättningar*. Lund: Studentlitteratur.

Aldrich, Howard and Marlene C. Fiol. 1994. 'Fools rush in?: the institutional context of industry creation'. *Academy of Management Review* 19(4): 645–70.

Aneesh, A. 2001. 'Skill saturation: rationalization and post-industrial work'. *Theory and Society* 30: 363–96.

Aspers, Patrik. 2001. *Markets in Fashion: A Phenomenological Approach*. Stockholm: City University Press.

Augustsson, Fredrik. 2001. 'Division of labour within and between firms: towards a new model to describe the organization of work'. *European Sociological Association Conference*, Helsinki, 2001.

Augustsson, Fredrik. 2002. 'Behind the scenes of creating interactive media: inter-firm collaboration and production networks in the Swedish field of interactive media production'. Paper for the *Nordic Sociological Conference*, Reykjavik, 2002.

Batt, Rosemary, Susan Christopherson, Ned Rightor and Danielle van Jaarsfield. 2001. *Networking: Work Patterns and Workforce Policies for the New Media Industry*. Washington: Economic Policy Institute.

Bell, Daniel. 1976. *The Coming of Post-Industrial Society: A Venture in Social Forecasting*. New York: Basic Books.

Bijker, Wiebe E. 1995. *Of Bicycles, Bakelites and Bulbs: Toward a Theory of Sociotechnical Change*. Cambridge, MA: MIT Press.

Bijker, Wiebe E., Thomas P. Hughes and Trevor J. Pinch, (eds). 1987. *The Social Construction of Technological Systems: New Directions in the Sociology and History of Technology*. Cambridge, MA: The MIT Press.

Bijker, Wiebe. E. and John Law, (eds). 1992. *Shaping Technology/Building Society*. Cambridge, MA: MIT Press.

Block, Fred. 1990. *Postindustrial Possibilities: A Critique of Economic Discourse*. Berkeley, CA: University of California Press.

Calhoun, Craig. 1995. *Critical Social Theory: Culture, History and the Challenge of Difference*. Oxford: Blackwell.

Castells, Manuel. 1996. *The Rise of the Network Society*. Malden: Blackwell Publishers.
Chandler, Alfred. D, Jr. 1962/1998. *Strategy and Structure: Chapters in the History of the American Industrial Enterprise*. Cambridge, MA: MIT Press.
Computer Sweden. 2001. Cell Network liknar ett nytt Mandator. http://computer-sweden.idg.se. 16.11.2001.16:00.
Davidow, William H. and Michael S. Malone. 1993. *The Virtual Corporation: Structuring and Revitalizing the Corporation for the 21st century*. New York: Harper Business.
van Dijk, Jan. 1999. *The Network Society: Social Aspects of New Media*. London: Sage.
Dosi, Giovanni, David J. Teece and Josef Chytry, (eds). 1998. *Technology, Organization, and Competitiveness: Perspectives on Industrial and Corporate Change*. Oxford: Oxford University Press.
Ekonomisk Debatt. 2000: 6. Tema: Den nya ekonomin.
Fligstein, Neil. 2001. *Architecture of Markets: An Economic Sociology of Twenty-First-Century Capitalist Societies*. Princeton, NJ: Princeton University Press.
le Grand, Carl, Ryszard Szulkin and Michael Thålin. 2001. 'Har jobben blivit bättre? En analys av arbetsinnehållet under tre decennier'. In *Välfärd och arbete i arbetslöshetens årtionde*. SOU 2001: 53. Stockholm: Ministry of Health and Social Affairs, ch. 3, 79–119.
Granovetter, Mark and Patrick McGuire. 1998. 'The making of an industry: electricity in the United States'. In *The Laws of the Markets*, edited by M. Callon. Oxford: Blackwell Publishers, ch. 6, 147–73.
Hansen, Lars H. 2001. *The Division of Labour in Post-Industrial Societies*. Göteborg: Göteborg University, Dept. of Sociology.
Helgesson, Claes-Fredrik. 1999. *Making a Natural Monopoly: The Configuration of a Techno-Economic Order in Swedish Telecommunications*. Stockholm: Stockholm School of Economics, EFI.
Himanen, Pekka, Linus Thorvalds and Manuel Castells. 2001. *The Hacker Ethic and the Spirit of the Information Age*. London: Vintage.
Hollingsworth, Roger J. and Robert Boyer (eds). 1997. *Contemporary Capitalism: The Embeddedness of Institutions*. Cambridge: Cambridge University Press.
Holmberg, Ingalill, Miriam Salzer-Mörling and Lars Strannegård, (eds). 2002. *Stuck in the Future?: Tracing 'The New Economy'*. Stockholm: Bookhouse.
Holmqvist, Mikael. 2000. *The Dynamics of Experiential Learning: Balancing Exploitation and Exploration Within and Between Organizations*. Stockholm: Stockholm University, School of Business.
Industry Standard 2001. 'Bittra känslor när Icon bantar'. http://standard.idg.se. 11.1.2001.17: 25.
Johansson, Conny. 2000. *Communicating, Measuring and Preserving Knowledge in Software Development*. Ronneby: Blekinge Institute of Technology, Dept of Software Engineering and Computer Science.
Johansson, Dan. 2001. *The Dynamics of Firm and Industry Growth: The Swedish Computing and Communications Industry*. Stockholm: Royal Institute of Technology, Dept of Industrial Economics and Management.
Kidder, Tracy. 1981. *The Soul of a New Machine*. New York: Avon Books.
Kjellberg, Anders. 2001. *Fackliga organisationer och medlemmar i dagens Sverige*. Lund: Arkiv Förlag.
Latour, Bruno. 1996. *Aramis or the Love of Technology*. Cambridge, MA: Harvard University Press.

Lennstrand, Bo. 2001. *Hype IT: IT as Vision and Reality – on Diffusion, Personalization and Broadband*. Stockholm: Stockholms Universitet, School of Business.

Magnusson, Lars. 2000. *Den tredje industriella revolutionen – och den svenska arbetsmarknaden*. Stockholm: Prisma.

Mattsson, Nicklas and Christian Carrwik. 1998. *Internetrevolutionen: 1000 dagar som förändrade Sverige*. Stockholm: Bonnier Icon.

Negroponte, Nicholas. 1995. *Being Digital*. New York: Knopf.

Pavlik, John V. 1998. *New Media Technology: Cultural and Commercial Perspectives*. Boston: Allyn and Bacon.

Pettersson, Anna and Viktoria Leigard. 2002. *Samling vid pumpen: Mediernas bevakning av IT-bubblan*. Rapport nr 2002: 4. Stockholm: Stiftelsen Institutet för Mediestudier.

Powell, Walter W. 1990. 'Neither market nor hierarchy: network forms of organization'. In *Research in Organizational Behaviour, Vol. 1*, edited by L. L. Cummings and B. Shaw. Greenwich, CT: JAI Press, 295–336.

Ransome, Paul. 1999. *Sociology and the Future of Work: Contemporary Discourses and Debates*. Aldershot: Ashgate.

Rehn, Alf. 2001. *Electronic Potlatch: A Study on New Technologies and Primitive Economic Behaviors*. Stockholm: Royal Institute of Technology, Dept. of Industrial Management.

Ritzer, George. 1998. *The McDonaldization of Society: An investigation into the Changing Character of Contemporary Social Life*. Thousand Oaks, CA: Pine Forge Press.

Rogers, Everett M. and Judith K. Larsen. 1984. *Silicon Valley Fever: Growth of High-Technology Culture*. New York: Basic Books.

Rosenberg, Nathan. 1994. *Exploring the Black Box: Technology, Economics and History*. Cambridge: Cambridge University Press.

Rosenqvist, Christopher. 2000. *Development of New Media Products: Case Studies on Web, Newspapers and Magazines*. Stockholm: The Royal Institute of Technology, Dept. of Manufacturing Systems.

Rössler, Patrick. 2001. 'Between online heaven and cyberhell: the framing of "the Internet" by traditional media coverage in Germany'. *New Media & Society* 31: 49–66.

Sandberg, Åke. 1998. *New Media in Sweden: The Swedish New Media and Internet Industry Survey*. Stockholm: Arbetslivsinstitutet.

Sandberg, Åke and Fredrik Augustsson. 2002. *Interactive Media in Sweden 2001: The Second Interactive Media, Internet and Multimedia Industry Survey*. Stockholm: Arbetslivsinstitutet.

Stael von Holstein, Johan. 1999. *Inget kan stoppa oss nu! En ny generation tar plats*. Stockholm: Ekerlid.

Strannegård, Lars and Maria Friberg. 2001. *Already Elsewhere: Om lek, identitet och hastighet i affärslivet*. Stockholm: Raster förlag AB.

The Swedish Metalworkers' Union. 1985. *Det goda arbetet*. Stockholm: The Swedish Metalworkers' Union.

The Swedish Metalworkers' Union. 1989. *Solidarisk arbetspolitik*. Stockholm: The Swedish Metalworkers' Union.

The Swedish Trade Union Confederation. 1991. *Det utvecklande arbetet*. Rapport till LO-kongressen 1991. Stockholm: The Swedish Trade Union Confederation.

Tapscott, Don. 1996. *The Digital Economy: Promise and Peril in the Age of Networked Intelligence*. New York: McGraw-Hill.

Thompson, Paul. and Chris Warhurst, (eds). 1998. *Workplaces of the Future*. London: Macmillan Business.

Uvell, Markus. 1999. *Rebeller: It-företagen och samhället*. Stockholm: Timbro Förlag.

Vision 2001. 'Ytterligare 400 får gå från Framfab'. www.vision.se. 22.2.2001.11:39.

White, Harrison C. 2002. *Markets from Networks: Socioeconomic Models of Production*. Princeton, NJ: Princeton University Press.

12
Expertise and Employability in Management Consulting

Staffan Furusten

Introduction: management consultation and ideals for a modern workforce

One form of work that in its very nature incorporates many of the ideals of the modern discourse of work is management consultation. It has, for instance, been observed that management consultants in order to be hireable, or employable, have to be versatile, constantly available, competent and unique but not deviant (Furusten, 2002a,b). To have the capacity to sell oneself and the firm one represents is also said to be one of the most important criteria that has to be met by anyone who wants to work as an expert on a consulting basis. Management consultants are also supposed to be flexible, task-oriented and multi-skilled. All these capacities are claimed to be important for a modern workforce (see chapters by Jacobsson, Chapter 3, and Garsten and Jacobsson, Chapter 14, in this book). This means that none of these capacities is unique for management consultants. Still, management consulting can be seen as an extraordinary form of service. Consultants can charge high for their work, but unlike other forms of expert service such as the practice of law or accounting, management consulting has no formalized barriers to entry such as passage rites in terms of documented experience of a certain kind, standardized codes of ethics or a shared body of knowledge.

With these circumstances as a point of departure this chapter discusses what are perceived to be the prerequisites in practice for becoming employable as a management consultant. In particular the chapter focuses on what types of knowledge and competence are viewed to constitute 'good' management consultation in (1) the discourse, (2) among buyers, and (3) among providers of management consulting services. The

discussions draw upon 23 interviews with consultants primarily working in small and middle-sized management consultancies in Sweden, as
well as a few interviews with representatives of large American-based
consultancies, and 13 interviews with buyers of small-scale management
consulting services, during the period between 1996 and 1999. The chapter
is structured as follows. First, some reflections on what management
consultancy work may represent are presented. This is followed by an
analysis of the tasks for management consultants as presented in the
literature among practising management consultants and organizations
that hire management consultants. Secondly, the issue of learning to be
employable as an expert is discussed in terms of knowledge and experience that seems to be accepted in practice as 'relevant' capacities for
employability on a consulting basis. Finally, the findings are discussed
in terms of tendencies towards individualism and institutionalization in
the kind of work management consultation represents.

I will argue that it is the form of work rather than the content that
constructs individuals as experts. I will also argue that the individual
consultant's capacity to establish trust is the single most important
factor in the becoming of a successful management consultant. Success
has little to do with formal prerequisites for expertise such as a certain
educational background or specific experiences. I will also argue that
although becoming employable as a management consultant is an
individual endeavour, it is a journey that has to follow already beaten
paths, but in an unexpected way.

Increasing demand for external expert services

Following Allvin's discussion in this volume (Chapter 2), management
consulting can be argued to represent an extreme form of modern work,
one that also represents an ideal form of work in the current work
discourse. Since the market for management consultation has grown
considerably, particularly during the last decade, it can be seen as an
example of a mode of work that is on the rise in modern western society,
with services provided by temporarily employed external experts.

The market for management consultation in Sweden tripled in size
between 1987 and 1998 (Furusten and Bäcklund, 2000; Furusten, 2002a).
Similar patterns have, however, been observed in several other European
countries (Kipping and Armbrüster, 1999). This development can, to some
extent, be explained by a tendency to commercialize management support tasks that organizations used to host internally. Today coordination
of these tasks has largely been outsourced from hierarchies to markets.

As argued above, management consulting is one example of the increase in the supply and demand for services of this kind. Other examples discussed in this book are the increase in the market for temporary employees and IT firms (see Garsten, Chapter 8, and Augustsson and Sandberg, Chapter 11, in this volume) and PR firms. The service management consultants provide represents a form of work and expertise that has become a more regular dimension in the everyday business of many organizations, private as well as public, and in which the discourse of employability is manifested in practice. Management consultants represent the very idea or image of the employable and competent individual.

Towards non-employment: expertise and trust

Management consultation can be seen as a form of non-employment that is on the rise as well as being legitimate in modern society. Consultants work on a project basis and are only hired for short periods of time. For self-employed consultants this means that when they are out of assignments they are not employed. However, consultancy work is not, at least not for everyone practising it, the same as being non-employed. Many consultants are in fact employed in large consultancies, but their salary is tightly connected to the fact that the firm has a constant inflow of assignments. Although consultants are employed in the consultancy, their positions are dependent on getting hired by their clients. So, to some extent, it is not a regular form of employment, and for many, especially seniors in large consultancies who are the ones responsible for selling projects and signing contracts, and those who are self-employed, it is a form of non-employment. It has also been argued that consultancy work represents a form of non-employment that is attractive for people who are in between regular positions (cf. Thedvall's contribution, Chapter 7, in this volume). Presenting oneself as a consultant directs attention away from unemployment, even if one may not have a regular inflow of assignments. Since no formal skills are required in order to claim that one is a management consultant (Furusten, 2002a,b), the label may be quite attractive when one is in between regular positions. To some extent, presenting oneself as a consultant is about building an image of an entrepreneurial, versatile, and competent professional.

Nevertheless, claiming that one is a management consultant and getting management consulting assignments may be two different things. Experienced consultants argue, for instance, that no one is a real consultant until he or she manages to sell projects – this is the single most crucial dimension of consultancy work. This is interesting in comparison with authorization of experts in similar forms of work in more traditional professions, such as the practices of law, accounting and medicine. When formal aspects of expertise are considered, the rules for expertise are quite clear. In order to be treated as an expert one has to pass certain exams, and have a certain experience (Abbott, 1988; Burrage and Torstendahl, 1991). It is the system of professions that is supposed to produce new professionals and control those who are already established (Larson, 1977). If this was true for consultancy work it would mean that clients would place trust in consultants just because they are representatives of a professional system. This would also mean that there would be certain management-related tasks in organizations that no one but formally authorized experts were allowed to do, as in the case of accountants. Then the formal prerequisites for what it takes to become such an expert would be clear.

However, management consultants and other not formally authorized experts live under other conditions. Individual consultants, or the firm where they are employed, have to present themselves as experts (Furusten, 2002a). Thus, they can hardly be seen as representatives of what Giddens (1990) defines as abstract expert systems. Consequently, trust for this kind of work is something that to a larger extent has to be constructed in single relations between consultants and their clients where the competence to sell projects and create trust is crucial (Furusten, 2002a). Framing oneself as a management consultant, thus using the label 'management consultant' in presentations of oneself or the firm one represents towards potential clients, might be a strategy to establish a first contact with a client. However, to frame oneself as a legitimate actor rather than a non-employed one is no guarantee of being hired. Thus, it is easy to claim that one is a management consultant, but it is much more complex to actually perform such management consultation that is accepted on the market. Of crucial importance in being accepted is that the consultant manages to establish trust in his or her relations to clients and potential clients. However, there is no standard way to make this happen. Contacts or earlier business or social relations are of great value here. But in situations when they are non-existent, the way in which single actors present themselves, their firm, the kind of service they claim that they can deliver and what good this would have for the possible client, are crucial. Consultants therefore make major efforts to arrange meetings with the potential client. Once they manage to do that it is often quite easy, some say, to convince the client that they will benefit greatly if they hire them.

Thus, although the label 'management consultant' may be a gate-opener in some situations, the construction of trust is to a large extent a local and individual process (Furusten, 2002a).

Organizing a weak profession

Although management consultation can be argued to represent a weak form of expertise it is not a form of work where anything goes. Thus, there are structures actors have to follow if they want to be regarded as legitimate and trustworthy. Attempts have, for instance, been made to organize this kind of work as a profession with formal prerequisites of whom is to be seen as a professional. The first attempt was the foundation of an association for professional management consultants in the US in the 1920s (McKenna, 1995). About two decades later a similar attempt was made in Sweden, followed about two decades later in several other European countries such as France, Great Britain and the Netherlands (Furusten, 2002a). Attempts have also been made to organize management consultation as a profession internationally. In the early 1960s the first international association for management consultants, FEACO (Fédération Européenne des Associations de Conseils en Organisation), was established and in 1989 a second association, the ICMCI (International Council for Management Consulting Institutes), was founded with the purpose of organizing all consultants in the world. Since 1991 the ICMCI has also run a certification programme for management consultants, the CMC (Certified Management Consultants) organized in different countries by the national management consulting association. These associations also constitute the members of FEACO and the ICMCI.

In the mid-1990s it was estimated that about 50 per cent of all practising management consultants in the world were members of a national association (Kubr, 1996). The success for professional associations in terms of attracting practising consultants as members varies, however, between different nations (Brunsson and Furusten, 2000; Furusten, 2002a). The British associations (one for individuals and one for firms) have been quite successful, while for example the SAMC (Swedish Association for Management Consultants) has had a more troublesome existence. In March 2002 it had, for instance, only 24 member firms. The scepticism towards the CMC in Sweden is probably even higher. Since it was first launched in Sweden by SAMC in 1991, only seven consultants have been certified. Questions can also be posed as to what membership means and whether the CMC has any organizing power. Swedish consultancies argue, for instance, that there is no point in being a member since the prerequisites of membership are too general. They represent, they say, what everyone does anyhow. This means that the attempts to centralize and standardize what professionalism in management consultation is supposed to be have not generally attracted the professionals themselves. Still, if there are structures everyone follows, there must be some mechanisms for stability, but it seems as though they are likely to be implicit and informal although widely institutionalized.

So, although there are attempts for active organization of the profession and setting rules for professionalism, they have not been successful. This means that the meaning of management consulting is ambiguous and is only partly determined in the prerequisites of membership in professional associations. To clarify the picture of what management consultancy work means, we turn below to the management consulting discourse and to voices from the field – to stories told by a selection of providers and buyers of management consulting services.

The practice of management consultants – as presented in the discourse

The general discourse of management consulting gives no clear answers about what consultants do and what it takes to become one. Some voices argue that they should be seen as organizational therapists (Rhenman, 1974; Schein, 1988) while others prefer to see them as agents of change (Greiner and Metzger, 1983) or specialists (Gummesson, 1991). In more critical analyses it is also argued that we should see them as carriers of ideology (Barley and Kunda, 1992; Saint-Martin, 2000), organizational witchdoctors (Clark and Salaman, 1996), salesmen of words and merchants of meaning (Czarniawska and Joerges, 1988), or messengers of incomplete beliefs about how organizations work and can be managed (Keiser, 1998). It has also been argued that it is not fair to see all consultants as representing the same category of professionals, since significant differences can be observed between large American-based strategy consultants such as McKinsey & Co., Boston Consulting Group and AT Kearney and large semi-American consulting firms such as Ernst & Young, PriceCoopersLybrand, KPMG, Andersen Consulting and Deloitte & Touche (Hansen *et al.*, 1999). They tend to offer different forms of services to different categories of clients (Furusten and Bäcklund, 2000; Furusten, 2002a).

These studies highlight different dimensions of what management consulting may represent. Probably all consulting projects, to some extent, can be described along these dimensions. It is, however, likely that some dimensions are more relevant in particular situations. Nevertheless, when taking a broad view on the discourse it seems there is divergence about what tasks management consultants are supposed to do. Still, the more practitioner oriented discourse, manifested primarily in the handbook literature, makes general claims regarding what professional management consulting should be in a rather purist manner.

The practice of management consultants in the handbook literature

In the handbook literature management consultation is seen as a profession having certain prerequisites. The authors of this kind of literature, who also often tend to practise management consulting themselves, seem to see as their task to develop, maintain and defend the profession. Considerable insight into what consultants see as the core of consultancy work is delivered. It is, for instance, emphasized that there are almost as many forms of management consultation as there are consultants (Sadler, 1998). This is, however, not seen as a complication for professionalism. Instead it is often claimed that the work of professional management consultants can be divided into two general modes of work. The first, has a functional meaning where the consultant is seen as a provider of all forms of help about contents, processes and tasks in organizations while not taking responsibility for the performance of the advice they deliver. In that sense it is open for almost anyone to become a management consultant. The second sees management consultation as a profession where certain prerequisites have to be fulfilled for those who want to act and call themselves management consultants. When this second argument is stressed, many authors refer to the following quotation (Greiner and Metzger, 1983: 7):

> Management consulting is an advisory service contracted for and provided to organizations by specially trained and qualified persons who assist, in an objective and independent manner, the client organization to identify management problems, analyse such problems, recommend solutions to these problems, and help, when requested, in the implementation of solutions.

When voices in the purist literature claim that management consulting is a professional advisory service it is often argued that consultants should be independent in terms of technique, finance and administration (Kubr, 1996). However, it is also argued that consultants are used for many different purposes, such as distributing information, offering specialist resources, working as lynch-pins between organizations, contributing expert opinions, diagnosing problems, developing plans for action, training and developing management and employees and contributing personal counselling.

Although emphasizing that there is a variety of tasks for management consultants, voices in the handbook literature often reduce professional management consultancy work to dealing with three general tasks, irrespective of the mode in which they work (Rassam, 1998): (1) identifying problems, (2) suggesting solutions and (3) helping clients out with implementation. These tasks are supposed to be performed professionally, which in this literature means meeting the needs of the client (and thereby not offering services they have no need for and do not demand), having integrity, being independent and objective and finally showing solidarity with the entire profession (Kubr, 1996; Lynch, 1998).

These assumptions of professionalism are based on the belief that there is a certain body of knowledge, codes of conduct and passage rites for professional management consultation. However, as argued above, the purist version of the tasks of management consultants is a picture not all agree with. It is a powerful version due to its emphasis in the practically oriented literature, which often reaches a wide readership. Nevertheless, when considering what more critical voices say about consultants being seen as witchdoctors, salesmen of words, merchants of meaning or preachers of ideology, what management consultants are up to in practice remains unclear. We will therefore now consider what buyers and providers of management consulting work say.

The practice of management consultants – as told by buyers and providers

The buyers' stories

A common story told by buyers of management consulting services is that management consultants sell specialized knowledge in a particular area where the organization is not self-sufficient. One example is the buyer in a middle-sized public organization who says that management consultation is 'a service performed by someone who is external whom I hire and pay for'. This means that management consulting services can be seen as representing commercialized, outsourced and specialized competence.

As revealed by a buyer at a similar kind of organization, the expertise of management consultants is described as a temporary form of expertise. According to him a consultant is a 'person that you purchase in order to provide a temporary achievement in an area where you normally use internal personnel but for some reason not at this particular moment'. Seen in this way management consulting is, at least to some extent, a staffing issue.

However, the consultant role is also claimed to be to support managers and the organization with competence they need, or as one buyer puts it, 'a consultant should be capable of being advisory when I am in need of it, whatever that will be'. Thus, as long as consultants have some competence the buyer experiences as relevant, consultants do not have to be specialized in a particular area or on a particular subject.

Another aspect of the practice of a management consultant is to perform in the role of an independent external resource with whom organizational issues can be discussed, that is, to be a speaking partner. However, consultants can also be seen as guides for managers who do not define problems or produce solutions. This is expressed clearly in the following quotation from a buyer in a middle-sized public organization, who says that a consultant is:[1]

> a person who can contribute with advice to someone who has a business responsibility, without acting in a management position. His contribution concerns know-how, advice, suggestions, planning and structuring. The consultant should be clever enough to find out and define a picture of the organization. He is someone who works for someone else without taking responsibility for the implementation phase. He has some form of contract.

Several buyers of management consulting services emphasize what is probably the most common understanding of the task of management consultants: that a consultant is someone organizations turn to for advice. This assumption is, however, likely to be combined with other meanings, such as a consultant being an 'advisor who brings with him competence I am missing', or 'a speaking partner, a resource, an expert on issues that I myself am missing'. The latter buyer also emphasizes that consultants often have to perform in different guises; partly as a sounding board, partly as a resource when organizations are missing a certain competence at a certain time, and partly in order to contribute with such expert competence the organization lacks.

To sum up the buyers' view of the tasks of management consultants, most respondents see a management consultant as an external resource representing a kind of expertise that is missing in the organization. Their expertise is often likely to be seen as constituted by specialized knowledge about something. A complementary assumption is that their expertise lies in a competence to act as supporters to management who assist them in taking decisions while standing in the background themselves.

This means that they are supposed to be able to perform a multiplicity of tasks and that it is difficult to clearly define what situations call for a certain consulting performance. The contents of their special knowledge may also have been acquired from quite different backgrounds: this is of lesser significance as long as it is regarded as a perspective the buyer organization perceives that they are missing.

The providers' stories

The buyers' and the providers' assumptions of the tasks of management consultants resemble each other quite well, as expressed in the quotation below from an interview with a self-employed consultant:

> A consultant is a catalyst, when things turn out well. Someone who is present and fertilizes processes without participating in the way employees do. The good consultant is a good catalyst and carrier of experiences and knowledge. He is a node who works on a light touch basis and who does not take over responsibility from anyone in the organization. He is a stimulator of processes and a sounding board, perhaps something of a mentor – it depends on the circumstances. He stands by and hopefully contributes to something good, but does not take over and manage.

This quotation suggests that consultants can be seen as back-stage actors. Their service does not necessarily have to be based on a certain expertise, at least not such expertise that can be associated with specific expert knowledge. This is also illustrated in the following quotation from an interview with a consultant who works in a larger medium-sized Swedish consultancy:

> Originally, consultants were hired because they were cleverer than internal people and their advice were obeyed. The consultant was also expected to take responsibility for the actual change. Thus, the consultant was the expert. Today a consultant is not more competent than the management in the organizations that hire them, but they may be more experienced in certain areas. Using a consultant is now more a way to get more information, more knowledge, better data for taking decisions, and to get more resources in order to implement

change. Today, the consultant works as a personal counsellor to CEOs, and it is common that they work in teams of consultants with a situation of change the members in the organization are competent to handle themselves, but do not have free resources to deal with.

Thus, according to this consultant, the task of management consultants today is to give advice, but also to provide information and knowledge to managers so that they have better data for their decisions and for possible change programmes. The consultant is thereby no longer likely to be seen as someone who parachutes in from the sky with a standard solution to all problems. This means that the contributions of particular management consultants do not have to be expertise in a technical sense. A senior consultant in a small consultancy, but with earlier experience from one of the largest Swedish consultancies, expresses this dilemma in the following way:

> Consultation is a profession...but what makes someone a professional has little to do with their technical competence. Many believe that consultants are specialists in something...and this leads many to believe that they can be clever consultants, just because they are clever at something. This was especially common in the late 1980s and in the early 1990s when many CEOs said 'well, I am so clever so I could be a consultant'. You have to be technically clever in some disciplines, such as managing or management, but you also have to be a consultant and this is not the same thing although it is what many people believe. To be that one has to have a capability to listen, to adapt to the situation, to act without prestige, only to provide help and not take the honour. One should also have an ability to identify problems and possible strategies to solve the problem in the actual situation. One also has to be extremely social and to have the competence to meet different kinds of people in different situations, to have a sense of timing for when certain things can be done, to combine, be strong, but not so strong that one takes over. Thus, a consultant is an advisor...if you go to another profession for advice you don't want eleven suggestions, you will have one piece of advice maybe complemented with strengths and weaknesses. A consultant has to stand up for his advice, and not imply that the client could do this or that.

The consultant just quoted expresses very well what most of the interviewed consultants mean by expertise. It has little to do with providing technical expertise. Still, it is a profession that requires certain competence: capabilities to listen, to identify problems, to suggest solutions, and to get management to listen and to take decisions and make results. In order to be able to do this one has to act without prestige, be prepared to adapt to situations, have the right timing, and give one piece of advice rather than a number of alternatives.

Institutionalized modes of behaviour

Following from the views of buyers and providers, it can be argued that management consultation is a sort of a profession without expertise. What distinguishes management consultancy work from other forms of management support work provided by internal actors in organizations seems to be the mode in which they work, not so much the content of the actual tasks they are hired to perform. As a consequence, it is quite unclear what professional management consultancy work should contain and what the tasks are, whereas there are clearer structures for *how* it should be performed. Management consultants struggle hard to present their services as varied in content and themselves as versatile enough to be hired for performing different tasks in order to find openings in relations with their clients. Such openings give them a chance to turn the meeting into a business relationship. To a large extent this entails efforts to establish trust in relations to clients. This means that the expert system in terms of tasks and contents for trustworthy management consultation is weak. Trust is something the providers of management consulting services believe has to be constructed locally. This does not, however, imply that there are no collectively shared assumptions about how professional management consultancy works. Consequently, it is appropriate to describe management consultation as a profession without expertise, even though there are institutionalized modes of behaviour that are more likely to be regarded as trustworthy.

Maybe this ambiguity is the reason why consultancies can charge so highly for their services? If the consultant cannot define what he or she does, and the client cannot be sure of what he or she wants, it will also be very difficult to judge what was really done. The result of management consultation is therefore very difficult to evaluate.

The construction of relevant experience and knowledge

It was argued above that neither the buyers nor the providers of management consulting services clearly define what being a professional management consultant means. Thus, there are no clear technical rules for expertise. Instead the interviewees emphasize that expertise in management consultation has more to do with individual capabilities. Still, although not explicitly pronounced, they also emphasize that individuals need experience and knowledge that clients judge as relevant! Again, what is likely to be regarded as relevant probably has less to do with the tasks, but more with the mode of working.

Relevant experience

According to the stories told by buyers and providers, one of the most important capacities a management consultant needs to have is a strong ego. If not, he or she risks being incapable of handling change, or open or latent conflicts within client organizations. Strong egos are, however, not something that automatically come with a particular background. The consultants interviewed had various backgrounds. Some had Master of Science degrees in management from the Stockholm School of Economics, while others had degrees in law, psychology, medicine, political science or sociology. Some had experience from politics, lobbying, research, evaluations, long-term planning, sales, marketing and different top management positions in either the public or the private sector. Obviously, experience is important, but not of a particular kind. According to the consultants themselves, the capacities needed are more individual and have much to do with their social and business talent and individual personality, although they also emphasize that it is important for a consultant to have special competence in one area at least. What that area is seems, however, to be of secondary importance. It can be almost anything from being specialized in handling conflicts to recruiting procedures, management accounting or a particular management technique such as Total Quality Management (TQM). Combining social, business, personal and special competencies is seen as the kind of capacity that creates trust in business relations with clients. Thus, there is no consensus in the field on what knowledge base such combinations should consist of. Some consultants believe that the construction of relevance has to do with a competence to balance knowledge and talent where what is considered as appropriate skills for particular projects emerges as the consultant muddles through.

Long experience as a management consultant in combination with experience from top management positions is referred to by many as an ideal background for being able to adapt to local problems and situations. However, at the same time as experience from management positions is seen as a strength, it is not seen as a prerequisite. Depending on what profile consultancies want to show, they emphasize the importance of different experience. Some claim that it is not enough to be clever in a special area or to have experiences from management positions. They also believe that the latter can be seen as a risk to the consultant's independence since his or her ability to be objective may be in danger. So, although experience from consulting and management positions is important, it has to be combined with experience of how to establish trust and sell projects.

To sum up, no clearly specified experience is needed for those who want to learn to become employable as experts on management consultation as long as they manage to establish trust and sell projects. Still, it is argued by many that management consultation is a profession. There are various ways in which trust may be established, but there are also rules for expertise. To some extent, the meaning of these rules varies between different situations. Any kind of experience may then have a chance to be seen as trustworthy. A prerequisite for legitimacy as an expert is that the experience concerned is considered relevant in local contexts. Thus, being an experienced consultant is of major importance, but the particular experience that makes someone employable is a matter constructed locally.

Relevant knowledge

Hitherto, it cannot be clearly defined what kind of knowledge management consultants need in order to be considered as representing expertise having good chances of becoming employable. One consultant says that it is a subtle kind of know-how where consultants see beyond the details and make the entirety work. He believes that a certain form of experience of a certain character in combination with technical know-how is central in order to have the competence to grasp the situation as a whole. This entails looking beyond the symptoms and seeing how things are connected. This is, however, an unspecified competence that only partly consists of being updated on well-established management techniques and fashionable tools. Therefore, it is common that consultants not only present themselves as experts in certain management tools (Furusten, 2002a,b). They also tend to mark what kind of education or experience they have, or what kind of clients they have been working with and what connections they have to research, education or other consultants in the country or abroad. Stressing connections to academia is common. This is meant to show that one is academically trained to think, to learn models, to conceptualize and to be critical of sources. Although knowledge of how to work in this, perceived, academic way is important, it has to be combined with knowledge that comes from personal experience and personal maturity. It is, however, also argued to be crucial to know how to listen and to develop a feel for timing, in other words a sense of 'now's the time' for listening, talking, being visible or stepping back and letting particular members of the client organization take over.

The knowledge necessary to have can only be learnt through experience, maturity and integrity. It is only in this way, in the consultant's view, that the feeling for timing and making important connections can be developed. This kind of knowledge can be defined as social. Social knowledge must, however, be combined with technical knowledge of two kinds. First, one has to have specialist knowledge in at least one area. Secondly, one has to have the technical knowledge of how to sell oneself in trustworthy ways. A key factor in the acquisition of long-term trust in the business is that consultants do not sell one thing and deliver another.

The competence to sell is very much an issue of creating trust, and when it comes to trust-building in vague services, the client's first impression is crucial. Careful management of their relations and contacts is therefore of major importance. Once contact is established, discussions of different forms of services can start. One consultant expresses this dilemma in the following way:

> Yes, it is difficult since it is hard with the specification. This is a pretty subjective type of knowledge, but of course, one tries all possible ways. If two companies announce they are going to merge, this is an opportunity to call them. Maybe I already have a relationship with one of them. I can give this person a call and say: hey, why don't we help you, we have experience of these kinds of questions. It is a bit weak, but I have to say something, don't I, and I also have to have a relationship with them in some way. But jumping on someone blindly, I never do that. It is too risky and there is little chance that you strike. That would probably be inefficient use of time. If you are going to sell, you have to strike every now and then. Then it is important that you choose your market channels carefully. I always try to make them at least meet me, so that we can start to discuss matters. Then, it is usually quite easy. The client, then, directly notices what you can do. They can hear whether or not you know what you are talking about.

Consultants often emphasize among themselves that the knowledge and talent that is required and the formation of services are subjective things that are varied and very difficult to specify. The nature of management consultancy work resembles everyday life for most people. One consultant says that people often tell him that what he is offering is only common sense. To that he answers 'OK, perfect, people make decisions on subjective grounds every day, how else could decision-making be done? Nevertheless, it is not enough only to have common sense knowledge, you also have to construct yourself as a trustworthy representative of this common-sense knowledge and have the competence to sell it to others who also have a close familiarity with it.'

Thus, it is not enough to be clever or have a good reputation if one cannot sell oneself or the firm to a client. Anyone who manages to sell also manages to construct him- or herself as representing relevant expertise towards this particular client in particular moments. Management techniques and tools that are generally known in the discourse as appropriate attributes for professionalism can be useful. However, one also needs to know that techniques and tools cannot be implemented literally, they need to be modified locally. 'It is in the nature of management consultation', as one consultant puts it, 'that everything needs its specific adaptation.' So, what they do can be described as improvising on standards in the discourse and in practice (Furusten, 2002a,b). This means that the consultants make personal interpretations on standardized management techniques and tools that are as commonly known as they work as a base for communication and practice in a particular area (Barret and Peplowski, 1998). This is what is meant by improvisation, and consequently different standards can be combined as long as the performance, in a particular setting, is accepted by an audience. The standards thereby constitute institutionalized components most people believe have something to do with the work of 'professional' management consultants. However, as they tend to use them as sources for improvisation, it seems as though it is also taken for granted that these standards need to be 'edited' (Sahlin-Andersson, 1996) or 'translated' (Czarniawska and Joerges, 1996; Røvik, 2000) to what is accepted locally as relevant form and content of the service. This means that although it is very much up to the individual consultant to produce him- or herself as an expert, a significant portion is nevertheless shared among those who practice management consulting.

Individualism and institutionalized structures

Although individualism is a crucial dimension of employability on a consulting basis, there are institutionalized structures in the field that to some extent make management consultancy work a collective endeavour. For some consultants these structures are more apparent than for others. In positions such as junior consultants what is required to become employable is quite clear. In such cases, the kind of learning required takes place at prestigious business schools. This kind of background is what large American-based consulting firms require from the juniors they hire, but it does not represent the kind of learning that makes these juniors hireable by the clients. When the clients hire this kind of consultant, it is as a representative of the large firm, not as an individual. This implies that it is not primarily the individual junior consultant that has to create trust. Trust is rather likely to be created by the reputation of the firm in combination with the behaviour of the seniors, who are usually centrally involved in processes that lead to clients buying projects.

For seniors, the kind of educational and professional background the consultant has is not crucial, it is their competence to create trust with clients and sell projects that creates value for their firms and themselves in the future. This kind of learning takes considerable time and involves a great deal of uncertainty since trust in senior consulting to a very large extent is a matter of how successful the individual consultant is in convincing clients of his or her capacity to deliver services that help. Thus, they have to be persuasive both in order to get the project and when they present the results, since management consulting services are often more or less impossible to evaluate (Alvesson and Kärreman, 1998). Senior consultants have to learn the kind of knowledge and the form of services that are likely to work in different situations: to learn to be intuitive, to earn a sense of timing, and to learn how to improvise on standards in trustworthy and attractive ways (Furusten, 2002a,b).

Seniors in the firms where juniors, or newly recruited seniors-to-be are employed, often initiate the newcomers in the management consultancy work. In the first case all newcomers to the firm all over the world are taught the firm way of consulting. In the latter case one has to be a more or less self-sufficient expert already when joining the firm. However, although seniors might introduce a newcomer to the field, one has not fully learned the ropes until the institutionalized structure in the field has been internalized.

Senior management consulting, therefore, does not represent a kind of work that can be fully taught through formal education. Some aspects of the work – a frame of reference and familiarity with certain management techniques – can be taught. But the most crucial dimension of management consultancy work, that of knowing how to sell projects, cannot be taught in schools. A junior consultant cannot be sent to sell advanced and unspecified management consulting services. A senior, on the other hand, might be looked upon by clients as a person who is likely to have relevant know-how and experience to deliver trustworthy services presented vaguely as – 'I'm clever at management, let me take a look at your organization and see what can be done in order to improve it!' This means that in order to become established as a senior, one has to introduce oneself in the field and produce oneself as an expert.

Thus, creating trust in management consulting is very much up to the individual consultant. This is, however, not unique to management consulting. To understand how professionalism is constructed in many modern forms of service work we have to consider more diffuse relations and formations of knowledge that are in different ways enmeshed together (Scarbrough, 1996). There are shared norms and expectations; but even these may not be articulated. There are structures that bind activities together socially, technically and transitionally, but those who are not initiated probably have considerable problems seeing them. This means that aspects of management consultancy work are institutionalized and shared, that is, there are institutionalized beliefs, standards and role-models that organizations are either forced to follow or cannot resist imitating (DiMaggio and Powell, 1983/1991). For example, consultants have to be familiar with the popular management discourse. They also have to be updated on the latest fads, but they do not have to deliver services that are built on them, although they have to be prepared to do so if demanded by the clients. Consultants are also supposed to be independent, objective, and convincing. These expectations of management consultancy work can be seen as widely institutionalized in the Western world, and although they are implicit, consultants cannot depart from them if they want to be seen as a professional.

Conclusions: improvising for employability

In this chapter it has been argued that there is no specified knowledge, no particular education or certain experience one has to have in order to become employable as a senior management consultant. However, one has to learn the institutionalized and implicit codes of conduct for management consultation. Consultants have to be familiar with the popular management discourse, updated on the latest fads, objective, convincing, independent and have to have social knowledge that builds up a sense of timing and a capacity to produce attractive improvisations. Thus, one must have a feel for how to combine and interpret new versions of standards that do not deviate from the collective beliefs of what professional management consultation is supposed to entail. To conclude, consultants must know how to improvise and make combinations of knowledge in ways that create trust in every local consulting situation. Learning how to make meaningful improvisations in different environments takes time and must be done through what can be described as 'on-the-job training', thus learning by improvising in real business relationships. Those who manage to sell will succeed, whereas those who do not will fail, no matter how high their technical or documented competencies are.

Being somewhat of an ideal and model for many employees in modern management support and administration work, management consulting also reflects demands placed on people in most forms of contemporary service work: the need to be versatile, have a sense of timing and a capacity to perform meaningful improvisations on institutionalized structures so that one looks unique while not being experienced as deviant. The case of management consulting may be more extreme in all this since its content is downplayed in favour of the form of work, which is what consultants are judged on. The important thing is not so much the actual content of a job or assignment, as the marketability of cumulative personal skills. Being employable in management consulting focuses less on filling specified and predetermined work roles, and more on cultivating and using versatile skills and marketable capabilities. Management consulting stands out as an example of the market-dependency of current forms of employment, while at the same time pointing to desirable skills and capabilities of employees beyond the field of consulting. Hence, even if the term employability may not be explicitly spelled out among consultants, its meaning comes across clearly and its impact has been shown not be underestimated. Other types of project-based and temporary work may entail similar work requirements but to a different degree. However, there is one common feature of temporary, project based and commercialized consulting work: if no deals are closed, the service providers will become non-employed!

Note

1. This and all other quotations from interviewees are my translations from Swedish to English.

References

Abbott, Andrew. 1988. *The System of Professions: An Essay on the Division of Expert Labour.* Chicago, IL: Chicago University Press.

Ackroyd, Stephen. 1996. 'Organization contra organizations: Professions and organizational change in the United Kingdom'. *Organization Studies*, 17(4), 599–621.

Alvesson, Mats and Dan Kärrman. 1998. *Taking the Linguistic Turn in Organizational Research: Challenges, Responses, Consequences*. Lund: School of Business Working Paper No 5.

Barley, Stephen and Gideon Kunda. 1992. 'Design and devotion: surges of rational and normative ideologies of control in managerial discourse'. *Administrative Science Quarterly* 37 (September): 363–99.

Barret, Frank and Ken Peplowski. 1998. 'Minimal structures within a song: an analysis of "all of me" '. *Organization Science*, 9(5), 558–61.

Brunsson, Nils and Staffan Furusten. 2000. *The organization of management consulting*. Paper presented at the 16th EGOS Colloquium, Helsinki, July 2000.

Burrage, Michael and Rolf Torstendahl, (eds). 1990. *Professions in Theory and History: Rethinking the Study of the Professions*. London: Sage.

Clark, Timothy and Graeme Salaman. 1996. 'Telling tales: management consultancy as the art of story telling'. Paper presented at the 3rd International Workshop on Managerial and Organizational Cognition. Strathclyde University, 14–16 June.

Czarniawska, Barbara and Bernward Joerges. 1996. 'Travels of ideas'. In *Translating Organizational Change*, edited by B. Czarniawska and G. Sevón. New York: Walter de Gruyter, 13–48.

Czarniawska-Joerges, Barbara. 1988. *Att handla med ord (To coin a phrase)*. Stockholm: Carlssons.

DiMaggio, Paul and Walter Powell. 1983/1991. 'The iron cage revisited: institutional isomorphism and collective rationality'. In *The New Institutionalism in Organizational Analysis*, edited by W. Powell and P. DiMaggio. Chicago: The University of Chicago Press, 63–82.

Furusten, Staffan. 2002a. *Managementkonsultation: reglerad expertis eller improviserat artisteri?* Lund: Studentlitteratur. Book manuscript.

Furusten, Staffan. 2002b. 'Learning to improvise: the jazz of small-scale management consulting'. Stockholm, SCORE (paper under review).

Furusten, Staffan and Jonas Bäcklund. 2000. 'Koncentration och differentiering på den svenska marknaden för managementkonsultation'. *Nordiske Organisasjonsstudier*, 2(1), 61–85.

Giddens, Anthony. 1990. *The Consequences of Modernity*. Stanford: Stanford University Press.

Greiner, Larry and Robert Metzger. 1983. *Consulting to Management*. Englewood Cliffs, NJ: Prentice-Hall.

Gummesson, Evert. 1991. *Qualitative Methods in Management Research*. Newbury Park, CA: Sage.

Hansen, Morten, Nitin Nohria, and Thomas Tierney. 1999. 'What's your strategy for managing knowledge?'. *Harvard Business Review*, 77 (March–April), 106–16.

Keiser, Alfred. 1998. 'Communication barriers between management science, consultancies and business companies'. Paper presented at Subtheme 7 of the 14th EGOS Colloquium, Maastricht.

Kipping, Matthias and Thomas Armbrüster, (eds). 1999. *The Consultancy Field in Western Europe*. CEMP-report. No 6. Uppsala: Department of Business Studies.

Kubr, Michel. 1996. *Management Consulting: A Guide to the Profession, third (revised) edition*, Geneva: ILO.

Larson, Magali Sarfatti. 1977. *The Rise of Professionalism*. Berkeley, CA: University of California Press.

Lynch, Paul. 1998. 'Professionalism and ethics'. In *Management Consultancy: A Handbook for Best Practice*, edited by P. Sadler. London: Kogan Page.

McKenna, Christopher. 1995. 'The origins of modern management consulting'. *Business and Economic History*, 24(1): 51–8.

Rassam, Clive. 1998. 'The management consultancy'. In *Management Consultancy: A Handbook for Best Practice*, edited by P. Sadler. London: Kogan Page.

Rhenman, Eric. 1974. *Organization for Long-Range Planning*. London: John Wiley.

Røvik, Kjell-Arne. 2000. *Moderna organisationer*. Lund: Liber.

Sadler, Philip. 1998. 'Consultancy in a changing world'. In *Management Consultancy: A Handbook for Best Practice*, edited by P. Sadler. London: Kogan Page.

Saint-Martin, Denis. 2000. *Building the New Managerialist State*. Oxford: Oxford University Press.

Sahlin-Andersson, Kerstin. 1996. 'Imitating by editing success: the construction of organizational fields'. In *Translating Organizational Change*, edited by B. Czarniawska and G. Sevón. New York: Walter de Gruyter, 69–92.

Scarbrough, Harry. 1996. 'Introduction'. In *The Management of Expertise*, edited by H. Scarbrough. London: Macmillan – now Palgrave Macmillan, 1–20.

Schein, Edgar H. 1988. *Process Consultation: Its Role in Organization Development*. Reading, MA: Addison-Wesley.

13
Competing for Employability: The Media Ranking of Graduate Business Education

Linda Wedlin

Introduction: ranking on the agenda

The relevance of education and training for business and for securing the employment of workers has been debated for a long time. As Aldcroft notes, a debate has been conducted about the value of education almost since the first universities were established (Aldcroft, 1992). Adam Smith, in his well-known work *The Wealth of Nations*, had already in 1776 criticized the education of that time for being unsuited to fill the needs of business and the economy at large: 'The greater part of what is taught in schools and universities . . . does not seem to be the most proper preparation for that business . . . which is to employ them [men] during the remainder of their days' (quoted from Aldcroft, 1992: 1). As this quote suggests, schools and universities are considered to have an important role in the training and educating of people for their future employment and working life. What demands are placed on today's education in order to serve businesses and the society at large?

In the current Western labour market, as addressed in the previous chapters, the focus on lifelong learning and competence development is clear. Employers seek learning individuals, and employees need to be employable and flexible to fit into the working environment. But where and how do individuals learn to be employable? To some extent, learning now takes place more at work, and continuously throughout one's working career (cf. Augustsson and Sandberg, Chapter 11 in this volume). This does not mean, however, that the role of universities and other educational institutions has diminished. Rather, as demand for continuous learning and competence development has increased, the interest in higher and continuing education has grown substantially as well. As will be shown, the pressures for learning and training in working life also put pressures on education systems and on the institutions providing educational programmes.

This chapter will elaborate on the link between the requirements of the labour market for learning experiences and learning individuals, and the demands placed on institutions for higher education in business and management through media rankings. Media ranking tables of business education programmes provide an example of the increased interest in education in society at large, and they comprise an arena where expectations and demands are expressed and formed. Major international newspapers and magazines such as *The Financial Times*, the *International Herald Tribune*, and *Business Week* provide rankings on business education today.

In this chapter, I will provide an overview of some of the rankings of business education institutions currently available, and discuss the criteria used in these rankings to evaluate programmes and schools. What are the features enhanced by these rankings, and thus the implicated picture of the graduates and the educational programmes provided through these assessments? I will also describe how the ranking process helps create pressures on business schools to educate 'employable' individuals, and thus how this employability is measured in the popular assessments of business schools and universities. The rankings thus reflect how employability is perceived and interpreted within business education.

These rankings have become a debated topic within business education. What are they and why do they exist? In this chapter, it will be argued that these rankings reflect a larger societal trend towards auditing and assessment of performances of all kinds, a trend labelled the 'audit society' (Power, 1997). The near explosion of auditing practices within many areas of society means that the term audit has been separated from the strict meaning of financial control, and has, in the case of education, become associated with terms such as performance, quality control, accreditation, accountability, transparency, efficiency, value for money, responsibility, external verification, etc. (Shore and Wright, 2000: 60).

Contrary to many other auditing procedures, the practice of ranking includes the idea of competition and exclusion; if a school moves up the list, another school will automatically move down, and if somebody wants to get onto the list, somebody else will have to be pushed out. This creates competition between institutions close to each other on the list, and between those in the rankings and those outside. It also, however, sends a message to potential students about which schools provide the most competitive places to study. Employability is, through these rankings, tightly connected to the idea of competition.

This chapter begins with an overview of the increased demands for audits and regulations in society at large, providing a theoretical background to the subsequent section that explores the development of an international market for rankings. This section shows how the market for rankings is closely linked to discourses on lifelong learning and continuous competence development, and how the rankings are linked to concepts of employability. The empirical section that follows describes the way the rankings measure and evaluate business education programmes, and how they create conceptions of learning and of the employability of business school graduates. The chapter ends with a discussion on how the concept of employability is understood and interpreted in this market and reflected in the rankings.

A growing market for audits and accountability in business education

The market for higher education in business and management is a diverse and competitive field. There are various types of programmes for graduate management training, for students with or without work experience as practising managers. The MBA is one of the more visible business education programmes in many parts of the world (Moon, 2002). The MBA, Master of Business Administration, was originally an American graduate degree but it has in recent years become widespread also in other parts of the world. The traditional MBA is a one or two-year, full-time programme aimed at students in their mid- or late 20s with limited experience as managers. There are also a variety of part time MBA programmes on the market, for instance the Executive MBA, designed for executives already employed as managers.

The American MBA-type programmes entered the European markets for higher education in the late 1950s (Mazza *et al.*, 1998; Sahlin-Andersson and Hedmo, 2000) and the market expanded very rapidly in Europe particularly during the 1980s and the 1990s. With 400 new business schools in Europe during the late 1980s, and with many of the traditional universities starting these programmes, the competition in the MBA market today is fierce (Daniel, 1998). With this development, the MBA has become an important credential for managerial positions, putting new demands on the employability of managers. Whether the MBA actually contributes to improved managerial practice is, however, a continuously debated topic (cf. Daniel, 1998).

With a large and extremely diverse market for MBA programmes and other business education programmes, the need for transparency, comparability and also standardization has been evoked. The diffusion of the MBA label has also created possibilities to compare programmes from different countries, regions or between different institutions, largely by creating expectations of similarity. The diffusion of the MBA title has thus provided conditions as well as incentives for international comparisons and new forms of regulations. This has caused a number of organizations, such as accreditation organizations and the media, to engage in standardizing and regulatory activities (Hedmo *et al.*, 2001).

Both accreditation and rankings as forms of regulatory mechanisms elevate an expressed tendency for the production of more external quality assessments and evaluations (Engwall, 1998; Trow, 1998), which arise from an obligation for universities and business schools to be accountable to their external supporters for pursuing their missions faithfully and meeting legitimate expectations. Trow (1998) argues that accountability is often used as a regulatory device through 'the kind of reports it requires and the explicit or implicit criteria it requires the reporting institutions to meet' (Trow, 1998: 16). Rankings are thus also reflections of, as well as results of, a trend to evaluate and audit performances of all kinds (Power, 1997).

Efforts to assess, evaluate, regulate and audit performances have been increasing in many areas of social life in recent years (Power, 1997; Rombach and Sahlin-Andersson, 1995; Miller, 1996). Such activities carry a technological element, that is, the particular tasks and routines performed by practitioners, as well as a programmatic content, which refers to the norms, ideas and concepts that follow the pragmatics and which attach the practice to broader policy objectives (Power, 1997; cf. also Miller, 1994). The normative element may also be described as the discursive representations and vocabulary that form the meaning of the practice (Miller, 1994: 3). Thus the demand for regulations and audits can partly be explained by the demands for accountability and transparency, and for quality improvements, following the developments of other forms of audits and accounting practices (Miller, 1994; Power, 1997).

The rhetoric of accountability and transparency seems to hide more regulatory and disciplining effects that these practices have been shown to have. Shore and Wright (2000) argue that the norms and the vocabulary following audit procedures have given rise to new ethics as well as to new politics of governance, or political technologies. These political technologies present themselves as objective and neutral, but 'revolve around normative statements and measurements which are used to construct evaluative grids – such as competitive league tables and performance charts – that simultaneously rank institutions and individuals against each other' (Shore and Wright, 2000: 61). It is in large part a dividing practice that works both as an external control system, and as an internalization of new norms that make individuals freely conform to the norms through which they are governed.

However, the large increase in audits, accounting practices and the subsequent demands for accountability calls for a critical review of the programmatic content that these types of practices bring along. Miller (1996) argues there are three dilemmas of accountability, each questioning the basic principle of evaluations conducted in the name of accountability. The first dilemma is one of principle: should we place trust in experts, and should for example, schools be held accountable to anybody but themselves? The second dilemma is one of meaning: what does it mean to be a customer in for example, education? The last point is the dilemma of mechanism, which refers to how these assessments are to enact accountability and how they assess performances. Can we place trust in numbers? (cf. Miller, 1996: 59).

These dilemmas all question basic assumptions about assessments, such as rankings, and the norms and standards set by such regulations and assessment activities. The following discussion on rankings will focus on the two last dilemmas, of meaning and mechanism. Who are the customers, and what does it mean to be a customer in higher education? How do the rankings measure performance of education? Not until we have some of the answers to these questions may we begin to have an opinion about the principles of rankings and similar assessments, and about what is gained and what is lost by these measures to ensure accountability.

A growing market for media rankings of business education

Business school rankings appeared as early as in the 1970s in the United States, and grew steadily throughout that decade. The *MBA Magazine* produced a ranking in 1974, which was followed by several others (Daniel, 1998). Since the early ranking attempts, rankings have been regarded as important measures of the status and attractiveness of MBA programmes and business schools, primarily in the United States. In the 1980s two of the best known current rankings of American MBA programmes started to publish their annual ranking features: the *US News and World Report* in 1983 and *Business Week* in 1988. Both these magazines rank national schools offering MBA programmes. These rankings are among the most widely cited American rankings, although they are not by far the only rankings featuring American business schools and programmes.

Although the interest in published rankings may seem to have its origin in the United States, the phenomenon is in no way restricted to particular regions. National rankings are published in almost all parts of the world, for instance *The Times* in Britain, *Der Spiegel* in Germany, and *India Today* in India. In 1999, the Swedish monthly magazine *Moderna Tider* published its first ranking of Swedish universities and university colleges, and has since published yearly rankings of undergraduate programmes in different disciplines. In 2000 the rankings featured undergraduate programmes in business studies (*Moderna Tider*, March 2000). Unlike for instance their British counterparts, Swedish universities and colleges have not been used to rankings and formal comparisons between educational institutions, and the rankings have generated extensive debates inside universities as well as between student organizations, employee unions, universities and the government. During a debate in March 2001, arranged by *Moderna Tider*, the editor-in-chief stated that the rankings are important in order to provide a 'consumer perspective' (author's translation) on education, which is intended to generate improvements in the educational programmes and institutions being ranked. Student organizations and employee unions are generally very positive about the initiative and the intent to survey student opinions, while university representatives criticize the methods used and the very principle of rankings (Seminar, 13 March 2001). Even internationally, the rankings are heavily debated and widely criticized.

However, a very powerful ideology supports the ranking system and that seems to bridge many of the concerns raised by business schools. Despite the complaints, business schools and universities, with very few exceptions, agree to being ranked and participate by submitting information and data (cf. Wedlin, 2002). They also use the rankings for marketing purposes and as a tool to position themselves against competitors (Wedlin, 2002). This points to the pervasive force of the rankings.

An international market

Apart from a number of national rankings featuring universities and colleges in different countries there has been a marked increase in the number of international rankings of business schools and management training programmes. The trend towards a more international market for higher education seems to have implied the desire for cross-country and cross-continental comparisons. Thus, the market that has been created is largely international in scope.

In 1999 the London-based *Financial Times* produced an international ranking list of MBA programmes, and a separate ranking of executive education courses. These rankings were among the first attempts to compare and rank schools from several continents and countries in one single league table. *The Financial Times* has since then expanded its ranking activities significantly and produces four different ranking lists every year.

In October 2000, *Business Week* published its biennial ranking of 'The best business schools', featuring 30 US business schools. The same year the magazine also included non-US schools in their surveys for the first time, and provided a separate ranking list of European and Canadian business schools. Under the heading 'A Global Report Card' *Business Week* presents the separate list of seven 'hot MBA programmes' outside the US (*Business Week*, 2 October 2000: 90). It stated:

> With deregulation sweeping through Europe, US-style, market-based business practices have been a fact of life in Europe for some time now. And that's put MBA-trained executives in hot demand. Plenty of American students, moreover, eager to start their careers abroad, are heading overseas for their degrees. For all these reasons, BUSINESS WEEK decided to launch its new ranking of non-US schools.

A third ranking made of US and European schools, although not compiled in one single ranking list, is published on the Internet as 'the Top 10 – the world's leading business programmes'. These ranking lists are produced by the Business Education Commission, a non-profit organization with a mission to promote 'high quality international business education' located in Brussels and Washington (www.top10.org, 27 February 2001). They present top-10 lists of American and European MBA programmes. Although Internet-based, the ranking is used by other newspapers and magazines to report on business school quality, for example, the *International Herald Tribune* (*International Herald Tribune*, 20 May 1999).

A market for learning

From the above, it seems clear that the demand for rankings has increased. To a large extent newspapers and magazines, which find the rankings a way to attract readers to the business press, have driven the development. This is related to the spread of the MBA label, as this has become an important credential for managers and managers-to-be. The business press has noted that MBA graduates have taken up important management positions in industry, and thus make up an important category of readers for newspapers like *The Financial Times* (Wedlin, 2002).

The demand for rankings is also driven by the increased competition between business schools. The rankings have been recognized as a means to profile and differentiate both the business schools and their programmes from their competitors' offerings (Wedlin, 2002). In particular, the MBA programmes are subject to this competition. The MBA can be regarded as a commercial degree, openly struggling to attract resources and students to the business schools. These programmes attract managers and executives at all levels, and the schools charge premium prices from companies and MBA students participating on these programmes. Annual tuition fees for the leading full-time MBA programmes in both the US and Europe range from about US$15,000 to US$35,000 (*Business Week*, 2 October 2000; www.top10.org, 4 April, 2002), while executive education courses can cost anywhere from around $1,400 for a short, three-day course to US$40,000 or above for longer courses (Crainer and Dearlove, 1999: 6). Tuition fees for the full-time MBA programmes are normally paid by individual students, while the employers pay the fees for executive MBA programmes and executive courses.

One of the ways business schools try to market their MBA and compete for students is through advertising of their programmes in business magazines and newspapers. These advertisements are currently common, and practically every business newspaper of some stature has advertisement sections for business schools in general and MBA programmes in particular. Browsing through *The Financial Times* supplement for business education, the advertisements for MBA programmes around the globe are competing for space, all with extraordinary arguments to why one should pursue an MBA at their school (*The Financial Times*, 22 January 2001):

> Give yourself a competitive advantage. A masters degree from London Business School will dramatically enhance your managerial and financial skills as well as fast tracking your career ... [programmes]

are practical and career-oriented, whilst maintaining high standards of rigour and scholarship. The pace is unrelenting but, at the end, you will rank as one of the most highly qualified professionals in the world. (London Business School, p. i)

Real world. Real learning: Get your MBA. Discover the world. Stay on the job. Build yourself for the future. (IMD, p. ix)

You have goals for your career and life. We know that. The Duke MBA – cross continent has been designed to allow you to reach those goals . . . to help you have it all in work, school, and life. (Duke University Fuqua School of Business, p. xii)

These statements show the belief in continuing education and in the MBA programme as an important programme in establishing continuous learning for managers and managers-to-be. Since the full-time MBA is directed towards individuals, not companies, these ads are addressed to prospective students and they reveal two quite distinct arguments to what the MBA is good for. One rests on career-building as the main argument for pursuing an MBA, like the London Business School stating that it creates a competitive 'advantage', and 'fast-tracking your career'. In other statements, the MBA programme is seen as a way to 'build your future', and to learn without any restrictions to nationality or your personal life. They make the argument that learning is for life, and that continuous learning for managers are good for both private and professional lives.

Together these ads thus build a discourse of competitiveness, learning, and employability which supports the notion of lifelong learning enhanced in much of today's discussions. Through their advertisements, business schools help create a market for their MBA programmes, creating expectations about what these programmes will contribute, and what students are expected to learn when attending these programmes.

Rankings as market guides

Considering the plethora of programmes and the many advertisements for MBA programmes currently available, choosing the right programme is not an easy task for students and participants. This is where the rankings claim to provide an aid. Rankings claim to be 'consumer guides' providing potential students and other interested parties with information about business schools and programmes in order to make their choice of school and programme easier. *The Financial Times* claims that rankings are important sources of information for prospective students:

'Courses can cost $100 000 or more, so students need guidance on finding value. The FT's MBA league tables will provide that.' (*The Financial Times*, 25 January 1999: 1)

Similarly, the editor-in-chief of *Business Week*, Stephen B. Shepard, goes further to argue that rankings are a service to the customers of business education. He writes in the MBA-ranking edition of *Business Week*:

When *Business Week* introduced its 'Best B-Schools' ranking in 1988, we knew then it was revolutionary. It was the first customer satisfaction survey based on a survey of consumers of business-school programmes: newly-minted MBAs and the recruiters who hire them. Since then, the biennial survey has not only been a crucial source of information about business schools, it has also spurred vast changes in B-school curriculums...Whether you read it in print or experience it online, our B-school coverage is service journalism at its best. (*Business Week*, 2 October 2000: 18, editor's memo)

The BEC (the Business Education Commission, providing the top-10 ranking on the internet) even claim that the ranking is the ultimate assessment of business school programmes, as the MBA programme can be defined solely in terms of market value or the value for students and future employers:

MBA is not simply an education, it is also a credential. Representing a credential, the utility of the MBA can be defined purely in terms of its market value. Brand names matter....If business schools want their products (MBA degrees) to succeed in the market place, they must listen to their customers (students and their future employers) and understand their needs. The next step in the reengineering process is therefore the installation of continuous feedback mechanisms... Ranking is the ultimate assessment, and as such, it should be left to professionals. (*Top10*, 27 February 2001)

Rankings are thus conducted in the name of transparency and accountability, claiming to provide students and parents with a comprehensive guide to the possible choices of business schools and programmes and an assessment of the quality of these programmes. This form of external quality assessment means placing the responsibility onto the market to decide the quality of educational programmes. This leaves the individual with the responsibility to assess the valued features of educational programmes, and, based on an 'educated' choice, decide on the best business school or programme. Rankings are thus a way to create market dynamics in the field of higher education by defining quality in terms of customer satisfaction.

Ranking method and criteria

The next section will review the methodology and criteria used in some of the current rankings. Three of the prominent international rankings will be described: *Business Week*, *The Financial Times*, and the *Top10*. The purpose is to show how the rankings assess the quality of business schools, and what picture of business schools, the programmes, and the graduates these rankings diffuse. The criteria used reflect how ideas about employability and learning are created and confirmed in current business education.

The two features of the rankings that will be discussed are the type of data collected and the criteria chosen to evaluate the schools. For the first feature, type of data, one ranking method is discussed as 'reputation' ranking, where business school representatives, students, or professors are asked for their subjective opinions about the schools' performance. Another method is to use quantitative criteria as a basis for comparison. The data used in the quantitative rankings can be gathered either from outside sources, for example, published statistics, or from the schools or students themselves.

The second feature of the rankings regards the criteria used for evaluating the schools' performance. Scott (1981/1998) identifies three types of indicators used for assessments: those based on processes, those on structures, and those on outcomes (Scott, 1981/1998: 354–9). Process measures focus on the quantity or quality of the activities carried out and the work performed, which in educational organizations relate to assessments of teaching, research and other activities carried out by the school. Process measures assess efforts rather than effects. Structural measures indicate the capacity of organizational structures to perform work effectively and focus on inputs of the organization, for instance features of the student body, faculty, and the facilities. This category is labelled 'inputs' in the following sections. Outcome measures relate to the effects of work procedures, and the 'output' of organizational efforts. This is for instance change in the knowledge or attitudes of students in educational organizations. The three categories used in the following sections are thus those of processes, input and output.

Business Week – the customer's voice

Business Week has undertaken rankings of graduate business schools since 1988, publishing a new list every two years. The initial purpose of their rankings was to serve 'customers' with information about schools and programmes:

> Let the customer speak. That's the philosophy behind BUSINESS WEEK's ranking of the best business schools. We think b-schools have two customers: the graduates, who trade their suits for backpacks; and recruiters, who seek out the best and brightest from among the business schools' ranks. (*Business Week*, 19 October 1998 www.businessweek.com)

The ranking is thus exclusively based on the reputation of schools among students and their recruiters, and is explicitly focused on the output as a measure of a good business school. The final rank is a combination of three sets of data: one for student satisfaction, one for recruiters' opinions, and one for intellectual capital. The latter component makes up 10 per cent of the final rank, with the remaining 90 per cent split evenly between students and recruiters.

In the 2000 ranking, MBA graduates from 82 different schools were surveyed about their opinion of and satisfaction with their graduate education. The selection criteria for these 82 schools are unknown. For the recruiter opinion, 419 companies were surveyed. The criteria are shown in Table 13.1. For the criteria 'intellectual capital', *Business Week* reviewed articles in 12 academic and professional journals, and it is claimed to be 'a measure of a school's influence and prominence in the realm of ideas' (*Business Week*, 2 October 2000: 80).

Focusing almost exclusively on graduates and company recruiters, the ranking chooses, also explicitly, to take the outcome perspective on the performance of schools. Many of the criteria are work related such as skills acquired and contacts with the business community both during the programme and afterwards in terms of job offers and wages. However, aspects of the quality of teaching and teaching material are also included in the survey.

The Financial Times – market value of the MBA

Contrary to *Business Week*, *The Financial Times* rankings are based largely on quantitative measures of process, inputs and outputs. The rankings are said to provide students with 'guidance on finding value' and they talk about market value of MBAs:

> The ranking provides a comprehensive assessment of the value of an MBA and the business schools that provide them. The criteria we have chosen reflect in our opinion the most important elements of an MBA programme, while allowing comparisons between schools globally.
>
> The position of a school in the table is determined by its perform-ance in three broad areas: the career progression accrued from the MBA – in particular its purchasing power in the marketplace – diversity and research. The impact or value of the MBA is measured through criteria such as salary and salary increases, career progres-sion and international mobility. (*The Financial Times*, 22 January 2001: II)

These declarations of purpose with the rankings express two important features of *The Financial Times* ranking: the international outlook and the 'value' criteria that focus on outcomes.

The 2001 full-time MBA ranking is based on two sets of questionnaires, one directed to business schools and one to all the alumni of 1997. The 137 schools selected to participate in the rankings had an accredited full-time MBA programme that had been running for at least three years. The questionnaire sent to the alumni resulted in eight criteria regarding the output of education (see Table 13.2) making up a total of 55 per cent of the final rank (*The Financial Times*, 22 January 2001). The second survey, sent to the business schools, reports on the 'diversity ranking' made up of nine criteria (seven input measures, one output and one process measure, see Table 13.2). Altogether the diversity rankings make up 20 per cent of the final rank. The last three criteria of the ranking assess the school's performance in research, a doctoral graduate rating and the number of faculty with doctorates. These three research ratings together count for 25 per cent of the final rank.

Using largely quantitative measures, *The Financial Times* ranking is focused on value criteria, in particular on value in relation to a market-place. Many criteria are related to salaries and the career progress of alumni as well as the ability of schools to provide students with career counselling and job opportunities. In this sense, there is a heavy bent towards outcome criteria. The ranking also measures the international experience of students and the characteristics of students and faculty, implying the value of business schools as a meeting place.

Top 10 – efficiency and customer satisfaction

The third ranking to be reviewed here is the *Top10* rankings of MBA programmes in the US, Europe, and Asia. One ranking list for each region is compiled. Information about the BEC and Best Education providing these rankings, as well as on the methodology used and the schools selected, is limited on the web page and no links to additional sites are provided. The organization has not responded to requests for additional information.

It is noteworthy that despite this apparent lack of information about the organization, its ranking has been picked up by the media and used as a legitimate source of information about MBA programmes. Hence, the legitimacy of the rankings does not seem to be strictly tied to the legitimacy of the organization conducting it. Also, the transparency and visibility claimed by the rankings, as claimed by audit practices in general, seem to be limited.

The Top10 rankings are based on the same notion of 'customer satisfaction' as the *Business Week*'s ranking of MBA's. The rankings are based on feedback from three different sources, namely students, professors, and the business community. The ranking philosophy is expressed as follows:

> We believe in 'customer satisfaction'.... We chose to target the 'end result' of Education as a concept, namely: efficiency in its particular setting. From that point on, it became obvious that we had to enter in close contact with the 'end user', and determine the degree of satisfaction found at the various educational institutions. (*Top10*, 27 February 2001)

The survey sent to professors for this ranking includes eight questions, including questions about the student body, student preparation for successful careers, firms recruiting on campus, and overall experience. The student survey is very similar to that used by *Business Week* in 1998. Of 23 questions, 20 are the same, and the same areas are covered in the two surveys (see Table 13.1). Although the student survey is very similar to that used by *Business Week*, the result of the two rankings vary (Wedlin, 2000). The third group of respondents, corporate recruiters, are asked about the quality of and their experience with graduates from the different schools.

Like the *Business Week* ranking, the *Top 10* explicitly takes the outcome perspective on education, surveying both students and corporate recruiters

Table 13.1 The 2000 *Business Week* ranking criteria: a reputation ranking, focusing on the opinion of graduates and corporate recruiters to evaluate business education

	Quantitative measures	Reputation
Process	Intellectual capital	Graduates Expectations fulfilled Quality of teaching (*2) Quality of Teachers (*2) Faculty availability Faculty awareness (*2) Responsiveness to students, demands (*2) Quality of teaching material Quality of coursework (*2) Skills stressed (*3)
Input		Calibre of class (*2) Technological tools (*3)
Output		Contacts with business comm. Value for money Usefulness of networks Employment opportunities (*2) Corporate recruiting on campus Practical job-info. (*2) Usefulness of skills (*2) Programme recommend *Corporate recruiters* Quality of and experience with graduates

* The asterisks indicate that there are more questions in the survey on which the ranking is based that delay to the criteria being described. For a fuller description on how the table is compiled, see Wedlin (2000).

about their experiences. This ranking also includes the opinion of professors. Both the survey of students and that of professors are largely focused on skills and preparations for future careers.

Ranking employability

The rankings reviewed above indicate a large and diverse field of management education rankings, with a variety of criteria used for measuring the performance of schools. The most striking feature of the rankings is the clear focus on outcome, and on the 'customer satisfaction' aspect of

Table 13.2   The 2001 *Financial Times* ranking criteria. Using mainly quantitative criteria, this ranking focuses on the characteristics of the learning experience and on the outcome, or employment value, of education

	Quantitative measures	*Reputation*
Process	Doctoral rating Research rating *Business schools* International experience	

Input	Faculty with doctorate
	
	Business Schools
	  International and female faculty
	  International and female students
	  International and female board
	  Languages	

Output	*Business Schools*
	  International mobility
	
	Alumni
	  Current salary
	  Salary increase
	  Value for money
	  Career progress
	  Aims achieved
	  Placement success
	  Employed at 3 months
		Alumni
		  Alumni recommendation

business education. This focus of rankings is apparent both in the choices of representative voices for the reputation surveys and in the choice of criteria.

Identifying customers

The rankings have to a varying degree chosen to rely on reputation as a means of deciding business school quality. Two of the rankings, *Top10* and *Business Week*, use reputation measures counting for more than 70 per cent of the final rank, while only *The Financial Times* ranking uses a majority of quantitative criteria. The rankings have targeted different interest groups for their surveys: students/participants or alumni, and recruiters and business representatives. By defining these interest groups as representative voices the rankings are defining the 'customers' of educational programmes. Apart from students, the business community is considered an important customer group.

Measuring employability and competence

The customer focus of rankings is also apparent when looking at the criteria for judging quality. Many of the rankings have an explicit focus on measuring the outcome of education, and thus a considerable number of output criteria in their tables. A substantial part of the criteria (more than 50 per cent) in both the *Business Week* and *The Financial Times* rankings are devoted to outcome criteria. This means an explicit focus on the employability of graduates, or the employment value of a business school degree.

The output criteria in the rankings include the value of contacts with the business community, the usefulness of skills and networks acquired during the programme, and practical job information provided to students. Outcome measures also include those relating to career progress, and employment and recruitment data. In particular, measures of salaries, salary increases, and 'value-for-money' are telling. One example is *The Financial Times* value-criteria, explicitly calculating the money gained by going to business school including the opportunity cost of lost income.

The process criteria in the rankings are for the most part reputation measures, and include opinions about the quality of teaching, teaching material and teachers. The quantified measures of academic quality used in two of the rankings regard criteria for research, calculated as the number of published articles in academic and practitioners' journals.

The Financial Times rankings use the input criteria quite extensively and have developed a number of quantitative criteria for this category, with a focus on the need to be international. 'International' is measured both in terms of opportunities for students to study abroad, and in the language requirements and the international agenda of the programmes and the schools. Most criteria on internationality, however, relate to the presence of an international student body, faculty and board. The schools, through this way of measuring, are viewed as a meeting place, presenting opportunities to meet the 'right', international people among students and faculty. This creates a view on competence as knowing the right people, and having the right networks for future careers.

Defining employability

This section has shown that the rankings create expectations and ideas about the employability of business school graduates. The discussion on rankings concerns both the discussion on who defines employability, and on how employability is defined. The rankings have chosen to take a customer approach to education, and they let employers and students/ graduates define employability and determine the employment value of education. The criteria chosen also reflect the implicit definition of employability. The rankings focus on the outcome of education, often defined in terms of economic measures of career success and employer and student satisfaction. The rankings thus bring in concepts of efficiency, value-for-money, and market value into education.

A market for learning: competing for employability

The rankings have been described as part of larger trends to audit performances of public institutions and ensure accountability. The rankings are a result of increased demands for new means of comparing, standardizing and regulating educational programmes. The efforts by the business press to rank business education institutions is widely debated, and many, foremost universities and business schools, have criticized the very principle of rankings. Despite the fact that they are critical, however, they have found the need to play along with the rankings, and to recognize the rankings as a means to create a position and a profile in the MBA marketplace. This tells us that it is a powerful ideology and discourse that lies behind these rankings, a discourse that may be assumed to influence the view of education of both the public and the educational institutions.

As has been shown, the rankings are not only a result of market mechanisms, but are also essential in constructing and enhancing market values and procedures in business education. The rankings identify customers of business education, students and businesses, and they introduce measures of 'customer satisfaction', market value, and efficiency into education. In the way they measure satisfaction, performance and value, the rankings also set criteria for how educational efforts are to be evaluated and compared. The empirical material from several rankings indicates strongly that the valued feature of business education today is the employability of graduates. Several rankings even explicitly stress the 'value added' by educational programmes, that is, the graduates' increased employment value, or their increased value on the labour market. Through these rankings, the MBA label is explicitly connected to the issue of employability.

Employability competition

These developments, in turn, mean that employability has become a means of competition for business schools and universities. Higher education institutions in business and management are assessed and compared on the basis of the employability of their students, and their graduates' success in the labour market. The particular way in which rankings and league tables evaluate institutions and rank them on a single scale means that schools to an increasing extent compete on these aspects. Competition is thus essential to the idea of employability.

There is also competition between students here. The ranking systems send messages to potential students about which schools they should attend in order to be employable. For the graduates of these programmes, the rankings hence become a measure of status – highly ranked programmes yield higher status and possibly make you more attractive on the labour market. A degree from a highly ranked institution may possibly also yield a higher salary, but does not necessarily guarantee that the knowledge and skills provided are better than those provided at other schools. The rankings thus create a classification of status and of employable individuals.

This classification of employability is primarily a sorting mechanism between individuals already employed, or at least those about to become employed when they leave business schools. It is not a sorting between those unemployed and those employed, which is normally the case of employability discourses. This employability classification separates the high-status employable individuals from those with less status and perhaps less attractiveness in the labour market. It does not apply, however, to individuals that are fully outside the labour market, striving to get in.

There are, however, a few concerns about this competitive view of education, and about employability as a quality measure in business education. The introduction of market mechanisms into higher education, such as those described above, may silence the demands for alternative sources of accountability and evidence of quality and relevance of education. Measuring quality in higher education is a difficult task for several reasons. The effects of education and learning are difficult to assess directly after the passage of a programme, since these may be delayed and appear only after a number of years in practice (Engwall and Morgan, 1999: 88; cf. also Hägg, 1975). In addition to this the effects may be entangled with other kinds of knowledge and experience, implying that educational efforts express weak relations in terms of cause and effect (Trow, 1998: 26).

The weak link between what is being taught and the effects of this knowledge also have another implication, namely that what is being taught in educational institutions is not necessarily the same as the knowledge that is required in practice. Trow (1998: 26) argues: 'A good deal of what is studied in college... may not have immediate market value – though what is learned there may have substantial value over the course of a lifetime.' Market forces and competition are thus not themselves adequate to guarantee or improve quality in education.

Conclusion: from learning to earning

The outcome measures used in the rankings and the advertisements for MBAs imply a very strict view on employability and the value of education. Output in this sense has very little to do with 'changes in knowledge or attitudes' as proposed by Scott (1981/1998), but rather concerns salaries and employment opportunities. This means that the criteria for judging educational efforts are those with 'immediate market value' rather than criteria assessing the skills acquired or the long-term benefits of educational programmes. This may standardize outcomes of educational programmes to what companies require today, which may not be what is valued in the long run. The outcome measures clearly reflect the interests of the student body, but also satisfy the business community. The employability criteria serve the interest of businesses since they can be expected to want a perfect match between educational outcomes, that is, graduates, and the needs of their businesses. Rankings today provide a picture of academic quality that serves businesses with this 'perfect match'.

Hence, rankings can be seen as a way to standardize educational efforts of business schools with the current needs of labour markets. There is a potential danger here that business schools, eager to satisfy students and perform well in rankings, will overemphasize features and issues that yield high market value today and downplay their role as a source of critical review and innovative thinking that may serve the community at large from a longer term perspective. There is also a risk that schools perceive the quality of themselves and their programmes to be outside their own control, and become more concerned about improving the rankings than improving their activities.

The rankings' apparent focus on short-term employment values is almost contradictory to the concepts of lifelong learning and learning for life that usually accompany discussions of employability. Regarding teaching and education as means to create employable graduates implies an instrumental view on learning and the outcome of learning processes. Individual learning is not the outcome or an end in itself, but simply the means of getting a good position in the workplace. The criteria measured by rankings tell that what students learn is not as important as what they can earn in the marketplace after they complete their programmes. The actual education and the quality of the learning processes, are thus less important. This also creates a market-oriented view on competencies, and the skills supposedly taught at business schools. Competence is equally less an assessment of the skills acquired or the knowledge gained through education. The rankings rather focus on features of the student body and the place of study that aids students in meeting and interacting with the 'right' people. It seems to be less important what is actually taught in class. Getting essential connections makes you employable. In this way, employability may not always go hand in hand with long-term learning investments.

References

Aldcroft, Derek. 1992. *Education, Training and Economic Performance 1944 to 1990*. Manchester: Manchester University Press.
Crainer, Stuart and Des Dearlove. 1999. *Gravy Training: Inside the Business of Business Schools*. San Francisco: Jossey-Bass.
Daniel, Carter. 1998. *MBA: The First Century*. London: Associated University Press.
Engwall, Lars. 1998. 'Att utvärdera för kvalitet'. In *Utvärdering: ett medel för att säkra eller utveckla kvalitet*, edited by L. Åberg. Forskningsrådsnämnden, Rapport 1998: 1, 61–6.
Engwall, Lars and Glenn Morgan. 1999. 'Regulatory regimes'. In *Regulation and Organization: International Perspectives*, edited by G. Morgan and L. Engwall. London: Routledge, 82–105.
Hägg, Ingemund. 1975. *Uppsala Business Students in Working Life: What They Think About Their Education in Business Administration*. Uppsala: Uppsala University.
Hedmo, Tina, Kerstin Sahlin-Andersson and Linda Wedlin. 2001. *The Emergence of a European Regulatory Field of Management Education*. Score research report 2001: 7.
Mazza, Carmelo, Kerstin Sahlin-Anderssson and Jesper Strandgaard. 1998. *MBA: European Constructions of an American Model*, Score research report 1998: 4.
Miller, Peter. 1994. 'Introduction'. In *Accounting as Social and Institutional Practice*, edited by A. Hopwood and P. Miller. Cambridge: Cambridge University Press, 1–39.
Miller, Peter. 1996. 'Dilemmas of accountability: the limits of accounting'. In *Reinventing Democracy*, edited by P. Hirst and S. Khilnani. Oxford: Blackwell, 57–69.
Moon, Hyeyoung. 2002. 'The globalisation of professional management education, 1881–2000: its rise, expansion and implications'. Unpublished doctoral dissertation. Stanford University.
Power, Mike. 1997. *The Audit Society: Rituals of Verification*. Oxford: Oxford University Press.
Rombach, Björn and Kerstin Sahlin-Andersson. 1995. *Från sanningssökande till styrmedel: Moderna utvärderingar i offentlig sektor*. Stockholm: Nerenius and Santérus.

Sahlin-Andersson, Kerstin and Tina Hedmo. 2000. 'Från spridning till reglering: MBA-modellers utbredning och utveckling i Europa'. *Nordiske Organisasjonsstudier*. 2(1): 8–33.

Scott, Richard. 1981/1998. *Organizations: Rational, Natural and Open Systems*. Fourth edition. New Jersey: Prentice-Hall.

Shore, Cris and Susan Wright. 2000. 'Coercive accountability: the rise of audit culture in higher education'. In *Audit Cultures: Anthropological Studies in Accountability, Ethics and the Academy*, edited by M. Strathern. London: Routledge, 57–89.

Trow, Martin. 1998. 'On the accountability of higher education in the United States'. In *Universities and Their Leadership*, edited by W. Bowen and H. Shapiro. Princeton, NJ: Princeton University Press, 15–64.

Wedlin, Linda. 2000. 'Business school rankings and the diffusion of ideas'. Paper presented at the 16th EGOS Colloquium, 2–4 July, Helsinki.

Wedlin, Linda. 2001. 'Negotiating field boundaries in business education'. Project plan presented at the Nordic Academy of Management Meeting, PhD conference, 13–18, August, Fejan, Uppsala.

Wedlin, Linda. 2002. 'Business school rankings as an arena for boundary-work'. Paper presented at the 18th EGOS Colloquium, 4–6 July, Barcelona.

Newspapers and Internet resources

Business Week, 2 October 2000. The best business schools. 75–100.

Business Week, 2 October 2000. Editor's memo. 18.

Business Week, 19 October 1998. The best business schools. www.businessweek.com

Financial Times, 22 January 2001. Business education: the top schools. Survey.

Financial Times, 22 January 2001. Three elements decide position. II.

Financial Times, 23 May 2000. Sea Change in the Market is Gathering Pace. I–IV.

Financial Times, 25 January 1999. Ranking can both help and rankle.

International Herald Tribune, 20 May 1999. Multiple choice for the seekers of today's MBA. 15.

Moderna Tider, March 2000.

www.top10.org, 27.2.2001

www.top10.org, 4.4.2002

14

Conclusion: Discursive Transformations and the Nature of Modern Power

Christina Garsten and Kerstin Jacobsson

This book has focused on a *discursive transformation* reordering relations between actors – including power relations – and shifting the distribution of risks and responsibilities between them. More precisely, the book has focused on how the discourse on employability as developed in the last few decades, is played out in situated local contexts. What expectations and demands are placed on individuals in public and private workplaces in Sweden?

In our view, discourses are performative. They give direction for daily practice, and they prescribe and encourage certain types of behaviour, sometimes supported by various types of practices, such as practices of evaluation and reward. However, generalized discourses are always *translated* into local contexts, where existing practices, traditions, and institutionalized ways of seeing things and doing things, transform and reformulate ideas in specific ways. In this sense, practice can also be said to impact on discourse. Moreover, discourses and their imperatives to action may also provoke resistance from actors. Rather than the influence going in one direction, a discursive transformation is a dynamic process characterized by negotiations, resistance and ultimately power struggle.

Discursive transformations involve changes in the ways people and organizations are to be understood as well as changes in assumptions regarding subjectivity, agency and responsibility and the type of knowledge and competences that are valued in firms, employment agencies and multilateral organizations. Discursive transformations may not involve a complete turnover of basic assumptions, but more often entail a gradual shift in understanding and framing (see for instance Hansson, 2002). Such transformations, we argue, are indicative of important shifts in the nature of economy and polity. They signify changes in culture and ideology. And they serve to recast responsibilities and powers.

From job security to employability security

Whilst employability in not a new key concept, it has assumed partly new meanings in the last decade. Employability has previously been used in reference to those who are unemployed. Improving people's employability has been a labour market policy instrument to increase labour force participation and to improve job matching. In the 1990s, employability has again gained salience as a policy concept, diffused by organizations such as the OECD and the EU, as shown by Jacobsson in Chapter 3 in this book. Employability is still a labour market instrument but is now something for the whole population – not just the unemployed. In a world with unstable patterns of work, employability is something that individuals – also those who are currently employed – need to work at improving and be prepared to assume responsibility for. 'Life time employability' is replacing 'life-time employment'. Thus, job security is redefined as 'employability security', the security derived from being employable (Bosco, 1998; Chabbert and Kerschen, 2001; Forrier and Sels, 2002).

Different parties can all have an interest in promoting employability. For the state, employability is an indicator of the chance for full employment. For the employer, it is an indicator of the possibility of matching labour supply and demand. For the individual, employability is an indicator of the chance of a job or a career (Forrier and Sels, 2002). The same is true of lifelong learning: for the enterprise it is a way of improving productivity by the efficient use of human resources; for the state it is a way to improve national competitiveness; and for the individual a way to secure employability and the prospect of employment also in the future. There is in the discourse on employability an emphasis on the commonality of interest and the need to share responsibility for employability.

The role of the state is, then, to support the employability of individuals, which entails a shift from providing jobs to providing employability, and from protecting from social risks directly to giving support to adaptability and the capacity to deal with change. It corresponds to a policy shift from full employment to full employability, where the lack of employability rather than the lack of jobs is the key problem.

Although there is in the discourse the notion of shared interests in, and responsibility for, improving employability, there is a strong emphasis on the responsibility of the individual for his or her competitiveness in the labour market. The trade unions, as shown by Huzzard's study of three Swedish unions, also tend to support the view that the individual worker must also be prepared to assume responsibility for his or her future employment prospects. In the trade union discourse, the notion of 'solidarity' is redefined to include not only equality of income but also equality of opportunity, for instance by the individual right to competence development at work.

The 'employable individual' as a normative category

The discourse of employability entails a transformation of the discursive arrangement of individuals in relation to firms, states and other organizations. It distributes them and circulates them in a changed network of relations and expectations. Not only do individuals shift among given points in given structures. New 'slots' are created in which to fit and enumerate people (cf. Hacking, 1986: 223). The discourse on employability has established the 'employable individual' as a normative category. In this volume, we have sought to discover by what mechanisms discourses operate and impact on social practice – to look at practices and devices used to regulate and shape the worker and his or her behaviour and work experience. Accordingly, by what norms and by what means is the 'employable individual' created in local contexts of Swedish working life?

In this section we will look more into detail at what is required of the 'employable individual'. We draw here on a Foucauldian perspective concerned with the governance of individuals through the 'conduct of conduct' (Foucault, 1991). In this perspective, governing becomes governance or self-regulation through the internalization of norms, a process in turn supported by various 'technologies of self', technologies understood as configurations of power and knowledge which are mobilized in particular ways in order to shape the way individuals perceive and conduct themselves (Shore, 2000: 30). 'Technologies of self' are accordingly to be understood as technologies by which a normative category is established, normalized and internalized.

New classifications imply new types of subjectivity (Shore, 2000: 30), thus affecting self-perception. This does not mean that regimes of governance *determine* forms of subjectivity. Rather, they encourage and support certain qualities, or, as put by Dean (1999: 32), they 'elicit, promote, facilitate, foster and attribute various capacities, qualities and statuses to particular agents. They are successful to the extent that these agents come to experience themselves through such capacities', qualities and statuses. The conduct of conduct is ultimately a moral activity in the sense that this activity always embodies a knowledge of what constitutes good, virtuous, appropriate or responsible conduct of individuals and collectives (Dean, 1999: 12). At the level of political discourse, as shown in Chapter 3 by Jacobsson and Chapter 4 by Faurbæk in this book, the employability and its related requirements are not unambiguous. Employability implies both education, training and, in the case of unemployment, activation, *and* being able to market and 'sell' oneself in a competitive labour market. This means that the employment policy agenda includes both measures to improve people's working capacity, their access to the labour market, their willingness and general attitudes to work and their self-presentation in relation to work.

It is clear that it is not enough to have appropriate education and training. A number of other qualities and attitudes are required too: the maintenance and development of employability requires an open-mindedness towards change (see also Bollérot, 2001: 54). It requires adaptability, flexibility, learning capacity, and generally a reflexive attitude towards one's work, worklife and role in the labour market at large. 'Soft' skills: teamworking, communication, problem-solving and inter-personal or self-managing skills rather than the upgrading of technical competence are increasingly coming into focus (Brown, 2001: 41; see also Chapter 9 by Lindgren and Sederblad in this volume). Entrepreneurship, an enterprising attitude, initiative, and the ability to sell oneself are other important characteristics (Jackall, 1988; Miller and Rose 1995; see also Chapter 12 by Furusten, Chapter 11 by Augustsson and Sandberg; and Chapter 7 by Thedvall in this volume). Also, the capacity for 'emotional labour' (Hochschild, 1983) – for self-observation and remoulding oneself accordingly – has become vital (see Chapter 8 by Garsten, and Chapter 9 by Lindgren and Sederblad, in this volume). The chapters in this volume illustrate the presence, and indeed salience, of normative expectations of employability in a number of different workplaces.

At the same time, the competencies that are required are often vague and the concept of employability partly fluid. What is expected from the individual is not always clear or outspoken. The insecurity of what is really expected of individuals may be stressful in itself, and even more so in combination with an insecure job situation.

Crespo and Serrano (2002) have argued that the rhetoric of adaptability and flexibility transform the instability and uncertainty of the economy into personal problems. As the chapters by Garsten, Oudhuis and Thedvall show, these problems are often repositioned as possibilities. To borrow Emily Martin's phrasing: 'The individual comes to consist of potentials to be realized and capacities to be fulfilled' (Martin, 1997: 247). A world of possibilities, exploration and development is opened up.

We have in our case studies also looked at techniques and procedures accompanying the vocabulary of employability in the creation of employable individuals. To recall, when focusing on self-regulation or governance, we are concerned not primarily with power as something external to actors but with power that presupposes the agency of individuals rather than denying it (Shore, 2000: 30). Thus we are concerned with techniques that *empower and activate forms of agency* (Haahr, 2002).

Several of the chapters in this volume give evidence of the logic of individualized responsibility and what may be called 'employability through incentives' (Raveaud, 2002: 173). Incentives are bestowed primarily onto individuals and in some instances to teams, more rarely to larger collective groupings. Awards, benefits, incentives, ratings and monetary compensations are examples of measures by which individuals are taught to be responsible and accountable.

An illustrative example is the reward system used to promote and encourage certain qualities of individuals. One such example is the award the Golden Ant given by the temporary staffing agency Olsten (see Chapter 8 by Garsten in this volume). The award accentuates and makes visible the value of being flexible, reliable and service-minded towards clients. Call centres often use visibilities such as diplomas on office walls, awarded to 'the collaborator of the year', 'the team of the year' as well as more specific ones: 'for the highest rate of debiting' or 'for an increasing rate of debiting'. Other rewards, material and/or symbolic, can be a personal parking space near the entrance, a study visit to a sister company in another country or a t-shirt with the emblem 'the collaborator of the quarter of the year' (Kadhammar, 2002). These visibilities function as reminders of the qualities worth striving for as well as rewards to those who have succeeded in meeting the expectations of management. A small note from the boss telling 'let's show the other groups that we are best' (Kadhammar, 2002) perform the same function of steering by encouragement. The chapters by Oudhuis and Thedvall also illustrate the frequent use of positive encouragement and the mobilization of positive feelings to achieve certain goals.

A certain tension between the notion of autonomous individuals and the notion of a need for adaptation to functional and thus external demands is discerned in the employability discourse. Governance techniques which encourage initiative and agency and at the same time steer individuals towards the demands of a competitive economy become instrumental here, such as the reward systems just mentioned. In practice, however, the dual imperatives of responsibility and adaptation are not always easy to reconcile and can cause stress on individuals. As demonstrated by Augustsson and Sandberg in their chapter, the way work is organized, in their case in the knowledge industry, makes little room for learning and developing the type of competence that is regarded necessary and in fact promised by the employer.

The governing of individuals also operates by techniques that work at a distance. Auditing as a governance technique has gained popularity during the last decade, the expansion of which has led authors to talk of the development of 'audit cultures' (Strathern, 2000) or even an 'audit society' (Power, 1997). As a governance technique auditing is comparatively inexpensive; it functions at a temporal and spatial distance from the organizational processes to which it is applied; it is possible to apply to a broad variety of areas: it is 'harmless' and difficult to object to but can be effective in that it aims not only at imposing external control but ultimately at actors internalizing norms, thus becoming 'self-managing individuals who render themselves auditable' (Shore and Wright, 2000: 57). Wedlin shows in Chapter 13 in this volume how the requirements for learning and the demands placed on institutions for higher education in business and management are manifested through media rankings. These rankings, Wedlin argues, are to be seen as audit practices, accentuating the idea of competition and exclusion among schools.

Comparing workers with each other is also an effective governance technique used by management. In some call centres, the work of individual employees is not only carefully registered but showed on a monitor to allow all workers to compare each others' results. This practice makes visible individual performance and may also be used as a follow-up in dialogue with management: how can your work performance be improved, do you think? (Kadhammar, 2002). In temporary staffing as well, continuous evaluation and rating of individual skills, competencies and desirable attitudes are used as governance techniques, as shown in Garsten's chapter.

Employability as a category can thus be used as an instrument to classify and sort individuals and direct measures at them. This was precisely what the category employed-unemployed did when used as an instrument of labour market policy, with measures tailed towards individual needs (Salais *et al.*, 1986; Zimmerman, 2001). This is partly the case also today in active labour market policy. In this sense, categorization can be empowering. But a category can also be used to distinguish who is worth investing in if resources are scarce. From the perspective of employees, there is a fear that the idea of employability serves to establish the priorities for dismissal: employability becomes a factor for potential exclusion (Bollérot, 2001: 58f). Since some employees may be more able than others to discern and realize the possibilities of improving their employability, there is a risk of differentiating among employees, where employers are more interested in supporting the employability of some workers than others. The category of employability, like other administrative categories which are at the same time social categories, may function to legitimize measures directed – or not directed – at actors which fall under the category.

The double character of social categories is also evinced in the simultaneous feelings of empowerment and powerlessness that individuals may experience (cf. Martin, 1994: 135). Individuals may simultaneously experience a sense of agency (I am able to do it myself by starting my own company!) or helplessness (since I may not introduce change, all I can do is adapt flexibly to what the client says). The 'employable individual' as a normative category brings with it both emancipatory potentials and suppressive powers.

Strategies of resistance

The case-studies in this volume show that workers are not necessarily passive objects to discursive influences. There are also examples of more or less active resistance or counter-strategies in response to various types of pressures. Lindgren and Sederblad show, in Chapter 9, that workers in the call centres studied develop strategies to handle the pressures they are exposed to through tight technical control and time pressure. One such strategy is to develop close personal and social relations at the workplace. It is also important, both for the workers and for management, to conjure up the feeling of being a 'team', although the possibilities for functional co-operation are in practice very low. Lindgren and Sederblad speak of such teams as 'empty teams'. For the workers, being a 'team' means a feeling of belonging together which makes work more enjoyable. For management, encouraging a team spirit is a way of securing loyalty to the company.

In the temporary staffing business, temporary employees may withdraw loyalty from the temporary staffing agency and focus more on themselves. Flexible work may thus be seen as a way for them to enter the labour market, to change career orientation, to get a broader scope of experience, or simply to raise enough money to set off on a long journey.

Garsten's chapter is illustrative of this more instrumental orientation towards the expectations of management.

There may be reluctance or resistance to identifying with the traits of character that management encourages. Thedvall shows in Chapter 7 how, in the course on entrepreneurship provided by the Public Employment Service, some of the participants express an unease and unwillingness to take on the characteristics of the self-employed entrepreneur.

We have thus been able to trace not only the converging impact of the employability discourse on individuals who embrace, accept, or subject themselves to it, but also various types of resistance. People may distance themselves from it, withdraw loyalty, or refuse to identify themselves with the desired characteristics of the employable individual. They may seek ways around control and cut themselves off from external or self-governance. Hence, the discursive transformation also involves the creation of alternative assumptions, latently or openly in conflict with the dominant ones.

Individualized responsibilities

We have argued that the discourse of employability reallocates responsibility among parties, so that the individual becomes in many instances the prime locus. The discourse positions the employable individual as a normative category, populated by self-reliant actors who assume agency. We have illustrated how not only unemployed people, but also plant workers, interactive media workers, 'temps', management consultants and call centre employees are taught to place trust in their own capacity of successfully navigating the labour market. To be employable thus requires individual responsibility, initiative and autonomy. This reasoning springs to a large extent out of a neo-liberal orientation, according to which employability and the realization of the positive freedoms associated with visions of 'good work' is a strictly individual affair.

Our view on employability as a multivocal concept (see Introduction) also involves a plurality of 'employability policies' with different views on who is to be seen as accountable for employability (Raveaud, 2002). Our accounts fit well with what Raveaud calls 'the logic of individualized responsibilities' in which policies are defined so as to make the (unemployed or employed) person behave in a certain way through incentives and constraints (Raveaud, 2002: 172–3). As shown by Huzzard, unions have also aligned themselves largely to this logic, now providing individual support and guidance, as well as subsuming the individual under the aegis of collective rights.

The practices implied render visible the individual as performer. The rationality of audit makes individuals amenable to comparison and legitimates differences according to alleged objective criteria of performance. Like the Foucauldian panopticon, it orders the whole system while ranking everyone within it. Individuals are made acutely aware that their performance is under constant scrutiny (Shore and Wright, 1997: 77).

Self-regulation or governance, in contrast to government by hierarchical authority, works by activating capacities and agencies, that is, by empowering individuals. The chapter by Oudhuis on a shift in a team model in a bus factory illustrates well the shift in management technique: from the creation of the 'good worker' by hierarchical control to the creation of the 'employable individual' by delegation and encouragement. By some workers, this shift was experienced as a relief and it allowed for a release of individual creativity, responsibility and initiative. By others, it was experienced as too demanding in terms of what was required from individuals and entailing false promises of learning and development in work. As put by an interviewee. 'They tell me it is up to me, but since I am not given the means to carry out my plans.' The focus on the individual may engender both motivation and frustration.

The individualization of responsibility serves to enhance and encourage reflexivity. Such reflexivity may be empowering, providing individuals with resources with which to deal with change and expectations and to be 'on top of things'. Reflexivity may, however, be circumscribed within institutional arrangements that render resistance little scope or potential. While we do not wish to give the appearance of the discourse as inescapable, we want to underline the importance of looking closely at the options and possibilities as well as constraints and conditionalities that follow in the thread of employability.

Placing responsibilities onto the individual also threaten to undermine the fabric of social relations and collegiality in the workplace. This is evinced in the case study by Lindgren and Sederblad, where 'empty teams' replace functionally based teams, becoming more volatile as a result. It is also to be seen in Garsten's case study, where temporary employees experience a lack of collegial community. Concepts such as colleague, competitor and client are often vague and interchangeable. In the long run, such tendencies may have severe consequences for the possibilities of collective action.

'Employability' in Sweden: continuities and changes

The book has focused on a discursive transformation which is general in its direction but with differential impact in different contexts. To what extent and in what respects has the global discourse on employability impacted on actual practices in Swedish working life? We will finally draw some conclusions on continuities and changes in the Swedish model of work relations. In our view, the Swedish labour market context, with traditions, institutions and labour market relations, talks back to and differentiates the penetration of the discourse.

True, the economic recession in the early 1990s hit the Nordic countries hard; unemployment rates rose sharply as did the number of social assistance recipients, which put the Nordic welfare states under strain (Kuhnle 2000; Johansson, 2001). Both the centre-right government of 1991–94 in Sweden and the Social Democratic government that came into office in 1994 tried to fight the economic crisis by a number of tough measures, including decreased benefit levels for sickness insurance, parental insurance and unemployment insurance, and the introduction of a waiting period before unemployment benefit was paid. However, in several cases, levels of benefit were restored at the end of the 1990s when the public finances allowed. It is probably fair to conclude that the Swedish welfare state managed to survive the crisis with its institutions and principles basically intact (universalism, comprehensiveness, the work strategy, a commitment to full employment and redistribution, etc). Structures in the tax and benefit systems have been slightly revised to strengthen the work incentive and avoid poverty traps, but this is largely along the lines of the traditional 'work strategy'. Even if work incentives have been strengthened in Sweden, it is clear that structures and institutions in the labour market are fairly stable, and that there has not been any drastic changes in this respect.

Despite the advice of both the OECD and the EU as well as the calls from the employers' organizations and the centre-right opposition in Sweden, the regulation of the Swedish labour market has not been notably flexibilized in recent years. There have been some changes in labour market regulation, including a revision of the law on employment protection so that the employer can exempt two key persons from the rules of the order of dismissal in case of scarcity of work. Usually the last individual employed would have to leave first. But, basically, the Social Democratic government does not agree with the view of for instance the OECD that Swedish labour market regulation is too rigid (Ministry of Finance, 2000). The number of employees on fixed-term contracts had increased to reach almost 14 per cent of total employment by 2002 (CEC, 2002: 26). The most 'flexible' form of temporary employment, 'on call' for temporary staffing agencies, has increased considerably since such agencies were allowed in 1992, but in 2001 still constituted only 0.87 per cent of the total labour force as compared to 1.5 per cent in the EU and 2 per cent in the US (Engman, 2002; SPUR, 2002). Moreover, when 'atypical' jobs (like those offered by temporary staffing agencies) have increased in numbers, labour unions have reacted and have managed to secure their regulation in collective agreements and legislation (Friberg *et al.*, 1999). There has also been a continuous striving to 'upgrade' the image and status of such jobs, for example by changes in terminology (agencies using the term 'consultants' rather than 'temporary' or 'flexible workers' or similar terms) as well as through attempting to recruit a larger number of well-educated individuals. This is also true of work in call centres, where employment contracts have been largely aligned to standard employment contracts. Thus, when new and 'atypical' working life phenomena have sprung up, they have after a period been incorporated into the Swedish tradition. Collective responsibility has been taken.

At the same time, some new ideas have found a certain resonance with the Swedish tradition. New influences, such as temporary staffing agencies, have come to be regarded as a welcome novelty to the extent that they can be brought to function according to established norms.[1] The idea is that if changes are supported in the proper way, they can bring new dynamics to the labour market which will in turn benefit individuals who will find employment opportunities. Structural transformation and industrial renewal are generally supported both by the political parties as well as the labour unions, even if the unions stress that adjustment to structural change is a collective rather than individual responsibility.

Moreover, as mentioned in the introductory chapter, neither the focus on individuals, nor the idea of supporting the employability of individuals by training and active labour market measures, are new to Sweden, even if the term 'employability' has not previously been used. The discourse on employability has also, against the background of traditional active labour market policy, resounded well with the Swedish labour market policy discourse.

Still, despite some important continuities, we see in our case-studies that the discourse on employability *has* penetrated and impacted on Swedish practices in working life as well as labour market policy. Thedvall shows in her chapter how the Public Employment Services give courses in entrepreneurship in order to encourage the unemployed to become self-employed (instead of merely mediating available jobs). Moreover, the PES in Sweden now provide computer services and encourage the unemployed to search for available jobs by themselves rather than through an appointment with an official. Thus, services are individualized and considerable responsibility placed on the unemployed individual. Oudhuis shows that workers in a Volvo bus factory are encouraged to think of their future employability: 'Only you can make yourself employable', as put by the new head of the plant at a seminar with the employees.

There is an increased emphasis on the responsibility of individuals for employability in general and lifelong learning in particular. As shown by Huzzard in Chapter 6 in this book, the trade unions also largely embrace this notion of individual responsibility for competence development.

Thus, even if the impact of the discursive shifts also differs between sectors and workplaces in Sweden, it is obvious that the discourse of employability is diffused in sectors and activities of very different kinds. The discourse of employability is thus shot through with different ideational influences, each bringing forth negotiations, adaptations and resistance. It is fair to say that the employability discourse has exerted a punctuated and fragmented influence on the Swedish scene, with differential degrees of impact across organizations.

Beyond employability...

The discourse on employability has been instrumental in bringing 'persons, organizations and political objectives into alignment' (Miller and Rose quoted in Shore and Wright, 2000: 71). The idea of employability acts as an instrument of governance by creating new normative categories, new subjects of power and new intermediaries. A new site of management opens up, and new entities emerge to do the management (cf. Miller and Rose, 1990). The workings of employability are not always easily discerned; they come with 'sibling terms' such as emancipation, freedom, and dynamics. They engage flexibly with existing structures and discourses and they emerge in a variety of organizational environments. This is also the nature of modern power; the ability to hide its own mechanisms (Foucault, 1978).

We have attempted to unmask some of these workings by looking at some of the sites in which they are constructed and then distributed and at workplaces where they are put to work. The discourse on employability is, in our view, indicative of a general market orientation in society, which has, in the case of the labour market, led to an emphasis on the labour market as *market*. This has, *inter alia*, reinforced pressures on individuals to be adaptable to market needs, and to be prepared to assume responsibility for their individual adaptation, for instance by undergoing continuous learning. Moreover, we see how the participation of people in the market, as employable individuals, as entrepreneurs, and as consumers increasingly defines social inclusion.

In the workings of employability, individual agency plays a key role. As Meyer and Jepperson put it: '[T]he constructed capacity for responsible agency is the core of modern actorhood' (2000: 106). Modern culture, and especially so the liberal tradition, depicts society as made up of 'actors', authorized agents for various interests. The individual is entrapped in standardized agency more than in explicit control schemes – in what they call an 'exaggerated actorhood' (2000: 110). The employable individual emerges as a normative category and as a category of assumed actorhood at the same time. The discourse of employability accordingly recasts insecurities and risks associated with contemporary labour markets into personal and individual problems (cf. Crespo and Serrano, 2002). 'Risk management' is to be handled by individuals, for example by engaging in lifelong learning and skills enhancement.

Not only are individuals emerging as central loci of the workings of employability. There are also other actors on the scene, such as the EU and the OECD, management consultants, manpower agencies, call centres, business schools, and the like, who work as intermediaries between the individual and the economy. These organizations are powerful forces behind a discursive transformation, encouraging economistic and market-oriented ways of thinking. They bring with them new generalized ways of thinking – 'invading' the present activities from the outside, so to speak (in contrast to new ways of thinking that develop from local practice). Other important intermediaries are the unions, who seek to combine the potential emancipatory and motivational prospects of employability with regulatory measures against threats to social exclusion.

Employability is, at least, a double-sided coin. At the very best, it entails an enterprising engagement with one's own career. At worst, it subsumes the individual under a hegemonic system of control.

What, then, can we expect beyond employability? We have hinted at a discursive transformation involving shifting constellations of actors and ideas, changes in the conceptualization of responsibility and accountability and in the rights and duties of citizenship. While this transformation is not changing the fabric of established structures and ways of thinking altogether, it does, however, signify a gradual shift in society, in economy and polity. This is also where a space for a new social policy and intervention opens up. The search for a form of governance of labour markets which combines labour market dynamism with the exercise of social rights should, in our view, recognize the embedded cultural assumptions, the ideational presuppositions and the structural framings that accompany governance structures. Not least, it should be attentive to the constraints and freedoms that follow in their wake. Amartya Sen has argued that 'economic development can be seen as a process of expanding the real freedoms that people enjoy' (1999: 3). This vision still awaits accomplishment.

Note

1. Temporary staffing agencies are, as a matter of fact, not entirely new to Sweden, but have existed previously albeit in different forms. What is new are the ways in which organizations rely on them for recruiting, outsourcing as well as a source of temporary workforce – that is to achieve flexibility, and the framing of work and workers.

References

Bollérot, Patrick. 2001. 'Two actors in employability: the employer and the worker'. In *Employability: From Theory to Practice*, edited by P. Weinert *et al*. London: Transaction Publishers, 51–90.

Bosco, Alessandra. 1998. 'Putting Europe into the systems: a review of social protection issues'. In *European Trade Union Yearbook 1997*, edited by E. Gabaglio and R. Hoffmann. Brussels: ETUI, 305–34.

Brown, Phillip. 2001. 'Skill formation in the twenty-first century'. In *High Skills: Globalization, Competitiveness and Skill formation*, edited by P. Brown, A. Green and H. Lauder. Oxford: Oxford University Press, 1–55.

CEC [Commission of the European Communities]. 2002. *Employment in Europe 2002. Recent Trends and Prospects*.

Chabbert, Isabelle and Nicole Kerschen. 2001. 'Towards a European model of employability insurance? Interaction between Europe and the member states'. In *Employability: From Theory to Practice*, edited by P. Weinert *et al*. London: Transaction Publishers, 91–112.

Crespo, Eduardo and Amparo Serrano. 2002. 'The EU's concept of activation for young people: towards a new social contract?'. In *Activation Policies for Young People in International Perspective*, edited by A. Serrano. Brussels: ETUI. Book manuscript.

Dean, Mitchell. 1999. *Governmentality. Power and Rule in Modern Society*. London: Sage.

Engman, Moa. 2002. 'Hon har ett jobb – men på tio olika arbetsplatser'. *Stockholm City*. 29 October.

Forrier, Anneleen and Luc Sels. 2002. 'Employability: the magic spell for a successful career'. Paper presented at the 18th EGOS Colloquium, Barcelona, 4–6 July.

Foucault, Michel. 1978. *The History of Sexuality. Volume one.* Harmondsworth: Penguin.

Foucault, Michel. 1991. 'Governmentality'. In *The Foucault Effect: Studies in Governmentality*, edited by G. Burcell, C. Gordon and P. Miller. London: Harvester Wheatsheaf, 87–104.

Friberg, Kent, Åsa Olli and Eskil Wadensjö. 1999. *Privat förmedling av arbete i Sverige.* Stockholm: Swedish Institute for Social Research (SOFI), Stockholm University.

Haahr, Jens Henrik. 2002. 'Open methods of government: advanced liberal government'. Paper presented at the ECPR 1st Pan-European Conference on European Union Politics, Bordeaux, 26–28 September.

Hacking, Ian. 1986. 'Making up people'. In *Reconstructing Individualism: Autonomy, Individuality, and the Self in Western Thought*, edited by T. C. Heller, M. Sosna and D. E. Wellbery. Stanford: Stanford University Press, 222–36.

Hansson, Johan. 2002. *Omtänkbara organisationer.* Stockholm: Stockholm University, School of Business Research Reports.

Hochschild, Arlie Russell. 1983. *The Managed Heart: Commercialization of Human Feeling.* Berkeley: University of California Press.

Jackall, Robert. 1988. *Moral Mazes: The World of Corporate Managers.* New York: Oxford University Press.

Johansson, Håkan. 2001. 'Activation policies in the Nordic countries: social democratic universalism under pressure'. *Journal of European Area Studies* 9(1): 63–77.

Kadhammar, Peter. 2002. 'Dokument callcenter'. *Aftonbladet.* 21 January, 12–17.

Kuhnle, Stein. 2000. 'The Scandinavian welfare states in the 1990s: challenged but viable', *West European Politics* 23(2): 209–28.

Martin, Emily. 1994. *Flexible Bodies: Tracking Immunity in American Culture – From the Days of Polio to the Age of AIDS.* Beacon Press.

Martin, Emily. 1997. 'Managing Americans: policy and changes in the meanings of work and the self'. In *Anthropology of Policy: Critical Perspectives on Governance and Power*, edited by C. Shore and S. Wright. London: Routledge, 239–57.

Meyer, John W. and Ronald L. Jepperson. 2000. 'The "actors" of modern society: the cultural construction of social agency', *Sociological Theory* 18(1): 100–20.

Miller, Peter and Nikolas Rose. 1990. 'Governing economic life'. *Economy and Society* 19(1): 1–31.

Miller, Peter and Nikolas Rose. 1995. 'Production, identity, and democracy'. *Theory and Society* 24: 427–67.

Ministry of Finance. 2000. *National Report on Economic Reforms. Product and Capital Markets – Sweden.* Stockholm.

Power, Michael, (ed.) 1997. *The Audit Society: Rituals of Verification.* Oxford: Oxford University Press.

Raveaud, Gilles. 2002. 'The European Employment Policy: from ends to means?'. In *Europe and the Politics of Capabilities.* Rapport de la Commission Européenne, Direction Général Emploi et Affairs Sociales.

Salais, Robert, Nicolas Baverez and Bénédicte Reynaud. 1986. *L'invention du chomage: Histoire et transformations d'une catégorie en France des années 1890 aux années 1980.* Paris: Presses Universitaires de France.

Sen, Amartya. 1999. *Development as Freedom.* Oxford: Oxford University Press.

Shore, Cris. 2000 *Building Europe: The Cultural Politics of European Integration*, London: Routledge.

Shore, Cris and Susan Wright. 1997. 'Policy: a new field of anthropology'. In *Anthropology of Policy: Critical Perspectives on Governance and Power*, edited by C. Shore and S. Wright. London: Routledge, 3–39.

Shore, Cris and Susan Wright. 2000. 'Coercive accountability: the rise of audit culture in higher education'. In *Audit Cultures*, edited by M. Strathern, London: Routledge, 57–89.

SOU 1997: 58 *Personaluthyrning*. Stockholm: Ministry of Labour.

SPUR. 2002. URL: www.spur.se, 24 September 2002.

Strathern, Marilyn, (ed.) 2000. *Audit Cultures: Anthropological Studies in Accountability, Ethics and the Academy*. London: Routledge.

Zimmermann, Bénédicte, 2001. *La constitution du chômage en Allemagne: Entre professions et territoires*, Paris, Ed. Maison des sciences de l'homme.

Author Index

Abbott, Andrew 234
Abercrombie, Nicholas 144
Åberg, Rune 55, 84
Abrahamsson, K. *et al.* 3, 20
Abrahamsson, L. 20
Aglietta, Michel, 30
Ahlstrand, Roland 173
Ahrne, Göran 212
Aldcroft, Derek 252
Aldrich, Howard 212
Allvin, Michael vii, xi, 4, 5, 15, 36, 76, 110, 126, 232
  et al. 39, 40
Alvesson, Mats 12, 13, 109, 247
Amin, Ash 107
AMS 149(n2)
Andersen, Niels Åkerstrøm 65
Anderson, Benedict 173
Aneesh, A. 211, 219
Armbrüster, Thomas 232
Aronsson, Gunnar 40
Arvidsson, Håkan *et al.* 112, 128
Aspers, P. 219
Atkinson, John 5, 33
Atkinson, Robert D. 110
Augustsson, Fredrik vii, 17, 145, 210, 213, 216, 217, 218, 227(n4), 233, 252, 277, 279
Austin, John L. 12

Bäcklund, Jonas 232, 236
Badeau, Nicholas 132
Bain, Peter 183, 184
  et al. 172, 180, 187
Barley, Stephen 110, 236
Barret, Frank 246
Batt, Rosemary *et al.* 211, 213, 219–20, 227
Baukens, Michèle 22
Bauman, Zygmunt 38, 169
Baverez, Nicolas 22, 288
Beck, Ulrich 4, 5, 144
Beckman, Sofia 184

Bell, Daniel 107, 212, 213
Benders, Jos 173, 177
Bennehall, Jerker 192
Berggren, Christian 173
Bergström, Jonas 76
Beronius, Mats 183
Biggert, Magnus 142, 144
Bijker, Wiebe E. 212
  et al. 212, 227
Björkman, Torsten 20, 85, 88, 89
Blackler, Frank 111
Blair, A. C. L. 54, 56
Block, Fred 212
Bollérot, Patrick 11, 22, 59, 277, 280
Bonoli, Guiliano 54–5
Bonvin, Jean-Michel 54–5
Börjesson, Mats xi
Bosco, Alessandra 10, 49, 50, 51, 275
Boyer, Robert 212
Braverman, Harry 127(n2), 175
Brown, P. 84, 85, 277
  et al. 2, 20, 59, 61, 83, 86, 104
Bruhn, Anders 113
Brunsson, Nils 235
Bruun, Niklas 37
Burchell, Graham *et al.* 200, 208
Burrage, Michael 234
Burton-Jones, Alan 112

Calhoun, Craig 212
Callaghan, George 129, 181
Callinicos, Alex 107
Campbell, John L. 63
Cantillon, Richard 132
Carlzon, Jan 32, 176
Carrwik, Christian 215, 216
Castells, Manuel 212, 216, 228
CEC *see* Commission of the European Communities
Chabbert, Isabelle 51
Chandler, Alfred D., Jr 212
Chassard, Yves 10

Christmansson, Marita *et al.*
    192, 208
Christopherson, Susan   227
Chumer, Mike   129
Chytry, Josef   228
Clark, Timothy   236
Commission of the European
    Communities (CEC)   5, 43,
    46–9, 51–2, 57, 59, 65–8,
    155, 284
Confederation of Swedish
    Enterprise   73–4
    see also SAF
Court, Randolph D.   110
Crainer, Stuart   259
Crespo, Eduardo   8, 58, 277, 286
Czarniawska, Barbara   64, 236, 246

Dahrendorf, Ralf   59
Danaher, Geoff *et al.*   200, 209
Daniel, Carter   254, 255, 256
Davidow, William H.   216
Davidsson, Per   133
De Geer, Hans   28
Dean, Mitchell   13, 276–7
Dearlove, Des   259
Delors, Jacques   65–6
Diamantopoulou, Commissioner   57
Dijk, Jan van   216
DiMaggio, Paul   248
Docherty, Peter *et al.*   127(n3),
    128
Donnellon, Anne   111
Dosi, Giovanni *et al.*   216, 228
Drøpping, Jon Anders *et al.*
    43, 61
Drucker, Peter   110
Durkheim, Émile   213

ECOSOC, 67
Edström, Anders   208
Ekonomisk Debatt   211
Ekwall, Göran   189
Ellström, Per-Erik   20
Engman, Moa   284
Engwall, Lars   255, 270
Esping-Andersen, Gösta   10
European Round Table of
    Industrialists (ERT)   46

Fairclough, Norman   12, 56–8
Fall, Gregor   187
Faurbæk, Lotte   vii, 15, 76, 277
Fayol, Henri   28

Ferrera, Maurizio *et al.*   6, 10,
    49, 50, 57, 60(n2), 61
Fiol, Marlene C.   212
Fligstein, Neil   212, 215, 220
Flynn, Padraig   49–50
Forrier, Anneleen   19(n3), 275
Forslin, Jan   128
Foucault, Michel   13, 14, 25, 65, 109,
    133, 153, 183, 200, 276, 285
Friberg, Kent *et al.*   154, 171,
    284, 288
Friberg, Maria   211, 216
Fridén, Lennart *et al.*   154,
    170(n3), 171
Friedman, Andrew   175, 182
Furusten, Staffan   vii–viii, 18, 231,
    232–6, 244, 246, 247, 277

Gallie, William B.   12
Garsten, Christina   viii, 4, 14, 16,
    160, 162, 166, 167, 231, 233,
    277, 278, 279, 281, 282
Gazier, Bernard   8, 19(n2)
Gerhard, Anette   21
Giddens, Anthony   107, 110,
    162, 234
Goffee, Robert   131, 136
Goffman, Erving   134
Gordon, Colin   208
Gough, J. W.   132
Government Bill (*Regeringens
    proposition*) 2000/01   83
Grand, Carl le *et al.*   213, 228
Granfelt, TiiaRiitta   133
Granovetter, Mark   212
Green, Andy   20, 61
Greiner, Larry   236, 237
Grey, Chris   4
Grillo, Ralph   13
Gummesson, Evert   236
Gyllenstierna, Tove   139

Haahr, Jens Henrik   278
Habermas, Jürgen   25, 38
Hacking, Ian   134, 140, 156, 276
Hägg, Ingemund   270
Hague, Jeremy *et al.*   111, 123,
    128
Handy, Charles   111
Hannerz, Ulf   135, 148, 161
Hansen, Lars H.   212
Hansen, Morten *et al.*   236,
    250
Hansson, Johan   274

Hansson, Per Albin   30
Härenstam, Annika   40
Harrison, Bennett   32
Harvey, David   5, 107
Harvey, Michael   155
Heckscher, Charles C.   111
Hedén, Ylva   171
Hedmo, Tina *et al.*   254, 255, 272
Heelas, Paul   142
Heikkillä, Matti   6, 10, 21
Helgesson, Claes-Fredrik   212
Hellmark, Ann-Britt xii
Helmersson, Stina   142
Hemerijck, Anton   10, 61
Henson, Kevin   157, 159
Hertog, Friso den   128
Himanen, Pekka *et al.*   216, 218, 228
Hirdman, Yvonne   30
Hjort af Ornäs, Anders   133
Hjorth, Daniel   133
Hochschild, Arlie Russell   158, 167, 173, 174, 176, 181, 186, 277
Hollingsworth, R. J.   212
Holmberg, Ingalill *et al.*   211, 212, 228
Holmqvist, Mikael   214, 215
Hörning, Karl H. *et al.*   5, 21
Houlihan, Maeve   183
Hout, Thomas M.   33
Hughes, Thomas P.   227
Hull, Richard   129
Hultman, Glenn *et al.*   85, 105
Hutchins, David   32
Huzzard, Tony   viii, 6, 7, 16, 20(n4), 89, 115, 118n, 124, 125, 126, 128, 214, 276, 281, 285
Hvinden, Bjørn   21, 61

Inglehart, Ronald   38, 110

Jackall, Robert   277
Jacobsson, Bengt   xi
Jacobsson, Kerstin   viii, 2, 4, 9, 15, 19(n3), 43, 66, 67, 68, 83, 108, 207, 212, 231, 275, 277
Jacques, Roy   4, 170
Jepperson, Ronald L.   286
Jessop, Bob   6, 55
Joerges, Bernward   64, 236, 246
Johannisson, Bengt   133, 136

Johansson, Anders   19(n3)
Johansson, Conny   211
Johansson, Dan   211, 217
Johansson, Håkan   10, 283
Johansson, Jan   20
Johansson, Kjell   135
Jones, Daniel T.   41

Kadhammar, Peter   278, 279
Karasek, Robert   90
Kärreman, Dan   12, 13, 109, 247
Kautto, Mikko *et al.*   10, 21
Keat, Russell   144
Keiser, Alfred   236
Kelly, Kevin   110, 112
Kerschen, Nicole   51, 275
Kidder, Tracy   216, 219
Kipping, Matthias   232
Kjær, Peter   64, 65
Kjellberg, Anders   213
Klasson, Alger   105
Kleinman, Mark   10
Knights, David   181
Korpi, Walter   87
Krugman, Paul   110, 112
Kubr, Michel   235, 237, 238
Kuhnle, Stein   283
Kullstedt, Mats   143
Kunda, Gideon   236

Landström, Hans   132
Larsen, Judith K.   216
Larson, Marie Sarafatti   234
Larsson, Allan   49, 52
Lash, Scott   166
Latour, Bruno   64, 212
Lauder, Hugh   20, 61
Law, John   212
Lefresne, Florence   8–10, 55–6, 59
Leigard, Viktoria   216
Lennstrand, Bo   216
Lindgren, Antony   viii–ix, 17, 89, 180, 277, 280, 282
Lindgren, Monica   111
Lindqvist, Rafael   xi, 19(n3)
Lipietz, Alain   29, 30
Littler, Craig R.   28
LO (Swedish Trade Union Confederation)   85–7, 214
Lødemel, Ivor   10, 43
Lönnqvist, Stefan   142
Luque, Emilio   45
Lynch, Paul   238
Lyttkens, Lorentz   135–6

Magnusson, Lars   19(n3), 24, 31, 212
Malinvaud, Edmond   60(n3)
Malone, Michael S.   216
Marcussen, Martin   43–4
Marginson, Paul   31
Marklund, Staffan   19(n3), 21
Martin, Emily   5, 133–4, 278, 280
Marx, Karl   26, 112, 213
Mattsson, Nicklas   215, 216
Mazza, Carmelo *et al.*   254, 272
McCabe, Darren   181
McGuire, Patrick   212
McHugh, David   184
McKenna, Christopher   235
Meager, Nigel   5
Medbo, Lars   208
Medbo, Per   208
Melin, Lars   143
Metzger, Robert   236, 237
Meyer, John W.   286
Michailow, Matthias   21
Miller, Peter   13–14, 133, 134, 135, 145, 200, 202, 203, 205, 208, 255, 256, 277, 285
Morgan, Glenn   270
Mueller, Frank   173, 177
Mulholland, Kate   175, 180
Mulvey, Gareth   187
Munro, Roland   166

Negroponte, Nicholas   216
Nilsson, Magnus   105
Nilsson, Tommy   125
Nohria, Nitin   250
Nordström, Kjell A.   112, 127
Normann, Richard   32
Nyberg, Mikael   86
Nyberg, Robert   162
Nyström, Örjan   84, 86

Okeke, Susanna   136, 149(n4)
Olli, Åsa   171, 288
Organisation for Economic Co-operation and Development (OECD)   7, 44–6, 60(n3)
Ottosson, Christina   53
Oudhuis, Margareta   ix, 14, 17, 89, 277, 278, 282, 285

Papakostas, Apostolis   212
Pavlik, John V.   216
Pedersen, Dorthe   65
Pedersen, Ove Kaj   64

Peplowski, Ken   246
Perrow, Charles   32
Pettersson, Anna   216
Pfeffer, Jeffrey   110
Pinch, Trevor J.   227
Pineschi-Gapènne, Marina   22
Piore, Michael J.   27, 32
Ploug, Niels   21
Potter, Jonathan   12
Powell, Walter W.   215, 248
Power, Michael   xi, 253, 255, 279
Prichard, Craig *et al.*   107, 110, 129
Procter, Stephen   173, 177
Pugh, Derek S.   123

Quesnay, François   132

Ransome, Paul   213
Rasmussen, Bente   90
Rassam, Clive   238
Raveaud, Gilles   10, 278, 281
Rehn, Alf   216
Reich, Robert B.   31, 124, 142
Reynaud, Bénédicte   22, 288
Rhenman, Eric   236
Rhodes, Martin   6, 10, 57, 61
Ridderstråle, Jonas   112, 127
Rightor, Ned   227
Ritzer, George   212
Rogers, Everett M.   216
Rogers, Richard   156, 157, 166
Rombach, Björn   255
Roobeek, Annemieke J. M.   30
Roos, Daniel   41
Rose, Nikolas   13–14, 133, 134, 135, 145, 200, 202, 203, 205, 277, 285
Rosenberg, Nathan   212
Rosenqvist, Christopher   210, 211, 214, 215, 217
Rössler, Patrick   216
Rothstein, Bo   76
Røvik, Kjell-Arne   246
Rubenson, Kjell   6, 7

Sabel, Charles F.   27, 32
Sadler, Philip   237
Sahlin-Andersson, Kerstin   xi, 246, 254, 255, 272
Saint-Martin, Denis   236
Salais, Robert *et al.*   7, 22, 279, 288
Salaman, G.   236

Salaried Employees' Union
  (HTF) 181, 183–4, 186(n3)
Salzer-Mörling, Miriam 228
Sandberg, Åke ix, 17, 34, 89, 145,
  190, 216, 218, 210, 227(n4),
  233, 252, 277, 279
Saxenian, Annalee 4
Say, Jean Baptiste 132
Scarbrough, Harry 248
Scase, Richard 131, 136
Scharpf, Fritz W. 10
Schein, Edgar H. 236
Schirato, Tony 209
Schmid, Herman xi, 43
Schmidt, Vivien A. 10
Schneider, Mark A. 161
Schön, Donald 123
Schröder, Gerhard 54
Schumpeter, Joseph Alois 132
Scott, Richard 262, 271
Searle, John R. 12
Sederblad, Per ix, 17, 89, 173, 175,
  180, 277, 280, 282
Sels, Luc 19(n3), 275
Sen, Amartya 287
Senge, Peter 110
Serrano Pascual, Amparo 2, 7, 8,
  10, 52–3, 58, 277, 286
Shani, Rami 128
Shepard, Stephen B. 261
Shore, Cris 14, 153, 161, 166, 253,
  255–6, 276, 278, 279, 282, 285
Simmel, Georg 213
Sisson, Keith 31
Smith, Adam 132, 252
Smith, Chris 107, 126
Stael von Holstein, Johan 216
Stalk Jr, George 33
Strandgaard, Jesper 272
Strannegård, Lars 211, 216, 228
Stråth, Bo 1, 5, 7, 8, 60
Strathern, Marilyn 153, 161, 166,
  279
Streeck, Wolfgang 5–6
Svensson, Lennart ix–x, 15, 16,
  55, 86
Sverke, Magnus 36, 126
Swedberg, Richard 132
Swedish Association of Temporary
  Work Businesses and Staffing
  Services (SPUR) 284
Swedish Labour Market
  Administration (AMV,
  Arbetsmarknadsverket) 84, 151n

Swedish Metalworkers Union
  (Metall) 114–15, 214
Swedish Trade Union Confederation
  (LO) 85–7, 214
Swedish Union of Clerical and
  Technical Workers in Industry
  (Sif) 116–17
Szulkin, Ryszard 228

Tapscott, Don 211, 216
Taylor, Frederick Winslow 27–8,
  123, 208(n1)
Taylor, Phil 183, 184, 187
Teece, David J. 228
Teubner, Gunther 37
Thålin, Michael 228
Thedvall, Renita x, 16, 155, 233,
  277, 278, 281, 284
Theorell, Töres 90
Therborn, Göran 27
Thompson, Edward P. 25, 27
Thompson, Paul 13, 107, 111,
  126, 181, 184, 213
  et al. 124, 129
Thorne, Marie 13
Thorvalds, Linus 228
Tierney, Thomas 250
Tilly, Charles 3
Tilly, Chris 3
Torstendahl, Rolf 234
Totterdill, Peter 128
Trickey, Heather 10, 43
Trow, Martin 255, 270–1
Trygged, Sven 135
Turtinen, Jan 160, 162, 166,
  167

Unell, Elisabeth 135
Uvell, Markus 215, 216

van Hootegem, Geert 173, 177
van Jaarsfield, Danielle 227
Vik, Kirsten 61

Wadensjö, Eskil 135, 171, 288
Wåhlin, Nils 111
Wallace, Terry 181
Walwei, Ulrich 22
Warhurst, Chris 111, 129, 213
Wass, Johan 208
Watson, Aileen 187
Webb, Jen 209
Weber, Max 213
Webster, Graham 112

Wedlin, Linda   x, 18, 257, 259, 265, 266n, 272, 279
Weinert, Patricia *et al.*   10, 22
Wetherell, Margaret   12
White, Harrison C.   212
Wiklund, Per   40
Williams, Raymond   12

Willmott, Hugh   129
Womack, James P. *et al.*   32, 41
Wright, Susan   253, 255–6, 279, 282, 285

Zimmerman, Bénédicte   279
Zuboff, Shoshana   25, 26, 111, 180

Subject Index

Key: f = figure/illustration; n = note; t = table; **bold** = extended discussion or heading emphasized in main text.

accountability   286
business education   253, **254–6**,
   261, 269, 270
   dilemmas   256
accreditation   253, 255
activation   10, 43, 53, 54, 55,
   56, 58, 277, 282
activation principle   135
active labour market policy   9, 10,
   19(n3), 50, 68, 71, 279, 284
active labour market policy measures
   (*arbetsmarknadspolitiska
   aktiviteter*)   135, 136
actorhood   286
actors   274, 278, 281, 286
ad hoc organization   **224–5**
adaptability   43, 45, 48, 50–1, 56,
   71, 78, 208, 275, 277, 286
adaptation   44, 45, 278, 279, 285
Adecco   170(n1)
adjustment   **57–60**
adjustment insurance   59
administrative principles (Fayol)   28
Adobe (software developer)   218
adult education   83, 96f, 97, 102, 104(n6)
AFA (formerly AMF insurance)   186(n1)
agency   274, 278, 280, 281, 282, 286
ALU (*arbetslivsutveckling*)   *see*
   Self-Employment Project – Work
   Experience Scheme
Amsterdam Treaty (1997)   47–8, 70
Andersen Consulting   236
appearance (personal)   166, 167
Apple   33
articulation   **63–82**
   competition   69, **72–6**, **76–8**, 79
   EU labour market discourse   **76–9**
   regulation   69, **70–2**, 73, 75, **76–8**,
      79, 81(n5)
AT Kearney   236
attitude   45, 53, 58, 157, 158–9, 160,
   164, 167, 174, 189, 194, 203, 206,
   262, 271, 277, 279

Audi   33
audit/auditing   **161–7**, 279, 282
   business education   253–4, **254–6**,
      265, 269
'audit culture' (Strathern)   161, 279
audit gaze   **169–70**
audit practices   265
'audit society' (Power)   253, 279
audit technologies   161
autonomy   110, 147
   responsible (Friedman)   175, 182
awards   165–6, 278

back office   178
balanced scorecards   89, 90
benchmarking   89, 90
best practice   89, 103
body   190, **200–6**
body of knowledge   231, 238
Borås: Volvo Bus Plant (1977–)
   189–209
Boston Consulting Group   236
breaks   175
bureaucracy   108, 111
business administration   149(n1)
business community   267, 268, 271
business concepts   137
business education
   media ranking   18, **252–73**
   programmes   253, 258, 262, 271
Business Education Commission
   (BEC, Brussels and
   Washington)   258, 261, 265
business owners   138, 141, 145–6, 147
business process   32, 34–5
Business Process Reengineering
   (BPR)   89, 90
business schools   255, 256, 269, 279, 286
   advertising/marketing   257,
      259–60, 271
   brand names   261
   competing for employability   **269–71**
   customers   **267**, 268, 269

business schools – *continued*
  'diversity ranking' 264
  employability and
    competence **268**
  graduates 263–72
  input 262, 263, 264, 266t, 267t
  intellectual capital 263, 266t
  international market **258**
  internationality 268
  management consultants 247
  measuring quality 270–1
  national rankings 256–7
  outcomes 262, 264, 268, 269, 271
  output 262, 263, 264, 266t,
    267t, 268
  process 262, 263, 264, 266t, 267t
  qualitative criteria 268
  quantitative criteria 267, 268
  recruiters 263, 265–6, 266t, 267, 269
  reputation 263, 267, 268
  structures 262
  student satisfaction 263, 265–6,
    267, 269
  teaching quality 266t, 268
  value-for-money 266t, 268, 269
Business Week 253, 257–9, 261–3,
    265–7
  customer's voice **263**
  ranking criteria (business
    schools) 266t
buyers (management consulting
    services) 231, 236, **238–40**

California 166
call centres 17, 86, 89, 90, **172–88**,
    278–81, 284, 286
  employability 185–6
  flexibility 184–5
  in-bound 184–5
  in-house 183
  out-bound 184–5
calls 175, 177–8, 180, 181
Canada 258
capital 75, 76, 193
  close cooperation with labour
    (Sweden) 87–8
  free movement 70
career advancement 215
career planning 116
careers, 'boundaryless' 111
cash benefits 54, 55
Cell Network 215
Certified Management Consultants
    (CMC, 1991–) 235

change 212–13, 275, 277, 282
chief executive officers (CEOs) 241
children 146, 149(n5), 162f
citizenship: rights and duties 286
class 97, 110
clients 172, 182, 278, 280
  management consulting 233, 234,
    236, 237, 243, 244–6, 247
co-determination 88
co-operation: functional 175
codes of conduct 238, 248
cohesion 57
collective action 60, 282
collective agreements 284
collective bargaining 29, 30, 168
collectivism 109, 110, 112–13,
    119, 126
  management consultancy 246–7
commitment 180, 182
communication 180, 184, 186, 277
communication skills 163
communications technology 110
community 197
community of fate 75, 81(n6)
companies (businesses/corporations/
    enterprises/firms) 30, 50, 51,
    57–60, 66, 71, 87, 102, 110,
    154, 163, 212, 269, 274
  business-school ranking 263
  capitalist 108
  client/customer 176, 178, 182, 185
  'flexible' 184
  high-technology 85, 216
  information technology 233
  Japanese 173
  knowledge-based 111, 121, 124,
    216
  large/larger 99, 137, 146, 217, 247
  manufacturing 85
  multinational/transnational 2, 32,
    65, 73, 152
  public relations (PR) 233
  small businesses/SMEs 86, 97, 98,
    103, 136, 145, 149(n4), 216–17
  see also interactive media firms
comparability 255
competence 53, 57, 58, 74, 92f,
    93, 95f, 98, 100, 101, 132,
    140, 165, 196, 239, 243, 244,
    272, 279
  alleged need **84–7**
  definition **92–3**
  individual 179
  specialized 238

competence accounts *see* learning
  accounts
competence alteration 213
competence development 17, 114,
  115–16, 119, 120, 122, 125, 126,
  193–4, 196, 252, 276, 285
  discourse in practice 220–5
  discourse in Sweden 213–15
  individualization 225
  interactive media workers **210–30**
  low priority 224, 225
  means of securing loyalty 225–6
  organization 224–5
  promises and realities 222–4
  resources 210–11, 222–4, 226
  sources 217–20, 220–2
competence gap 85, 101
competence levels 215, 220
competence mix 215
competencies 173, 184, 186, 215,
  220, 221, 222, 226, 243, 249,
  272, 274, 277, 279
  core 172
competent individual:
  construction **107–30**
competition 6, 49, 57, 58, 60, 68,
  70, 101, 140, 141, 155, 206–7,
  212, 271, 279
  business education 253–4
  global 36, 58, 110
  international 31, 55, 122
  temporary staff 168
  versus regulation **63–82**
competition articulation 69, **72–6**,
  76–8, 79
competitive
  advantage 66, 110, 260
  corporatism 6
  economy 279
competitiveness 6, 7, 46, 47, 48,
  50, 52, 57, 58, 98, 99, 111, 113,
  122, 125
  labour market 276
  national 55, 275
computer services 285
Computer Sweden (journal) 215
computers 114, 163, 177, 182, 186
conduct (behaviour/manners) 59,
  158, 160, 164, 166–7, 205, 207,
  274, 276, 277
conduct of conduct (Foucault) 200, 276
Confederation of Swedish
  Enterprise 69, 73, 74, 75
  see also SAF

conflict resolution 199, 243
constraints 281, 282
construction of relevance 243
consultants 137, 146, 227(n3),
  284
consumption 30–1, 38
content developers 220
continuous learning **163**, 167, 202,
  206, 286
  right to use working time 154
control **180–4**, 281, 286
  bureaucratic 180, 181, 186
  direct 175, 180
  governmental 181
  ideological 174, 177, 179, 186
  normative 177, 179, 181, 186
  technical 180, 181
  technological 180
courses
  entrepreneurship 281, 284–5
  interactive media 220, 221
  multimedia 217
  self-employment 136, 139, 142
creation of meaning 63, 64, 68,
  78–9, 80, 80(n2)
  ideological boundary 75, 80
creolization 148
culture 275, 286
  cultural assumptions 287
  cultural engineering 135
customer
  contact 186
  demand 214
  satisfaction 269
  service 175–6
customers 32, 141, 147, 173, 177–8,
  180–4, 186, 192, 256
  needs 172
customization 172

decision-making 143–4, 195, 200,
  201, 205, 240, 246
decommodification 55
delegation of tasks 189, 198, 200,
  202, 282
Deloitte & Touche 236
Delors I and II (budget reforms) 67
Denmark 76, 80
deregulation 5, 46, 50, 74, 78, 79,
  154, 258
deskilling/downskilling 100, 175
determinism 212
  linguistic 109
'Developmental Work' (DUVA) 115

DG ECFIN, DG Economic and Financial Affairs　47
DG Employment and Social Affairs　49
DGV　79
　see also DG Employment and Social affairs
dialogue　199, 279
digital design　216
disabilities　86
disciplinary techniques　190, 202
discipline　36, 100
disciplining techniques　200, 205, 207
discourse　xi, 1, 2, 3, 14, 15, 20(n4), 43, 52, 58, 107
　competence development　254
　competence development and employability (interactive media industry)　**210–30**
　competent individual　16, **112–13**, 115, 122, 123, 127(n3)
　concept　**12–13**
　definitions　81(n2)
　emancipatory　6
　employability　8, 153, 155, 169, **189–91**, 275, 276, 277, 281
　entrepreneur/ entrepreneurship　147
　EU　9, 10, 15, 79
　EU labour market (Swedish articulation)　**63–82**
　flexibility　153, 169
　generalized　274
　'good worker'　**200–1**, 203, 207
　impact of practice　274
　individualizing　169–70
　learning　85
　lifelong learning　254
　management　248
　management consulting employability　**231–51**
　media rankings (business schools)　269
　'muscular'　13, 109
　new economy　112
　OECD　9, 15, 79
　performative　18, 274
　political　42–3, 52, 277
　post-industrial　107–8, **109–13**, 127(n1)
　structural　67–8, 70–1, 74, 77, 79
　trade union (continuity and change)　**125–7**
　trade unions and post-industrial　**113–22**
　workplace reality　**117, 119–22**
　see also employability; labour market
discourse analysis　64
discrimination　68, 72, 78, 86, 101
discursive
　couplings　78–9, 80
　field　12
　influences　12
　practice　13, 15, 43, 69, 179
　shift　11, 56, **114–17**, 119
　terrain　69, 75, 76, 78, 80
　transformations　18–19, **274–89**
　transition　17
disincentives　52
division of labour　179, 225
dotcom crisis (2000)　214, 216, 218, 226
downsizing　90, 91, 156
dress code　158, **159–60**
Drugco AB (pseudonymous pharmaceutical multinational)　114, 120–2, 123, 124
dynamics　285

e-centres　94
economic
　development　287
　downturn　136
　dynamism　57
　growth　66, 67, 68, 72, 78, 83, 101
　performance　50
education　3, 45, 46, 50, 55, 68, 71–2, 74, 78, 79, 87, 101, 135, 174, 196, 244, 248, 252, 253, 256, 257, 262, 265, 270, 272, 277
　adult right to leave of absence for studies　94, 97
　formal　210, 213, 215, **217–18**, 219, 220, 221, 222, 247
　higher　161, 270, 279
EES　9–10, 43, 46–9, 52, 54, 57, 68, 132
efficiency　208, 253, 265, 269
elderly　86, 87
emotion work　173, 179, 181
emotional labour　158, 166, 169, 173, 174, 181, 185–6, 277
　intense forms　180, 182–3, 184
　praxis in call centres　**177–80**
emotions　190, **200–6**

employability   1–22, 68, 71, 76–80,
     94, 99, 102, 103, 108, 115,
     124–7, 148
  beyond   285–7
  call centres   172–88
  central union concern   117
  change of discourse   189–91
  competition for   269–71
  concept   7–11, 19(n2)
  continuities and change
     (Sweden)   283–5
  defining   53, 268–9
  discursive dynamics and
     techniques   11–19
  discursive transformations   274–89
  double-sided coin   286
  'duty'   132, 133
  embodying   207
  ethos   53–4
  EU discourse   42–3, 46–52, 52–4,
     57, 58, 60(n1)
  EU labour market discourse in
     Sweden   64
  European politics   42–62
  flexibility and security   49–50
  full   83
  gap   116–17
  graduate business education   252–73
  improvization   248–9
  interactive media workers   210–30
  management consulting   231–51
  'multivocal concept'   281
  nature of modern power   274–89
  normative expectations   173
  OECD discourse   42–3, 43–6, 49,
     52–4, 57, 58, 60(n1)
  OECD–EU discourse in
     summary   52–4
  political technology   152–71
  politics of adjustment   57–60
  post-industrial discourse   109
  provision   111
  shifting responsibilities   54–7
  temporary staffing business   152–71
  Volvo Bus Plant   189–209
'employability through
     incentives'   278
employability insurance   59
employability security   51, 275–6
employable individual   190, 203, 205,
     270, 278, 282
  construction   201–2, 207
  normative category   276–80,
     281, 286

employee loyalty   176, 181, 202,
     225–6, 281
employees   43, 75, 87, 102, 119,
     122, 126, 141, 143, 144, 146,
     172–84, 189, 210, 213, 215,
     226, 252, 280, 283
  'constituted as legal entity'   37
  less-qualified   101
  permanent   220, 227(n3)
  salaried   136
  time for competence
     development   222
  see also workers
employers   40, 43, 87, 90, 98, 100,
     102, 117, 122, 125, 147, 154,
     172, 174, 177, 183, 184, 186,
     213, 226, 252, 283
  lacking   73
  media ranking of business
     schools   261
employers' associations/
     organizations   72–3, 88, 283
  see also Confederation of Swedish
     Enterprise, SAF
employers' rights   29
employment   55, 249
  'atypical'   284
  full   2, 5, 7, 9, 60, 60(n3), 67, 71,
     77, 83, 275, 283
  full-time permanent position
     preferred   145
  J-curve   66
  low-skilled   84, 99, 102
  part-time   84, 86, 87
  quality   87, 101
  regular salaried   154
  skilled   85
  temporary   84, 184
  unskilled   85, 86
employment agencies   274
  see also PES
employment conditions   183
employment contracts/work
     contracts   50, 59–60, 155
  de-standardization   152
  fixed-term   5, 283–4
  permanent (preferred)   213
  rolling   152
  short-term   152, 156
  stationary   154
employment security   51, 58, 72, 73,
     77, 78, 125, 154, 275–6
employment value   271–2
empowerment   278, 279–80, 282

enabling state   56, 58, 59, 60
'enchanted milieu' (Schneider)   161
encouragement   199–202, 205,
    278, 282
'enriching production' (Volvo)   190
enterprising self   133, 148
entrepreneurs   131, 133, 137–8,
    141–3, 148, 216
    self-employed   281
entrepreneurship   43, 48, 58, 71, 78,
    131–5, 137, 140, 142, 145, 277
    idea 'more influential'   132
    see also courses
equal opportunities   43, 48, 71, 87
equal rights   94
equality
    income   59, 276
    opportunity   57, 59, 115, 126, 276
    outcome   57, 115, 126
    'through mobility and
        opportunity'   57
Ericsson   34
Ernst & Young   236
Essen: European Council (1994)
    47, 49
ethnic minorities   86
Europe: business education   254,
    258, 259, 265
European Centre of Public Enterprises
    (CEEP)   65
European Commission   43, 46–7, 49,
    51, 59, 65, 66, 74, 77, 155
European Community   66
European Council: social action
    programme (1974)   65
European Employment Strategy
    (EES)   9–10, 43, **46–9**, 52, 54,
    57, 68, 132
    see also EES
European Round Table of
    Industrialists (ERT)   46
European Social Fund (ESF)   42, 43,
    52, 65
European Trade Union Confederation
    (ETUC)   65
European Union   2, 10, 11, 55, 83,
    103(n2), 155, 212, 275, 283,
    284, 286
    decision-making process   63, 64,
        75, 76, **79–80**, 81(n4)
    employability discourse   42–3,
        46–52, **52–4**, 57, 58, 60(n1)
    employment guidelines   49, 68,
        71, 81(n7)

employment strategy   56; *see also*
    EES
    internal market   66, 67, 70, 73
    lack of job creation   73
    Objective 3 programmes   85, 96f
    Objective 4 funds   85, 104(n5)
    social dimension   63, 65
    social and labour market policy   15
European Union discourse
    labour market (Swedish
        articulation)   **63–82**
    two phases   64–8
evaluation   162, 163–5, 247, 274, 279
Evaluation Form
    (*Utvärderingsblankett*)   164
expectations   248, 274, 276, 277, 278,
    281, 282
    business education   255
experience   221, 222, 240, 242, **243–4**,
    245, 248, 249, 270, 276, 280
expert system   176, 180, 182, 234
expertise   **233–5**, 238, 239–40,
    241–4, 246
experts   246, 248, 256
    legitimacy as   244
    self-sufficient   247

faculty   262, 264, 266t, 267t, 268
family   72, 78, 204
*Fédération Européenne des Associations
    de Conseils en Organization*
    (FEACO)   235
Federation of Salaried Employees in
    Industry and Services (PTK)   89
Federation of Swedish County
    Councils   69
feedback   200, 204, 261
Financial Times   253, 258, 259, 260–1,
    262, 267, 268
    market value of MBA   **263–4**
    ranking criteria (business
        schools)   267t
flexibility   8, 15, 16–17, 33, 43,
    49–50, 56, 59, 60, 100, 111, 124,
    145, 152, 173, 277, 278, 287(n1)
    'A' list   157
    attitude   157–9
    call centres   **184–5**
    financial   185
    functional   184, 185
    gendering   160
    individual   58
    interactive media firms   220
    lacking in labour markets   46

limits 157
normative tool 153, 166
numerical 185
organization of work (Volvo) 89
pay 60(n1)
positive 78
'positive' v. 'negative' 50
temporary staff **156–61**, 163, 169
willingness to adapt 157, 158
work organization 47
working conditions 39
flexibilization 10, **152–5**, 169, 283
'enchanted milieu' (Schneider) 161
labour law 5
labour markets 5, 8
performative power 161
flexible production 32
flexicurity (flexibility +
security) 60(n2)
flight attendants 186
flight crew 181
FLiSa (Flexible Teamwork in
Co-operation) 191, 208(n4)
Folkhem (Hansson) 30
'following Joe around' 219
Fordism 4, 6, 111
Fordist regime of accumulation **30–1**
Foucauldian panopticon 282
Framfab 215
France 8, 235
freedom 127, 143, 144, 156,
158, 285, 287
freelancers 227(n3)
front-line 176, 178
Frontloader AB (pseudonymous
manufacturer in northern
Sweden) 114, 119, 123, 124
frustration 195, 198, 201, 202, 203,
205, 282
Funky Business (Nordström and
Ridderstråle, 2000) 112–13

gaps/'gaps' 48
education system versus production
system 84, **97–9**, 100
employability 116–17
see also labour market/mismatch
problem
gender equality 65
gender mainstreaming 43
generation gap 113
global network of commerce **31–4**, 40
globalization 31–2, 39–40, 44, 52,
54, 85, 99, 100, 172, 211

golden chains 211, 226
'good work' 115, 117, 125, 127,
214, 281
'good worker' 189–90, 203, 204,
207, 208(n1), 282
construction **200–1**
gossiping 168
governance 153, 169, 200, 256,
276, 278, 279, 282, 285
of temp work 161, 163, 164
government 104(n6), 169,
257, 282
governmental technology 133, 135
governmentality 133, 153
graduates
business schools 263, 264, 265
career counselling and job
opportunities 264
career progress 268, 269, 270, 271
employability **268–9**
job offers 263, 265
wages/salaries 263, 264, 267t, 268,
270, 271
Growth, Competitiveness, Employment
(CEC White Paper, 1993) **46–7**,
49, 50, 66
guidance (individual) 58

handbook literature (management
consultants) **237–8**
Harley Davidson 33
health 68
health and safety at work 65, 66,
72, 78
Heatplates AB (pseudonymous
manufacturing plant) 114, 117,
120, 121, 123
'sound production flow
control' 119
hierarchy 200
high-skill society 86–7
hiring (management consultants)
233, 234, 240, 247
household 30
household type of economy 24
housing 30, 68
HTF *see* Salaried Employees' Union
human capital 50, 55, 84, 86
human resource management
(HRM) 89, 180
strategic 122
human resources 7, 50, 125, 275
'investment' 48
humiliation 200, 201, 203

Icon Medialab 215
ideational presuppositions 287
identification 177, 181–2, 186
identity (construction) 169
ideology 170, 238, 257, 269, 275
  management consultants 236
IF *see* Swedish Industrial Workers
  Union
ILO conventions 154
image 141, 233
imagined community
  (Anderson) 173
imbalances 84
immigrants 94, 149(n1)
improvization 246, **248–9**
incentives 58, 75, 77, 278, 281
  to enterprise 48
  to work 48
independence: management
  consultants 244
India Today 257
individualism 113, 119, 232, **246–8**
individualization **23–41**, 42, 59,
  108, 110, 112, 117, 122, 126,
  167–9, 170, 202, 225, **281–2**
individuals 1, 14, 16, 19(n3), 97,
  101, 102, 133–4, 142, 163, 181,
  201, 275, 281, 282, 284, 286
  autonomous 278
  'competent' 16, 38
  employability 58
  entrepreneurial 133, 142
  independent 189, 208
  new business logic **111–12**
  new ways of control 168
  qualities 43, 59
  right to skills upgrading 115, 125
  rights 103
  self-employed 138
  self-managing 279
  self-perception 148
  self-reliant 145, 157, 281
  self-steering 200, 206, 208
  subsidized education packages 102
industrial
  capitalism 27
  dynamics (interactive media
    firms) 217
  organization 215
  relations 24, 37–8, 283
  revolutions 24, 25–6, 27
industrialization 38
Industry Agreement (1997) 125
Industry Standard (journal) 215

inequality 39, 84, 86, 87, 100,
  101, 103
  regional 66, 67, 72
inflation 7, 60(n3), 71
information 89, 176, 237, 240, 241
information and communications
  technology (ICT) 172, 174,
  179, 182
  ICT literacy 51
information society 206, 208
information technology (IT) 176,
  183, 185, 213–14, 216–18,
  220, 233
initiative 220, 221–2, 277, 278
  employer-driven 173
innovation 99, 100, 110, 132,
  213, 216
insecurity 86, 286
institutional history 65, 80(n2)
institutionalization 232, 248
institutionalized structures
  246–8, 249
instruction/s 176, 177–8, 181
insurance 154
integrity 159, 245
intellectual capital 263
interaction face-to-face 182–3
interactive media 281
  definition 216, 227(n1)
interactive media firms/
  producers 211–13, **216–17**,
  218–24, 227(n3)
  functioning 214–15
  inter-firm collaboration 217, 225
  mergers, acquisitions, consolidation,
    restructuring 217
  tight financial situation 215
interactive media solutions 219,
  221–2
interactive media workers
  competence development
    210–30
  seductive discourses in dynamic
    industry **210–11**
interface zone **134**, 142, 143, 147,
  148
intermediaries 285, 286
internalization (of norms) 276
International Council for
  Management Consulting
  Institutes (ICMCI, 1989–) 235
International Herald Tribune 253, 258
internet 163, 172, 179, 182–3, 215,
  216, 219, 258, 261

interviews   81(n4), 114, 117, 119–22,
    127(n4), 137, 143–7, 153, 158–60,
    164–6, 168, 170(n4), 174, 183,
    184, 190, 194, 232, 239–41, 245,
    249(n1), 282
intranet   172, 216
investment   46, 110, 141

Japan   50, 66
job centres   155
    see also PES
job creation   74
job opportunities: state monopoly
    over allocation (1935–early
    1990s)   153–4
job redesign   125
job rotation   124
jobs for life   119
journals   215, 263
just-in-time production   32, 193

Keynesianism   6, 7
knowledge   74, 92, 108–10, 112,
    115–16, 120, 124, 126, 127(n2),
    240–2, **244–6**, 262, 270–1, 272,
    274, 276–7
    combinations   249
    specialized   238, 248
    subjective   245
    tacit   219
knowledge capital   225
knowledge management   89, 90
knowledge work   107, 111, 113,
    123–4
    limits   **124**
knowledge-based economy/'new'
    economy   6, 33, 45–6, 52,
    58, 60, 84–6, 99, 101, 110,
    112, 145, 211–12
knowledge-based firms   111, 121, 124
knowledge-based society   68, 84, 111
KPMG   236

labelling   156, 207, 213, 233, 235
Labor and Monopoly Capital
    (Braverman, 1974)   127(n2)
labour   34, 75, 76
    close cooperation with capital
        (Sweden)   87–8
    crisis   31–8
    discipline   25–6
    disorganized   38–40
    emergence   25–7
    individualization   **23–41**

institutionalization   27–31
    private and public   36
    rise   24–7
    social category   15, 38
    social role   31, 38
    supply and demand   275
Labour Force Surveys
    (Sweden)   103(n1)
labour law   **37–8**
labour market   1–7, 11, 13, 15–16,
    40, 42–3, 54–7, 60, 70, 85–9,
    98, 100–3, 114–15, 124, 132,
    153, 169, 193, 210, 218, 252–3,
    269, 271, 280–1, 283–4, 286–7
    access   58
    choice of business school   270
    competitive   2, 23, 39, 83, 154,
        164, 172, 277
    demand side   71, 77, 83
    deregulation   113, 154
    dynamic   170
    equity   57
    European   160
    future   145, 147
    government interference absent
        36–7
    harmonization (EU)   155
    marginalization   86–7
    mismatch problem   71, 77–8;
        see also gaps
    'new'   183–4
    segmentation   86–7, 185
    supply-side   67, 69, 71, 74, 77, 83
    winners and losers   185
Labour Market Board   154
labour market dynamism   287
labour market flexibility   52, 55,
    68, 74, 101, 133, 142–3, 144–5,
    161, 166
    'double flexibility'   47
    lacking   46, 73
labour market policy   2, 9, 14, 15, 16,
    19(n3), 48, 58, **63–82**, 133, 135,
    148, 275, 279
    ideological shift (Sweden,
        1980s)   132, 136
labour market reform   52
labour market situation   215, 226
labour mobility   74
labour movement   27, 29
'labour power'   38
labour process   110, 176
labour process theory   174
labour shortage   101

labour standards 78
language 12–13
　constitutive power 'overstated' 109
late modernism (Giddens) 107
layoffs 214, 215, 218
　hire and fire 215, 226
leadership: organizational 189
leadership style (Volvo Bus
　Plant) 189, **191–9**, 202
　coaching 189–90, 193, 198, 199,
　　201, 204
　experiences of change **198–9**
lean production 32, 90, 172
learning 1–22, 58, 107–10, 116,
　125, 180, 253, 270, 279
　alleged need **84–7**
　collective 219
　continuous 252, 260
　definition **92–3**
　diversity **122–4**
　double-loop 123
　false promises 282
　formal 84, 91–3, 96f, 98, 99, 103
　group-based 219
　informal 84, 91–3, 96f, 99, 103
　lost 219
　management consultants 247
　market for **259–60**
　'mechanism for inequality' 87
　non-formal 93
　off-the-job 211, 219–22
　on-the-job 211, 214, 217, **218–20**,
　　221–2, 225
　personal/individual 221,
　　222, 271
　reflected/reflective 92f, 93
　single-loop 123
　see also lifelong learning
learning ability 163
learning accounts (individual)
　19(n1), 114, 127
learning capacity 277
Learning Centres 94, 96
learning how to learn 51
learning individuals 252, 253
learning for life 271
learning logic 84, **87–91**, 100
　emphasis 90–1
learning opportunities/possibilities
　193, 195, 197, 200, 202,
　205–6
learning for work 101
legislation 284
liberalism 27, 286

liberalization 66
life-wide learning 102
lifelong learning 1, 6, 7, 11, 14,
　15–16, 45, 46, 48, 51, 58, 64,
　68, 71–2, 74–9, **83–106**, 112,
　115, 124, 126, 206, 208, 210,
　271, 275, 285
　barriers to successful strategy 84
　components 96f
　limits and prospects **99–103**
　positive agenda **101–3**
　positive aspects 96–7
　problems 97
　role of education system **91–9**,
　　103(n2)
　strong discourse, weak
　　practice **83–4**, 99
　three strategies 101–2
line leaders 190, 193, 195, 197,
　199, 204
LO　*see* Swedish Trade Union
　Confederation
local authorities 51, 83, 163
local community 24
London Business School 259–60
losers **206–8**

macro-economic policy 55, 56,
　60(n3)
macroeconomics 112
magazines 142, 259
'making up people' (Hacking) 134,
　156
management 25, 121, 122, 124, 180,
　181, 182, 183, 201, 202, 207, 241,
　278, 279, 280, 281
　experience 243–4
　negotiation meetings with
　　unions 114
　solutions to problems 237
management catchwords 32
management consultants 232,
　281, 286
　'flexible, task-oriented,
　　multi-skilled' 231
　handbook literature **237–8**
　junior/senior, 247–8
　practice (buyers' stories, providers'
　　stories) **238–42**
　practice (as presented in
　　discourse) **236–8**
　relevant experience **243–4**
　relevant knowledge **244–6**
　tasks 238

management consulting 18
  ability to sell projects 233–4, 244,
    245–6, 247–8, 249
  demand 232–6
  expertise and employability
    231–51
  ideals for modern workforce 231–2
  many forms 237
  'staffing issue' 239
  weak profession 235–6
management fads/fashions 85,
  244, 248
management strategies 162, 186
management techniques 244,
  246, 247
managers 90, 184, 214, 254, 260
Manpower 157
'manufactured uncertainty' (Giddens)
  162
market 18, 286
  clearing 67
  failure 72
  forces 1, 271
  mechanism 269, 270
  research 140
  value 207, 261, 263–4, 269, 271,
    272
marketability 249
marketization 172, 179, 185
markets 26, 167
  competitive 91, 98
  global 23, 91, 111
Marxism 134
mass production 29, 32, 110, 176
Master of Business Administration
  (MBA) 254–72
  effect on managerial practice
    254–5
  Executive MBA 254
  market value 263–4
  tuition fees 259
maturity 245
MBA Magazine 256
McKinsey & Co 236
means of production (Marx) 112
media 145, 147, 212, 216, 217,
  218, 265
  newspapers and magazines 18
media ranking 279
  agenda 252–4
  consumer perspective 257
  criteria 253, 262–6, 267t
  graduate business education
    252–73

growing market 256–7
  identifying customer 267
  international market 254
  market guides 260–2
  method 262–6
  normative element 255
mentorship 219
meta-learning 4
Metall see Swedish Metalworkers
  Union
Method Time Measurement (MTM)
  system 88
Microsoft 218
mind 190, 200–6
  'major asset of society' 112, 127
mobility 59, 173
models
  Anglo-Saxon 9, 56
  European social 47, 48, 57, 58
  lean organization 202
  Nordic 56
  Scandinavian 9, 10
  Swedish 87–8, 283
  United States 48
Moderna Tider (Sweden) 257
modernism 107
modernization 58
multi-skilling 115, 124, 125
multimedia 217, 227(n1)
municipal agencies 154
Municipal Schools for Adult
  Education 94, 98
municipalities 94, 135

National Action Plans 43
  Swedish (Regeringskansliet) 71
negotiated identities 148
negotiation 274, 285
neo-classical economics 45, 52
neo-liberalism/neo-liberal
  discourse 49, 133, 134, 142,
    144, 161, 172, 179, 281
net-universities 96
Netherlands 60(n2), 235
network skills 221
networking 103, 139
networks 266t, 268
neue Mitte (Schröder) 54
New Deal (Roosevelt) 30
New Labour 56, 57
newsletters 165, 179
newspapers 18, 259
Nike 33
non-employment 233–5, 249

'normalizing gaze'   165
normative
    argument   60(n2)
    categories   18–19, 285, 286
    framework   57
norms   180, 183, 248, 255–6,
    276, 284

obedience (workers)   200, 203, 205
OECD (Organisation for Economic
    Co-operation and Development)
    2, 11, 275, 283, 286
    employability discourse   42–3,
        43–6, 49, **52–4**, 57, 58, 60(n1)
OECD Jobs Strategy (1994–)   43,
    44–6, 60(n3)
Office Angels   168
oil price crises (1970s)   65
Olsten Personalkraft   153, 157–60,
    163–6, 168, 278
    Bullen (newsletter)   165
    internal documents   153, 170(n4)
oppression   200
organization   238, 239, 240, 248
organizational change   89
organizations: multilateral   274
organized labour   29, 31
outsourcing   33, 34, 90, 172, 184,
    185, 220, 232, 238, 287(n1)
over-education   55–6
over-production (1930s)   29
over-qualification   84, 86, 99, 101
over-regulation   74, 79

parental insurance   283
parental pay   154
participant observation   153, 190
passage rites   238
pension rights   154
performance   163, 180, 237, 240,
    246, 253, 269, 282
    education   256
    individual   279
    temporary staff   161
performers (individual)   **167–9**
perquisites   215
personal characteristics   140
personal/social relations   175, 176–7,
    179, 180, 181, 185–6, 280
personality   221, 243
personality test   **139–40**, 148
personalization   59
PES   *see* Public Employment Service,
    job centres

Pharmacia (pharmaceutical
    company)   34
polarization   84, 86
    Volvo Bus Plant   206
political
    parties   284
    rationality   133, 135
    technology   **152–71**, 256
portfolio workers (Handy, 1996)
    111–12
post-industrialism   107, 108
post-materialistic values   113
post-structuralism   13
postmodernism   107, 109
poverty   45, 68, 283
    'deserving and undeserving'
        poor   7
power   15, 60, 100, 101, 112, 127,
    153, 161, 172, 183, 200, **274–89**
praise   200, 201, 202, 205
prevention   49, 53
PriceCoopersLybrand   236
Principles of Scientific Management
    (Taylor)   28, 208(n1)
private sector   87, 89
private training institutions   **218**,
    219, 221, 222
problem-solving   93, 219, 221–2,
    237, 277
production logic   84, **87–91**, 96, 100
    emphasis   91
production networks   217, 220, 225
production process   34–5
production systems   89
productivity   7, 29, 30, 45, 51, 52,
    98, 101, 120, 275
professional associations   235–6
professionalism   158, 159–60, 161,
    167, 237, 238, 246, 248, 249
professionalization: management
    consulting   235–6
professionals   235, 236, 241, 261
professions   237, 241, 244
professors   265, 266
profitability   58
    importance of training   98
profits   30, 34, 87, 91, 100, 136,
    140, 141–2, 145, 147, 148,
    154, 181
project managers   210, 215, 216,
    220–3, 225
proportionality   73
providers (management consulting
    services)   231, 236, 237, 238

Public Employment Service (PES, Sweden) 16, **131–51**, 281, 284–5
  part of supportive stratum 135–7
  see also job centres
public sector 87, 89, 137
punishment 200

qualifications 68, 71, 78, 85, 100, 103
quality assessment 261–2
quality control 90, 253, 255
questionnaires 174, 179, 184, 264

rating 278, 279
rationality 208
rationalization 91, 100
readiness to work 49
recession 65, 70, 72, 283
recommodification 55
recruitment 243, 287(n1)
redistribution 6, 54, 57, 58, 283
reflexive attitude 167, 277
reflexive projects (Giddens) 110
reflexivity 166, 282
  female 160
  structural conditions 166–7
'regimes of truth' (Foucault) 14
regulation 169, 254
  competition versus **63–82**
  labour market 283
  'technologies' (Foucault) 14
regulation articulation 69, **70–2**, 73, 75, **76–8**, 79, 81(n5)
rehabilitation 49
reliability 157, 169, 208, 278
  see also awards
relief workers 86
repression 201
reputation 208, 246, 247
research 244, 262, 264, 267t
research and development 120–1, 124
resistance 2, 3, 13, 174, **180–4**, 185, 274, **280–1**, 282, 285
resource allocation 33, 34
responsibility 135, 143, 200, 202, 206, 240, 253, 274–5
  'active citizen' 142
  collective 7, 8, 9, 284
  employer 116
  individual/personal 1–4, 7–9, 15, 23, 43, 53–4, 56, 60, 100–1, 107–8, 112, 116, 120, 132, 133, 144, 157, 189, 193, 210,

212, 225, 261–2, 276, 278, 279, 285, 286
  individualized **281–2**
  lack of 183
  shared 163
  shifting **54–7**
  social 116
  state 60
restructuring 83, 85, 125
reward 274, 279
rhetoric of reconciliation 57, 58
right to strike (transnational) 70
right to work/right to employment 108, 132
rights (collective) 282
rights and obligations **56–7**
risk 131, 132, 138, 139, 140, 143, 145, 146, 148, 244, 274, 275, 286
  financial, 185
  individualization 169
rotation 189, 192–5, 197, 202, 203
rules 25–6, 35, 37–8, 39, 181

SAF (Swedish Employers' Association) 29, 89
  see also Confederation of Swedish Enterprise
Salaried Employees' Union (HTF) 154, 170(n2), 183–4
salaries 115, 178, 267t, 268
sales 184
Saltsjöbaden Agreement (1938) 88, 76
  General Agreement of 1938 (LO/SAF) 29, 36
SAP (Swedish Social Democratic Party) 29, 30, 37, 88
Scandinavia/Nordic countries 10, 27, 283
schools 102, 252
  folk high 94, 96
  upper secondary 94
schools of technology 218
science 89
scientific management *see* Taylorism
scripting 177–8
Seat 33
secondary schools 170(n3), 221
  media programmes 227(n2)
security **49–50**, 60
  loss of 146, 148
  through skills 59
segmentation 185
self-acting 189
self-confidence 142, 147, 201

self-employed   131–2, 136, 142–3,
    145, 146, 285
  role   **145–6**
  successful personality type   139
self-employers   132, 142
self-employment   5, 16, **131–51**
  expectations and perspectives
    143–7
self-employment grant (Sweden,
    1984–)   133, 136–7, 138,
    149(n2, n4)
  'start-up grant'   149(n2)
  'support for entrepreneurial
    start-ups'   149(n2)
Self-Employment Project   133, 134,
    135, 136, 145, 147, 148
  articles   **142–3**, 144, 148
  first day   **137–8**
  mediation   **138**
  negotiated identities   **148**
  'Our Roles in the Project'   138
  pedagogical techniques   **140–2**
  personality test   **139–40**, 148
  teaching to think like
    self-employed   **147**
Self-Employment Project – Work
    Experience Scheme (*starta eget
    projekt arbetslivsutveckling*)   16,
    132, 136, 149(n1)
'self-evaluative gaze'   166
self-governance   281
self-managing skills   277
self-monitoring   169
self-regulation   17, 153, 169, 207,
    276, 278, 282
self-reliance   144, 147, 157
service   176, 245, 248
service management   32
service sector   84, 85, 86, 99, 102,
    173, 175, 180
service work/workers   172, 173, 186
service-mindedness   184, 278
servicing states   55
shareholder value   124
sickness insurance   283
SIF/Sif   *see* Swedish Union of
    Clerical and Technical
    Workers in Industry
skill levels   225
skills   74, 102, 114, 116, 121, 163,
    164, 175, 184, 217, 224, 233,
    243, 263, 268, 271, 279
  inter-personal   277
  personal   249

social   51
technical   51
see also training
Skoda   33
social
  behaviour   43
  competence   51, 53, 220, 221
  contracts   43, 56, 57, 59, 172
  dumping   66, 67, 70, 73,
    78, 79
  exclusion   6, 47, 59, 68, 70–1, 87,
    103, 280, 286
  identity   169
  inclusion   43, 48, 286
  justice   57
  knowledge/skills   116, 208, 245
  partnership   48, 60(n3), 83, 87–8,
    101–2
  policy   **63–82**, 287
  practices   152
  processes   109
  protection   50
  quarantine   136
  rights   59, 60, 287
  security   6, 73, 135, 145
  security/benefit systems   19(n3),
    42, 43, 46–7, 48, 51, 53, 72–3,
    144, 148, 283
  state   135
Social Insurance Office   135
socialization   53, 142, 156
  temporary employees
    ('temps')   152–3
software   155, 163, 218
solidaristic work (Metall, 1989)   115,
    125, 127
solidarity   6, 36, 39, 40, 49, 113,
    125, 141, 147, 148, 197, 276
sparsely populated areas   149(n1)
specialization   185
Spiegel   257
SPUR (Swedish Association of
    Temporary Work Businesses and
    Staffing Services)   170(n2)
standardization   167, 169,
    255, 271
state   7, 43, 51, 55, 101, 102,
    108, 135, 142, 148
state agencies   154
state role   1, 275
status   270
stock options   211, 226
Stockholm: Public Employment
    Office   137

stories 236
buyers' (management consultancy
    services) **238–40**, 243
providers' **240–2**, 243
stress 90, 199, 277, 279
structural
    funds 67
    reform 44, 47, 52, 55, 60(n3)
    transformation 284
students 260, 261, 262,
    265, 269
    allowances 94, 97
    organizations 257
study circles 103, 104(n4)
subjectivity 153, 161, 245–6,
    274, 276
subordination 200
subsidiarity 73
Sun (software developer) 218
supply-side policy **54–6**, 58
supporting systems 94, 96f,
    97, 102
supportive stratum **135–7**
surveillance 186
    direct 181
    electronic 180
Sweden 3, 9, 11, 19(n1), 170(n1),
    189, 212
    adjustment insurance 59
    articulations of EU labour market
        discourse **63–82**
    call centres 173–4, 183, 184–5,
        186
    centre–right government
        (1991–4) 283
    competence development
        discourse 211
    'competent individual'
        discourse 110, **112–13**, 115,
        122, 123, 127(n3)
    education system 94
    employability (continuities and
        change) **283–5**
    expectations and demands on
        individuals 274
    golden years 30, 36
    government 136
    industrial landscape 27
    interactive media activity
        217, 220
    investment overseas 31
    labour market 23
    labour market policy
        (ideological shift) 132

lifelong learning 83
management consulting market
    (1987–98) 232
social democratic government
    70, 71, 72, 74–5, 77, 80,
    81(n5), 283
temporary staffing sector 153
trade unions 16, 108
travel agencies 173
universities (media ranking) 257
Sweden: Ministry of Finance 81(n5)
Sweden: Ministry of Heath and Social
    Affairs 69, 70, 81(n5)
Sweden: Ministry of Industry,
    Employment and
    Communications 69, 70,
    71, 81(n5)
Swedish Agency for Government
    Employers 69
Swedish Association of Local
    Authorities 69
Swedish Association for Management
    Consultants (SAMC) 235
Swedish Association of Temporary
    Work Businesses and Staffing
    Services (SPUR) 170(n2)
Swedish Confederation of Professional
    Associations (SACO) 69
Swedish Cooperative Wholesale
    Society (KF) 29
Swedish Employers' Association
    (SAF) 29, 89
Swedish for Immigrants 94, 98
Swedish Industrial Development
    Fund 139
Swedish Industrial Workers Union
    (IF) 108, 125
    'Developmental Work' (1995) 115
    'IF club' 121
Swedish Metalworkers Union
    (Metall) 102, 108, 120, 122
    Congress (1985) 89
    Congress (1999) 114
    'Good Work' (1985) 89, 115, 117,
        125, 127
    'Knowledge for Development'
        (1999 slogan) 114
    'Metall club' 117, 119
    'Solidaristic Work' (1989) 115
Swedish Research Council xi
Swedish Social Democratic Party
    (SAP) 29, 30, 37, 88
Swedish Trade Union Confederation
    (LO) 29, 69, 70, 72, 86, 89

Swedish Union of Industrial and
   Technical Workers in Industry
   (SIF, later Sif)   108, 113–19,
   126, 127
   action programmes (1987,
      1996)   116, 117
   career development facilitator   117
   Competence Development Project
      (1989–93)   116–17
   'high time for competence' (slogan,
      1997)   115
   identities, images, norms   118t
   'Sif club'   119, 121
   website   115
   symbols   178

tax incentives   19(n1)
taxation   31, 45, 48, 58, 72, 74, 78,
   79, 283
Taylorism (scientific management)
   27–8, 84, 86–91, 100–1, 120–1,
   123–4, 173, 175, 190, 208(n1)
   modern version/neo-Taylorism
      89–91
   negative effects   88
team cohesiveness   181
team concept   186
team model   191, 192, 193, **194–6**,
   282
   problematic aspects   **197–8**
team spirit   184
team-leaders   181, 186, 201,
   205, 206
teams   177, 183, 280
   'collective spirit' (Benders and
      van Hootegem)   173
   definition   173
   'empty'   177, 280, 282
   informal relations   177
   'defined subjectively'   185–6
teamwork   115, 123, 124, 125, 217,
   219–20, 225, 277
   call centres   **172–88**
   case-studies   173–4, 179
   cooperation and relations   **174–7**
   Japanese   177
   way of organizing work   **172–4**
technical
   competence   241, 277
   control   280
   development   213
   knowledge   245
   systems   212
technologies of self   153, 200, 276

technology   51, 66, 67, 85, 86, 99,
   115, 180, 212, 215, 216
telephone operators   177–8, 182
telephones   173, 179, 186
   cellular   34
Temping: Insider's Guide (Rogers, 1996)
   156–7
temporary staff ('temps')   **152–71**,
   233, 249, 279, 281, 282
   audited   **161–7**
   'disciplinary subject'   170
   educational level   170(n3)
   evaluation by agency/client   163–6
   identity   166
   lack of collegial community   282
   'manufactured uncertainty'
      (Giddens)   162
   recipe for success   157
   transnational regulation   155
   service-minded   158–9
temporary staffing agencies   16,
   152–71, 185, 278, 280, 284,
   287(n1)
   client organizations   152, 157, 158,
      159, 164, 166, 167–8
   expectations of temping   **156–61**,
      165, 169
   transnational   154, 157, 170(n1)
   see also Olsten Personalkraft;
      temporary staff
test calls   181
third way   54, 56, 58
time pressure   **210–30**, 280
Time-Based Management (TBM)
   32–3, 89, 90
Times   257
timing   245, 248, 249
Top10 (Business Education
   Commission)   258, 259, 261,
   262, 267
   efficiency and customer
      satisfaction   **265–6**
Total Quality Management
   (TQM)   33, 89, 90, 243
trade deficit   31
trade union organization   112
trade unions (labour unions)   6, 16,
   19(n3), 30, 37, 50, 70–2, 75, 80,
   83, 87–8, 100–3, 144, 154, 214,
   257, 276, 281, 284–6
   blue-collar   108, 112, 121, 126, 127
   call centres   181, 183, 186(n3)
   construction of competent
      individual   **107–30**

legitimacy 35–6
negotiation meetings with
    management 114
officials 90
post-industrial discourse **113–22**
rights 29
role **124–5**
temporary staff 168
white-collar 108, 109, 115, 126
training (vocational) 45–6, 47, 51–2,
    56, 83, 85–8, 96–7, 98, 103, 103(n1),
    114–15, 121–2, 135, 174, 179, 202,
    218, 221–2, 252–3, 277, 284
cause and effect 104(n3)
flexibility 99
formal 85
on-the-job 249
skills enhancement (updating/
    upgrading) 45, 48, 50, 51, 53, 55,
    57–9, 68, 71–2, 77, 100, 108, 115,
    125, 154–5, 163, 167, 195, 286
see also over-qualification; skills;
    under-qualification
translation 68, 69, 211, 246, 274
transnational organizations 1
Transnational Regulation and the
    Transformation of States
    (Treo-project) xi
transparency 253, 255, 261, 265
travel agencies 173–4, 178–9, 182, 186
face-to-face interaction 182–3
new competitors 182–3
Treaty of Rome (1957) 65
trust 35, 194, 232, **233–5**, 243–6,
    247, 248, 256, 281

under-qualification 84, 86, 99
underemployment 5
unemployed 51–2, 68, 72, 77, 94,
    96, 101–3, 135, 137, 138, 270,
    275, 281, 285
long-term 47, 50, 71
projects and courses 131
unemployment 4, 7, 8, 36, 44, 52,
    56, 63–8, 74, 84–8, 100, 156, 214,
    233, 283
disguised 87, 131
'islands' 19(n3)
relief work 135
structural 46, 60(n3), 68, 70–1,
    73, 78–9
youth 10
unemployment benefit 10, 55, 75,
    77–8, 79, 135, 136, 137, 149(n1)

unemployment insurance 59, 283
Union of Industrial and Employers'
    Confederations of Europe
    (UNICE) 65
United Kingdom 56, 67, 108, 166,
    181, 186, 235
business schools (media ranking) 257
United States of America 8, 27, 30,
    47, 50, 66, 108, 157, 162, 166,
    220, 284
business education (MBA) 254,
    256–7, 258, 265
competence development
    discourse 211
management consultants 235
MBA tuition fees 259
social model 48
universities 94, 96f, 102, 220, 221,
    243, 255, 258, 269
business education 254
media ranking 257
'play along with media
    rankings' 269
university education 87, 137, 218
Upjohn 34
US News and World Report 257

value-added 111, 269
value-for-money 253, 266t, 268, 269
verification 253
Vision (journal) 215
vocabulary 255, 278
Volkswagen 33
Volvo 34, 89, 190
Kalmar car factory 89, 190
Uddevalla plant 34, 89, 190
Volvo Bus Plant, Borås (1977–) 17,
    189–209, 282, 285
assembly stations 191–8, 203, 205,
    208(n3)
docks 191
frustration 195, 198, 201, 202,
    203, 205
individualized payment
    systems 201–2
new head (spring 2001–) 193,
    198, 285
quality assurance station 191, 192,
    195, 198
seminars 190, 193, 200–2, 285
teams model 191, 192, 193, **194–8**
winners and losers **206–8**
work organization, leadership
    style **191–9**

Volvo Way (Volvo, 2000)   190
Vredeling directive   65

wage
    differentials   36
    moderation   60(n3)
    negotiations   114
    policy   47, 89
wage-earner funds   136
wage-earners/wage–labour   147,
    148, 170
wages   71, 88, 183, 215
    minimum   44
    'solidaristic'   122
Wealth of Nations (Smith, 1776)   252
websites   115
    www.businessweek.com   263
    www.spur.se   154
    www.top10.org   258
welfare benefits   9, 44, 58,
    278, 283
welfare state   4, 5, 6, 15, 23, **30**,
    36, 37, 40, 48, 55, 58, 88
    basic principles intact
        (Sweden)   283
    Swedish   154
welfare traps   10, 52
    poverty trap   45, 283
    unemployment trap   45
welfarism   135
winners   196, **206–8**
women   47, 86, 87, 89, 137, 149(n1),
    153, 154
work   249, 277
    arena for disciplining mind, body
        and emotions   **189–209**
    contingent   5
    de-standardization   5
    and family   78
    flexible   113, 280
    individualization   202
    'juridicalization'   5
    management consulting   247
    service   249
    standardization   5
work experience schemes   136
work incentives   283
work organization   88, 173, 174,
    181, 189, **191–9**, 214, 279

work performance   204, 206
work practices   113, 175
    social technologies   169
work strategy (*arbetslinjen*)   19(n3)
work systems, sustainable   127(n3)
workers   67–8, 69, 71, 90, 102, 190,
    214, 280, 281
    blue-collar   28, 59, 112, 121, 123,
        124, 125, 126, 127, 191, 201
    competent   71
    consultation in multinational
        firms   65
    core   60(n2)
    'flexible'   284
    free mobility   65, 74
    individualized   202
    low-income   74
    multifunctional   189, 206
    multiskilled   192, 206
    from overseas   94
    private sector   113
    temporary   60(n2)
    white-collar   28, 108, 112, 113,
        114, 121, 122, 124, 191
    see also employees
Workers' Educational Association
    (ABF)   29
workers' rights   65
    EC charter (1989–)   66–7, 70
workfare   10, **231–2**
    Schumpeterian workfare state
        6, 55
working conditions   38, 40, 72, 155
'Working conditions at call centres
    and travel agencies'   186(n1)
working hours   183
    non-working hours   213, 225
working life   **3–7**
Working Life Funds   104(n5)
working for oneself   141
workplace reform   127(n3)
works councils   73
World War I   28
World War II   28, 29
    post-war era (1945–)   36, 38,
        88, 110

youth   10, 45, 47, 50, 51, 59, 86,
    113, 184, 213, 218